THE
DICTIONARY
OF
CHICANO SPANISH

2nd Edition

EL
DICCIONARIO
DEL
ESPAÑOL CHICANO

2ª Edición

Originally Compiled by
Roberto A. Galván, Southwest Texas State University
Richard V. Teschner, University of Texas-El Paso

This Edition
Revised and Augmented by
Roberto A. Galván, Southwest Texas State University

Printed on recyclable paper

National Textbook Company
a division of *NTC Publishing Group* • Lincolnwood, Illinois USA

Contents/Índice de materias

A Note to Users

Unless otherwise indicated, nouns or adjectives ending in *-o* or *-a* are masculine and feminine respectively.

Likewise, unless otherwise indicated, nouns and adjectives ending in *-ón* and *-ona* are masculine and feminine respectively.

Since Spanish is almost always pronounced as it is written, this dictionary does not provide phonetic transcriptions for its entries.

Nota al lector

De no indicarse lo contrario, los sustantivos y adjetivos que terminan en *-o* y *-a* son respectivamente masculinos y femeninos.

De igual manera, a menos que se indique lo contrario, los sustantivos y adjetivos que terminan en *-ón* y *-ona* son respectivamente masculinos y femeninos.

Como el español casi siempre se pronuncia como se escribe, este diccionario no ofrece transcripciones fonéticas.

Preface

This volume has been designed to introduce speakers of English to the richness and vitality of *Español Chicano*, Chicano Spanish, the special vocabulary and expressions of Mexican-Americans. At the same time, this dictionary provides speakers of Spanish a convenient and authoritative means for translating this special vocabulary to standard English. *The Dictionary of Chicano Spanish–El Diccionario del Español Chicano* contains the special colloquial, euphemistic, slang, and commonplace expressions of the speech of Mexican-American citizens in the United States, along with the spelling and pronunciation variants common to Chicano Spanish.

As a fourth-generation Mexican-American, I have witnessed the growth and development of this dynamic segment of American society. Changes in society are often reflected in language, and this dictionary contains a record of the linguistic adjustment of Spanish speakers to the influence of the other cultures of North America.

My hope is that this volume will serve to acquaint English speakers with the special vocabulary of their Mexican-American neighbors. We are sure that both Spanish speakers and English speakers will find this dictionary useful in opening new lines of communication and fostering greater understanding in the exciting future we will share.

Jerry Apodaca
Former Governor of New Mexico

Prólogo

Se dedica este tomo a presentar a los angloparlantes a la riqueza y la vitalidad del español chicano, el lenguaje y los modismos singulares de los mexicano-americanos. Al mismo tiempo, este diccionario procura proporcionar a los hispanoparlantes un recurso de comodidad y de uso autorizado para traducir este vocabulario tan distintivo al español normativo. En *The Dictionary of Chicano Spanish–El Diccionario del Español Chicano* figuran los coloquialismos únicos, los eufemismos, la jerga y los modismos del lenguaje cotidiano del habla de los mexicano-americanos dentro de los Estados Unidos, todo ello acompañado de las variantes típicas de ortografía y de pronunciación del español chicano.

Como miembro de la cuarta generación de una familia mexicano-americana, he sido testigo del crecimiento y del desarrollo de este dinámico segmento de la sociedad norteamericana. Los cambios sociales a menudo se hacen sentir en el lenguaje mismo, y este diccionario registra los ajustes lingüísticos que han hecho los hispanoparlantes a las varias influencias de otras culturas de Norteamérica.

Es de esperar que este tomo sirva para familiarizar a los angloparlantes con este vocabulario tan singular de sus vecinos mexicano-americanos. Estamos seguros de que tanto para los hispanoparlantes como para los angloparlantes este diccionario será de gran utilidad en abrir nuevas vías de comunicación y en fomentar mejor entendimiento del porvenir desafiante que los dos grupos comparten.

Jerry Apodaca
Antiguo Gobernador de Nuevo México

Author's Preface

The Chicano language, as it is spoken and written in the United States today, is constantly in flux. New words are coined to express various cultural and technological changes, while old words acquire slightly different meanings and pronunciation slowly evolves. *The Dictionary of Chicano Spanish* will serve as an invaluable reference for anyone involved with the dynamic Chicano culture. The word list of this unique dictionary comprises 9,000 items frequently used in the Chicano language.

Designed for students, business people, educators, and service professionals, *The Dictionary of Chicano Spanish* features words and expressions not usually found in standard references and purposely excludes words easily located in commonly available dictionaries. In this way, it is an excellent supplement to any monolingual Spanish or bilingual Spanish and English dictionary.

Many terms in *The Dictionary of Chicano Spanish* have been labeled according to their current usage in Chicano speech: *slang, colloquial, vulgar, euphemistic, antiquated,* etc. Thus, users of this dictionary will be able to know quickly the appropriate social connotations of the words they look up.

Also included, as separate or coordinate entries, are words whose pronunciation results in a variant spelling—thus avoiding the need to search for words pronounced differently from standard Spanish. For example, the word *degual* is listed as a variation of the word *desigual; malición* is listed as a rustic variation of *maldición.* Likewise, *espeletiar* appears alongside *espeletear; maniar* alongside *manear.* Words containing variations such as *güe-* or *bue-* for *hue-* (*huerta > güerta, huevo > buevo*) and *j* for *h* (*hijo > jijo*) are also listed separately. Because of the relative simplicity of the change, the dropped *d* close to or at the end of words (e.g., *bondad > bondá* or *hablado > hablao*) has not been shown in separate entries.

At the back of the book you will find an appendix of 650 up-to-date proverbs and sayings commonly used in everyday speech as well as a bibliography of secondary sources. The practical bibliography provides both a scholarly list of resources consulted in compiling this dictionary and a rich source of reading and research material for all those wishing to expand their knowledge of the Chicano language.

Prólogo del autor

Una característica de todo idioma vivo es su constante cambio. Con el fin de expresar cambios culturales y avances tecnológicos se idean nuevas palabras, algunas voces adquieren nuevos significados y la pronunciación cambia gradualmente.

El diccionario del español chicano será un libro de consulta de incalculable valor para todo aquél que se relacione con la dinámica comunidad chicana de los Estados Unidos. Su léxico de 9.000 artículos refleja el habla chicana, verbal y escrita, de los Estados Unidos de hoy.

Los estudiantes, empresarios, educadores y profesionales del campo de servicios encontrarán en *El diccionario del español chicano* palabras y expresiones que no se suelen hallar en los libros de consulta tradicionales. Como suplemento a los muchos diccionarios monolingües o bilingües actualmente en venta, es una obra incomparable. Sus autores han excluido específicamente la mayoría de las palabras que figuran en uno o más de los diccionarios de mayor circulación.

Tras largos años de investigación de campo y de revisión de fuentes primarias y secundarias, los autores han clasificado muchas voces según su uso actual en el habla chicana: voces jergales o caló (slang), coloquiales (colloquial), vulgares (vulgar), eufemísticas (euphemistic), anticuadas (antiquated) y así sucesivamente. De este modo, el usario de este diccionario podrá sentirse seguro de conocer las connotaciones sociales de la palabra consultada.

El diccionario del español chicano es fácil de usar. Para hallar un artículo en él no se necesita ser un especialista en lingüística. Con miras a facilitar su uso, los autores han incluido palabras que se pronuncian y deletrean de varios modos, evitándole así al lector tener que buscar aquí y allá palabras cuya pronunciación varía del español corriente. Estas palabras pueden figurar como artículos separados o en el mismo artículo en que aparece la forma principal. Por ejemplo, la palabra *degual* aparece como una variación de *desigual*; *malición* aparece como una variación rústica de *maldición*. Del mismo modo, *espeletiar* está catalogada al lado de *espeletear* y *maniar* al lado de *manear*. Las palabras que contienen variantes como *güe-* o *bue* por *hue-* (*huerta > güerta*; *huevo > buevo*) y *j* por *h* (*hijo > jijo*) también se presentan por separado. Debido al cambio relativamente simple de la supresión de la *d* al final de algunas palabras (e.g., *bondad > bondá* o *hablado > hablao*), no aparecen por separado. De este modo, *El diccionario del español chicano* consta de artículos que reflejan el uso, la pronunciación y la escritura actual, no sólo en la conversación y escritura informal, sino en la dinámica y vigorosa literatura chicana.

El apéndice titulado *Proverbios y refranes/Proverbs and sayings* presenta una lista actualizada de 650 proverbios y refranes que le añaden vivacidad al habla chicana de todos los días.

Un tercer apéndice contiene una bibliografía de fuentes secundarias que se consultaron en la elaboración de este diccionario. Además de documentar las obras de consulta revisadas, dicha bibliografía ofrece a los lectores interesados en ampliar su conocimiento del léxico chicano un importante caudal de materiales de lectura e investigación.

List of Abbreviations Used in This Dictionary/Abreviaturas usadas en este diccionario

abbrev.	abbreviation / abreviatura
adj.	adjective / adjetivo
adv.	adverb / adverbio
Ang.	Anglicism (word or phrase historically Spanish but altered in meaning through English influence) / anglicismo (palabra o frase de origen castellano pero que se alteró luego por influencia del inglés)
ant.	antiquated / anticuado -da
aut.	automotive, automobile / automovilístico -ca, carro
cf.	compare / compárese
coll.	colloquial / coloquial
conj.	conjunction / conjunción
dim.	diminutive / diminutivo
e.g.	for example / por ejemplo
Eng.	word from English borrowed into Spanish / palabra prestada del inglés al español (cf. Ang.)
esp.	especially / especialmente
et al.	and others / y otros -tras
euph.	euphemism, euphemistic / eufemismo, eufemístico -ca
expr.	expression / dicho
fam.	familiar / familiar
f.	feminine / femenino -na
fig.	figurative / figurado -da
fpl.	f. plural / plural f.
fsg.	f. singular / singular f.

ger.	gerund / gerundio
hum.	humorous(ly) / festivo -va
id.	identical (to) / lo mismo (que)
i.e.	that is to say / es decir
imperf.	imperfect tense / tiempo imperfecto
ind.	indicative (mode) / (modo) indicativo
infra	below / abajo
interj.	interjection / exclamación
iron.	irony, ironic / ironía, irónico -ca
m.	masculine / masculino -na
mf.	either m. or f. according to sex of human referent / m. o f. según el sexo
m. & f.	word taking either gender / palabra de ambos géneros
mfsg.	singular (either m. or f.) / singular (o m. o f.)
mpl.	m. plural / plural m.
msg.	m. singular / singular m.
n. place	no place of publication indicated / no se indica el lugar de imprenta
orthog.	orthographic / ortográfico -ca
pej.	pejorative / peyorativo -va
pers.	person (e.g., 1st person sg. = yo) / persona (e.g., 1ª persona de sg. = yo)
pl.	plural
pol.	polite / formal
poss.	possible / posible
pr.	pronounced / se pronuncia
pres.	present tense / tiempo presente
ppart.	past participle / participio pasado
prep.	preposition / preposición
pret.	preterite tense / tiempo pretérito

prob.	probably / probablemente
pron.	pronoun / pronombre
q.v.	which see / véase
ref.	reference, refer(s) / referencia, se refiere(n)
resp.	respectively / respectivamente
rus.	rustic, rural or small town / rústico -ca, rural o de pueblo chico
s.	see / véase
sg.	singular
Std.	standard Spanish, normative usage / español normativo
subj.	subjunctive (mode) / (modo) subjuntivo
supra	above / arriba
underw.	underworld / del hampa
va.	active (transitive) verb / verbo activo (transitivo)
var.	variant / variante
vn.	neutral (intransitive) verb / verbo neutral (intransitivo)
vr.	reflexive verb / verbo reflexivo
vulg.	vulgar, obscene / obsceno -na, ordinario -ria

A

a: a ca (var. of) *a casa de*: "Voy a ca mamá" 'I'm going over to mom's house'; **a carrilla** hurriedly, rapidly; **a cas de** (var. of) *a casa de*: "Voy a cas de Chucho" 'I'm going to Chucho's house'; **a cas e** (var. of) *a casa de*; **a como dé lugar** one way or another, any way it can be done: "¿Cómo piensan hacerlo? — A como dé lugar"; **a fe que yo** (a fixed expression usually followed by a negative statement) as far as I'm concerned, as for me: "A fe que yo, yo nunca la perdonaría" 'As for me, I would never forgive her'; **a fuerza que sí** most likely, in all likelihood, more likely than not: "¿Tendrán frío los gatos? — A fuerza que sí 'Are the cats cold? — More likely than not'; **a huevo** by force, forcibly; **a la brava** seriously; genuinely; **a la buena** voluntarily, willingly; **¡a la!** I'll be!; **¡a la chingada!/¡a la fregada!/¡a la jodida!** (vulg., slang) I'll be God-damned!; **a la buena o a la mala** willingly or else: "Lo haces a la buena o a la mala" 'You'll do it willingly or else'; **a la hora de la hora/a l'hora de l'hora** when it comes right down to it, at the moment of truth, when all is said and done; **a la mala** by force

(cf. **a la buena**); *a la mejor* probably, likely as not (cf. Std. *a lo mejor*); **a las quinientas** after a long period of time (often ref. to a delayed reaction, also ref. to solutions or assistance coming too late to be of any good); **al no ser que** (var. of) *a no ser que*; **al rifín** let's eat; **a manos** tied (in a sports competition); even, all paid up; **a patín** (slang) on foot; **a pespunte** (slang) on foot; **a pincel** (slang) on foot; **a plata limpia** innocent, blameless; **a poco** perhaps (often used as interj.): 'You don't say!' (used when the speaker dares a braggart to make good a threat; also used to register surprise or incredulity); **a poco rato** shortly, soon thereafter; **a raiz** (said of a person dressed too sparingly for the weather); **a(l) rato** afterwards, in a while; **a tiro de que** although, despite; **a toda fuerza** in full swing: "El baile estaba a toda fuerza" 'The dance was in full swing'; **a toda madre** super, great, tremendous (etc.); rapidly, quickly; **a toda máquina** very fast, rapidly; **a todo dar** very good, tremendous, great, super (etc.); **a todo esto** while we're speaking about that, while we're on the subject: "Bueno, y a todo esto, ¿qué hiciste con el reloj?" 'Well, while we're on the subject, what did you do with the watch?'; **a todos tiros** always; **a todo tren** very good, excellent, super (etc.); **a todo vuelo** very good, excellent, super (etc.): "Esa fiesta estuvo a todo vuelo" 'That party was super'; **¡A volar!** (interj.) Get out of here!, Beat it! (coll.); **¡A volar con alas!** Beat it! Scram!; **al ratón** (var. of) *al rato* in a short while

abanicar el aire (slang) vn. to strike out (in baseball)

abanico (slang) easy out (ref., in baseball, to person who strikes out easily); **abanico de enfriar** air conditioner

abarrotes mpl. groceries; groceries and other items sold at grocery stores

abocanado -da running wild (ref. to horses); footloose, wild, fancy-free (ref. to persons, hum.)

abocanar vr. to rear up and run wild (said of horses and hum. of persons)

aboliado -da (see **abolillado -da**)

aboliar (see **abolillar**)

abolillado -da (coll.) gringo-like, gringoized (see also **bolillo -lla**)

abolillar va. to cause to become like a gringo, gringoize; vr. to act like a gringo

abrelio (var. of) *Aurelio* (proper name)

abremos (var. of) *abrimos* (1st pers. pl. pres. ind. of *abrir*)

abricias (var. of) *albricias*

abridero -ra act of opening a door, a container, a drawer, etc., repeatedly: "Siempre anda con esa abridera y cerradera de puertas" 'He just keeps on opening and

closing the doors'

abrido -da (vars. of) *abierto -ta* (ppart. of *abrir*)

abridura act of repeatedly opening a door, a container, etc. (cf. **abridero -ra**)

abriles (usually mpl.) (coll.) years, years old: "¿Cuántos abriles tienes?" 'How old are you?'

abrora (var. of) *aurora* dawn

abrora (var. of) *Aurora* (proper name)

abruja (var. of) *aguja*

abuelito -ta (slang) friend

abuja (slang, underw.) joint of a narcotic cigarette; injection (of a narcotic substance), fix (slang); (var. of) *aguja*

abujazo (slang, underw.) injection of a narcotic substance; fix (slang) (cf. **abuja**)

abujerado -da (vars. of) *agujerado -da*

abujerar (var. of) *agujerar*

abujero (var. of) *agujero*

aburi (var. of) *bure* et al. (see also **de aburi** et al.)

abusado -da bully; clever person; wealthy person; miser

abusar vr. to be alert; to become alert

abusón -sona abusive, bully-like

acá: acá García (see **García, ir acá García**); **acá la chingada** (**chingá, fregada, fregá, jodida, jodía, mierda**) (see also **acá tiachingada [tiachingá]**) (vulg., slang); **acá la madre de los burros** or **acá la madre de los caballos** (fig.) a long way away, half way to hell and gone (slang), way the hell out there (slang); **¿de cuándo acá?** or **¿de dónde acá?** Since when? What do you mean by that? (statements indicating incredulity and often intended as a form of challenge to the speaker): "Ya no me emborracho. —¿De cuándo aca?" (see **¿desde cuándo?**)

acabado -da   old, worn out

acabar   va. to age, wear down, fatigue: "Me estás acabando con tus pleitos"; vr. to wear oneself down, become run down; to die; **parar acabarla de chingar (fregar, joder)** (vulg.) to make matters worse, as if that were not enough (see also **de pilón**)

acaprichar   (var. of) *encaprichar*

acarrear or **acarrear chismes**   va. to spread tales, bear rumors

acartonado -da   lean, thin (ref. to persons)

acarriar   (var. of) *acarrear*

acatarrado -da   said of one suffering from a head cold

acatarrar   vr. to get the sniffles, get a runny nose as when suffering from a head cold

ace   (Eng.) mf. ace (person who excels in an activity)

acomedido -da   accommodating, obliging

acomedir   vr. to serve or help without being asked; to be helpful, accommodating

accento   (Eng.) accent

aceitar   (var. of) *aceptar*

aceite   m. kerosene; **aceite de carro** motor oil; **aceite de castor** (Ang.) castor oil (cathartic) (Std. *aciete de ricino*) **aceite de comer** cooking oil, olive oil

acelda   fsg. (var. of) *acelga*

acelga   fsg. spinach

acero   frying pan

acetar   (var. of) *aceptar*

ácido   msg. amphetamines; (slang) acid ("hard" drug used for narcotic purposes)

acomodado -da   opportunistic

acordión or **cordeón** or **cordión**   m. (vars. of) *acordeón* (Std.)

acorralado -da   corralled, trapped

actobús   (var. of) *autobús*

actomovil or **actomóvil**   (vars. of) *automóvil*

actor -tora   mf. (vars. of) *autor -tora*

actual   (Ang.) actual, real, factual

acú   interj. (nonsense syllables said to babies, probably onomatopoetic) coo, kitchy-kitchy coo

acuaducto   (var. of) *acueducto*

acual   (var. of) *cual*

acultrado -da   (pejs.) gringo-like, gringoized

acupar   (Ang? or var. of?) *ocupar*

achacar: achacársela a alguien   to blame it on someone (ref. to a wrongdoing: a crime, a double cross, a treacherous act, etc); to make a mistake

achantar   (var. of) *chantar*

achar   (var. of) *echar*

achicopalar   vr. to lose one's nerve, chicken out (slang)

achichorranar   (var. of) *achicharrar*

achinado -da   curly (ref. to hair)

achinar   (var. of) *chinar*

Adelfina   (var. of) *Delfina*

adió   (interj. of incredulity) Really?, You don't say?!

aditorio   (var. of) *auditorio*

adolorado -da   hypochondriac

adolorido -da   hypochondriac

adoptado -da   adoptive; artificial, unreal

adotado -da   (vars. of) *adoptado -da*

afane   mf. thief, robber; m. theft

afectado -da   tubercular, suffering from tuberculosis

afectar   vr. to become tubercular

afilar vr. to form a line; to stand in line; to march in a line; to take a walk

afileriar (slang) va. to knife

afiloriar (slang) va. to knife

aflojadora a female who puts out (slang) (ref. to a female who grants sexual favors indiscriminately)

aflojar va. to let out (clothing); (coll.) to cough up (money), pay; to put out (slang) (ref. to women who grant sexual favors indiscriminately); vr. to fart (vulg.), break wind

afrañar va. to understand

agabachado -da (pejs.) gringo-like, gringoized

agachado -da humble, lowly

agarradera (var. of) *agarradero*; fpl. love handles (slang), small rolls of fat on the waist; breasts; **tener buenas agarraderas** to have a good shape (ref. to female body), to be sexually attractive

agarradito -ta: tener bien agarradito -ta a alguien to have someone wrapped around one's little finger (slang), to have someone eating out of one's hand (usually ref. to a woman who dominates her husband, boyfriend or fiancé utterly and effortlessly)

agarrado -da: tener agarrado -da to have under arrest

agarrar va. to catch on, get (coll.), comprehend; to take in, reduce the dimensions of (e.g., clothes that are too large); to arrest; to capture; to employ: "¿Por qué no buscas trabajo allí? Dicen que allí sí agarran mujeres jóvenes" 'Why don't look for work there? They say that they do employ (take) young women there'; to tune into a radio station; to get a call through on the telephone; to fall prey to a vice; **agarrar abajo** to keep someone in his/her place, keep down (coll.); **agarrar ai(g)re** to get caught in cold air (folk medicine's belief is that such exposure will precipitate muscular pains or spasms); (Ang.) to go outdoors to get a breath of fresh air; to scram (slang), go (leave) abruptly; **agarrar a alguien de mandadero -ra** to use someone as an errand boy/girl repeatedly (he/she usually complains by saying "Ya me agarraste de mandadero -ra"); **agarrar a alguien de su cuenta** to have someone on a string (fig.), maintain in a position of dependency: "Ya déjalo, ya lo agarraste bastante de tu cuenta"; **agarrar a alguien de vacil/agarrar a alguien de vacilón** to pick on someone, make him/her bear the brunt of one's kidding (teasing); **agarrar bien agarradito -ta** to grasp very tightly; to trap a criminal beyond the possibility of escape; **agarrar chanza** (Ang.) to take a chance, to risk; **agarrar clases/cursos** to take courses (in school); **agarrar de carrito** to harp on the same subject, talk constantly about the same thing (see also **carrito** and **tener**); to hound someone to death (fig.), annoy in an extreme fashion; **agarrar de puro pedo** to hound someone to death (fig.); **agarrar de una cuenta** to harp on the same theme; to hound someone to death (fig.), annoy in an extreme fashion; **agarrar descuidado -da a alguien** to take someone by surprise; **agarrar el chivo** (Ang.) to get someone's goat (fig.): "Juan le agarró el chivo a Pepe, por eso se peliaron (pelearon)" 'Juan got Pepe's goat, and that's why they got into a fight'; **agarrar el sueño** to get to sleep: "Me tomé una píldora pero no pude agarrar el sueño" (Std. *conciliar el sueño*); **agarrar en** to fall into the habit of, to take a notion to: "En estos días ha agarrado en comer huevos y tortillas" 'Recently he's taken a notion to eating eggs and tortillas'; **agarrar pa(ra) (a)trás** (Ang.) to retract, take back (i.e., something someone one has said); **agarrar correntía** vn. to gain momentum; to get a running start; **agarrar (el) gusto** to develop a taste for: "Ya le agarró (el) gusto a la cerveza" 'He's already developed a taste for beer'; **agarrar el trago (el vicio, la botella, la bebida, la tetera, la tomada)** or **agarrarla** to hit the bottle (coll.); to drink to excess habitually; **agarrar la onda** to catch on (coll.), to understand; **agarrarla (agarrarlo) mal** to take it (a remark, gesture, attitude, etc.) the wrong way, take offense, take exception to: "Yo te dije la verdad para que ya no te engañen; no la agarres mal" 'I told you the truth so that they won't deceive you anymore; don't take it the wrong way'; **agarrarla con alguien** to pick on someone (fig.), get on someone's case (fig.), get on someone's back (fig.); **agarrarla suave** (coll.) to take it easy, be unconcerned; **agarrar para** to go off to, head for: "¿Pa(ra) dónde agarró Pepe?" 'Where did Pepe go off to?'; **agarrar patada de** (Ang.) to get a kick out of (coll.), receive gratification from; **agarrar por** to get into the habit of: "Pedro ha agarrado por parquiarse (estacionarse) en la banqueta (acera)" 'Peter has gotten into the habit of parking on the sidewalk'; **agarrar tesón con** to harp on (a subject); to use or wear (repeatedly): "Agarró tesón con la corbata nueva" 'He kept on wearing the new tie'; **agarrar vuelo** to get a running start; to gain momentum; to grow fast: "Las plantas agarraron vuelo", 'The plants grew fast'; **agarrarle sabor a algo** (fig.) to develop a liking for something: "Pedro ya le agarró sabor al trabajito" 'Peter has already developed a taste for his job; vr. to fight, come to blows; **agarrarse a cabronazos (cancos, chingadazos, chingazos, fregadazos, fregazos, reatazos, riatazos)** (vulg.) to come to blows (in a fight); **agarrarse al tirón** to fight; **agarrarse a porrazos** to fight, get into a fight; **agarrarse a las mechas** or **agarrarse de las mechas** to pull hair while fighting (usually said of women); **agarrarse con alguien** to take up (relations) with (ref. to amorous relationships): "Dicen que Cuca se agarró con un cubano" 'They say that Cuca has taken up with a Cuban' (Note: it is usually the woman who is said to take up with the man, not the reverse)

agarrón (see **dar un agarrón**)

agorsomado -da (vars. of) *amosomado -da*

agosomar vr. to become frightened or intimidated

agresivo -va aggressor

agricoltura (var. of) *agricultura*

agringado -da (pejs.) gringo-like

agringolado -da (pejs.) gringo-like

agringolar va. to gringoize, cause to act like a gringo (Anglo-Saxon); vr. to become or act like a gringo

agrito prickly desert shrub

agruras fpl. acidity, acid stomach condition; gaseous stomach conditon, stomach gas

agua f. rain; (interj.) Watch out!; **darle (llegarle) a uno la (el) agua hasta la cabeza (el pescuezo)** (fig.) to have a hard time keeping one's head above water (fig.); be in a tight spot (slang), be in trouble, be in a predicament; **de agua** adj. soft, delicate (ref. to persons); wimpy; effeminate; **hacer (algo) como agua** to perform a task with ease: "Para hacer eso se requiere bastante inteligencia. — Pues yo lo hago como agua"; **hacer agua** (var. of) **hacer aguas menores** to urinate; **marrano de agua** hippopotamus; **pato del agua** (vulg., slang) homosexual, pansy; pantywaist (slang), weak, effeminate man; wimp

aguacates mpl. (slang) testicles

aguaceral m. heavy rain shower, cloudburst

aguado -da dilute, watered (said of liquids that lose the desired thickness when excessive amounts of water or, in the case of paint, thinners are added); soft, delicate; doughy; sodden, heavy and soggy (said of food improperly cooked); flabby, flaccid (ref. to muscles), saggy (flesh); **pantalones aguados** baggy trousers; **venir aguado** to be no match for: "Sé que ese tipo me viene muy aguado" 'I know that guy is no match for me'

aguador m. water boy; (fig.) person always alert to shifts in the political wind

aguantador -ra patient, forebearing

aguantar: aguantar buri barilla (slang) to tolerate heavy kidding; **aguantar la vara como venga** (coll.) to withstand whatever comes, take whatever fortune brings; **aguantar muleta** to tolerate heavy kidding; vr. to resign oneself, be resigned to

aguante m. strength to endure heavy emotional and physical stress

aguantón -tona patient, forebearing, able to tolerate a great deal

aguazal m. downpour, heavy rain, shower

agüelo -la (Std. fam. var. of) *abuelo -la*

agüerado -da or **ahuerado -da** fair, light-complexioned, blondish

aguerrido -da stubborn; relentless

agüevar (var. of) *ahuevar*

agujerar va. to deflower, take away a woman's virginity

Águila, El (coll., Hispanization of) Eagle Pass, Texas

¡águila! (interj.) Watch out!, Be careful!; **¡águila ahí!** (interj.) (Ang.?) of eagle eye, Watch out!, Be careful!; **¡águila con los velises!** (interj., coll.) Watch out!; **águilas** (interj.) Watch out!; adj. alert, quick, careful, shrewd; **andar águila** to be on the alert, be watchful; **ponerse águila** to become alert, get smart (coll.)

aguilía (var. of) *aguililla*

aguililla buzzard (Buteo)

¡aguiluchas truchas! (interj., slang) Watch out!, Be careful!

agüita drizzle, persistent light

rain; annoyance, bother (frequently used as interj.: "¡Qué agüita!" 'What a bother!'

agüitado -da downcast, sad; afflicted; frustrated; nervous; frightened; tired

agüitar va. to make sad; to bore; to tire out; to frighten; to afflict; to make nervous; vr. to become frustrated, afflicted, frightened, bored, sad, tired, nervous, etc.

agüite m. sadness; fear; fatigue; boredom; nervousness

agujerado -da (ref. to a baseball player who fails to snare grounders or other hits rolling on the ground); (vulg.) f. (ref. to any woman who is no longer a virgin)

agujero -ra (vulg.) m. anus; vagina; f. hairpin

aguzadillo -lla (coll.) smart-aleck kid, mischievous child

aguzadío -a (vars. of) *aguzadillo -lla*

aguzado -da (vars. of) *abusado -da*

ahi (var. of) *ahí*

ahí: ahí es donde él le dijo a ella or **ahí está el detalle** or **ahí está el huasumara** (Eng. = What's the matter?) There's the rub (Std. *Allí está el busilis*); **ahí está (ahi 'sta)** I told you so, Didn't I tell you (that would happen?); **por ahí (por ahi)** more or less, thereabouts, approximately: "¿Te robaron veinte y cinco billetes de a cinco? — Por ahí." 'Did they steal twenty-five five-dollar bills from you? — Thereabouts.'

ahijado -da ward (person, usually a child, under the protection of an adult guardian)

ahincado -da (vars. of) *hincado -da* kneeling

ahincar (var. of) *hincar*

ahogadito ring (child's game played with marbles)

ahogado -da (slang) dead drunk; **andar (a)hogado -da** to be dead drunk

ahogar vr. (slang) to get soused (coll.), get very drunk

ahora adv. today; **ahora lo verás (verá, verán)** Now you're going to get it (a spanking, scolding, reprimand, beating, etc.); **ahora sí que estás (están, estamos) curioso (curiosos)** this is a fine how-do-you-do, this is a fine state of affairs; **ahora sí que la chingué (chingaste, chingó, chingamos, chingaron)** (each of these exprs. is made emphatic by the speaker when he/she adds **y bien chingada)/ (a)hora sí que la fregué (fregaste, fregó, fregamos, fregaron)** (each of these exprs. is made emphatic by the speaker when he/she adds **y bien fregada) / (a)hora sí que la jodí (jodiste, jodió, jodimos, jodieron)** (each of these exprs. is made emphatic by the speaker when he/she adds **y bien jodida)** (vulg., slang) Now I (you, he/she, we, they) really botched it (good and proper), Now I (you, he/she, we, they) really put my (your, his, her, our, their) foot in it (but good); **ahora pronto** recently: "¿Cuándo pasó todo eso? — Ahora pronto"

ahorcar vr. (slang) to get married

ahorita: ahorita or **sí, ahorita** (iron.) That'll be the day! (general expression of incredulity) (see **ser: ¡no vaya a ser tan de repente!**)

ahoy (var. of) *hoy*

ahua (var. of) *agua*

ahuerado -da (vars. of) *agüerado -da*

ahuevado -da adamant, insistent, stubborn

ahuevar vr. to become or to be stubborn, be (act) pigheaded; to resist

ahuichote m. pimp, whoremaster

ahuichotear or **ahuichotiar** to encourage, stimulate

ahuitado -da (vars. of) *agüitado -da*

ai (var. of) *ahí*

aigre m. (var. of) *aire*; **agarrar aigre** (Ang.) to go outdoors to get a breath of fresh air; to scram (slang), go (leave) abruptly

aigro -gra or **aigrio -gria** (vars. of) *agrio -gria*

aigronazo or **aironazo** violent wind

aigroso or **airoso** windy

aire: agarrar ai(g)re (Ang.) to go outdoors to get a breath of fresh air; to scram (slang), go (leave) abruptly

aire m. (anal) gas; (interj., coll.) Scram!, Beat it!, ¡aire al queque! (slang) Scram!, Beat it!, Bug off! (slang); **darle (el) aire a alguien** to get rid of someone; to fire someone from a job; to give someone the brush off (slang), dismiss; **en tanto que el aire** in a jiffy, in a split second, in no time at all

airepuerto (var. of) *aeropuerto*

airioplano (var. of) *airoplano*

airopla (var. of) *airoplano*

airoplano (var. of) *aeroplano*

airopuerto (var. of) *aeropuerto*

airoso (var. of) *aigroso*

aiscrim (Eng.) (var. of) *aiscrín*

aiscrín (Eng.) m. ice cream

aiscrinero -ra ice-cream vendor

ajá yes; so (that's what you're up to, that's the way it is)

ajear vr. to become wrinkled

ajera (var. of) *afuera*

ajilar (var. of) *afilar*

ajolote m. salamander

ajuera (var. of) *afuera*

ajuevado -da (vars. of) *ahuevado -da*

ajuevar (var. of) *ahuevar*

ajuitado -da (vars. of) *agüitado -da*

ajuitar (var. of) *agüitar*

ala: ¡a volar con alas! Beat it! Scram! **dar alas** to give free rein to; to side with someone

alacranado -da mad, angry; blond; (slang) feminine

alacranesco -ca evil-tongued, malicious, viciously gossipy

alagarto (var. of) *lagarto*

alambrazo telephone call; telephone message

alambre eléctrico (hum.) thin, skinny (ref. to persons)

alambrista mf. illegal Mexican immigrant into the United States (so named for his/her skill in jumping or otherwise crossing the wire fence that forms the border between California and Baja California)

alambrito intrauterine device, coil, loop (form of contraception)

alarma: alarma de lumbre fire alarm

alarme m. (var. of) *alarma*

alavantar (var. of) *levantar*

alba: ¡al alba! (interj., coll.) Cut it out!, Stop it!; Watch out!, Be careful!; **ponerse al alba** to become alert, be careful; **ser alba** to be clever, astute, alert

albajón m. (var. of) *arvejón*

albayalde m. face powder

albocharnar (var. of) *abochornar*

alborotado -da: andar alborotado -da con to have a crush on, be smitten by; **pelo alborotado** unkempt (uncombed, tousled, disarranged) hair

alborotador -ra   rouser; coaxer

alborote   m. usually **alborotes** mpl. (vars. of) *alboroto, alborotos*

albun   (var. of) *álbum*

alcagüete   mf. (var. of) *alcahuete*

alcanforín or **alcanforina**   (vars. of) *bola de alcanfor* mothball

alcaso   (var. of) *acaso*

alcatraz   m. paper bag

alcoholista   mf. alcoholic

alcol   m. (var. of) *alcohol*

aldaba   f. small latch, catch (i.e., of a screen door, window screen, small box, etc.)

aldilla   groin

aldrede   (var. of) *adrede*

ale   (Eng.) m. alley

alebrastar or **alebrestar**   vr. to brighten up, cheer up, regain one's good spirits (often said with ref. to sick persons on the road to recovery); (coll.) to smarten up, get smart

alegar   vn. to dispute, argue

alegrón   -grona   flirt; goodtime Charlie/Charlotte (coll.); f. woman of ill repute, prostitute

alelado -da   stupid, simple-minded

aleluya   mf. (pej.) Protestant

alerto -ta   intelligent

alevador   (var. of) *elevador*

alevantar   va. & vn. (var. of) *levantar*

alferecí   (var. of) *alferecía*

alfider   m. (var. of) *alfiler* m.

alfilear or **alfiliar**   va. to cut (someone) with a knife, stab

alfiler   f. or **alfirel**   m. (vars. of) *alfiler* m. (cf. **alfider**)

alfileriar   (slang) va. to knife

alfombría or **alfombrilla**   (type of verbenaceous plant used as a ground cover in dry climates); German measles, rubella

alfrente   (var. of) *enfrente*

algo: andar en algo   to be up to something, be up to no good

algodón   m. cottonwood tree (Populus deltoides)

algodonero -ra   freeloader, sponge (slang)

algotro -tra   (vars. of) *algún otro/ alguna otra* (Std. *otro -tra*)

alguate   m. cactus sticker, cactus spine

alguen   pron. (var. of) *alguien*

aliento -ta   illegal Mexican immigrant to the United States

alimal   mf. (var. of) *animal*

alimar   mf. (var. of) *animal*

alineado   -da or **aliniado   -da** dressed up, elegant; straight (slang) (i.e., not in trouble with the law)

alinear or **aliniar**   vr. to get dressed; to go straight (slang), cease to be in trouble with the law

aliñar   (var. of) *alinear/aliniar*

alistar   va. to dress up; vr. to get dressed up

aliviado -da   well, cured (of an illness)

alivianado -da   (slang) "high" on narcotics, "turned on" by a narcotic drug

alivianar   va. to straighten (someone) out (e.g., to straighten out a criminal, assist a criminal in reforming); to lend a helping hand; vr. to go "straight" (cease to engage in criminal behavior)

aliviar   va. to cure; vr. to get well, cease to be sick; to end pregnancy by giving birth

Áliz or **Aliz**   (Hispanization of) Alice, Texas

alma: como cuando Dios se lleva

un(a) alma in the twinkling of an eye (coll.), quite rapidly; **es como si dijera/dijiera (dijeras/dijieras, dijera/dijiera, dijéramos/dijiéramos, dijeran/dijieran) mi alma** It's as if I (you,he/she, etc.) were talking to a wall; **tener el alma en el cuerpo** to wear one's heart on one's sleeve

almedón m. (var. of) *almidón*

almetir (var. of) *admitir*

almirar (var. of) *admirar*

almitir (var. of) *admitir*

almohada: consultar la almohada to sleep on a matter before making a decision (fig.)

almuada (var. of) *almohada*

almuerzar (var. of) *almorzar*

aló (Eng.) hello

¡aloja! (interj., coll.) (Hispanization of the Hawaiian *aloha*) Hello!, Hi there!; Goodbye!

alquerir (var. of) *adquirir*

alrevesado -da (vars. of) *al revés*

alta (see **dar de alta**)

altanero -ra disrespectful, discourteous, rude

altero m. high pile of objects

alto: parar el alto to put a stop to abusive behavior or to personal excesses: "Se está atacando mucho; hay que pararle el alto" 'He's becoming very abusive; we'll have to make him cut it out' (coll.); to put someone in his/her place, cut someone down to size (coll.); **ponerse alto** (coll.) to get high, get drunk; **dar de alta** to discharge, fire (from a job); **parar la alta** (var. of) *parar el alto*

altonón -nona very tall, of great height (ref. to object or person)

alumbrado -da (slang) drunk; **andar alumbrado -da** to be all lit up (coll.), be dead drunk

alumino (var. of) *aluminio*

aluzar va. to light up, cause light to shine or enter into (a room, etc.)

alvertir (var. of) *advertir*

alzadito -ta (coll.) imprisoned

alzado -da mf. loner, lone-wolf (coll.) (said of person who dislikes the company of others); put away (coll.) in a penal or mental institution

alzar va. to put away, return to an assigned place of storage (e.g., clothes, toys, etc., to their respective drawers); to put away in a penal or mental institution; **alzar la casa** to clean house; **alzar los tenis** (var. of) *colgar los tenis*; **alzarse una bola** to rise up, form a lump (said of wounds on the human body): "A Juanito se le alzó una bola en el brazo" 'Juanito got a lump on his arm'

allá: allá a las quinientas or **allá a las cuantas** after a long period of time (often ref. to a delayed reaction, also ref. to solutions or assistance coming too late to be of any good); **allá él (tú, ella, Ud., etc.)** that's up to him (you-fam., her, you-pol., etc.), that's his (your-fam., her, your-pol., etc.) business (coll.)

allí: allí es donde él le dijo a ella/allí está el detalle/allí está el huasumara (Eng. = *What's the matter?*) There's the rub (Std. *Allí está el busilis*); **de allí no lo sacas (saca/sacan, etc.)** (a set expression, used to refer to a person who refuses to yield to reason or logic); **por allí** more or less, thereabouts, approximately: "¿Pagaste seis dólares por ese libro? —Por allí"

amá (var. of) *mamá*

amacanar vr. to grab something tightly; to refuse to budge from a place, refuse to move

amacizar va. to tighten; to get a firm grip on; vr. to brace oneself; to make love, possess sexually: "Se amacizó con ella" 'He had his way with her' (coll.)

amachado -da stubborn, insistent

amachar vr. to be stubborn, to resist

amachimbrar vr. to surrender, give up

amachinar vr. to take what one wants: "Se amachinó con el libro" 'He made off with the book'; to strike a blow; to take sexual possession; to neck (coll.), pet (ant. slang), engage in noncopulative amatory activities

amachón -chona stubborn

amar: saber lo que es amar a Dios en tierra ajena to know firsthand what trouble really is

amarihuanar(se) (var. of) *enmarihuanar(se)*

amarrado -da (Ang.?) married, tied down (slang)

amarrador -ra employee who ties or bundles (e.g., vegetables into bunches, wool into packs, etc.)

amarrar va. to marry; vr. to get married, tie the knot (slang); **amarrarse la tripa** to tighten one's belt (fig.), economize; to endure hunger; **amarrarse las naguas** or **amarrarse los pantalones** (fig.) to act resolutely

ambalancia (var. of) *ambulancia*

ambasador -ra (Eng.) ambassador

ambustero -ra (vars. of) *embustero -ra*

amejorar (var. of) *mejorar*

amenorar (var. of) *aminorar*

americano -na (non-pej.) Anglo-Saxon, gringo

americonado (var. of) *amariconado*

amiguero -ra person who makes friends easily

amilcado -da (Eng.) milk, containing milk

amolado -da ruined, down and out (coll.)

amolar va. to ruin, harm; vr. to ruin oneself, harm oneself; **de a tiro la (a)muela(s)/(a)muelan** (a set expression used to reprimand abusive behavior) 'You're really something', 'You're a mess', 'You're a lulu'; **pa(ra) (a)cabarla de amolar** on top of all that, to make things worse (fixed expressions): "Y para acabarla de amolar, (se) robaron también la ropa y el carro"

amolinar (var. of) *arremolinar*

ámonos (var. of) *vámonos*

amos (var. of) *vamos*

amosomado -da dull; ill-humored, sour (fig.)

amosomar (var. of) *agosomar*

anca prep. at the house of: "Estoy anca Juan" 'I'm at Juan's house' (Std. *Estoy en casa de Juan*)

anclar vn. to arrive

anclear or **ancliar** vn. to settle down permanently, establish permanent residence

ancheta (coll.) thingamagig, thingummy (said with ref. to an item whose name one has forgotten)

anda, vete or **andavete** (command) Get out of here!

andada distance covered by foot; very long walk

andadito -ta manner of walking, gait, carriage

andancia light epidemic

andar: anda (ande, anden) al arroyo

(usually employed as an imperative) go jump in the river (lake) (slang), go fly a kite (slang); go to the devil, go to hell; **¡ándale!/ ¡ándele!/¡ándate!/¡(ándese, ándense) paseando!** Good for you! (expression of approbation); Hurry up!, Get a move on! (coll.); That's it! Now you've got it! (i.e., the correct answer to a question, the solution to a problem, etc.); **andar alumbrado -da** (slang) to be drunk, be lit up (slang); **andarle a alguien** to be in a very tight spot (fig.), be in serious trouble: "Ya me andaba" 'I was really up against the wall' (fig., slang); **andar a la línea** to be well dressed; **andar al alba** to be on the alert, careful; **andar al trote con algo/andar al trote con alguien** to be wrapped up in something/someone (fig.), be very involved with something/someone: "El niño anda al trote con el juguete que le compramos"; **andar a medios chiles** to be tipsy, be slightly drunk; **andar águila** to be on the alert, be careful, be eagle eyed (coll.); **andar agüitado -da** to be downcast, sad, frustrated, tired, nervous (etc.); **andar (a)hogado -da** to be dead drunk; **andar alumbrado -da** to be all lit up (coll.), be dead drunk; **andar andando** to be up and about after an illness (said with ref. to persons who are sufficiently recuperated to be able to leave their sickbeds); **andar avispa** (slang) to be alert, be eagle eyed (coll.); **anda(n) que no se sienta(n)/ anda(n) que no se aguanta(n)** he's/ they've got ants in his/their pants (slang), he's/they're extremely restless; **andar bailando** to be missing; **andar bombo** to be drunk;

to be dazed; **andar brujo** to be penniless, stone broke (coll.) (note: only a man may *andar brujo*); **andar caballón -llona** to be drunk; to be high on narcotic drugs; **andar canica(s)** to be passionately in love; **andar carga** to be carrying narcotic drugs; **andar cargado -da** to be carrying (to have possession of) narcotic drugs; **andar catarrín** to be drunk; **andar cayendo** to be coming down with an illness (usually a cold or the flu); to be falling in love; **andar clavado -da** to possess stolen money; to be in the money (coll.); to possess a certain quantity of money in excess of the amount one is accustomed to have; **andar como burro sin mecate** to run wild and free (said with ref. to persons); **andar con alguien** (coll.) to go steady, date one person exclusively; **andar con el rabo caído** to feel depressed, low (coll.); **andar con (en) la garra** to be on the rag (slang), be having one's menstrual period; **andar con la tienda abierta** to be going around with one's fly open; **andar con las nalgas de fuera (pelonas)** to be wearing rags (coll.), be dressed in threadbare or tattered clothing; to be poverty stricken; **andar con pelota** (vulg.) to be passionately in love with (someone); to be carrying the torch for someone (coll.), suffer from unrequited love for; **andar cortado -da de dinero** to be low on funds; **andar corto -ta** to be low on funds; **andar crudo -da** to have a hangover; **andar charca** to be well dressed; **andar chiflado -da** to be lovelorn, obsessively in love; **andar chueco -ca** to be involved in shady deals (coll.), be involved in dubious business practices; **andar dando malos pasos** or **andar en malos pasos** to be up to no good (i.e., to be involved in shady deals, or to be having an affair); **andar de atiro** or **andar diatiro** to be very drunk; **andar de cabrón -brona** to be up to no good (coll.); **andar de jacalero -ra** to go from house to house visiting or gossiping; **andar de jilo** to run rapidly, go like a bat out of hell (coll.); **andar de malas** to be in a bad mood; **andar de mojado -da** to be an illegal immigrant from Mexico (see also **mojado -da**); **andar de paseo** to be out on the town, to celebrate publicly (in various places of entertainment); **andar de puche** to act as if one were the boss; **andar de puntas** to walk on tiptoes; **andar (de) suelto -ta** to run around wild and free; **andar de hoquis** et al. (see **di hoquis** et al.); **andar detrás de alguien** to be making a play for a member of the opposite sex; to be harassing someone; to be pestering someone; **andar el cuerpo** to defecate (cf. **hacer el cuerpo**); **andar eléctrico -ca** to be drunk, be lit up (coll.); **andar empalmado -da** to be heavily bundled up (for protection against cold weather); **andar empelotado -da** to be passionately in love with (someone), to be carrying the torch for (someone), suffer from unrequited love for; **andar en (+ años de edad)** to be __ years old: "Andrés anda en los 34"; **andar en algo** to be up to something, be occupied with (usually up to no good); **andar encanicado -da** to be passionately in love; **andar en el babay** to be out on the town, to celebrate publicly (in various places of entertainment); **andar en el resbalón** to be having a love affair, having sexual relations; **andar en la línea** to be drunk; **andar en la movida** (slang) to sleep around (slang), have sexual relations frequently and promiscuously; to sow one's wild oats (fig.), behave wildly (esp. while one is young); to carouse; **andar en las nubes** to be drunk; **andar en malos pasos** to be keeping bad company; to be involved in shady deals; to be having an affair; **andar en pedo con** (slang) to be in trouble with; **andar en pelotas** (vulg.) to go around naked (vulg.), walk around completely nude; **andar entonado -da** to be drunk; **andar entrado -da** to be tipsy, slightly drunk; **andar ficha** to be broke, without money; **andar ficha lisa** (coll.) to be flat broke, completely without a cent; **andar hasta el copete** (slang) to be very drunk; **andar hasta el queque** (slang) to be lit up like a birthday cake (fig.) (slang), be very drunk; **andar hasta la raya colorada** to be very drunk; **andar hasta las cachas / andar hasta las cachitas** to be very drunk; **andar hasta las manitas** to be very drunk; **andar iluminado -da** to be lit up (like a Christmas tree) (slang), be very drunk; **andar juntos** to go steady (coll.), date one person exclusively; **andar lana morado -da** to be in love (note the process of disguise: enamorado>lana-morado); **andar loco -ca** to be drunk; to be high on narcotic drugs, **andar locote** to be drunk; to be high on narcotic drugs; **andar mal** to be involved in an illicit love affair; to be involved in a shady (questionable) business deal; **andar medio suato -ta** to be tipsy; **andar moteado -da/andar motiado -da** to be high on marihuana; **andar moto -a** to be high on marihuana; **andar motorol -ola** to be tipsy, slightly drunk; **andar manito / andar muy manitos** to be real buddy-buddy (slang), be on very friendly terms; **andar pando -da** to be staggering drunk, falling-down drunk; **andar para arriba y para abajo / andar pa' 'riba y pa' 'bajo** to run around like a chicken with its head cut off (fig.), to rush about rapidly; **andar pedo -da** to be drunk, to be gassed up (slang), tanked up (slang); **andar piocha** to be dressed neatly; **andar pisto -ta** to be drunk; **andar plocha** to be dressed neatly; **andar puerco -ca** to be dirty, filthy; **andar que apenas** to be extremely drunk (so drunk one can scarcely walk); **andar quebrado -da** (Ang?) to be broke, without money; **andar quedando bien** to be trying to make a very favorable impression on someone (usually the object of one's amorous intentions — most often said of a male trying to ingratiate himself with a female): "Héctor anda quedando bien con Yolanda"; **andar rayado -da** to have money on hand; to be in the money (coll.), be unaccustomedly wealthy; **andar recortado -da de dinero** to be very low on funds; **andar rosado -da** (see **rosado**); **andar sobres** (andar sobre alguien) to pursue a member of the opposite sex; run after someone (coll.); **andar socado -da** to be cleaned out (said of someone who has lost his/

her money in a game of chance); **andar socas** to be cleaned out (cf. **andar socado**); **andar solares** to be alone (cf. **andar a solas**); **andar sonámbulo -la** to be high on narcotic drugs or alcohol; **andar soqueado -da / andar soquiado -da** to be cleaned out (cf. **andar socado**); **andar subido -da** to be high on narcotic drugs or alcohol; **andar tiniado -da** (Eng. thinner) to be high from sniffing paint thinner; **andar uno en su jai** (Eng.) to be on one's high horse (fig.), be disdainful or conceited, be putting on airs of superiority; **andar uno que toca lumbre** to be hard up, be in dire need (usually said of a person who stands ready to resort to any means to resolve his economic situation); **andar volado -da** to go beserk; to be distracted; to be smitten with (slang), be in love with; **andar volando bajo** to be feeling low (coll.), sad, depressed; **andarle cayendo a alguien** to be making a play for someone (coll.); "Mario le anda cayendo a Juanita" 'Mario is making a play for Janie'

andariego -ga m. adulteror; f. adultress

andarino (var. of) *andarín*

andaron (var. of) *anduvieron* (3rd pers. pl. pret. of *andar*)

andaste (var. of) *anduviste* (2nd pers. fam. sg. pret. of *andar*)

¡ándate paseando!/¡ándate pasiando! (coll.) That's it! Now you've got it! (i.e., the correct answer to a question, the solution to a problem, etc.)

anduriego -ga (vars. of) *andariego -ga*

ángel de la guardia (var. of) *ángel de la guarda*

anginas fpl. tonsils

ánimas: ¡ánimas (santas) que...! interj. If only...! (similar in intent and function to Std. *Ojalá que...*)

anjí (var. of) *ansí*

antes: de más antes of former days, of yesteryear, of olden times

anonero -ra exaggerator

anque (var. of) *aunque*; (var. of) *anca* (q.v. supra)

ansí (var. of) *así*

ansia: comer ansia(s) to be impatient

antecristo (var. of) *anticristo*

anteojos: anteojos de larga distancia binoculars (Stds. *gemelos, prismáticos*); telescope (Std. *telescopio*)

antes: más antes once, formerly; in times gone by (Std. *antes*)

ántico -ca identical; similar

anticonceptivo -va contraceptive

antifrís (Eng.) m. antifreeze

antigüidad f. (var. of) *antigüedad*

antinoche (var. of) *antenoche* or *anteanoche*

antiojos (var. of) *anteojos* (Eng. eyeglasses)

antonces (var. of) *entonces*

anuncio: decir un anuncio to announce; to advertise

añales mpl. many years

añidir (var. of) *añadir*

año del caldo (coll.) very old; m. yesteryear, olden days, times gone by; **comerse uno los años** (said of persons who look much younger than they really are); **completar años** to have a birthday (Std. *cumplir años*); **una vez por año/una vez al año** once in a blue moon, very seldom

aoler (var. of) *oler*

apá (var. of) *papá*

apachado -da (vars. of) *apapachado -da*

apachar (var. of) *apapachar*

apachurrado -da smashed, crushed; wrinkled (ref. to clothes)

apachurrar va. to smash, crush, squash; **apachurrar (la) oreja** (slang) to sleep; vr. to become smashed, crushed, squashed

apachurrón m. act of smashing, crushing

apagadora fire engine

apagar: apagar el ojo to give (someone) a black eye (in a fight): "Le apagaron el ojo en el bochinche" 'They gave him a black eye in the brawl'; **apagarle las luces a alguien** (Ang.) to turn out the lights on someone (slang), knock out, render unconscious

apalancar vr. to lift with a lever; to open with a lever

apaleador -ra or **apaliador -ra** person who knocks off fruit from a tree with a pole

apaliar (var. of) *apalear*

apantallar vn. to act important, show off

apañar va. to steal; **apañar aire** to escape from (someone): "Tuvieron que apañar aire porque vieron venir a la polecía (policía)" 'They had to escape because they saw the police coming'

apapachado -da spoiled, pampered (ref. to children)

apapachar va. to spoil, pamper (ref. to children); to encourage

aparador m. showcase, store counter; grass catcher (type of basket attached to rear or side of a lawnmower)

aparar va. to buy

aparatito intrauterine device, coil, loop (contraceptive)

aparato msg. buttocks

aparencia (var. of) *apariencia*

apartado part (division in human hair)

aparte reserved, somewhat standoffish (ref. to people); **ser muy aparte** to be a loner, be shy of human company

apear vr. to get off from atop a partner of the opposite sex after having had sexual intercourse

apelativo -va surname (cf. Std. *apellido*)

apenado -da ashamed

apenar va. to shame, make someone feel ashamed; vr. to be ashamed

apenas: andar que apenas to be extremely drunk, be falling-down drunk; **apen(it)as** just, just now: "Apen(it)as llegó" 'He just (now) arrived'

apendis m. (var. of) *apéndice*

apéndix m. (Eng.) appendix; **estar malo -la del apéndix** to have appendicitis

apenterar va. to frighten; to surpass; to degrade, humiliate

aperlado -da pearl-colored (ref. to skin coloration midway between "white" and "brown")

apestar vn. to get old (fig.), to become bothersome, get on one's nerves: "Esa canción la has tocado tanto que ya apesta" 'You've played that song so much that it's getting on my nerves'

apestoso, el (vulg.) the anus

apladir (var. of) *aplaudir*

aplanadora steam roller

aplanar va. to press, bear down upon

aplastar va. to leave speechless, cut down, put in one's place; vr. to overstay one's welcome; to sit down with the intention of staying

a long while; to butt in, enter unwelcomed into (e.g., a conversation)

aplastón m. unexpected scolding or punishment, reprimand; **darle (echarle) a alguien un aplastón** to put someone in his/her place

aplicación (Ang.) f. application (for funds, a job, admission to a school, etc.) (Std. *solicitud*, etc.)

aplicante (Ang.) mf. applicant (for a job, admission, political office) (Std. *solicitante, aspirante*)

aplicar (Ang.) va. to apply for (job, admission, political office) (Std. *solicitar*)

aplogar vr. to regain one's composure, become calm

aplomar vr. to be slow to react (because of inability, laziness, lack of preparation, etc.)

aporreado -da / aporriado -da beaten up, thrashed (in a fight, etc.)

aporrear or **aporriar** vr. to fight

apoyo last squirt of milk from a cow's udder

aprebar (var. of) *aprobar*

aprecio: hacer aprecio to pay attention

aprender (Ang.) to find out, become aware of: "Aprendí que iba a venir el jueves" 'I found out that he was coming Thursday'; **para que aprendas (aprenda, aprendan)** Let that be a lesson to you (Std. *escarmentar: para que escarmiente[s], escarmienten*)

aprenterar va. to outshine; to belittle; to scare

apretado -da tight-fitting (ref. to clothes): "El vestido le queda muy apretado" 'The dress is very tight on her'

apretador m. brassiere

apretar: apretar el mono to bewitch, hex: "A Pedro le están apretando el mono; por eso se está portando así"

apretones (see **dar apretones**)

aprontar vr. to arrive unexpectedly

aprovechado -da bully-like (said of persons), viciously aggressive

aprovechar vr. to bully someone

¡apucha! interj. (expression of surprise or astonishment)

apuchar (Eng.) (var. of) *puchar*

apuercado -da poorly dressed

apuración f. haste, hurry

apurado -da in a hurry; in a tight spot (fig.), in trouble

apurar vr. to hurry

apurón -rona impatient (ref. to people)

apurreado -da / apurriado -da (vars. of) *aporriado -da*

aquélla (see **de aquélla**)

aquello: por aquello de las dudas just in case: "Lo voy a llamar por teléfono por aquello de las dudas"

aqueo -a (vars. of) *aquello -lla*

aquí: aquí así right here (Note: this fixed expression is accompanied by the speaker's pointing with his/her finger; **Y que aquí y que allá y que fue y que vino** (coll.) et cetera, et cetera, and so on and so forth

araclán m. (var. of) *alacrán* m.

Araiza (slang) Arizona

arañado -da stolen

arañar va. to steal; (coll.) to try to get something for nothing

arañon m. scratch

aras (var. of) *arras* fpl.

arbolera (var. of) *arboleda*

arcas fpl. (seldom fsg.) armpits

arco: arco ires (var. of) *arco iris* m.

aredor (var. of) *alrededor*

arengue m. trouble, difficulty

arentro (rus.) (var. of) *adentro*

arfiler (var. of) *alfiler* m.

argente mf. accommodating

argolla wedding ring

argüenda m. piece of gossip

argüendero -ra gossiper, gossip-monger

argullo (var. of) *orgullo*

argumento (Ang.) argument, dispute, verbal fight

ariscar va. to fight; **ariscar mangas** (coll.) to roll up one's sleeves (in preparation for a fight)

arisco -ca suspicious, distrustful; skittish; jealous

arismética (var. of) *aritmética*

armado -da flushed (slang), loaded (=possessor of considerable money or other assets)

armador m. (var. of) *desarmador* (Std. *destornillador*) screwdriver

armar vr. to have it made (coll.), be assured of success or fortune; to have a stroke of good luck, come into good times; **armarse la jicotera** for all hell to break loose (fig.), for the trouble to start

arme (Eng.) m. army

aroplano (var. of) *aeroplano*

aropuerto (var. of) *aeropuerto*

arvejón m. chick-pea (Cicer arietinum)

arracada any type of earring

arracle mf. show-off

arranado -da (hum.) married, hitched (hum.); peaceful; docile

arranar va. to marry, marry off, hitch (hum.); vr. to get married, get hitched (hum.); to sit comfortably

arrancado -da penniless, broke (slang)

arrancar vr. to move off rapidly

from a standing position

arrane m. matrimony, married state

arranque: ser de arranque(s) to be unpredictable; to be temperamental; **arranques** mpl. periods of strange and unusual behavior; **tener sus arranques** to anger quickly; to become angry unexpectedly

arrastradero: irse por el arrastradero to be guided by the tracks of an animal

arrastrado -da mean, despicable; mischievous, tricky; (slang) lousy, crummy, damned (coll.): "¡Sosiégate, huerco arrastrado!" 'Stop it, you damned little brat!'

arrastrar va. to be good at doing things, excel: "A Juan le arrastra para jugar al tenis" 'Juan is very good at playing tennis'; **arrastrarle a alguien el aparato** for someone to be good at doing things, excel

arreador -ra or **arriador -ra** chauffeur, driver of a car

arrear or **arriar** va. to drive (horses, mules, etc.); to drive any vehicle (including motorized vehicles)

arreglada fsg. repairs; act of straightening out (the life of a person previously engaged in crime or otherwise "crooked" business); act of hexing or bewitching

arreglar va. to hex, bewitch; **arreglar cuentas** to settle a matter; vr. to reform, straighten oneself out (fig.)

arrejuntar vr. (coll.) to cohabitate, live together out of wedlock, shack up (vulg., slang)

arremachar (var. of) *remachar*

arrempujón m. (var. of) *rempujón*

arrendar va. to return, give back: "¿Qué hiciste con la camisa? ¿Se la arrendaste?" 'What did you do with the shirt? Did you give it back to him?'; vr. to turn back after having started out, return: "Se arrendó antes de llegar a la casa"

arrepentir vr. to change one's mind

arrequintado -da tight-fitting; tightly pressed together (ref. to persons, e.g., in a crowd); mf. high-pressure artist (person who puts others under pressure, keeps them in a state of tension)

arrequintar va. to tighten (a wire); to get someone into trouble; to force someone into a corner; vr. to press tightly against someone (esp. while dancing)

arrestrar (var. of) *arrestar*

arriador -ra (vars. of) **arreador -ra**

arriar (var. of) **arrear**

arriba: hasta pa(ra) (a)ventar pa(ra) (ar)riba (coll.) with much to spare, in excess; **irse pa(ra) (ar)riba** (fig.) to climb the ladder of success, go to the top (of one's trade or profession)

arriesgar: arriesgar el cuero (pellejo) va., vr. to risk one's neck

arrimado: estar de arrimado(s) to live with someone and be dependent upon them (often said with ref. to relatives who move in with a family)

arrimar vr. to move in with a family (often relatives) and depend on them financially; **arrimarle a alguien la chancla** (coll.) to spank; **arrimarle a alguien una joda** to give someone a rough time, make it hard for someone (fig.)

arrinconar va. to put in a corner

arrolear or **arroliar** (coll.) to go for a ride (in a car); to go for a walk

arroña (var. of) *roña*

arroyo: ¡anda (¡ande, ¡anden) al arroyo! go jump in the river (lake)! (slang), go fly a kite! (slang); go to the devil!, go to hell!

arruinar: pa(ra) (a)cabarla de (ar)ruinar to make matters worse (set expression)

arrumbado -da (vars. of) *rumbado -da*

asarruchar (var. of) *aserruchar*

asco (see **poner a alguien del asco**)

ascrinero -ra (vars. of) *aiscrinero -ra* (Eng.)

asegún (var. of) *según*

aseguranza (var. of) *seguranza*

asegurar: no asegurar to not expect someone to live: "No la aseguran" 'They don't expect her to live'

aseguro (var. of) *seguro*

asentar va. to tamp down, smooth, level, smooth out (press clothing lightly with a clothes press or an iron)

así: así es que so, therefore (conj.): "Nos quieren allí a las seis de la tarde en punto, así es que no vengas tarde"; **así sí (se vale)** That's more like it (general expression of approval); **así no (se vale)** That's not it at all, That's just not right; That's not fair (Note: **así no** enjoys greater frequency than **así sí**); **así y asado -da** so-and-so (used to ref. to person whose name one wishes to avoid mentioning): "¿Por qué te pones a hablar con ese así y asado?" 'Why do you talk with that old so-

and-so?'; S.O.B.; **¡cómo así!** (expression of surprise) You don't say!, Really!; (expression of doubt) How can that be?, Really?: "Se llevaron a Juan a la cárcel.— ¿Cómo así?" 'They took John to jail.— How can that be?'

asiento: asientos mpl. coffee grounds

asigún (var. of) *(a)según*

asilenciar (var. of) *silenciar*

asina (var. of) *así*

asistente mf. or **asistenta** f. (Ang.) assistant (Std. *ayudante*)

asistir vr. to serve oneself (food); to eat

asoleado -da or **asoliado -da** scatterbrained, lame-brained, stupid; crazy, loony (slang); (said of a person dazed or stunned from overexposure to the sun's rays); **tonto -ta asoleado -da** crazy old fool

asolear or **asoliar** vr. to overexpose oneself to the rays or heat of the sun; to show the effects of being out in the hot sun (by perspiring, being short of breath, etc.)

asperina (var. of) *aspirina*

aspirino -na (coll.) person who becomes intoxicated by aspirins, person who "turns on" with aspirins

asquela mosquito (Culicidae)

asqueroso -sa squeamish

astracto -ta (vars. of) *abstracto -ta*

astronota mf. (var. of) *astronauta*

asuavizar (var. of) *suavizar*

asumir (Ang.) to assume (i.e., that something has happened), suppose, conjecture (Std. *suponer*, etc.)

asustón -tona (coll.) fraidy cat

(coll.), person easily frightened

atacado -da (coll.) stuffed, full, filled (e.g., with food); opportunistic; abusive, vulgar, gross; tight-fitting: "El vestido le queda muy atacado" 'The dress is too tight-fitting on her'

atacar vr. to overdo in a vulgar or greedy fashion; to behave abusively; to take more than one should (e.g., food), (coll.) to make a pig of oneself through overeating

atacón -cona bully (-like), abusive; stingy, cheap, parsimonious

atado: atado de cigarros a pack of cigarettes

atajo (pej.) bunch, group (of persons); **atajo de pendejos** bunch of idiots (fig.), group of fools

atarantado -da in trouble; absent-minded, in a daze

atariado -da (vars. of) *atareado -da*

atascadero mess, jam (coll.), difficult situation

atascado -da ignorant; good-for-nothing; mean, base, vile; filthy, dirty (see **dar una atascada**)

atascar va. to jam (an object) into an opening; **atascarla** (vulg.)to insert the male organ into the vagina; to force one's way in, crash (e.g., a party) (slang)

atascoso -sa muddy

ataúr (var. of) *ataúd* m.

ataurista mf. (derivative of *ataúd*) undertaker, mortician; funeral director (usually a male)

atender (Ang.) va. to attend, be present at, go to (Std. *asistir*)

atendiente mf. or **atendienta** f. clerk, attendant

atener vr. to depend upon someone to do one's work or discharge one's responsibilities: "Si vienes a atenerte, es mejor que te vayas"

atenido -da dependent upon others to do one's work

atexanado -da Texanized, Texan-like

atexanar va. to Texanize, cause to act like a Texan; vr. to become or act like a Texan

atibiarse: atibiarse a hacer algo to get a move on (fig.), get busy doing something: "¡atíbiate!" interj. 'Move it!', 'Get a move on!', 'Shake a leg!' (coll.)

atirantado -da dead

atirantar vr. to go to bed, stretch out (fig.)

atiriciado -da sad, depressed

atiriciar vr. to become sad

atizar va. to stir, poke (a fire); to strike (someone); "¡atícele!" ("¡atízale!") interj. 'Move it!', 'Get a move on!', 'Shake a leg!' (coll.)

atocar (var. of) *tocar*

atol m. (var. of) *atole*

atole m. drink made of water, corn meal, sugar and sometimes chocolate and other ingredients; m. cream of wheat (cereal); **atole/atole de avena** oatmeal (cereal); **dar atole con el dedo** to deceive one's husband with another man; **después de atole** too late to do any good; **hacer atole** to flatten, break every bone in one's body (ref. to person run over by a heavy vehicle); **hacerse atole** to become over-dilute, watery (usually said of food losing consistency while being prepared): "El arroz se hizo atole porque le echaste(s) mucha agua y lo dejaste(s) una hora sobre la lumbre"

atolero -ra person who makes or sells *atole*; (also, pej. designation for any vulgar or ill-mannered person)

atolladero tight spot, jam (coll.), difficulty

atollar va. to anger; vn. to wander, roam; vr. to get confused, mixed up

atomobil (var. of) *automóvil* m.

atomóbil (var. of) *automóvil* m.

atontado -da dazed, stunned (as from a blow on the head)

ator -ra (vars. of) *autor -ra*

atornillado -da prudent, having common sense

atotachado adv. rapidly

atrabancado -da reckless

atrabancar vr. to act recklessly

atragantar vr. (coll.) to stuff oneself, make a pig of oneself by overeating

atrancado -da constipated (Std. *estreñido -da*)

atrancar va. to latch (usually a screen door), lock (a door), bar; vr. to become constipated (Std. *estreñirse*)

atrás: coquena pa(ra) (a)trás ant lion

atrasado -da (coll.) backward, slow to learn, dense; half-baked (coll.); relapsed, set back (said of medical patients); willfully ill-informed; **estar atrasado -da** to be incorrigible (as a reprimand for abusive behavior): "¡Estás atrasado!" 'You're really something else again!' (iron.)

atrasar va. to cause a medical patient to suffer a relapse: "El doctor, en vez de aliviarlo, lo atrasó"; vr. to have a relapse, suffer a setback: "Anoche estaba muy bien, pero esta mañana se atrasó"

atrevido -da insolent, abusive

atrocidado -da opportunistic, abusive

atrojado -da behind, running slow (ref. to clocks and watches); behind schedule

atrojar vr. to fall behind, run slow (ref. to clocks and watches): "Voy a darle cuerda a mi reloj para que no se atroje otra vez"; to fall behind in one's work, on one's payments, etc.: "Me van a quitar la casa porque me atrojé en mis pagos"

atufar vr. to become proud

atullar (var. of) *atollar*

aucupado -da (vars. of) *ocupado -da*

auditor (Ang.?) m. bookkeeper

aúja (var. of) *aguja*

aunque: aunque sea at least: "Dale dos dólares aunque sea" 'Give him two dollars at least'

aura (var. of) *ahora*

auroplano (var. of) *aeroplano*

autobusero -ra bus driver

autoridad fsg. the police, police force

aventar va. to push; to throw (an object); vr. to fight; to excel, do well; **aventar a león** to ignore; **hasta pa(ra) (a)ventar pa(ra) (ar)riba** with much to spare, with many to spare, in excess

aventón m. lift, ride (in a car); push, shove

averiguación f. dispute, argument

averiguadero dispute, argument

averiguador -ra argumentative person

averiguar va. to argue; vn. to argue; vr. **averiguárselas** to resolve one's problems: "Carlos nunca se las va a averiguar"

averiguata noise and confusion created by an argument

avergüenzado -da (vars. of) *aver-gonzado -da*

avergüenzar va. (var. of) *aver-gonzar* va.

aviente mf. decoy; police informer

avirote adj., mf. naked, nude

aviso sign, board, placard, poster

avispa bee; mf. alert; astute; intelligent; **andar avispa** (slang) to be alert, be eagle eyed (coll.)

avispero: ponerse (en el) avispero to become alert

avitorio (var. of) *auditorio*

avocado or **avocaro** (Spanish, *aguacate*/to English, *avocado*/to Spanish, *avocado* or *avocaro*) avocado

ay: ay 'stá/ahi está/ahí está I told you so, Didn't I tell you (that would happen)?; ¡**ay tú!/ ¡ay tú Pepe!/ ¡ay tú Pepe, cuidado que te voy a pegar!/ ¡ay tú tú!/ ¡ay tú Pepe, tú la trais!/ ¡ay tú chochón!** interjs. (hum. or pej.) (used to mark or make fun of an effeminate person or else to mark or make fun of an effeminate-sounding statement); (var. of) *ahí*, *allí*; interj. Will you look at that!; ¡**ay mira nomás!** Will you look at that!; **ay nos vemos/ay nos vidrios** (slang) /**ay te guacho/ay te miro** (coll.) See ya 'round, So long, Be seein' you (coll.); **ay te miro, Casimiro/ay te guacho, cucaracho** (slang) (roughly equivalent to Eng. 'See ya later, alligator', etc.); **ésa es de ay** or **ése de ay** (general expression of approval) (slang) Right on! (slang), That's right!; **por ay/por ay nomás/por ay va** (just) over there; more or less, approximately; **ay voy** I'm coming (also **ay vamos, ay van,** etc.)

azadonear or **azadoniar** (vars. of) *azadonar*

azonzado -da stunned, dazed (from a blow, overexposure to the sun, etc.)

azonzar va. to stun, stupify; vr. to become stunned, bewildered

azorrillar va. to intimidate, frighten; vr. to become frightened; to become confused

azotar va. to give (a present); to pay, fork over (coll.); vn. to yield, submit; to die; vn. to fall down hard, fall down with a bang; **azotar la res** (var. of) *caer la res*; **azotar muy feo** (slang) to die tragically

aztlán m. ancient homeland of the Aztec people, roughly coincident with what is now the southwestern part of the United States (Texas, New Mexico, Arizona, California, etc.)

azucadera (var. of) *azucarera*, sugar bowl

azufre (slang) m. heroin

azul (slang) m. policeman, "man in blue"

azurca f. (child language, var. of) *azúcar*

azurumbado -da (vars. of) *zurumbado -da*

B

baby (Eng.) bye-bye (<good-bye); **ir de babay** to take a walk; **ir al babay** to "go out" (coll.), leave in search of amusement

babiche msg. beet(s); bitch; son-of-a-bitch (vulg.) (origin of **babiche** uncertain—possible blend of *baba* and *biche*/bitch?)

Babito (dim.) (Eng.) Bobby

babosada foolish act; stupid idea or remark

babosear or **babosiar** vn. to talk nonsense, act foolishly

baboso -sa ignorant, stupid

babuch (slang) foolish; stupid

bacalado (var. of) *bacalao*

baciero chief shepherd

bacín m. bassinet; bed pan; slop jar

bacicleta (var. of) *baisicleta*

bacha cigarette butt; (Eng.) (slang) badge, identification plate; barge, flat boat

bachicha (slang) cigarette butt (esp. marihuana cigarette butt)

badía (var. of) *bahía*

bai (Eng.) interj. good-bye; **bai bai** or **ba bai** good-bye; **ir al bai bai/ir al ba bai** to go bye-bye (coll.), go out for a walk or a car ride; go out to enjoy oneself

baic or **baica** (Eng.) bike, bicycle

baicicleta (Eng.) bicycle

baicico (Eng.) bicycle

bailadero -ra continuous and/or excessive dancing

bailadora mf. fond of dancing; good dancer

bailar: bailarse a alguien to whip or spank someone; to defeat someone in a fight

baile: baile-cena (Ang.) m. dinner-dance; **baile zapateado/baile zapotiado** Mazurka (type of dance)

baisa (coll. & underw. slang) hand (prob.< *baes* 'manos' in Spanish Romani [Gypsy] language)

baisicle (Eng.) m. bicycle

baisicleta (Eng.) bicycle

baisíquel (Eng.) m. bicycle

baiso -sa (slang) young person

bajar: va. to turn down the volume of a radio receptor (a televison set, etc.); **bajar pa(ra) (a)bajo** (pleonasm) to go down, descend; to get off, climb down from; **bajar de arriba** to leave prison legally; **bajarle la luna a alguien/bajarle la regla a alguien** to flow (said of menstrual fluid), have one's period

bajos mpl. lower floors (of a building)

bala mf. clever person, astute person; flirt; (f.) loose woman

balaceada or **balaciada** act or effect of firing a volley of shots (bullets); riddling (of a person with bullet shots)

balacear or **balaciar** va. to riddle or spray with bullets, fire a volley of bullets

Balde (dim. of) *Baltasar*

balerina (var. of) *bailarina*

balone or **baloni** (Eng.) m. baloney sausage; (hum.) penis

balún (Eng.) m. balloon

bamba Cuban dance; trick; accident

banco (Ang.) river bank; **banco de madera** lumber yard; **banco de sangre** blood bank

banda (Ang?) bandage, band-aid

bandeja washbasin; **bandejas** fpl. pots and pans: "¿Por qué no has lavado las bandejas?"

bandolero -ra lazybones (coll.), indolent (person)

banquear or **banquiar** (Eng.) va. to bank, deposit money in a bank

banquetear or **banquetiar** vn. to have a good time

baño: baño de pies foot bath; **baño de regadera** shower bath; **baño de toalla** sponge bath; **darse baños de pureza** to glorify oneself, take a holier-than-thou attitude (coll.)

baptismo (Eng. influence?) or (var. of) *bautismo*?

baquear or **baquiar** (Eng.) va. & vr. to back up (a car), cause to move backwards; to support, back up; to back down, go back on one's word, chicken out (slang)

baraja: leer la(s) baraja(s) to read someone's fortune with cards

barajear or **barajiar** va. (vars. of) *barajar* to mix, jumble together; vn. to mix with a crowd (said of persons)

barajero -ra card freak (slang), inordinately fond of playing cards

baraña unkept head of hair; (coll. & underw.) tomorrow; (coll. & underw.) (slang) morning; fsg. thickets, branches

barata bargain sale; **barata de quemazón** fire sale (sale at reduced prices of merchandise slightly damaged in a fire)

baratear or **baratiar** vr. to mix with a crowd (said of persons)

barato deadbeat (coll.), person unwilling to pay and eager to borrow

baratón -tona ill-bred, coarse, vulgar

barba: hacer la barba to applepolish (coll.), flatter; **barba de elote** corn tassel (Zea mays) (herb prepared as a tea and used to treat kidney ailments); **barbas tengas** or **barbas tengas y con ellas te mantengas** fpl. (expression used mainly by children to taunt other children, roughly equivalent to Eng. "Phooey on you!")

barbacoba (var. of) *barbacoa*

bárbaro -ra excessive; tremendous, wonderful, marvellous; daring

barbear or **barbiar** va. to applepolish (coll.), flatter

barer (var. of) *barrer*

barra bar (of metal); bar (barroom counter; the barroom itself)

barraca (Ang.) barrack (military)

barral (coll. & underw.) m. muscular man

barranco slope, hillside

barranqueña: hacer barranqueña to gather and take possession of a large number of articles for one's own use

barreada or **barriada** citizenry of

a *barrio* (collective reference to all persons in a given neighborhood)

barredero -ra continuous and excessive sweeping

barredora (var. of) *barredora eléctrica* vacuum cleaner (Std. *aspiradora*)

barrendero -ra m. janitor, f. "janitoress"; f. maid

barrer va. to make the sign of the cross with wide, sweeping motions on a person's body to break the spell of a hex or an incantation (the act is performed by the healer as he/she recites several Our Fathers, Hail Marys and Credos)

barrilito -ta (coll.) chubby, tubby

barrio neighborhood (esp. with ref. to a Mexican-American neighborhood)

barro acne

barrón -rrona m., f. materialist(ic)

barrote m. rafter

bas (Eng.) m. bus

basca vomit

báscula (coll. & underw.) search; **dar báscula** to frisk

base: base por bolas (baseball slang) base on balls

basquear or **basquiar** vr. to vomit

basudero -ra (vars. of) *basurero -ra*

basura scum of society (pej. ref. to persons); **basura blanca** (Ang.) (pej.) white trash (lower-class Anglo-Saxons); (see also **poner de la basura**)

basurita foreign object that has gotten into one's eye

bataría (var. of) *batería*

bate m. penis

batear or **batiar** (Eng.) va. to bat a ball (in baseball)

bateo (Eng.) act or effect of batting a ball (in baseball)

batería (electrical) battery; flashlight; a hard time: "No quiero que me den tanta batería" 'I don't want them to give me such a hard time'; **caerse la batería** (said of a battery which has lost its electric charge; the expression usually makes reference to a car battery): "¿Por qué no comienza el carro? —Se le cayó la batería" 'Why doesn't the car start? —Its battery has gone dead'

batero -ra (Eng.) batter (of a ball in baseball)

batiador -ra (Eng.) (vars. of) *bateador -ra* (Eng.)

batiar (Eng.) (var. of) *batear*

batidero disorderly and messy place; **hacer un batidero** to botch, mess up a job or other commitments; to mess up a place (coll.), make it dirty, soiled or untidy; **hacer (un) batidero y medio** to mess up and then some (coll.) (ref. to a place or a job)

batido -da dirty, soiled (often ref. to persons)

batir vr. to get dirty: "Acabo de cambiarte; no te vayas a batir con ese chocolate"

batismo (var. of) *bautismo*

bato -ta (coll. & underw.) m. guy, dude (slang); f. gal; **bato calote** big guy; **bato de colegio** educated person; guy who thinks he's smart; **bato loco** (slang) cool dude (slang); **bato relaje** punk; ridiculous punk; **bato tirilí** Pachuco (q.v.); **bato tirilongo** member of an adolescent or criminal gang; dude (slang); hood (slang)

baul (var. of) *baúl*

baxeo (var. of) *boxeo*

bayito -ta light complexioned

bayonesa (var. of) *mayonesa*

bebedero -ra continuous and excessive drinking of any kind of liquid

bebeleche or **bebelechi** mf. kindergarten pupil

beber va. to drink intoxicating beverages

bebida act or effects of drinking intoxicating beverages; **agarrar la bebida** to take to drink, develop drinking as a habit

becerro -rra ignorant person

Beches (slang) Batesville, Texas

bedero (var. of) *babero*

beibi (Eng.) mf. (var. of) *bebé* (cf. **bebe**)

beibisira (Eng.) mf. baby-sitter

beibisirin (Eng.) m. baby-sitting

beiquinpauda or **beiquinpaura** (Eng.) m. baking powder

beis (Eng.) m. base (in baseball)

belduque m. knife

bendecido (var. of) *bendicho* (ppart. of *bendecir*)

bendéi (Eng.) m. band-aid

bendito: bendito de Dios good luck (said by the speaker to the person who refuses to follow advice); **poquito porque es bendito** (This statement is made by the person serving when a scarcity of the food prepared or available obliges him to serve out smaller portions than he would normally do under more favorable circumstances); **¡Bendito sea Dios!** That's a fine how-do-you-do!, That's a fine state of affairs!; The Lord works in mysterious ways

Benito (dim. of) *Benjamín*

benquear or **benquir** or **benquiar** (vars. of) *banquear / banquiar* (Eng.)

beo -a (vars. of) *bello -lla*

bequear or **bequiar** (vars. of)

baquear / baquiar (Eng.)

bequenpaura or **bequinpauda** or **bequinpaura** (Eng.) m. baking powder (cf. **beiquinpauda** et al.)

Berne or **Berni** (Eng.) Berny

berrongo -ga bothersome (person)

besbol (Eng.) m. baseball

besotear or **besotiar** va. to kiss repeatedly

besuquiar (var. of) *besuquear*

bet (Eng.) m. baseball bat

betabel msg. sugar beet(s) (Std. *remolacha azucarera*)

betabelero -ra harvester of sugar beets

betear or **betiar** (vars. of) *batear/ batiar* (q.v.)

beteo (var. of) *bateo* (q.v.)

betero -ra (vars. of) *batero -ra* (q.v.)

Beto -ta (dims. resp. of) *Alberto -ta, Gilberto, Heriberto, Humberto, Roberto -ta*

Bi (Eng.) (dim. of) *Beatriz*

Bíbel or **Bibel** (Hispanizations of) Beeville, Texas

bica (slang) money

bicarbonato: bicarbonato de soda bicarbonate of soda

bicecleta tricycle; bicycle

bici f. (var. of) *bicicleta*

bicicleta: bicicleta de gasolina or **bicicleta de motor** motorcycle

bicicletería bicycle shop

bicoca (slang) money

bicorbonate (var. of) *bicarbonato*

bien: bien dado -da wealthy, rich; (with ref. to a blow to the body) good solid blow, thorough blow or beating: "Te voy a dar una paliza bien dada"; **¡bien haiga!** or **¡bien haya!** Good for you! (expression of approbation); **bien parecido -da** handsome; **bien sentado -da** rich, sitting pretty (coll.); **cerrar la**

puerta (**ventana, gaveta,** etc.) **bien cerrada/abrir la puerta** (**ventana, gaveta,** etc.) **bien abierta** (infinitive) + (noun) + *bien* + (ppart. of said infinitive) to close the door (window, drawer, etc.) good and tight/to open the door (window, drawer, etc.) good and wide; **decir bien** to be right (Std. *tener razón*): "Es mejor que vuelvas temprano —Dices bien"; **salir hasta bien** to turn out for the best, be a blessing in disguise: "Salió hasta bien que no pasaras el examen; ahora no te van a reclutar" 'It turned out for the best that you didn't pass the examination; now they won't draft you'

bil (Eng.) m. bill of sale; tab, restaurant check; **bil de la luz** (**del teléfono, del agua,** etc.) (Eng.) light (telephone, water, etc.) bill

billar: bola de billar (Ang.?) billiard ball; (hum.) baldy; bald head

bingo (Eng.) (game of) bingo

binoculares (Ang.) mpl. binoculars

bironga (coll. & underw.) beer

bironguear or **bironguiar** (coll. & underw.) to drink beer; to drink any alcoholic beverage

bironguero -ra (slang) beer-drinker

birunga (var. of) *bironga*

birote m. French bread

bírrea or **birria** barbecue; (Eng.) beer

birrionga (slang) beer

bísquete (Eng.) m. biscuit

bítaro beet; sugar

bitoque m. nozzle of a syringe used for enemas; nozzle of a hose

Biure (Hispanization of) Buda, Texas

biure chap or **biuri chap** (Eng.) m. or f. beauty shop, beauty parlor

blaf (Eng.) m. bluff (deception, deliberate misleading)

Blancanieve (var. of) *Blancanieves*

blanquillo -lla (pej.) Anglo-Saxon; m. (euph.) testicle, ball (vulg.)

blanquío (var. of) *blanquillo*

blich or **bliche** or **blichi** (Eng.) m. bleach

blichar or **blichear** (Eng.) va. to bleach (hair)

blíchers (Eng.) mpl. bleachers (for seating spectators)

blóaut (Eng.) m. blowout (of a car's tire)

bloc or **bloca** (Eng.) m. block

blofe (Eng.) m. bluff (deception, etc.) (cf. **blaf**)

blofeador -ra or **blofiador -ra** (Eng.) bluffer (deceiver)

blofear or **blofiar** (Eng.) va. to bluff, deceive

blonde or **blondi** (Eng.) mf. blondy, blondie

bloque (Ang.) m. city block; cement block

Bobito (dim.) (Eng.) Bobby

bobito eye gnat (hippelates)

bobo -ba (slang) drunk; crazy, nuts (coll.); m. balloon

boca: boca de chancla thick-lipped; **boca del estómago** esophagus, gullet; **boca grande** (coll.) big mouth, excessive talker; **hacerse (de) boca chica** or (**de**) **boca chiquita** to pretend to be a small eater; **tener boca chica** to talk very little

bocón -cona (coll.) defamatory; defamer; liar; gossiper; foul-mouthed person; loudmouth (excessive and noisy talker)

bochinche m. gathering or crowd of lower-class or delinquent persons; party, celebration; melee

bofo -fa soft, spongy; fat; **vieja bofa** fat old bitch (vulg.); whore

boganvilla or **boganvilia** (vars. of) *buganvilla*

bogue (Eng.) m. buggy (esp. baby buggy)

boicote (Eng.) m. boycott

boicotear or **boicotiar** (Eng.) va. to boycott

boi escaut (Eng.) m. boy scout (Std. *explorador*)

boila (Eng.) boiler

¡boítelas! interj. (coll.) Hot damn!, Gol-lee!

bola dollar; group of people; mob, disorderly gathering; baseball (Std. *pelota*); pack, bunch, number of similar or related persons or things: "No me junto con ellos porque son una bola de mentirosos" 'I don't associate with them because they're a pack of liars'/"Estoy enojado con Pedro porque me echó una bola de mentiras" 'I'm angry at Peter because he told me a pack of lies'; fpl. knots (type of tissue swelling): "Dicen que las bolas en la nuca vienen de la nerviosidad"; **bola de billar** (Ang.?) billiard ball (slang); (hum.) bald head; **bola de carne** meatball; **bola de la puerta** door knob; **hacer bola** to confuse, puzzle, bewilder; **hacerse bola** to mill around (said of groups of people); to become confused; **volverse bola** to become confused; (see also **dar con bola**); pl. testicles, balls (vulg.)

bolado -da m. adulteror; f. adultress

boleada or **boliada** shoeshine

boleador or **boliador** m. shoeshine boy

bolear or **boliar** va. to shine shoes

boler (var. of) *oler*

bolero -ra m. shoeshine boy; f. mumps

boleto ticket; (pej.) gringo, Anglo-Saxon

bolevear or **beleviar** vn. to dance

bolillada (pej.) action or behavior typifying a Bolillo (Gringo); a group of Bolillos (Gringos): "No quería ir al baile porque allí estaba toda la bolillada" 'He didn't want to go to the dance because all the Bolillada was there' (See **bolillo**)

bolillo -lla (pej.) gringo, Anglo-Saxon; **bolillo con cola prieta** gringoized Mexican-American, coconut (slang, ref. to Chicano who is "brown on the outside but white on the inside")

bolío -lía (vars. of) *bolillo -lla*

bolita yolk of egg; clay marble (used in game of marbles)

bolo dollar; peso; gift; bunch of pennies traditionally thrown to children at baptisms by godfathers

bolón m. multitude

bolsa pocket (in trousers); **bolsa chiquita** watch pocket; **bolsa de aguas** amniotic sac: "El feto crece en la bolsa de aguas"; douche bag; enema bag; **navaja de bolsa** (Ang.? or var. of?) *navaja de bolsillo* (Std. *cortaplumas, navaja*) pocketknife, penknife

bolsita watch pocket, small pocket for storing watches

bolsudo -da (coll.) monied, loaded (coll.); (said of clothes having an excessive number of large pockets)

boludo -da lumpy, full of lumps; m. (vulg.) (said of a male with large testicles)

bombo -ba (slang) rich, wealthy; tired; **andar bombo -ba** to be drunk; to be dazed: ¡**viejo bombo!**/ ¡**vieja bomba!** interjs. (pej.) You damned old bastard! / Bitch!

bombones mpl. okra

bompa (Eng.) (automobile's) bumper

bompear or **bompiar** (Eng.) va. to bump, bump into

bómper (Eng.) (automobile's) bumper (cf. **bompa**) (Stds. *guardabarros, guardafangos*)

bonche or **bonchi** (Eng.) m. bunch, handful; (coll.) gang, bunch (of persons)

bóngalo or **bongaló** (Eng.?) bungalow

bonito -**ta** handsome; ¡**qué bonito!, ¿no?** (iron.) Nice going! (iron.) (expression used to reprimand people for their improper behavior)

bonque (Eng.) (slang) m. bunk (type of bed); **tirar bonque** (coll.) to sleep

bonquear or **bonquiar** (Eng) vn. to sleep

boñelo (var. of) *buñelo*

boquineta m. cleft palate

borcelana small chamber pot; **mearse fuera de la borcelana** to miss the mark; to fail to resolve a problem; to mess up a job (coll.), bungle, botch a job

borchinche (var. of) *bochinche*

bordera (Eng.) owner and operator of a boarding house

bordo small dam or dike; (Eng.) food dispensed in a boarding house

borlo dance; movie theater; agitated situtation; any festivity

borlote m. noise, agitation, tumult; scandal; trouble; **hacer borlote** to make trouble; to liven things up, raise hell (coll.)

borlotear or **borlotiar** vn. to raise hell (coll.), liven things up; to make trouble; to dance

borlotero -**ra** troublemaker; agitator; turbulent, noisy, rowdy

Borne or **Borni** (Eng.) Barney

borol or **bórol** (Eng.) m. bottle

boruca: hacer boruca to confuse, disorient

boruquear or **boruquiar** va. to confuse, disorient

borrachales (usually) mfsg. habitual drunkard, lush (coll.)

borrachento -**ta** habitual drunkard

borrachín -**china** habitual drunkard

borrachinto -**ta** (vars. of) *borrachento* -*ta*

borracho -**cha** dizzy, giddy

borrado -**da** greenish-colored (esp. ref. to eyes)

borrar vr. to beat it (coll.), scram (coll.); **borrar del mapa** (coll.) to kill (someone)

borrego -**ga** sheep; veal

borreguero -**ra** country person, hick (coll. & pej.)

bos (Eng.) m. bus; boss

bosero -**ra** bus driver

bosgo -**ga** glutton

boslain or **bosláin** (Eng.) m. transportation network, busline; bus terminal

bostecear or **bosteciar** (vars. of) *bostezar*

bostezada yawn

bosteceada or **bosteciada** (vars. of) *bostezada*

botana taco given free to tavern patrons

bote m. (slang) jug (slang), slammer (slang); pail, bucket; bottle (in general); baby bottle; (Eng.) buddy, friend: "Hórale, bote, hazte (a) un lado" 'Okay, buddy, step aside'; (slang) **echar en el bote/echar al bote** to hex, bewitch; (slang) to jail

botea (var. of) *botella*

botelata m. (var. of) *bote de lata* canned food

botella fsg. intoxicating beverages; **agarrar la botella** to take to the bottle (fig.), become a habitual drunkard

boti (var. of) *bote*

botijón -jona large-bellied (usually ref. to women)

boto -ta alcoholic; **ponerse las botas** to take advantage of a situation; to have a ball (coll.), have a very good time

botón very young boy who constitutes the male half of the "miniature couple" at formal Catholic wedding ceremonies

box (Eng.) (var. of) *boxeo* m.

bóxar or **bóxer** (Eng.) m. boxer (Std. *pugilista*)

boxiar (var. of) *boxear*

boxin (Eng.) m. boxing, fisticuffs

braca (Eng.) break, chance, opportunity

bracero day-laborer, esp. one of Mexican origin; (by extension) Mexican immigrant to the United States

brandi (Eng.) m. brandy

bravo -va: a la brava by force

brazo: más valen las piernas que los brazos (said by mothers when they see their sons paying more attention to their wives than to mother)

breca (Eng.) break, rest period; brake (on a car or other vehicle)

brendi (Eng.) (var. of) *brandi*

breña (var. of) *greña*

breque (Eng.) m. brake (aut.)

brequear or **brequiar** (Eng.) va. to

brake, apply the brakes to stop a moving vehicle

brete m. eagerness to act

brich or **briche** (Eng.) m. bridge (card game)

brilla (var. of) *brillantina*

brillantina (Eng?) brilliantine, hair tonic, hair oil

brincacharcos msg. high-water pants; msg., pl. person who wears (persons who wear) high-water trousers

brincar: brincar el charco to cross the river (understood to ref. to the Rio Grande/Río Bravo between Texas and Mexico); (by extension) to immigrate from Mexico to the United States; **brincarle a alguien** (Ang.) to jump on someone (coll.) (fig.), snap at someone

brisa fog, mist

brizna drizzle, light rain; crumb; chip, splinter, piece

brócolo (Eng.) m. broccoli (Stds. *brécol* m., *brócoli* m.)

broda (Eng.) m. (coll.) brother

broíta (Eng.) m. (var. of) *brodita* (dim. of *broda*, q.v.)

Brómfil (Hispanization of) New Braunfels, Texas)

Brónsvil (Hispanization of) Brownsville, Texas

bruja broke (coll.), without money; **andar bruja** to be penniless

brujo medicine man, *curandero*

brujear or **brujiar** to go without sleep

brutal (coll.) super, terrific, great, keen (etc.) (adj. of general approbation); f. sexually attractive

brutálico -ca (coll.) super, terrific, great (etc.) (adj. of general approbation); f. sexually attractive

bruto -ta (coll.) intelligent;

tremendous, terrific; (said of problems or tasks that are very difficult to resolve or complete); stupid, dumb; f. sexually attractive; **ponerse bruto -ta** to get stupid drunk (coll.); to get high on drugs

buca (slang) (var. of?) *ruca* girl

buchaca billiard table pocket

buche (vulg.) m. ass, buttocks; **pesarle a alguien el buche** to be lazy; said of one who has a big buttocks; **hacer buches (de sal)** to fill one's mouth with warm salt water so as to kill germs and lessen the pain of a toothache or a sore throat

buelito -ta (vars. of) *abuelito -ta*

buen adv. well (used instead of Std. *bien*)

bueno -na fine (e.g., **buen tiempo** fine weather); **buen tiempo** (Ang.) good time, enjoyable experience; **bueno para nada** (Ang.) good for nothing, lazy, useless; **bueno y sano** healthy; **de (a) buena suerte** fortunately, luckily, it's a good thing: "De (a) buena suerte que vino temprano" 'It's a good thing he came early'; **estar bueno** to be enough (said with ref. to actions the speaker finds excessive and wishes to terminate): "Ya está bueno con esa canción" 'That's enough of that song'; **estar de buenas** to be in a good mood

buenote -ta (slang) sexually attractive, very good-looking

buevo (var. of) *huevo*

buey m. cuckold; ignorant, dumb

bueyada (var. of) *boyada*

buganvilia (var. of) *buganvilla*

búiga, búigas, búiiga, búigamos/ búiganos, búigan (vars. of) *bulla, bullas*, etc. (pres. subjunctive of *bullir*)

búigo (var. of) *bullo* (1st pers. pres. ind. of *bullir*)

bujerar (var. of) *abujerar*

bujero (var. of) *agujero*

búlava (Eng.) boulevard (Std. *bulevar* m.)

bulchitear or **bulchitiar** (Eng.) (vulg.) to bullshit (vulg.)

bulchitero -ra (Eng.) (vulg.) bullshitter (vulg.)

bule (Eng.) mf. bully (person who intimidates others)

bulío -a (vars. of) *bolillo -lla*

bullir va. to incite, provoke; **bullir la lengua** to gossip, speak ill of (someone); to talk frequently

bulto ghost, phantom

buqué (Eng.<Fr.?) m. bouquet (of flowers)

buquear or **buquiar** (Eng.) va. to book (i.e., to enter a purchase as debit against future wages; this practice is typically carried out by owners of company stores)

Búquer (var. of) *Albuquerque*

buqui -quia m., f. child, kid, youngster

bure or **buri** (slang) much, many, very

burlista mf. (var. of) *burlón -lona* (Stds.) joker; mocker

buruca (var. of) *boruca*

burro (fig.) dumbbell (coll.), stupid; **entre menos burros más olotes** the less you eat the more there'll be for someone else

bus m. (var. of) *autobús*

buscamoscas mfsg. agitator, troublemaker

buscapleitos mfsg. troublemaker; person who is always looking for a fight

buscar va. to look for trouble; to incite, provoke; **buscarle la cara a alguien** to seek someone out so as to effect a reconciliation; **buscar pedo** to look for trouble; **buscarle ruido al chicharrón** to make trouble for oneself needlessly, borrow trouble; **el que la busca la halla** if you look for trouble you'll find it; (see also **lado: buscarle a alguien por su lado**); **buscarle mangas al chaleco** to complicate matters

buscatoques (slang & underw.) mfsg. addict in search of a narcotic fix

buscón -cona troublemaker; sharpie (coll.), wheeler-dealer (slang); arriviste; person on the make (coll.)

busgo -ga dog; glutton; **ser un busgo** to have a hollow leg (coll.), desire to eat incessantly

buso -sa (vars. of) *abusado -da* clever, smart

busquita little extra advantage obtained in a business deal

butaca (var. of?) *petaca* hope chest

bute or **buti** (vars. of) *bure* and *buri* (q.v.)

butlega or **butléguer** (Eng.) mf. bootlegger

C

caballada (coll.) group of disorderly or riotous persons

caballitos (var. of) *caballito* merry-go-round

caballo clumsy person; **caballo cuatroalbo** horse with four white hooves; **caballo pinto** pinto horse; **meter caballo** (coll.) to put in a bad word about someone

caballón -llona high on drugs: "Pepe anda caballón" 'Pepe's high on drugs'; large; tall (both with ref. to persons)

cabanuelas (var. of) *cabañuelas*

cabar (var. of) *acabar*

cabaretear or **cabaretiar** vn. to go to nightclubs; to work in a nightclub

cabaretero -ra frequenter (habitué) of nightclubs

cabecilla head (of a bed, table, etc.) (var. of) *cabecera* head of a bed

cabecita (euph.) head of penis; **cabecita de vena** red dots on the skin, angiomata

cabellera wig, toupee

caber: cabiera, cabieras, cabiera, etc. (vars. of) *cupiera, cupieras, cupiera,* etc. (imperfect subjunctive of *caber*); **cabo** (var. of) *quepo* (1st pers. sg. ind. of *caber*)

cabeza (underw.) African American;

cabeza cuadrada (Ang.?) (pej.) square head, German; **cabeza de búfalo** (pej.) U.S. black; **darle (llegarle) a uno la (el) agua a la cabeza (al pezcuezo)** (fig.) to have a hard time keeping one's head above water (fig.), be in a tight spot (slang), be in trouble, be in a predicament; **echar a alguien por la cabeza** to tell on someone (coll.), betray a confidence; to blow someone's cover (coll., fig.); **tener buena cabeza** to have a good head (coll.), be intelligent; **¡qué cabeza!** (an expression directed at a stubborn or dense person or at oneself when one forgets an important date, commitment, etc.); **voltearle a alguien la cabeza** to give someone a swelled head (fig.), cause someone to assume an exaggerated sense of importance

cabezoncito -ta bigheaded, with a big head (note the augmentative and diminutive suffixes)

cabezudo -da hard-headed, recalcitrant

cabinete (Eng.) m. cabinet

cablar (var. of) *clavar*

cable: cable de boca word of mouth

cabo (var. of Std.) *quepo* (1st pers. sg. ind. of *caber*)

cabói (Eng.) m. cowboy (Std. *vaquero*)

cabra: cabra que da leche (said of a person with great promise)

cabrón -brona m. one deceived by an adulterous spouse; (general term of insult, usually vulg.: son of a bitch, bastard, etc.) **andar de cabrón -brona** to be up to no good (coll.)

cabronada: hacerle a alguien una cabronada to play a dirty trick on someone; give someone a dirty deal, do someone a bad turn

cabronazo hard blow (with fist or blunt instrument); **agarrarse a cabronazos** (vulg.) to get into a scrap (slang), fight, get into a fight

cabronzote -ta m., f. large; tall (ref. to persons)

cábula discord; mf. competitor

cabulear or **cabuliar** va. to complete a chore; to joke, jest

caburro (hum.) cowboy (Std. *vaquero*)

cabús (Eng.) m. caboose; (hum.) buttocks; large buttocks, big butt (coll.) (ref. is usually to the posterior region of the female)

caca (vulg.) excrement (Std. *mierda*); **hacer (la) caca** (vulg.) to (take a) shit (vulg.), defecate (Std. *cagar, hacer aguas mayores*); **no valer caca** (vulg.) not to be worth a shit (vulg.), not to be worth a damn (see also **no valer mierda** and **no valer un cacahuate**)

cacahuate m. pill; barbituate pill; **no valer un cacahuate** (slang) not to be worth a damn

cácara (slang) girl; person with acne; acne

cacaraquear or **cacaraquiar** (vars. of) *cacarear* or *cacariar*

cacaraqueo (var. of) *cacareo*

cacarear or **cacariar** vn. to gossip

cacerola cooking pot

cacha: andar hasta las cachas/ andar hasta las cachitas to be dead drunk

cachar (Eng.) va. to catch; to cash (a check, etc.)

cachetada slap

cachetar va. to slap (the face) (see also **cachetear**)

cachete m. cheek; **el otro cachete** Mexico (= el otro cachete de la misma cara)

cachetear or **cachetiar** va. to slap

cachetón -tona plump-cheeked; **cachetón del puro** m. fat man (esp. one who smokes cigars constantly)

cachirul m. large comb, back comb

cacho -cha m. bit, small amount, fraction: "Son las siete y cacho" 'It's a little after seven o'clock'; fpl. facial expression of worry or displeasure; side of a gun's handle; **andar hasta las cachas** to be dead drunk; **traer las cachas colgando** to be wearing a long face, have a hangdog expression (coll.)

cachucha drug supply; heroin or drug capsule; (pej.) police, police force; hat

cachuchazos: darse cachuchazos said of two or more persons (usually two) who try to outdo one another in a competitive effort

cachuchón m. mean or vengeful policeman

cachudo -da stern-faced

cachumbear or **cachumbiar** va. to nick, chip; (fig.) to neck (kiss and embrace)

cachuquear or **cachuquiar** (slang) va. to blow a job (coll.), mess up (coll.); to double-cross

cada: (de) cada en cuando or **(de) cada vez en cuando** from time to time; once in a while

cadena: cadena de televisión television channel; **cadena de tiendas** chain stores

cade (var. of) *Cadilaque* m.

cadernal m. (metathesis of) *cardenal*

Cadilaque (Eng.) m. Cadillac (brand of automobile); any large, expensive car

Cadilec (Eng.) m. Cadillac (cf. **Cadilaque**)

caedré, caedrás, etc. (vars. of Std.) *caeré, caerás,* etc. (future forms of *caer*)

caer va. to swoop down upon, catch off guard, fall upon; vr. to come across with (coll.), pay up, pay one's debts; vr. to scratch (in pool or billiards); **andar cayendo** to be coming down with an illness (usually a cold or the flu); to be falling in love; **andarle cayendo a alguien** to be making a play for someone; **caer agua(s)** to rain; **caer atravesado** to rub someone the wrong way; **caerle a alguien la chancla** to receive a reprimand; **caer como la basura/caer como la chingada** to be repellent; **caer como la fregada** to be repellent, repulsive; **caer con algo** to catch or come down with (coll.) a disease; **caer en cara** to be fed up with (coll.), be extremely tired or disgusted with, be satiated with: "Ya les cayó en cara la comida de la cafetería" 'They're already fed up with the cafeteria food' (see also **dar en cara**); **caer de ésa/caer como la patada** to be repellent, repulsive: "Ese bato me cayó como la patada" 'That guy really

turned me off'; **caer de aquélla** to please, turn on (slang), be attractive to; **caer en gracia** to strike one as being funny or cute (ref. to gestures, comments, ideas, etc.); **caer gacho/caer gordo/caer pesado/caer peseta/caer sura** to displease, turn off (slang), be unattractive to, be repellent, etc. (cf. **caer como la basura**, supra); **caer guango** to compare unfavorably (often in the physical sense): "Alfredo me cae guango" 'Alfred is a pushover for me' (i.e., it will be easy for me to defeat him in physical combat or in games of competition); **caer la res** to fall into a trap (ref. is made to a careless or slow-witted person); **caer tierra** to get into trouble, get caught; **caerle la tierra a alguien** to surprise, sweep down upon by surprise; to yield, fall into a trap (said of someone who falls prey to the calculating advances or machinations of the opposite sex in a romantic involvement); **caer tostón** to turn off, displease, be repellent, etc.; **caerse la batería** (said of a battery which has lost its electrical charge; the expression usually makes ref. to a car battery); **no tener en qué caerse muerto** to be destitute, dirt-poor (coll.); **¡cáete! / ¡cáete muerto!** (coll.) Pay up!, Fork over!

café: café con leche brownish or tan-colored; **café con llantas** (hum.) coffee with doughnuts; **café con mosca** (hum.) coffee with a sweet roll; **café negro** (Ang.?) black coffee, coffee without cream

cafecero -ra coffee fiend, person who drinks a great deal of coffee

cafeses (var. of) *cafés* (Std. pl. of

café)

cafiro (slang) coffee

cafirucho (slang) bad-tasting coffee

cafro (slang) coffee

cagadera (vulg.) diarrhea

cagadero (vulg.) bathroom, toilet; pile of excrement; diarrhea

cagado -da (vulg.) angry, infuriated; f. (vulg.) excrement; (underw.) heroin; (vulg.) brat, obstreperous child; f. blunder, mess: "Hizo su cagada como siempre" 'He blew it as usual'

cagar (vulg.) va. to bawl out (coll.), scold, reprimand strongly; **cagar bien cagado -da** (vulg.) to bawl out good and proper (coll.); **cagar uno a un hijo o a una hija** (vulg.) to breed (produce) a child who is one's spitting image, said of a parent whose child (children) bears (bear) a striking resemblance to him/her; (vulg.) vr. to get very angry; to shit in one's pants, panties or diapers (vulg.); **cagarse de risa** (vulg.) to laugh uncontrollably; **cagarse de miedo** to be frightened out of one's skull (slang), be extremely frightened; **cagarse de frío** to shiver uncontrollably as a result of the cold temperature or out of fear

Cagarrubias (hum.) (var. of) *Covarrubias* (surname)

cagón -gona (said of persons who defecate with frequency); quick-tempered (person)

caguillas mfsg. quick-tempered person; scaredy-cat, person who is easily frightened

Cai (Hispanization of) Kyle, Texas

caiba, caibas, caiba, cáibamos/cáibanos, caiban (vars. of) *caía, caías,* etc. (imperf. forms of *caer*)

caido -da (vars. of) *caído -da*

caidré, caidrás, etc (vars. of) *caedré, caedrás,* etc. (future forms of *caer*)

caindo (var. of) *cayendo* (ger. of *caer*)

caine f. (var. of) *carne* f.

cair (var. of) *caer*

cairé, cairás, etc. (vars. of) *caeré, caerás,* etc. (future forms of *caer*)

cais, cai, caimos/cayemos/cayimos, cain (vars. of) *caes,* etc. (pres. ind. forms of *caer*)

caite (Eng.) m. kite

caja: caja de colores crayon box; **caja de correo** (Ang.) mailbox (Std. *buzón*)

cajeta small round wooden box containing caramel candy

cajetuda sexy (said of women); f. headache

cajón de cartas (Ang.) m. letter box, mailbox (Std. *buzón*)

cajonería mortuary

cajonero -ra box-maker; funeral director

calabacita squash (vegetable); (coll. & hum.) woman's leg; fpl. little white lies (coll.), minor untruths

calabaza dummy, stupid person; air filter of an automobile's carburator; (see also **dar calabazas**)

calaboz m. (var. of) *calabozo*

calaburnia stupid; eccentric

calaca death; sigh of death

calambre m. part of the human body fallen into a comatose state: "Tengo un calambre en la pierna derecha" 'My right leg has fallen asleep'

calango -ga ambitious

calar va. to try out, test; to attack (e.g., hunger pangs): "Me está calando el hambre"; to hurt (fig.), offend: "Me caló lo que me dijo" 'What he said offended me'; to stab, knife; vr. to have a try (at doing something), give it a try: "Se me hace que no lo puedo hacer porque ya me calé"

calavera drunkard; stupid person, dullard; reveler; combination tractor and plow

calcear or **calciar** vn. to walk barefooted

calceta stocking, sock; **desenrollar la calceta** (hum.) to dance

calcetín: calcetín de seda (hum.) upper class, silk-stocking (fig.)

calco (slang) shoe

calcomanía decal; process and result of transferring a design to a wet surface

caldeado -da or **caldiado -da** angry, boiling mad

caldear or **caldiar** va. to anger; to make love to; vr. to become angry, become boiling mad

caldo soup; **año del caldo** yesteryear, days gone by

calentadora: ¡calentadoras! interj. (slang) Shut up! (form of linguistic disguise — note the partial resemblance between the first syllables of this form and *cállate*)

calentar va. to excite sexually; vr. to be in heat (said of animals), become sexually excited (said of persons); **calentársele a uno la sangre** (var. of) *encendérsele a uno la sangre*

calentón: dar un calentón to arouse sexually; to arouse anger; **darse un calentón** to become aroused sexually; to become angry

calientar (var. of) *calentar*

caliente hot, sexually excited; **estar caliente** to be sexually excited; (Ang.) to be hot (ref. to the weather); (Ang.) to be hot, feel hot (ref. to one's body temperature); **ser caliente** to be hot, be sexually excitable by nature

Califa(s) or **Rifas** (slang) California; m. & f. Californian

cáliz: hacer el cáliz to try, make an effort: "No sabe si puede ganar, pero quiere hacer el cáliz"

calmante m. snack before meals; **¡calmantes montes!** (slang) interj. Quiet down!, Knock it off! (coll.), Take it easy!, etc.

clamar vr. to wait

¡calmeroz! (slang) interj. Take it easy!, Knock it off!, etc.

calo nickle, five cent piece; penny; attempt, effort

caló slang (esp. Pachuco slang); dialect; jargon

calofrío hot flash (of the sort experienced by women reaching menopause), hot spells

calorcito intense heat

calorón m. heat wave

calota (slang) beautiful woman

calote (slang) mf. big; politically active; effective in politics

calvito (slang) God, the Deity

calzoncillos or **calzoncillos largos** mpl. man's long underwear, long johns (coll.)

calzoncíos (var. of) *calzoncillos*

calzones mpl. man's undershorts; woman's panties; trousers

calzonudo -da (said of person wearing baggy trousers)

calle: quedar(se) en la calle (fig.) to be left (out in the street), penniless, lose everything

calleja alley

callo: pajuelear/pajueliar el callo to stink (said of feet); **tener callo** to be experienced; to be callous

camada: ser de la misma camada

(slang) to belong to the same generation; to be on the same social level

camaleón or **camalión:** m. horned toad; **fumar como un cameleón** to smoke like a chimney (fig.), smoke excessively

camará (var. of) *camarada*

cambachear or **cambachar** (vars. of) *cambalachear* or *cambalachar*

cambeado -da or **cambiado -da** m. homosexual; f. lesbian

cambear (var. of) *cambiar*

cambiar: cambiar chaqueta to change allegiance, be a turncoat; **cambiar el disco** to change the subject; to stop harping on the same theme

camedor -ra or **camiador -ra** hard worker

camear or **camellar** (vars. of) *camiar*

camello or **cameo** (slang) work, labor; job, employment

camiar (slang) to work, labor

camino: camino de fierro railroad (Gallicism? of *chemin de fer*)

camita baby's bed, crib; (slang) (var. of?) *camaradita* buddy, friend

camotazos (slang) blows with the fists or with a solid object

campamocha walking stick

campana electrical buzzer

campear or **campiar** vn. to go camping

campechano -na countrified; country person, peasant; f. type of Mexican sweetbread

cámper (Eng.) m. camper (recreational vehicle)

campión -piona (vars. of) *campeón -ona*

campionato (var. of) *campeonato*

campo: campo turista (Ang.) tourist camp; motel

camposantero -ra cemetery caretaker

cana: sacarle a uno canas verdes (used by parents to reprimand children when they misbehave): "Espérate, tú también vas a ser padre, y tus hijos te van a sacar canas verdes" (the implication is that the next generation will be even harder to manage if the present generation misbehaves; **canas verdes** is roughly equivalent to 'premature gray hairs')

canalear or **canaliar** va. to cut

canalero -ra canal worker

canco (slang) blow with the hand or fist; mpl. fistfight; **agarrarse a cancos / darse cancos / meterse cancos** to have a fistfight; to beat up (coll.) on one another

cande m. (Eng.? or Arab.?) candy (Std. *azúcar cande* or *azúcar candi*)

Cande (dim. of) *Candelario -ria*

candelía or **candelilla** icicle

candeliar or **candelillar** vn. to fall lightly (said of freezing rain or hail)

candi m. (var. of) *cande* m.

candilar va. to lure into a trap

canica: andar canica(s) / cargar canica (slang) to be passionately in love with, carry a torch for (coll.)

canijo -ja mischievous person, little devil (coll. & hum.)

canilla wrist

canquear or **canquiar** va. to beat someone up in a fight; vn. to fight with the fists; vr. to have a fistfight; to beat up on (coll.) one another

canquiza beating, thrashing (in a fight)

cantar (slang) va. to ask for; to degrade, humiliate; to tell off (coll.), reprimand severely; **cantar pa(ra) (e)l carnicero** (slang) to die

cantear or **cantiar** vr. to incline, lay on edge

cantinera dance hall girl

canto (slang) house; home

cantón (slang) m. house; **el cantón de la perra galga** (hum.) the Greyhound bus terminal

cantonear or **cantoniar** vn. to live, dwell, reside

canutillo herbal tea used to treat anemia ("Mormon tea," Ephedra trifurca)

canuto (see **salir canuto**)

cañoneta (var. of) *camioneta*

capa raincoat; (slang) heroin capsule; **capa de agua** raincoat

capable (Ang.) capable

capaceta or **capacete** m. convertible top (of an automobile)

capear or **capiar** va. to catch; to put heroin in capsules; vn. to tattle on someone

capirotada m. dessert made out of bread, cheese, raisins, honey and shortening; the same type of dish made with meat and without any form of sweetening

capiruche or **capirucho** m. captain

capital f. capitol (building) (Std. *capitolio*); **castigo capital** (Ang.) capital punishment (Std. *pena capital*)

capón -pona sterile (ref. to persons unable to bear or procreate children)

capote (see **dar capote**)

capoteada (see **dar capoteada**)

capotear or **capotiar** va. to snatch an object (usually a ball) on its way to its intended receiver; to leave scoreless in an athletic competition, to blank (coll.)

capotiza: dar una capotiza to leave scoreless, blank (in an athletic competition); to shellack (coll.), achieve a high number of points while leaving the opponent scoreless

capotudo: ojos capotudos bulging eyes, pop eyes (slang); drooping eyelids

cápsul (Eng.?) (var. of?) *cápsula* capsule

captivo -va (vars. of) *cautivo -va*

caquis fsg. fecal matter (euph. often applied to babies' feces); **estar caquis maquis** "El bebito está caquis maquis" 'The baby is dirty' (i.e., the baby had defecated in his/her pants)

cara: dar or **caer en cara** to be fed up with (coll.), satiated with; **echar en cara** to hold something over someone: "Después del favor que me hiciste ahora quieres echármelo en cara"; **hacer (poner) cara de hacha** to make (put on) an expression of intense displeasure; **tener cuerpo de tentación y cara de arrepentimiento** to have a beautiful body and a homely face (said of a woman); **torcerle or voltearle (voltiarle) la cara a alguien** to snub, slight, give someone the cold shoulder (coll.); (see also **dar en cara**)

carácter (Ang.) personage in a play, character; oddball (slang), eccentric person

carácteres (var. of Std. pl.) *caracteres*

carajada boo-boo, stupid thing, dumb act

carajazo blow (with fist or object)

carajo -ja mischievous, tricky; mpl., interj. difficult, hard to resolve (mild or violent according to intonation): "¿Qué carajos quieres?'' 'What in the Sam Hill/ tarnation (etc.) do you want?'

caramelo peppermint stick

caranchada trick, mischief; stroke of bad luck

carancho -cha mischievous, tricky

carantizar va. (var. of) *garantizar*

carátula (slang) face

carbulador m. (var. of) *carburador* m.

carcacha old car, jalopy (coll.)

carcaja (slang) (var. of) *carcacha*

carcaje (Eng.?) carcass

carcajear or **carcajiar** vr. to laugh heartily, guffaw

carcamonía (var. of) *calcomanía*

carceleja type of children's game played with marbles

careado -da or **cariado -da** at par, beginning a sports competition on an equal footing; f. sports competition not involving a handicap

carga (slang & underw.) load of narcotics

cargado -da bothersome; over-bearing; boring; strong (e.g., strong coffee): "El café está muy cargado" 'The coffee is very strong'; thick (e.g., beard or hair); heavy: "El tráfico está muy cargado" 'The traffic is very heavy'; **andar cargado -da** (underw.) to be carrying drugs

cargador m. pallbearer

cargar (Ang.) va. to charge (merchandise to an account); **cargar canica** to be passionately in love with, carry the torch for (coll.); **cargar(se) la calentura** to increase or persist (ref. to fever): "Anoche se le cargó la calentura al niño" 'The child's fever went up last night'; **cargar la carreta** for one person to do most of the work in a supposedly cooperative ven-ture, to take the lion's share of the burden; **cargar la educación en la punta de los pies/cargar la educación en los talones** (ref. to an educated person who behaves in an ill-bred manner); **cargar pelota** (slang) to be passionately in love with, carry the torch for (coll.); **cargársele a alguien mucho** to take someone's death very hard: "A Julio se le cargó mucho la muerte de su bisabuela"

cargo: hacerle cargos a alguien (Ang.) to bring charges against someone (in a law suit)

carguero freight train

cariñoso -sa likeable

carita flirt, tease

carlango -ga raggedy; m. coat (in general)

carlanguiento -ta raggedy; sickly-looking

carmesa (var. of) *quermés* or *quermese* (also spelled *kermés, kermese*)

carmín m. lipstick

carnajal mf. a person (usually a drug addict) wishing to purchase drugs illegally

carnal (slang) (shortened form of the Std. *hermano carnal* blood brother?) m. brother

carnala (slang) (shortened form of the Std. *hermana carnal*/blood sister?) sister

carnalismo comradeship

carnalongo -ga (slang) m. big brother; f. big sister (see **carnal**)

carne: bolas de carne meatballs; **carne del diablo** devilled ham; **carne molida** hamburger meat, ground meat; **carne picada** ham-burger meat, ground meat

carnicero: cantar pa(ra) (e)l carnicero (slang) to die

carnival (Eng.?) (var. of?) *car-naval* carnival

carnosidad: carnosidad del ojo fleshy eye growth (pterigium)

carpanta multitude

carpeta (Ang.) carpet; rug

carta: leer las cartas (var. of) *echar las cartas* to tell someone's fortune with cards

cartelón m. placard

cartita small card (e.g., a filing card)

cartuchera holster

cartucho a package of marihuana cigarettes

cartún (Eng.) m. cartoon

carranclán m. type of cloth used for women's dresses

carrazo luxurious automobile

carrerear or **carreriar** va. to hurry someone along; vn. to hurry, rush

carrería mass or bunch of auto-mobiles

carretía or **carretilla** spool (e.g., spool of thread)

carretón m. child's toy wagon

carría or **carrilla: ¡carrilla!** interj. Hurry up!; **agarrar a carrilla** to give chase to; **dar carrilla** to bother, pester; **echar en carrilla** to give chase to; **hacer algo a carrilla** to do something hurriedly

carrito streetcar, tram; **agarrar de carrito a alguien** to hound some-one to death (fig.), annoy him/her in an extreme fashion; **tener car-rito** to harp on the same subject

carrizo fishing rod

carroferril m. (var. of) *ferrocarril* m.

carrucha or **carrucho** (coll.) ja-lopy, clunker (slang), old worthless car

carruchar va. to cart off, carry off; vn. to ride in a car

carrumfla (slang) jalopy, old car; (hum.) face

casa: casa de alto two-story house; **casa de apartamentos** (Ang.) apartment house, apartment build-ing; **casa de borde** or **casa de borderos** or **casa de bordos** (Ang.) boarding house; **casa de cambio** currency exchange; **casa de corte(s)** (Ang.) courthouse; **casa de (los) viejitos** nursing home, old folks' home; **casa de renta** (Ang.) house for rent; rented house; **casa grande** (Ang?) (slang) big house (i.e., penitentiary); **casa mortuoria** funeral home; **casa redonda** (Ang.) round house (for the switching and repairing of trains); **levantar la casa** to clean the house, tidy up

Casanova m. adulterer

cascar va. to ask for and receive something

cáscara or **cascarita** scab (of a sore or healing wound)

cascarear or **cascariar** vn. to use one's last ounce of strength in order to accomplish something

cascarón (used mainly in mpl.: **cascarones**) egg shells filled with confetti, then painted, and sub-sequently broken over people's heads, festively, at Eastertime

cas: cas de (see **acas de**)

case prep. at the home of: "Está case Felipe" 'He's at Felipe's house'

casera baby-sitter; person who enjoys doing household chores; homebody

casimiento (var. of) *casamiento*

Casimiro: ahi (ahí) te miro Casimiro see you later alligator (slang) (see also **ahi (ahí) te guacho cucaracho**); **Casimiro**

Guerra (slang & hum.) (a play on words: "Casi miro guerra" 'I'm about to see the war') m. young man about to be drafted

casita outhouse, privy; **la casita de los tíquetes** (Eng.) (Std. *taquilla*) box office (theater), ticket office (railroad depot)

caspiento -ta full of dandruff

casqueta masturbation; **hacerse la casqueta** to masturbate

casquetear or **casquetiar** va. & vr. to masturbate

casquilla cartridge case; empty cartridge

castaño or **castaña** chest, trunk

castigo: castigo capital (Ang.) capital punishment (Std. *pena capital*)

castor: aceite de castor (Ang.) castor oil (cathartic) (Std. *aceite de ricino* m.)

casualidad: ¡qué casualidad! That'll be the day! (general expression of incredulity); How convenient! (iron.)

catágalo or **catágolo** (vars. of) *catálogo*

cataplún (var. of) *cataplum* (interj.)

Catarino -na (vars. of) *Catalino -na*

catarriento -ta (vars. of) *catarroso -sa*

catarro: catarro constipado chronic headcold (coryza); hay fever

Cate (dim. of) *Catalino -na, Catarino -na*

cateado -da or **catiado -da** victim of a beating

catear or **catiar** (slang) va. to beat up (in a fight); vr. to beat up on one another in a fight

catiza (slang) beating, thrashing (in a fight)

cato (slang) blow with a fist; pl. fistfight; boxing match; **agarrarse a catos** to have a fistfight; **meterse catos** to beat up on one another in a fight

catolecismo (var. of) *catolicismo*

¡catorce! interj. (of varying intensity according to intonation) (euph.)

catorrazo heavy blow with the fist; heavy slap

catrín m. dandy, fop, dude, (slang)

caubói (Eng.) m. cowboy

cauch or **caucho** (Eng.) m. couch, sofa

cáusula (var. of) *cápsula*

Cavarrubias (var. of) Covarrubias (surname) (see **Cagarrubias**)

cayer (var. of) *caer*

cayí, cayiste, cayimos (vars. of) *caí, caíste, caímos* (various pret. forms of *caer*)

Cayo (dim. of) *Arcadio*

cazo large kettle used for boiling clothes; bowl

cazueleja children's game played with tops

cebolla (hum.) watch, wristwatch

cebollita children's game similar to tug-of-war

cedrón m. bucket

celefán or **celaféin** (Eng.) m. cellophane

celebrar: ¿qué celebras? (set expression) What are you up to?, What are you doing?; What is wrong with you?

célebre mf. thankful; cute

celebre mf. (var. of) *célebre*

celebro (var. of) *cerebro*

celga (var. of) *acelga*

cemeterio (var. of) *cementerio*

cemita (var. of) *acemita* bran bread

cencia (var. of) *ciencia*
cenicera (var. of) *cenicero* ashtray
centro: centro abarrotero shopping center
centura (var. of) *cintura*
cenzoncle or **cenzonte** or **cenzontle** m. mockingbird (Mimus polyglottos) (Std. *sinsonte* m.)
cequia (var. of) *acequia*
cer (var. of) *hacer*
cerca mf. stingy
cercas (var. of) *cerca*
cerebro nape (of the neck), back of the neck
cerillo (var. of) *cerilla* any type of match (general Std. *fósforo*)
cero kindergarten
cerote large-statured, tall
cerquero -ra fencer, one (usually male) who erects or repairs fences
cerquitas (var. of) *cerquita*
cervecear or **cerveciar** vn. to drink beer
cervecero -ra very fond of beer
cerrado: cerrado de barba thick-bearded
cerrar: cerrar el pico (coll.) to shut up, be quiet
cestón m. kitchen cupboard
cicleta (var. of) *bicicleta* bicycle; tricycle
ciegar (var. of) *cegar*
cielo (vocative) darling
cien (var. of) *ciento* (when Std. requires the full form, e.g.: "cien treinta"); (also in adjectival constructions: "¿Cuántos libros tienes? — Cien.")
científico -ca well-educated, knowledgeable
cierto -ta: ciertos elotes (verdes) / ciertos elotes y cañas heladas certain so-and-sos (said to avoid naming someone specifically)
cigarrera ashtray

cigarro: atado de cigarros a pack of cigarettes
cimentero -ra (vars. of) *cementero -ra*
cimento (var. of) *cemento*
cinc (Eng.) m. sink (for washing dishes) (Std. *fregadero*)
cinco nickel, five cents; **dar cinco** (Ang.): "Dame cinco" (slang) 'Shake hands', '(Give) me five' (slang), 'Put'er there' (slang)
cincho (Eng.) (slang) cinch, sure thing; **de cincho** certainly, for sure
cinia (Eng.) zinnia
cinque (coll.) five; fifteen
cinta shoelace
cinto woman's belt (never ref. to male's belt)
cintura small of back, area surrounding the small of the back; **dolor de cintura** backache, back pain, back soreness (usually at the waist level); **sufrir de la cintura** to have back trouble, have a bad back
cinzoncle or **cinzontle** m. (vars. of) *cenzoncle* m. et al. (Std. *sinsonte* m.)
ciodí (Eng.) m. C.O.D. (abbrev. of Collect On Delivery; the abbrev. has been reconstituted in Spanish as *cobrar o devolver*)
cipote m. straw for sucking up a liquid, for sipping a drink
cirgüela f. or **cirgüelo** m. (vars. of) *ciruela*
cirquero -ra fond of circuses; circus performer; person working for a circus
cisca shame
ciscar va. to frighten away
Cisco (dim. of) *Francisco*
cisnero -ra liar
(c)ito -ta (dim. suffixes) (iron.) quite, very "Ese muchacho está grandecito" 'That boy is very big'

cizote   m. sore; wound

clab   (Eng.) m. (var. of) *club*

claco   (slang) nickel, five cents

clapiar   (Eng.) va. to clap, applaud; to cut in on someone at a dance; vn. to clap, applaud

claridoso -sa   frank, blunt

clas or clasia   (vars. of) *clase* f.

clavado -da   (underw.) stolen; echarse un clavado/tirarse un clavado to dive into water

clavar   (slang) vr. to steal, pocket, appropriate: "Se clavó con el dinero" 'He pocketed the money'; to fail to return a borrowed item; clavar la uña to sell (often through high-pressure tactics); to borrow money; to stab

clavel   (slang) mf. thieving; thief

clavelito -ta   (slang) mf. thieving; thief

clavete   (slang) adj. thieving; m. thief (ref. to male thieves only)

clavetear or clavetiar   vr. (slang) (vars. of) *clavar* vr.

clavetín   (slang) m. robbery

cleimiar   (Eng.) va. & vn. to claim

clemo   (slang) penny, one-cent piece

clepear or clepiar   (Eng.) (vars. of) *clapiar*

clepto -ta   (var. of) *cleptomaníaco -ca*

Cleta   (dim. of) Henriqueta

cleta   (var. of) *bicicleta* and *tricicleta*

clíners   (Eng.) mpl. cleaners, dry cleaners; llevar a los clíners (Ang.) (slang) to take to the cleaners (coll.), to clean someone out (fig.), impoverish someone

clipa   (Eng.) (usually clipas) clippers, shears

clipeado -da or clipiado -da   (Eng.) clipped, sheared; cheated, overcharged

clipear or clipiar   (Eng.) to clip, shear; to cheat, overcharge

clob   m. (var. of Eng.) *club* m.

cloche   (Eng.) m. clutch (automotive) (Std. *embrague* m.); meter el cloche to step on the clutch (of a vehicle)

cloche or croche   m. (Eng.) crutch (aid in walking)

clorax or clorox   (Eng.) m. bleach, chlorine

cloroforme   m. (var. of) *cloroformo*

cobija(s): pegársele a alguien la(s) cobija(s)   to oversleep

cobrador -ra   persistent in collecting money that is due

cobre   m. penny, one-cent piece

cobrón -brona   persistent in collecting money that is due

coca   cocaine

cócciz   m. tailbone, coccyx

cocedor   m. oven

cociniar or cociñar   (vars. of) *cocinar*

coco   (hum.) head, skull; (child language) hurt, injury

cocoles   mpl. beans

cocomaletas or cucomaletas   msg. bogeyman

cocolmeca   herbal tea (sarsaparilla, Smilax mexicana) used to treat kidney ailments

cócono   turkey; gigolo; (slang) male homosexual; mf. person high on drugs

coctel or cóctel or cocteil   (Eng.) m. cocktail party; cocktail (alcoholic drink)

coche   (Eng.) m. coach, athletic trainer

cochino -na   nasty; indecent

cochito -ta   conformist, square (coll.)

cochotas: cochotas de papá   (term

of endearment with a slight tinge of vulgarity to it; possible Eng. equivalent: 'Daddy's sweet mama')

cochote -ta m. sugar daddy; f. sweet mamma (terms of endearment, often used in the vocative; cf. **cochotas** supra); mf. fat person

codo stingy; **empinar el codo** to drink (usually intoxicating beverages)

cófiro (slang) coffee

cogedera (vulg.) fornication; sexual orgy

cogedor -ra m. sex fiend, satyr; f. nymphomaniac

coger (vulg.) va. to fornicate; **coger en las moras** (coll.) to catch red-handed; **coger frío** (Ang.) to catch cold, get a cold; **coger pa(ra)** to head toward, go in the direction of; **cogerse algo** to steal

cogido -da (vulg.) screwed (vulg. slang); f. screwing (vulg.), fornication: "Le dieron su buena cogida" 'They really screwed her over'

coil (Eng.) m. intrauterine device, coil, loop (contraceptive)

cojín m. adulteress; unmarried woman who enjoys sex frequently

cola fsg. buttocks; (Eng.) long distance telephone call; (fig. and slang) tail, shadow; probation officer (i.e., anyone who "follows" a criminal, a suspect or an ex-criminal); **cola afuera** (Eng.) long distance telephone call; **cola larga** sly, astute, tricky; **cortar la cola** (hum.) to baptize; **poner cola** (Ang.?) to put a tail on (someone) (e.g., to have someone follow a suspect); **salir con cola** to travel with one's family; to leave prison on parole; **tener cola** to be on probation; **no tener cola que le**

pisen to have nothing to be ashamed of, have no skeletons in the closet; **traer cola** to have underclothing showing

colar vr. to slip in and out, sneak in and out

colcrim or **colcrín** (Eng.) m. cold cream

colcha: ¿cuáles colchas? interj. 'What do you mean?', 'What the hell are you talking about?' (esp. with the implication: 'I didn't promise you anything'); **pegársele a alguien las colchas** to oversleep: "A Luis se le pagaron las colchas, por eso llegó tarde"

colear or **coliar** va. to follow, tail (slang); to grab by the seat of the pants or by the skirt; to borrow; (var. of) *colorear* to color

colectador -ra collector (e.g., of taxes)

colectar va. to collect

colegiante mf. student; college student

colerear or **coleriar** va. to borrow

colero -ra sponger, freeloader (coll.)

colgar: colgar jeta(s)/colgar chica(s) jeta(s)/colgar tamaña(s) jeta(s) (slang) to pout; **colgar los guantes** (fig.) to retire from boxing; **colgar los tenis** (fig. & hum.) to die

coliche mf. tagalong, person (usually youngster) who follows others wherever they go

colmar: colmarle a alguien el plato to cause someone to come to the end of his/her rope (coll.): "Ya me colmaste el plato con tu abuso. ¡Vete!"

colmena bee

colón m. (Eng.?) or (var. of?) *colonia* cologne, eau-de-cologne

colopear or **colopiar** (Ang. of *columpiar* to swing?) to go out on the town (coll.), have a good time in nightclubs, etc.

color m.: pl. type of children's game; **dar colores** to show off

colorada (slang) secconal capsule; blood; **sacarle a alguien la colorada** to give someone a bloody nose

colote m. (var. of) *culote* m.

colote m. laundry bag

coltura (var. of) *cultura*

coludo -da showing, hanging out (said of underclothing, shirttails, etc.)

columpio -pia tightwad (coll.), person who never pays; person who walks with an exaggerated swinging gait; **cada chango a su columpio y a columpiarse luego** let each one attend to his/her own affairs

coma (var. of) *goma*

combate: fuera de combate unwell, out of sorts: "Por qué no vino Pedro a la fiesta? — Porque se sentía fuera de combate" 'Why didn't Peter come to the party? — Because he felt under the weather'

combiar (Eng.) va. to comb

comelón -lona glutton (Std. *comilón -lona*)

comemierda mf. (vulg.) a shit-ass (vulg., slang), son-of-a-bitch, (vulg.), no-good bastard (vulg., slang), highly contemptible or objectionable person

comenzón (var. of) *comezón*

comer: comer ansia(s) to be impatient; **comer con la vista** to devour with glances; **comer gallo** to become aggressive; to hit foul balls (note bilingual pun: foul — baseball term is equated with fowl — *gallo*); **comerse una carta** to fail to answer a letter; **comerse a una persona** to browbeat someone; **comerse a alguien con los ojos** to stare at someone with hatred or anxiety; **comerse a alguien vivo** to tell someone where to get off (slang) in no uncertain terms, reprimand someone severely; **comerse alguien sus palabras** (Ang.) to eat one's words (fig.), retract something one has said, eat crow (coll.); **comérsela** for one to keep to oneself, not let out of the bag (coll.); **comerse uno los años** (said of persons who look much younger than they really are)

comido -da full, awash with, blighted by: "Tiene la cara comida de espinillas" 'His face is full of pimples'; **comida de bufé** (Eng.) buffet supper; **comida empacada** canned food

comidor m. (var. of) *comedor* m.

comilón -lona (Std. vars. of) *comelón -lona* (Latin America)

cominos: no valer tres cominos (coll.) (var. of) *no valer un comino* to be worthless (ref. to persons or things)

como: como alma que (se) lleva el diablo/como cuando Dios se lleva un(a) alma in the twinkling of an eye (fig.), very rapidly; **¡cómo así!** You don't say, Really! (used to register surprise or incredulity); **como él solo** as only he can be: "Es loco como él solo" 'He's crazy as only he can be' (also: **como ella sola, como ellos solos,** etc.); **¿cómo te (le, les) quedó el ojo?** (slang) How does that grab you?, How do you like them apples? (slang); **como quien dice** so to speak, as they say; **es como si dijera/dijiera**

(**dijeras/dijieras, dijera/dijiera, dijéramos/dijiéramos, dijeran/dijieran**) **mi alma** It's as if I (you, he/she, etc.) were talking to a wall

compa (<*compadre*) (slang) m. Mac, Bub, Jack, mister, etc. (frequent vocative used to address a person whose name one does not know): "Ese, compa, páseme un frajo" 'Hey Mac, gimme a cigarette'

companía (var. of) *compañía*

compañero: el ____ ese mi compañero (ironic or festive reference to a quality shared by both the speaker and the person referred to; the remark is sometimes made to take revenge on an initial criticism from the person referred to, e.g., "El chaparro ese mi compañero" 'That guy was just as short as I am')

compita m. (var. of) *compadre, compa* m.

compleaños or **compliaños** msg. or mpl. (vars. of) *cumpleaños*

completar: completar años (var. of) Std. *cumplir años* to have a birthday; **completar con** to take care of as well, finish up the job with (you) too: "Y si tú te entremetes, completo contigo" 'And if you stick your nose into this, I'll take care of you afterwards' (i.e., after having defeated the original antagonist, as in a fight)

componedor -ra handy man, Mr. Fix-It (coll.); distorter of the truth

componer va. to cast a spell, bewitch; vr. to reform, go straight (after a life of crime); to clear up (said of cloudy skies); **componerle** to fabricate, distort, add on to change a present or previous statement, to cover up a lie or a fault: "¡Qué pronto le compusiste! ¿A poco crees que te (lo) van a creer?", 'How quickly you added on (to your statement)! Do you really think they're going to believe you?'

comprar: comprar a tiempo (Ang.) to buy on time (coll.), buy on the installment plan

compromiso debt

compuestito -ta (coll.) straightened out (i.e., after having led a life of crime); bewitched, hexed (often used in the context of 'I-told-you-so' or 'He-had-it-coming-to-him': "Pues ya está compuestito" 'I told you they would put a spell on him sooner or later')

con (Eng. or var. of?) *cono*: **con de nieve** (var. of?) *cono de nieve* ice cream cone

con prep. **con razón** no wonder (coll.), that's reason enough: "Se le quemó la casa de María—Con razón no vino a visitarnos" 'Mary's house burned down—No wonder she didn't (come) visit us'; **con safos or con zafos** (insulting) The same to you!, The same goes for you!, Now I've said the last word!; **con el gordo** hitchhiking (Ang.?) to thumb a ride; (see also **con don** —v.s. **don**)

concencia (var. of) *conciencia*

concuño -ña (vars. of) *concuñado -da*

Concha (dim. of) *Concepción*

conchabar vr. to live in free union, form a common-law marriage

condenado -da (pej.) bastard, son-of-a-bitch (terms of insult)

condo (rus.) (var. of) *cuando*

condotor -ra or **condutor -ra** (vars. of) *conductor -ra* (Stds.)

conducí, conduciste, condució, conducimos, conducieron (vars. of) *conduje, condujiste*, etc. (pret. forms of *conducir*)

conductor -ra or **condutor -ra** railroad conductor, ticket collector

Cone (Eng., dim. of) Connie

conectación (var. of) *conexión*

conejo msg. biceps

conferencial m. meeting; small conference meeting

confidencia (Ang.) confidence, trust

confidente -tad faithful; m. sofa (in general)

conformar va. to adjust, harmonize, reconcile; vr. to reconcile

conforme mf. reconciled

conga type of Cuban dance

congal (slang) m. brothel, whorehouse; beer joint

cono: cono de nieve ice cream cone

conocencia acquaintanceship, group of friends

conquián m. type of card game similar to whist

conciencia: tener la conciencia limpia to have a clear conscience; **tener la conciencia sucia** to have a guilty conscience

consecuentar va. to tolerate, bear with

conservatista (var. of) *conservador -ra* (Stds.) conservative (usually in the political sense)

conservativo -va stingy, tightfisted; (Ang.) conservative (usually in a political sense (Std. *conservador -ra*)

consiguir (var. of) *conseguir*

constipado -da (Ang.) constipated, unable to move one's bowels

consistir: consistir de (Ang.?) or

var. of?) *consistir en* (Std.)

consultar: consultar la almohada to sleep on a matter before making a decision

contado -da few, far and in between (coll.), rare: "Son contadas las visitas que nos hace su familia" 'His family's visits to us are few and far between'

contar: contar las muelas to pull the wool over someone's eyes (coll.), to deceive

contentar va. to reconcile; vr. to become reconciled

contento -ta reconciled

contestable (var. of) *condestable*

contimás (var. of) *cuantimás* at least

contino -na (vars. of) *continuo -nua* adjs.

contoy todo (var. of) *con todo y todo* lock, stock and barrel (coll.), absolutely everything

contra (see **dar la contra**)

contrabandista mf. illegal immigrant (esp. one from Mexico to the United States)

contrabando illegal (male) immigrant

contrecho -cha contradictory

control -la (slang) m. gang leader; f. (hum.) wife

convenencia (var. of) *conveniencia*

convenienciero -ra or **convenenciero -ra** opportunistic

convertible m. (Ang.) convertible (car with folding roof); pick-up truck

convienencia (var. of) *conveniencia*

convite m. group of persons announcing a forthcoming event from a truck

cónyugue (var. of) *cónyuge*

copala perch (Perca flavescens)

copear (var. of) *copiar*

copeón -eona or **copión -iona** copycat

copequiec (Eng.) m. cupcake

copetón -tona (ref. to person whose hair is piled up high in front)

coperar (var. of) *cooperar*

copete m. top rim of a measuring glass; **andar hasta el copete** to be very drunk; **estar hasta el copete** to come to the end of the road (fig.), be completely fed up with (fig.), want nothing more with: "Ya estoy hasta el copete con Enrique" 'I've just come to the end of the road with Henry'; **tener a alguien hasta el copete** "Ya me tienes hasta el copete" 'I've just had it up to here with you'

copetear or **copetiar** va. to fill a glass to the brim

copqueic (Eng.) (var. of) *copequiec*

coquena: coquena pa(ra) (a)trás ant lion

cora (var. of) *corazón* m.; (see also **de cora**)

coraje m. pathologically angry condition believed to cause miscarriage, spoil breast milk, etc.; **da-coraje** (hum. or ironic) m. Cadillac (or any other expensive brand of automobile)

corbata: corbata de gato (hum.) bow tie (Std. *corbatín* m.)

corbatero tie rack (perch for hanging neckties); man fond of wearing neckties

corbeador -ra or **corbiador -ra** freeloader, sponge(r) (coll.)

corbero -ra freeloader, sponge(r) (coll.)

corcholata or **corchelata** bottle cap

cordeón (var. of) *acordeón* (Std.)

cordión (var. of) *acordión*

cordón m. string; street curb

cormillo (var. of) *colmillo* (Std.)

corona V.I.P., big shot (coll.), important or influential person; **corona de San Diego** climbing red rose (Antigonon leptopus)

Corpos (Hispanization or var. of) Corpus Christi, Texas

corsaje (Eng. influence: <Fr.<Lat.?) m. corsage

cortado -da: f. (var. of) *cortadura*; **andar cortado de dinero** to be low on funds

cortar va. to put down (slang), put someone in his/her place, deprecate; vr. (slang) to leave; **cortar el mito** to stop talking (used esp. as a command: "¡Corta el mito!"); **cortar la cola** (hum.) to baptize; **cortar las nubes** to "cut" storm clouds (according to folk belief, if an innocent child makes the sign of the cross with a knife out of doors, storm clouds will break up and then disappear gradually); **cor-tarse la calentura** (for a fever to break, cease to be intense): "Anoche se le cortó la calentura" 'His fever broke last night'

corte (Ang.) f. court, courthouse; slight trim (haircut); **casa de corte(s)** (Ang.) courthouse

cortina: ¡cortinas! (slang) (var. of) *¡córtatela!, ¡córtesela!*, etc. Cut it out!, Stop it!

corto -ta f. short film preceding the main feature; m. (coll.) brush-off; (electricity) short circuit; **andar corto -ta (de dinero)** to be low on funds

cortón m. brush-off, snub

corvas: temblarle a alguien las

corvas to be afraid

corre (slang) (var. of) *casa de corrección* (underw.); f. prison, jail

correa immigration or customs officer (esp. U.S. immigration officer on the U.S.-Mexican border)

correctar (Ang.) va. to correct

corredera diarrhea

correlón -lona scaredy-cat (slang) (said of person who consistently runs away from a situation which he/she finds threatening)

correllón or **correón** m. thick belt (article of clothing)

correntía impetus, momentum; **agarrar correntía** to get a running start

correntón -tona common, ordinary, cheap

correr va. to chase; (Ang.) to run off (on photocopy machine), reproduce, duplicate: "¿Cuántas copias corriste?"; (Ang.) to operate, run (e.g., a business); va. (Ang.) to run, supervise; vn. (Ang.) to run, recur, persist: "Esa enfermedad corre en la familia" 'That ailment runs in the family'; **correr el cuerpo** to defecate; **correr la cabeza** to talk excessively; **correr para una oficina** (Ang.) to run for political office

corretear or **corretiar** va. to run ragged

corrida: en corrida written by hand

corriente ordinary, common, cheap, low class

cosa: creerse la gran cosa/hacerse la gran cosa to act superior; **cosa que** conj. therefore, and so, hence; **dejando de cosas** (set expression) all kidding aside, seriously speaking; **la otra cosa** (any narcotic drug substitute); **¡qué cosas!** (fixed expression of endearment and approbation frequently used with ref. to a child's actions) How nice!, How adorable!, etc.

cosita: hacer cositas fpl. (euph.) to copulate

cosota: cosotas (de mamá) fpl. (term of endearment usually used when addressing one's female sweetheart; poss. Eng. equivalent: 'Sweet mamma'); **cosotas (de papá)** (term of endearment with a slight tinge of vulgarity; poss. Eng. equivalent: 'Daddy's sweet mamma'); (cf. **cochotas** et al.)

costal: ser harina del mismo costal to share the same charcteristics, be cut from the same cloth (fig.); **ser harina de otro costal** to belong to a different tribe (fig.), belong to someone else (often said sarcastically by parents to married offspring who seldom return to the parental home to visit)

costalazo precipitous tumble, heavy fall; **dar el costalazo** to keel over, go down like a sack of meal (fig.)

costear or **costiar** to be worth the trouble, worthwhile

costilla f. girlfriend; m. boyfriend; f. girl who keeps a gigolo

costillita: ser muy costillita to be a stinker (slang), be disagreeable to others

costipado -da (vars. of) *constipado -da*

costroso -sa grimy, grubby, filthy, heavily soiled (ref. to persons): "Báñate; andas muy costroso" 'Take a bath; you're very filthy'

costurería seamstress's shop

cotaco (Eng.) m. Kotex (female sanitary napkin)

cotachís (Eng.) m. cottage cheese

cotín m. cloth used to cover chairs or sofas; slip cover

cotinchón -chona meddler (usually ref. to man who meddles in women's affairs)

cotorrazo blow, heavy hit

cotorrear or **cotorriar** vn. to converse amiably, gossip, chat

cotorro -rra talkative person, chatterbox, gossip

couc (Eng.) f. Coca-Cola (soft drink)

couch (Eng.) mf. coach, trainer

coyote mf. youngest member of a family (Std. *bejamín* m. 'youngest son'); person easily frightened; exploiter-contractor, one who transports illegal aliens across the Mexican-U.S. border; unscrupulous politician; half-breed; person who works for a commission (fixed rate of pay)

coyotear or **coyotiar** va. to rob; vn. to goof off (slang), fool around, enjoy oneself aimlessly

cozco devil

craca (Eng.) wisecrack, would-be clever remark

cranque (Eng.) m. crank (tool); crank (grumpy person)

craqueado -da or **craquiado -da** (Eng.) cracked (slang), crazy

craquear or **craquiar** (Eng.) va. to crack, break open

creada (var. of) *criada*

creatura (var. of) *criatura*

crecer vn. to mature, gain experience

crecidote -ta ponderous and overgrown young person

creer: creerse la divina garza envuelta en tortilla (slang) / **creerse la divina gracia** / **creerse la gran cosa** / **creerse la gran caca** (vulg.) / **creerse muy maldito -ta** (slang) / **creerse muy chicotudo -da** (slang) / **creerse muy chicho -cha** / **creerse muy chingón -gona** (**chingonón -nona**) / **creerse muy grande** / **creerse sabroso -sa** (slang) to consider oneself superior / **creerse muy machín** (slang) to consider oneself to be a real stud (slang): "Él se cree muy machín" 'He thinks he's a real stud'; ¡no creas! (interj., iron.) Don't doubt it for a moment!

creiba, creibas, etc. (vars. of) *creía, creías,* etc. (imperf. conjugation of *creer*)

creído -da credulous, gullible; vain, presumptuous

creido -da (vars. of) *creído -da* (ppart. of *creer*)

crenquear or **crenquiar** (Eng.) va. to crank a car

crep or **crepé: crepé romano** type of coarse cloth

crepa (Eng.) (vulg.) crapper (i.e., toilet)

crequear or **crequiar** (Eng.) (vars. of) *craquear* or *craquiar*

crer (var. of) *creer*

cresta: ir la cresta to rise (said of bodies of water during floods)

creyer (var. of) *creer*

creyón (Eng.) m. crayon

criar: criar con pecho to breastfeed

Cris (dim. of) *Cristóbal*

Crismas or **Crismes** (Eng.) msg. Christmas (season); (in lower case) Christmas present

cristal m. multicolored marble; mf. (mildly pej.) Anglo-Saxon; (capitalized) Crystal City, Texas

cro (var. of) *creo* (1st pers. sg. pres. ind. of *creer*)

croum (Eng.) chrome, chromium

crucifico (var. of) *crucifijo*

crudo -da hung over; person suffering from a hangover (Std. *resaca*)

crúner (Eng.) crooner, singer of popular love songs

cruz f. opium; **hacer la cruz** to make one's first sale of the day (said of merchants)

cruzacalles mfsg. gadabout, loafer

cruzado -da half-breed

cuaco horn of an animal; mpl. animal horns; handle bars of a bicycle

cuacha chicken dung; **hacer cuacha** (vulg., slang) to make mincemeat of (fig.), beat up soundly (in a fight); **no valer cuacha** (vulg.) to not be worth a shit (vulg.), to not be worth a damn

cuachalote ugly; bad; clumsy

cuachón -chona fat and flabby; slovenly dresser, infrequent bather

cuachonón -nona very fat and flabby

cuadrada: cabeza cuadrada (Ang.?) (pej.) square head (pej.), German

cuadro field for cultivation; field under cultivation

cuai (<*cuate*) m. buddy, pal (slang)

cuajar vn. to lie, tell falsehoods

cualquiera prostitute, whore

cuando: (de) cada en cuando or **cada vez en cuando** from time to time

cuantimás (coll.) at least; let alone

cuanto -ta: ¡A las cuántas! It's about time!, **¿A quién y a cuántos?** What business is that of anyone?

cura (Eng.) quarter (coin)

cuardado -da (metathesis of)

cuadrado -da

cuarentaidós or **cuarentaiuno** (slang) male homosexual (so named after the disputed number of men caught by the police *in flagrante delicto* at a private party in Mexico City in the late 1930's)

cuarentena forty days following parturition (birth of a child): "Antes, las mujeres tenían que evitar baños y varios alimentos durante la cuarentena" (women are advised by their doctors or midwives not to engage in sexual intercourse during that interim)

cuarta belt (article of clothing)

cuartada spanking or whipping with a belt

cuartalazo: dar el cuartalazo to keel over, go down like a sack of potatoes (slang)

cuartazo msg. single blow with a belt; mpl. spanking, whipping with a belt; **dar el cuartazo** (var. of) *dar el cuartalazo*

cuarterón -rona person of mixed Hispanic and African ancestry

cuartilla quarter, twenty-five cent piece

cuartito outhouse, outdoor toilet

cuartiza spanking or whipping with a belt

cuarto: cuarto redondo (Ang.) quarter round (piece of corner furniture similar to a night stand)

cuate -ta twin; pal, buddy (coll.); peer, equal; m. double-barreled shotgun; mpl. (slang) testicles

cuatezón -zona intimate friend

cuatrojos (slang) mfsg. four-eyes (i.e., person who wears eyeglasses)

cuatro: cuatro reales/riales fifty cent piece or any combination of coins that total fifty cents

cuay m. guy, fellow

cubrido (var. of) *cubierto* (ppart. of *cubrir*)

cucaracha (coll.) jalopy, old car

cucarachero place infested with cockroaches

cucaracho (var. of) *cucaracha*; **ahi te guacho cucaracho** see you later, alligator

Cuco or **Cuca** (dims. of) *Refugio* (m. & f.)

cucomaletas (var. of) *cocomaletas*

¡cúchale! or **¡cúchele!** interj. Sic 'em! (said to animals as encouragement to attack someone or retrieve something)

cuchara: cuchara de viernes busybody, interfering person

cuchía or **cuchilla: pantalones de cuchilla** bell-bottomed trousers

cuchillero -ra troublemaker

cucho -cha twisted, misshapen; harelipped

¡cuela/cuélale/cuélate/cuele/cuélele/ cuélese! interjs. (slang) Scram!, Beat it!, Bug off!, etc.

cuello: cuello de matriz cervix, entrance to the uterus

cuenta: agarrar algo de una cuenta to keep harping on something; **hacer de cuenta que** (var. of) *hacer cuenta de que* to suppose, assume

cuentazo several related pieces of gossip (all of which make for a long story)

cuento pretext: "Ahora con el cuento de que está enfermo se porta como niño" 'Acting now under the pretext that he is sick, he's behaving like a child'; **cuento chino** (often mpl.) lie, falsehood; **con el cuento de que** under the pretext that: "Con el cuento de que estaba enfermo, no quiso hacer el trabajo"; **estar malo el cuento** (said of situations which have become precarious): "Si mandaron traer (a) la ley, es que está malo el cuento" 'If they sent for the cops then things have really gotten bad'

cuera (slang) girlfriend, sweetheart; (pej.) mistress, kept woman; woman of considerable beauty

cuerazo (slang) sexually attractive or very beautiful woman

cuerdo -da (slang) reckless, bold; (slang) f. boss, leader; **¡cuerda!** interj. Wham!, Bam!, Pow!; **cuerda de leña** cord of wood

cuerería leather goods shop

cuerín m. scab (over a wound on the skin); trap for small animals (e.g., mousetrap)

cuerito scab (over a wound on the skin), a small piece of dead skin that is partly detached from the rest of the skin found on a wound; prepuce, the foreskin that covers the head of the penis

cueriza spanking

cuerno -na mean; wicked; **poner cuernos** to deceive one's spouse through adultery

cuernado -da buck-toothed; lean-faced

cuero -ra (slang) m. handsome; f. pretty; m. fiancé; f. fianceé; m. & f. sweetheart; m. man living in free union with a woman, common-law husband; m. gang, circle of friends; **arriesgar el cuero** to risk one's life, risk one's hide (slang); **cuero de rana** dollar bill, greenback (slang)

cuerpazo sexy female body

cuerpo (slang) woman with a sexy body; **andar el cuerpo / correr el cuerpo** to defecate; **cuerpo de coca-cola** shapely (ref. to a woman's body); **cuerpo de estu-**

diantes (Ang.) student body, totality of students (Std. *estudiantado*); **hacer el cuerpo** to defecate; **hacérsele el cuerpo chinito a alguien** to get goosepimples; **tener el alma en el cuerpo** to be sensitive about things, wear one's heart on one's sleeve (coll.)

cuerta (var. of) *puerta*

cuervo (pej.) African American

cuestar (var. of) *costar*

cuestión (Ang.) f. question (i.e., one that asks for information (Std. *pregunta*)

cuetazo pistol shot; shot from any weapon

cuete mf. drunk, high as a kite (coll.); m. drunken binge; gun, pistol; **cuetes** mpl. curls, ringlets

cuetear or **cuetiar** va. to shoot

cueva (vulg. slang) vagina

cueveno -na light-colored (usually said of eyes)

cuidado: poner cuidado to pay attention; (imperative) **pon cuidado** watch and see, just wait and see: "A Juan lo van a arrestar; pon cuidado" 'They're going to arrest John; you wait and see'

cuidadora babysitter

cuidandera babysitter

cuidaniños fsg. babysitter

cuidar: cuidar a la esposa for a man to ejaculate outside of the uterus

cuija personal defect attracting sympathy

cuilca (Eng. by acoustic equivalence?) quilt, cover, blanket

Cuilmas: San Cuilmas (hum.) San Antonio, Texas; (hum.) (name applied to any town one wishes to burlesque)

cuilta (Eng.) quilt, blanket

cuininche mf. uncooperative person

cuira (slang) quarter, twenty-five cent piece

cuiza (slang) prostitute (cf. **huiza**)

cuitear or **cuitiar** (Eng.) va. to quit

cula (slang, vulg.) (var. of) *culo*

culebra: culebra de agua sudden storm, cloudburst

culebrí or **culebrilla** undulating line

culeco -ca brooding (said of hens); m. recently become a father (said of a man whose first child has just been born)

culequillas: en culequillas (var. of) *en cuclillas*

cúler (Eng.) m. water cooler, drinking fountain

culero -ra cowardly, fearful; eccentric; m. (slang & vulg.) homosexual; mf. (slang & vulg.) son-of-a-bitch; gash hound (slang), skirt chaser, womanizer

culo fear, fright; **culo aguado** large, flabby ass (vulg.; ref. is usually to the feminine posterior); **fruncírsele a alguien el culo** to be afraid, become frightened

culón -lona (slang & vulg.) son-of-a-bitch

culote m. female buttocks (ref. may be pej. or flattering, depending on the context)

culuquillas or **culuquías** (vars. of) *cuclillas*

cumpriaños (var. of) *cumpleaños*

cuñado (term used to address a stranger or a buddy who has a sister to annoy him or to hint that he [the speaker] is interested in dating her)

cuotizar (Ang.?) va. & vr. to quote, set the price on an article

cuquear or **cuquiar** (Eng.) va. to cook

cuqui (Eng.) f. cookie

cura (slang) fix (of a narcotic drug); medicinal preparation for someone with a hangover

curandero -ra witch doctor-cum-herbalist

curar va. to remove a hex or spell; to provide an addict with a fix (slang); **curar de susto** to cure, by sorcery, the afteraffects of a traumatic experience; **curarle a alguien los callos** to stop annoying someone; **curarse (de) la cruda** to "cure" a hangover by drinking more alcohol; to cure a hangover by drinking *menudo* (q.v.)

curiosito -ta f. cartoon film or humorous short feature shown before the main feature in movie theaters; m. & f. comic relief, in a play or movie

curioso -sa funny, humorous; fpl. comic strips in a newspaper; comic relief in a play or movie; **(a)hora sí (que) estás curioso -sa / (a)hora sí que (estamos) están curiosos -sas** this is a fine how-do-you-do, this is a fine state of affairs; **hacerse uno curioso -sa** to play (act) dumb, pretend not to know what is going on

curita (Eng., through metonymy from Curity) Band-Aid, bandage

cursi embittered, sour

cursiento -ta diarrhetic, suffering from diarrhea

cursio (var. of) *curso*

curso (normally msg.) loose bowels, diarrhea

curvar (Ang.) va. to curve, grade on a curve (manner of assigning grades on examinations)

curvas (Ang.?) female body curves (ref. to her bosom, hips and/or buttocks)

curvia insinuation, innuendo

cusquear or **cusquiar** va. to pick up with a utensil; to eat

cute (Eng.) m. coat

CH

chabacán (var. of) *chabacano* apricot

Chabela (dim.of) Isabel(a)

chacotear or **chacotiar** vn. to engage in lewd behavior

chacuaco (slang) cigarette; cigar butt

chachalaca talkative

chachalaquero -ra talkative

chacho -cha (vars. of) *muchacho -cha*

chafo -fa worthless, substandard; cheap, inexpensive; tired, fatigued

Chago (dim. of) *Santiago*

chágüer or **cháhuer** or **chahua** (Eng.) m. shower (bath and apparatus); party (at which gifts are given in honor of a newborn baby or a woman engaged to be married

chain (Eng.) m. shine, polish; shoeshine; **dar chain** to shine or polish (esp. shoes)

chainada (Eng.) shine, polish, (esp. of shoes); **dar una chainada** to shine or polish (esp. shoes)

chainar or **chainear** or **chainiar** (Eng.) va. to shine or polish (esp. shoes)

chaineada or **chainiada** (Eng.) (vars. of) *chainada*

chainero (Eng.) shoeshine boy

chairo -ra (slang) crazy, nutty, cracked (coll.); f. (slang) watch chain; mf. sweetheart; f. fiancée

chalán m. shoe; skiff, flat-bottomed boat

chalar (used only as interj.): **¡chálese!** or **¡chale!** Shut up!, Cool it!, Knock it off!, etc.

chale (vulg.) m. penis; (capitalized) (dim. of) *Carlos*

chaleco: buscarle mangas al chaleco to complicate matters; **de chaleco** as a freeloader, without paying; free, gratis

chalice (Eng.) m. & f. chalice

chalito (vulg.) penis; (capitalized) (dim. of) *Carlos*

chalupa shoe

Challo -lla (dim. of) *Rosario* m. & f.

chamaco -ca m. boy; son; f. girl; daughter

chamagoso -sa sloppy, slipshod, poorly made or done job

chamarra sweater

chamba (coll.) job

chambear or **chambiar** vn. to work at a job

chambelán or **chamberlán** or **chabeláin** m. escort

chambón -bona sloppy, slipshod, poorly made or done job

chambonada a poorly done job

chambonear or **chamboniar** vn. to do a job awkwardly

chamorro   calf (of the leg)
champéin m. (Eng.?) (French?) (Eng.<French?) (var. of?) *champaña*
champión -piona (Eng.) champion
championato (Eng.) championship
champú (see **darse champú**)
champucero -ra (vars. of) *chapucero -ra*
champurrado gruel made of sugar, chocolate and corn meal
chamuco devil
chamuscado -da scorched, burnt
chanate mf. black adj.; m. coffee; mf. (pej.) African American; mf. child
chancaquía or **chancaquilla** thistle, burr
chancla slipper (bedroom slipper); **arrimar la chancla** (slang) to dance; **arrimarle a alguien la chancla** (slang) to spank; **caerle a alguien la chancla** (slang) to receive a reprimand (esp. said of husbands whose wives put a stop to their flirtations or other misbehavior); **tirar chancla** (slang) to dance (see also **tirar chancle**)
chanclar or **chanclear** or **chancliar** (slang) va. to spank; (slang) vn. to dance; to walk
chanclazo (slang) spanking; dance, party (see also **chancleo**)
chancle m. (slang) dance; **tirar chancle** (slang) to dance (see also **tirar chancla**)
chancleo (slang) dance, party
chancletear or **chancletiar** (slang) (vars. of) *chanclar* et. al.
chanclón -clona (slang) good dancer
¡chane (su pico)! or **¡chánese!** interjs. Shut up!, Cool it! (slang) etc.
changarrete m. business estab-

lishment
changle mf. & adj. useless, good-for-nothing (usually ref. to persons)
chango -ga monkey; (slang) young person; (pej.) African American; (slang) fiancé(e); f. tomboy; f. amusing little show-offish girl; **cada chango a su columpio y a columpiarse luego / cada chango a su mecate y a darse vuelo** everyone (should) mind his/her own business; every man for himself; **ponerse chango** (slang) to become alert, get smart; to get all dressed up
changuear or **changuiar** (slang) va. to imitate, mock, ape (coll.)
Chano (dim. of) *Feliciano, Graciano, Luciano*
chanquilear or **chanquiliar** (slang) vn. to walk, take a walk
chansa (common orthog. var. of) *chanza*
chansiar (slang) va. to two-time (slang), commit adultery
chantar (slang) vn. to live, dwell; vr. to get married; (coll. & vulg.) to shack up (Std. *vivir amancebados*)
chante m. (Eng.?: *Shanty* or Nahuatl? *chan -tli*) house, home
chantón m. (slang) (blend of *chante* and *cantón*?) (var. of?) *cantón* house, home
chanza (Eng.) chance, opportunity; risk; mumps; adv. perchance, perhaps; **agarrar chanza** to take a chance, risk; **(hay) chanza que** there's a chance that, it's possible that
chapa doorknob; door latch; (Eng.) pork chop; any chop of meat; pl. (Ang.) false teeth, choppers (slang)

chapanecas: las chapanecas popular Mexican dance

chapaneco -ca short-statured

chapaña (var. of) *champaña*

chaparral m. roadrunner (Geococcyx californianius)

chaparro -rra short person; ¡qué suerte tan chaparra! What lousy luck!

chapeado -da or **chapiado -da** flushed (said of cheeks)

chapear or **chapiar** vr. to blush; to apply rouge to cheeks

chapel: jijo de la chapel (<*La Chapelle*, the name of a San Antonio street found in the central part of that city); (expression of surprise, incredulity, displeasure, etc.)

chapeta earring; diaper

chapete m. shawl; poncho; f. (var. of) *chapeta*; ¡Qué chapete! What a bod! (slang, said of an attractive woman); **chapete's pleis** (Eng.) (said of a sexually attractive woman's body): "¿Tú conoces a Mariana? — Uj, ¡Chapete's Pleis!"

chapeteado -da or **chapetiado -da** rosy-cheeked

chapetear or **chapetiar** va. to rouge one's cheeks; to fornicate

chapetona stacked (slang), shapely, curvacious, sexually attractive woman's body: "¡Qué chapetona!" 'What a bod!' (slang)

chapetuda sexy woman

chapetura (var. of) *chapetuda*

chapín -pina misshapen (said of legs)

chapo -pa (vars. of) *chaparro -rra* short-statured (person); (coll. & hum.) Japanese

chapopote (var. of) *chapapote*

chapote m. live oak tree (Quercus virginiana)

chapucear or **chapuciar** va. to deceive, cheat

chapucero -ra cheat, deceiver

chapul m. child

chapulín -lina grasshopper

chapulinada group of children (fig.); swarm of grasshoppers

chapuza fraud, deception; **hacer chapuza a alguien** to cheat someone

chapuzar va. to cheat, deceive

chaquetear or **chaquetiar** va. to betray

chaquetero -ra turncoat, betrayer

cháquira (Eng.) (slang) jacket

chara (Eng.) charter

charamusca taffy in twisted or spiral form

charca: andar charca to be well dressed

charco: ahogarse en cualquier charco to be incapable of doing anything right, not able to fight one's way out of a paper bag (fig.); **brincar el charco** to cross the Rio Grande/Río Bravo (Texas-Mexican border) (said with ref. to persons immigrating from Mexico to Texas)

charchar (Eng.) va. to charge purchases on a charge account

charchina jalopy, old car; (slang) girl

charife (var. of) *cherife* (Eng.)

charlador -ra liar

charola tray (of whatever sort); pl. pots and pans

charpiar (Eng.) va. to sharpen

charrasquear or **charrasquiar** va. to scar with a knife

charreada or **charriada** party or get-together of *charros*

chasís m.: **ser el puro chasís** to be nothing but skin and bones (coll.), be extremely thin

chat (Eng.) m. shot, injection

chato -ta (term of endearment used between husband and wife); f. marihuana; **chatos** mpl. crab lice (usually found in the genital region); **hacerse chato -ta** to turn a deaf ear (coll.)

chaval -la sweetheart; fiancé(e)

chavalón -lona child

chaveta (slang) head (Std. *cabeza*); fiancée; sweetheart f.

chavo -va (slang) young person; sweetheart

Chayo (dim. of) *Eduardo*; **Chayo -ya** (dim. of) *Rosario* m. & f.

chayote m. tomboy; (slang) dollar

checadita (Eng.) checkup, examination

checador -ra (Eng.) (vars. of) *chequeador -ra, chequiador -ra*

checar (Eng.) va. to review; to verify; to check; to correct; to examine

cheche -cha m. & f., resp. young child, little shaver (coll.)

chef m. (Eng.) chef

cheiquear or **cheiquiar** (Eng.) va. to shake, agitate

Chela (dim. of) *Graciela, Celia*

Chelo (dim. of) *Consuelo*

Chema m. (dim. of) *José María*

chembi (slang) adv. perhaps, maybe

Chencho -cha (dim. of) *Cresencia, Cresencio* m. & f., *Inocencio* m.& f.

Chendo -da (dims. of) resp. *Rosendo, Rosenda*

Chente -ta (dims. of) resp. *Vicente, Vicenta*

chepe mf. hypocrite

cheque (Eng.) m. investigation, examination (see also **dar su cheque**)

chequeada or **chequiada** (Eng.) (vars. of) *chequeadita, chequiadita, checadita*

chequeadita or **chequiadita** (Eng.) (vars. of) *checadita*

chequeador -ra or **chequiador -ra** (Eng.) checker, inspector

chequear or **chequiar** (Eng.) (vars. of) *checar*

chequeo (Eng.) check, checkup, examination

chérbet (Eng.) m. sherbert

cherife (Eng.) m. sherriff

chermés m. silk cloth

Chevi (Eng.) m. Chevy, Chevrolet (auto make)

chi f. (vulg.) urine; **hacer (la) chi** (Std. *hacer chis*) to urinate

chiapaneco -ca (vars. of) *chapanico -ca*

chicabacho -cha (a cross of *chicano -a* and *gabacho -cha*) Chicano (Mexican-American) who acts and thinks like an Anglo-Saxon (*gabacho*, q.v.)

chicago (slang, vulg. & hum.) toilet, restroom, bathroom (etc.) (< *chi* 'urine' + *cago* 'I defecate')

chicales mpl. cornmeal stew

chicles mpl. cornmeal stew

chicanada (slang) action or behavior typifying a Chicano; group of Chicanos; chicanery

chicaneada or **chicaniada** (slang) (vars. of) *chicanada*

chicanear or **chicaniar** (slang) vr. to behave like a Chicano; (coll., said of Chicanos) to do one's thing (slang), act as one feels like acting

chicaneo action or behavior typifying a Chicano

chicanería (slang) (id. to **chicaneo**)

chicanglo (a cross of *chicano* and *anglo*) Chicano who acts like an Anglo-Saxon; Anglo-Saxon who identifies with the Chicano and the Chicano cause(s); the mixture of Spanish and English which characterizes the vernacular of the Chicano

chicanismo ideology and ethnic spirit typifying the Chicano Movement(s)

chicano **-na** Mexican-American, person of Mexican heritage born and raised in the United States or person born in Mexico of Mexican ethnic background who has become a United States citizen or permanent resident; any person of Mexican ethinic background; the Spanish vernacular of the Chicano

chicle m. tar; asphalt; pest, uninvited person, tagalong (coll.)

chicloso -sa pest, tagalong (coll.); m. (vulg.) anus

chico -ca mockingbird (Mimum polyglottos); (iron.) big, large; **colgar chica(s) jeta(s)** (slang) to pout; **chicas patas** mfsg. Mexican: "Él es un chicas patas"; **a las chicas patas** in the Mexican fashion;

chicolito -ta small, tiny

chicotazo whiplash, bow with a whip

chicote (slang) m. penis

chicoteada or **chicotiada** whipping, lashing

chicotear or **chicotiar** (slang): **chicotearle a alguien el aparato (el mango) / chicotearle a alguien para hacer algo** to excel at doing something: "A él le chicotea para jugar a la pelota" 'He is really good at playing ball'

chicotudo -da very large; difficult; m. extremely handsome male, an Adonis (coll.); (slang) V.I.P., person of considerable importance

chicura ragweed herb (Ambrosia ambrocoides) (its roots are made into a douching solution)

chícharo pea, green or sweet pea (Lathyrus odoratus); (slang) pl. household goods (e.g., furniture, etc.)

chicharro (hum.) cigar

chicharronear or **chicharroniar** va. to burn to a crisp

chicharrón: buscarle ruido al chicharrón to look for trouble; **hacer chicharrón** to burn to a crisp

chiche or **chichi** f. breast (female); sinecure, soft job (coll.) often obtained as a political favor; **dar chiche** to breast-feed a child; **mamar chiche** to sponge (coll.), live off other people, live at someone's expense

chichecano -na or **chichicano -na** (slang) Chicano who enjoys a sinecure (cf. **chiche/chichi**) (the word appears to have been born in 1968 at the Kelly Air Force Base in San Antonio, Texas)

chichero (coll. & mildly vulg.) brassiere, bra

chichita welt; (var. or derivative of) *bachicha* cigarette butt

chicho (dim. of) *Narciso*

chicho -cha crazy, daffy, screwy (slang); wonderful, great

chichón **-chona** large-breasted (usually f., ref. to women)

chiflado -da daffy, scatterbrained (coll.); stuck up (coll.), presumptuous; smitten, head over heels in love (coll.); **andar chiflado -da** to be smitten in love

chiflar va. to elate; to cause to swell with a (false) sense of pride or self-importance; to spoil, pamper; vr. to swell with a (false) sense of pride; to go overboard (fig.), show a great deal of enthusiasm; to be carried away, be moved or excited greatly: "No te chifles tanto con Juanita; es casada" 'Don't get so carried away with Janie; she's a married woman'

chifleta   (var. of) *chiflete* (m.); (var. of) *chufleta*; sarcastic remark, innuendo

chiflón   **-flona** person very susceptible to the flattery of others

chifón   m. chiffon

chifonía   (Eng. < Fr.?) chiffonier, chest of drawers

¡chihuá!   or   **¡chihuahua!** interj. Holy Toledo! (of varying intensity of meaning, according to intonation, e.g., everything from 'Goodness gracious!' through 'Hell!')

chile   m. penis; **andar a medios chiles** (slang) to be slightly drunk, be tipsy; **chile parado** erect penis, hard-on (slang); **chile pelón** (in the sexual act, penis not encased in a condom); **ir hecho chile** to go like a bat out of hell (slang), move very quickly; chili pepper (and the following variant types) **chile ancho** bell pepper; **chile bolita** small round red pepper; **chile cascabel** dry red pepper whose seeds rattle inside the cask; **chile del monte** round red pepper measuring one centimeter in diameter; **chile dulce** sweet pepper; **chile en escabeche** chile preserved in vinagre; **chile jalapeño** large and piquant green pepper; **chile japonés** elongated piquant red pepper about four centimeters in length; **chile piquín** very piquant caper-size green or red pepper; **chile pisado** large red dry pepper measuring about ten centimeters in length and six in width; **chile pitín** (var. of) *chile piquín*; **chile relleno** large green pepper filled with meat and sauces and then baked

chilero   **-ra** fond of eating chili peppers; m. small yellow bird with gray wings (Pitangus sulfuratus)

chilete   m. (id. to *chilipiquín* or *chile piquín*) (Capsicum baccatum)

chilpasía   dry and ripe chili artificially dried in the sun

chilpayate   mf. small child

chilpitín   (var. of) *chile piquín/ chile pitín*

chiluca   (slang, underw.) head (human)

chiludo   (vulg.) man with a big penis

chilla: estar en la chilla   to be hard-pressed financially (usually for just a short time)

chillador   **-ra: trompo chillador** windup top which makes a whining noise when spinning; **(víbora) chilladora** rattlesnake

chillante   mf. loud (said of colors)

chillar   vn. to cry; vr. **chillarse** or **chillarse de coraje** to become very angry

chillón -llona   crybaby

chimenea: tener la chimenea muy cerca   to be very hot-tempered

chiminea   (var. of) *chimenea*

chimenía   or **chiminía** (vars. of) *chimenea*

chimolear   or **chimoliar** (vars. of) *chismorrear* or *chismorriar*

chimolero -ra   (vars. of) *chismolero -ra*

chimpa   hair

chimuelo -la   lacking teeth, with some teeth missing

chinanero   any stick used to remove a hot lid from a kettle

chinar   va. to comb; vr. **chinársele**

el cuerpo a alguien to get goose-bumps (goosepimples)

chinocorrazo blow on the head

chincuales mpl. type of small skin eruption; (fig.) nervousness: "Parece que traes chincuales" 'You look like you have ants in your pants' (coll.) (said of persons, usually children, who are restless and who continually squirm around)

chincuís m. ocular sty

chinche mf. miserly; **chinche pedorra / chinche perroda** stink-bug (Pentatomida); **hacerse chinche** to act stingy, miserly; to overstay one's welcome; **tener (la) sangre de chinche** to be repugnant to, repellent to (said of persons)

chinchería squalor, filth; place infested with chinch bugs (bed bugs)

chinchero messy room; messy house; any room, mattress, etc., infested with bed bugs; (hum.) small business establishment; jail

¡chínelas! interj. (slightly euph.) 'Son of a…!'

chingado -da (lit., woman on whom the act of coition has been performed) (vulg.); **acá la chingada** or **acá la chingá** (vulg. slang) a long way away, half way to hell and gone (slang), way the shit out there (vulg. slang); **¡A la chingada!** (vulg., slang) I'll be God-damned!; **¡Con una chingada!** (vulg.) Dammit the hell!, Hell's bells!; **estar como la chingada** to be as ugly/mean/timid/insensitive (etc.) as one can possibly be; **¡hijo de la chingada madre!** interj. (strongest and most vulg. interj. possible); **¡hijo de tu chingada madre!** (very vulg.); **mandar a la chingada** to

tell someone to go to hell; **¿Qué chingados tienes (tiene)?** or **¿Qué chingados te (le, les) pasa?** What the hell's wrong with you (him, her, them)?; **¡¿Qué chingados quieres?¡** (very strong and vulg.) What the hell ya want?; **¡Me lleva la chingada!** (strong and vulg.) I'll be God-damned!; **ser más + adj. + que la chingada** to be + comparative adj. + than hell: "Ese bato es más malo que la chingada" 'That dude is meaner than hell'; **¡Vámonos a la chingada!** Let's get the hell out of here!

chingadazo (var. of) *chingazo*; **agarrarse a chingadazos** (vulg.) to get into a scrap (slang), fight, get into a fight

chingadera nuisance, annoyance; damn (ed) thing; bitching, complaining: "Ya déjate de (tus) chingaderas" 'Stop your bitching now'; **dejando de chingadera** all damn joking aside; **¿Qué chingaderas traes?** / **¿Qué chingaderas te cargas?** What the hell are you up to?

chingal: un chingal a great deal, to a high degree (cf. **un chingatal**)

chingar (vulg.) va. to copulate (etc.); to cheat; to avenge; to defeat (in a contest); to get what one is after: "Ya chingó" 'He got what he wanted'; to break, put out of order: "El estúpido de tu hermano chingó la baica" 'That stupid brother of yours broke the bike'; vr. (slang & vulg.) to get married; **¡chinga cagada!** interj. (very strong and vulg.); **chingar la pac(i)encia** to bother; **De a tiro la chingas (chinga, chingan)** (used to reprimand abusive behavior)

You're really something else;
You're a real lulu (all used ironically with critical intent); **No la
chingues (chingue/chinguen)/ Ya
ni la chingas (chinga/chingan)**
(set expression used to reprimand
abusive behavior) (see also **fregar**
and **joder**); **para acabarla de
chingar** to make matters worse; **Te
chingas que no** or **Te chingas si no**
(set expressions used by one to
contradict emphatically a negative
statement made by another) the
hell it isn't, the hell you're not, the
hell he's not, etc.: "Juan no va a
venir más a tu casa.— Te chingas
que no." 'John isn't coming to your
house anymore.— The hell he
isn't.' (see also **fregar** and **joder**)

chingatal: un chingatal a great
deal, to a high degree (cf. **un
chingal**)

chingazo blow with the hand or
with a heavy object; pl. a fistfight;
agarrarse a chingazos (vulg.) to
get into a fistfight

chingón -gona: large; tall (ref. to
persons); **creerse chingón -gona** to
consider oneself superior; **el mero
chingón/ la mera chingona** (hum.)
the big boss, the big cheese (slang)

chingonón -nona (vars. of) *chin-
gonote*; **creerse chingonón -nona** to
consider oneself superior

chingos adj. several, many; adv. a
great deal, to a considerable
extent

chinguiza (see **dar una chinguiza**)

chinita: ¡chinita por tu amor!
interj. (slightly euph.) Son of a
bitch!; **¡chinitas!** interj. (slightly
euph.)

**chinito: hacérsele a alguien el
cuerpo chinito** to get goose-
bumps (goose pimples); **traer los**

ojos chinitos to have sleepy
(looking) eyes

chino -na m. curl (of hair); comb
(in general); comb for removing
body lice or hair lice; mf. darling
(term of endearment); **china
poblana** Mexican regional cos-
tume (worn by women); **papel de
china** tissue paper

chipiar vn. to drizzle, rain very
lightly

chipil or **chípili** mf. spoiled or
overindulged child (cf. **chiple**)

chipón -pona spoiled child

chiqueador -ra or **chiquiador -ra**
mf. pamperer (person who pam-
pers); adj. fond of pampering

chiquear or **chiquiar** va. & vr. to
spoil, pamper; vr. to play hard to
get, be evasive (esp. in amorous
games)

chiqueo act or effect of pampering

chiqueón -ona or **chiquión -ona**
spoiled child; person who enjoys
being pampered

chiquero dirty and messy place, a
shambles, pigpen (fig.)

chíquete m. chewing gum; asphalt;
tar

chiquiningo -ga or **chiquirringo -ga**
or **chiquitingo -ga** small child

chiquito -ta son/daughter who
bears the first name of the parent
of the same sex (esp. used after
parent's first name with ref. to the
child, e.g., "Eva chiquita"; also
used when ref. to a child who
imitates the parent, even though
the two are not identically
named); m. (slang) buttocks;
(vulg.) anus; **Éntrale chiquito -ta
(chiquitito -ta)** Have a go at it, Go
get'em tiger (slang), (an expr. used
to encourage someone to accept a
challenge)

chira (Eng.) mf. cheater, deceiver

chiriar (Eng.) va. & vn. to cheat, defraud

chirinola gossiper; group of gossips; fuss, bother

chirife (Eng.) (var. of) *cherife*

chirión -riona cheater, deceiver

chiripada (var. of) *chiripá*

chirrión m. penis

chirriona (var. of) *chirona*

chisca or **chiscura** bicycle

chismarajo gossiping, gossip

chismolear or **chismoliar** (vars. of) *chismorrear*

chismolero -ra gossiper

chispa f. (ref. to both men and women) astute, sly, sharp; **¡chispas!** (mild interj.) Holy cow!, Golly!, Great balls of fire! (coll.)

chispudo -da m. curly (said of hair); mf. daffy, crazy, screwy (coll.)

chisqueado -da or **chisquiado -da** (slang) adv. very rapidly, like crazy (coll.)

chisquear or **chisquiar** va. to drive crazy, madden; vr. to become crazy, to go off one's rocker (slang)

chistar or **chistear** or **chistiar** vn. to complain (esp. with interj. ichst! as to request silence in a theater), to shush

chiste m.: **no tener chiste** to be worthless, of no importance; to be dull (said of persons); to be easy to accomplish: "Eso no tiene chiste" 'There's nothing to doing that'; **pasarle a una el chiste** said of a female who becomes pregnant out of wedlock or unexpectedly

chito -ta (<*muchachito -ta*) m. (dim.) little boy; f. (dim.) little girl

Chito -ta (dims. of) *Jesús, Jesusa*, resp.; *Felícito, Felícita*, resp.

chiva heroin

chivas trinkets, objects of little value; (slang) interj. Give me whatever you have! (used for example by a thief to a victim: 'Hand it over!)

chivato -ta mischievous youngster, "kid" (coll.)

¡chive! (slang) interj. Don't be frightened!

chivear or **chiviar** vr. to back down, back out, retract (a statement); to be afraid or bashful

chivero -ra skittish person, scaredy-cat (coll.); (pej.) Anglo-Saxon; m. goatherd; f. young girl

chivetal m. fold for goats (young goats)

chivete m. fear

chivetero -ra frightened; m. fold for kids (young goats)

chivinolera gossipy person

chivo -va (slang) afraid, shy; handsome, beautiful; (slang) coward; f. ten dollar bill; heroin; thingamagig (used as a substitute for a forgotten designation); coin; nanny goat; **agarrar(le) el chivo a alguien** (Ang.) to get someone's goat (fig.): "Juan le agarró el chivo a Pepe, por eso se peliaron" 'Juan got Pepe's goat, and that's why they got into a fight'; **hacerle a alguien los tamales de chivo** (fig.) to deceive a spouse, commit adultery

chivote (slang) m. handsome man

cho (Eng.) show, spectacle, exhibition; movie theater

choc (Eng.) m. shock; choke (automotive); chalk (writing instrument)

chocado -da at odds with one another (said of two or more persons); **estar chocados** not to be on speaking terms

chocante mf. repugnant; presumptuous

chocantería repugnant act

chocantón -tona repulsive, repugnant (usually ref. to persons)

chocar va. to shock, repel, be repulsive to: "Ese tipo me choca mucho"; vr. to become enemies; to cease to be on speaking terms: "¿Por qué no invitaste(s) a María y a Juana? — Porque ayer se chocaron"; **chocar las manos** to shake hands

chocle (Eng.) m. chalk (writing instrument)

choche m. small boy; (Eng.) George; (Hispanization of) George West, Texas (city in south Texas) (cf. **yoche**)

chocho -cha chubby; slow-moving; f. small girl

chochón -chona (term of endearment)

chofero -ra chauffeur, driver of a car

choflear or **chofliar** (Eng.) vn. to shuffle

Chola or **Chole** (dim. of) *Soledad* f.

¡chole! or **¡chólese!** (slang) Shut up!, Knock it off!, Cool it!, etc.

cholenco -ca weak, worn, weary; (said of persons who appear to be coming down with an illness); sickly, prone to infirmities

cholenque mf. (var. of) *cholenco -ca*

chompa or **chompe** or **chompeta** (slang) f. head (human)

Chon or **Chona** (dims. of) *Asunción, Encarnación* (m. & f.); (dims. of) *Concepción* (f. only)

chones mpl. (var. of) *calzones* long underwear

chongo knot of hair tied up in the back of the head; **agarrarse de los chongos** to fight by pulling one another's hair

chongueada or **chonguiada** fight wherein one woman pulls another's hair

chonte m. mockingbird (Mimus polyglottos)

chopa f. or **chope** m. (Eng.) shop, store

chopetear or **chopetiar** (slang) vn. to have sexual intercourse

choquear or **choquiar** (Eng.) va. to choke, manipulate the choke (on a car); vr. (var. of *chocar* to shake hands)

chopo (hum.) nose

chopucero -ra (vars. of) *chapucero -ra*

chora sweetheart, fiancée; cigarette butt

choralo -la small child

chorcha (Eng.) (little used) church; (more frequently) group of people; **hacerse la chorcha** for a group to form, congregate

chore (Eng.) m. short-statured

choricero -ra sausage vendor; member of the family of a sausage vendor

chorizo type of Mexican sausage; (vulg.) penis

chorreado -da or **chorriado -da** dirty, soiled; grimy, grubby

chorrear or **chorriar** va. to soil with a liquid, make dirty; vr. to spill a liquid on oneself; to drip: "La pompa está chorriando"

chorrera or **chorrería** diarrhea; (id. to *chorrero*)

chorrero long string of (things or persons): "Traiba un chorrero de huercos" 'He had with him a long string of brats' (see also **chorrera**)

chorro diarrhea; multitude (of people); (euph.) gonorrhea; **llover a chorros** to rain cats and dogs (fig.), rain heavily

chorros sure (slang) (affirmative response to a question): "¿Vas al pueblo? — Chorros"; diarrhea

chot (Eng.) (var. of) *chat*

chota (slang) policeman; police force

choteado -da or **chotiado -da** (slang, vulg.) promiscuous, loose-living (usually ref. to women), with a lot of mileage on (slang)

chotear or **chotiar** va. to use to excess; to abuse; to ridicule; to defame, ruin; to make a fool of someone; to caress heavily, pet (slang)

choteo act and effect of using to excess, abusing, ridiculing, defaming, etc. (see **chotear**, supra)

chou (Eng.) (var. of) *cho*

Chuco, El (slang) El Paso, Texas

chuco -ca (slang) (var. of) *pachuco -ca*; m. the vernacular of the Pachuco

chuchalucar va. to take advantage of a woman sexually

chucho -cha (dims. of) *Jesús, María de Jesús*

chucho -cha sly, astute, foxy (coll.); m. dog

chuchuluco little toy

chueco -ca twisted, not straight, tilted; bowlegged; crooked (coll.), dishonest

chuga (Eng.) (pej.) African American; (Eng.) sugar

chúingom (Eng.) m. chewing gum

chulada cute remark or gesture (can be used ironically, e.g.: "¡Qué chulada!" 'Well isn't that just something!')

chulear or **chuliar** va. to caress; to speak affectionately to; to flatter (usually 'to flatter a woman'); to primp; vr. to primp

chulo -la pretty (often said to children)

chupacharcos (slang) mfsg., pl. tennis shoes; homosexual

chupada pull, inhalation (on a cigar or cigarette)

chupadera act of smoking; chain smoking, continual smoking of cigarettes

chupador -ra smoker; heavy smoker

chupamiel m. unscrupulous politician

chupón -pona (slang, vulg.) homosexual

chuponcito puff on a cigar or cigarette

chuparrosa humming bird (Trochilidae)

chusar or **chusear** or **chusiar** (Eng.) va. to choose, select

chuseador -ra or **chusiador -ra** (Eng.) person who does the choosing

chutar or **chutear** or **chutiar** (Eng.) va. to shoot

chuteado -da or **chutiado -da** embarrassed

chuteo (Eng.) act of shooting; shootout (with guns, between two or more people); (var. of) *choteo*

Chuy (dim. of) *Jesús*

D

da-coraje   (see coraje)

daga   (slang) doped cigarette

dagazo   stab with a dagger

dailear or dailiar or dalear or daliar   (Eng.) va. to dial (a telephone)

daime   (Eng.) m. dime, ten cent piece

Dallas   (see ir a Dallas)

dama de honor   bridesmaid

damiana   damiana (Turnera diffusa) (herb prepared as a solution and either drunk or else used as a douch for treatment of *frío de la matriz*, q.v. infra)

dar   va. to show, project (a film); va. (iron.) to sell: "¿A cómo dan esas naranjas?" 'What are you selling those oranges for?'; **A mí no me la(s) das** You can't fool me; **andar dando malos pasos** to be up to no good (i.e., to be having an affair or to be involved in shady deals); **dar a bajar** to ill-treat, mistreat; **dar aire** to fire, discharge; to dismiss one's boyfriend/girlfriend, give him/her the air (slang); to give cause to suspect: "No le des aire de lo que ha pasado aquí"; **dar alas** to give someone free rein; to side with someone (in a dispute, etc.); **dar a oler** to give cause to suspect: "No

le den a oler que su amigo se murió ayer" 'Don't give him cause to suspect that his friend died yesterday'; **a como dé lugar** one way or another, any way it can be done: "¿Cómo piensan hacerlo? — A como dé lugar."; **dar apretones** (folk medicine) sharp squeezes administered from behind to a sick person, typically one with a cold and aching bones and muscles; the sick person grabs himself by the hands behind the neck so that the elbows jut out from the body at a 90° angle; the treatment is said to cure the cold and relieve the muscular ache; **dar atole con el dedo** to deceive one's spouse with another person, have adulterous sexual relations; **dar báscula** to frisk for concealed weapons, stolen goods, etc.; **dar bebito** (coll.) to impregnate, make pregnant; **dar calabazas** to give someone the air (slang), reject (as a suitor); to make a fool out of someone; **dar capote** to blank (sports slang), hold an opponent to zero points in a game; **dar capoteada/dar capotiada** to blank (sports slang), achieve a very high score while holding the opponent to zero points; **dar capotiza** (id. to dar capoteada); **dar carrilla** to bother, molest; **dar catos** (coll.) to beat someone up, usually with one's fists; **dar color** to show something off (usually a new possession); **dar champú** to shampoo someone's hair; **dar de alta** to discharge (i.e., from a hospital); to discharge from the armed forces (usually ref. to an honorable discharge); **dar de pecho** to breast-feed; **dar de sí** to yield, be reasonable, be willing to compromise (the expression is used more frequently in the negative); to budge (door, window, etc.): "La ventana dio de sí después de que le di dos golpes fuertes con el martillo" 'The window budged after I gave it two hard blows with the hammer'; **no dar de sí** to be adamant, uncompromising, hard to convince, etc.; to stretch (said of clothing); **dar el cuartalazo/dar el cuartazo** to keel over, go down like a sack of potatoes (slang); **dar el golpe al cigarro** to inhale deeply on a cigarette; **dar en cara** to be fed up with (coll.), satiated with: "Ya me dio en cara esa sopa"; **dar en el (mero) mate** to hit where it hurts; to hit right on the button; **dar en el moco** to punch on the nose; to administer a beating (usually in a fistfight); **dar en la madre** (id. to **dar en el moco**); **dar en la mera madre** to administer a severe beating; **dar en la torre** to administer a beating (usually in a fistfight); **dar en toda la madre** to give someone a severe beating (usually in a fistfight): **dar fama** to praise, eulogize; **dar guerra** to annoy, irritate, bother; **dar la contra** to contradict, oppose, disagree with; **dar (la) lata** to bother, pester: "Llévate ese niño pa' fuera, está dando mucha lata"; **dar la patada** to dismiss, fire (from a job); to sever ties, break with, terminate (e.g. an amorous relationship); to stink, emit a foul odor; **darlas** to have sexual intercourse promiscuously, be up for grabs (slang) (usually said of women), put out (slang) (cf. **ir a Dallas**); **dar las doce** to be in a tight spot: "Ya me daban las doce" 'I was sure in a tight spot'; to be worried stiff: "Ya me daban las doce con el niño porque tenía una calentura de 150°"; **dar las nalgas** or **darlas** (hum.) to lose in a game or sports contest; to have sexual intercourse promiscuously, put out, be up for grabs (slang) (usually said of women); **dar lástima con** to feel sorry for: "Me dio lástima con Juan" 'I felt sorry for Juan'; **dar la suave** to humor; **dar la vuelta** to look in on (someone): "Dame la vuelta mientras me baño, no vaya a ser que me desmaye" 'Look in on me while I'm taking a bath, just to make sure I haven't fainted'; **darle al gas** (Ang.?) to step on the gas (fig.), hurry; vn. to hurry, speed up, get a move on (slang); **darle (llegarle) a uno la (el) agua a la cabeza (al pescuezo)** (fig.) to have a hard time keeping one's head above water (fig.), be in a tight spot (slang), be in trouble, be in a predicament; **darle (el) hipo a alguien** to scare someone; to get scared; **darle de reversa** to back up, reverse (a vehicle); **darle duro a alguna actividad (empresa, vicio,** etc.): "Pancho le dio duro a la botella" 'Pancho hit (took to) the bottle as if there were no to-morrow'; **darle gas** to speed up (esp. a motor vehicle); **dar lija** to put the finishing touches on a job; **dar luz** to give the go ahead, approve a request; (Ang.) to give a light (to someone lighting a cig-arette, etc.); (var. of) *dar a luz* to give birth to; **dar madera** to flatter, apple-polish (coll.), give a snow job (slang); **dar más quedo (quedito)** to turn down the volume of a radio receptor (a television set, a record player, etc.); **dar pa' dentro** (vulg.) to copulate **dar patadas de ahogado/diogado** to be in a tight spot, in a precarious situation; to fight a losing battle: "Ese pobre señor está dando patadas de ahogado"; **dar pa' fuera** to fire, dismiss (from a job); **dar pa' tras** (Ang.) to return, give back; to back up, reverse: "Le dio pa' tras al coche" 'He backed up the car'; **dar pena** to embar-rass: "Me da mucha pena" 'It embarrasses me a lot'; **dar picones** to pique, make remarks calculated to provoke envy, jealously, resent-ment, anger, etc.; **dar piquetes** to incite, provoke, insult; **dar por** to take a notion to: "Le dio por irse temprano" 'He got it into his head to go early'; **dar(le) a uno por su lado** to humor, indulge or side with someone: "Dale por su lado para que te dé lo que quieres"; **dar cuidado** to give cause to worry; **dar puerta** to show the body's "private parts" (genitalia, etc.) or to show one's under-garments unintentionally; **dar quebrada** (Ang.) to give a break,

allow to have a chance; **dar reatazos/riatazos** to administer a beating (usually with the fists); **dar su cheque** to fire (coll.), dismiss, discharge from a job; **dar su lonche** to put someone in his/her place, tell someone where to get off (slang): "Mamá te está esperando para darte tu lonche" 'Ma is waiting to give you what you've got coming to you'; **dar un agarrón** to scold; to browbeat; (vulg.) to copulate (with); **dar un aplastón** to humiliate, cut down (coll.); **dar un chain** (Eng.) to shine or polish (esp. shoes); **dar un reatazo/riatazo** to strike a blow with one's fist; **dar una atascada** (vulg.) to copulate; **dar una chainada (chainiada)** (Eng.) to shine or polish (esp. shoes); **dar una chinguiza** to administer a beating (usually with the fists); **dar una freguiza** to beat up (coll.), administer a beating (usually with the fists); **dar una manita** to lend a helping hand; **dar una mano** (id. to **dar una manita**); **dar una metida** (vulg.) to copulate (coll.); soundly triumph over (in a sport's competition); **dar una pichoneada/pichoniada** to pet heavily (the male usually being the aggressor); **dar una reatiza/riatiza** to give a severe beating (usually with the fists) (cf. **dar reatazos, dar un reatazo**); **dar una tamboriza** to administer a severe beating, beat to a pulp (coll.); **dar una tirada** (vulg.) to copulate (vulg.); vn. to go off in a specific direction (usually used as a command): "Dale una tirada pa' la casa" 'Get on home'; **dar abasto** to suffice, be enough (usually employed in the negative): "Estas tortillas no dan abasto" 'These tortillas aren't going to be enough' (to feed the number of people expected); to be coped with: "Estos niños no dan abasto; se ensucian la ropa cuatro veces por día"; **dar con bola** to realize one's goals; **dar la vuelta** to pass by, drop by (a place), drop over (for a visit): "Mañana no dejes de dar la vuelta" 'Don't forget to come by tomorrow': **dar una vuelta** to make a complete turn; to go for a stroll or a ride; **dar un round** (Eng.) to last out a round (said of boxers in a boxing match); vr. to give up, yield, produce: "Este año se van a dar muchas nueces"; to submit to sexual advances; **darse a bajar** to act in such a manner as to bring on ill treatment or abuse: "Te tratan así porque te das a bajar" 'They treat you like that because you bring it on yourself'; **darse baños de pureza** to boast of one's decorum and behavior; to justify one's words and deeds; **darse cabronazos** to beat up on one another (usually in a fistfight); **darse cachuchazos** said of two or more persons (usually two) who try to outdo one another in a competitive situation; **darse cancos/darse catos** to have a fistfight; **darse champú** to shampoo one's own hair; **darse chingazos** to beat up one another (usually in a fistfight); **darse de santos** to thank one's lucky stars (coll.), be thankful for favors received; **darse en** to bump: "El niño se dio en la cabeza con la mesa" 'The child bumped his head on the table'; **darse fregadazos/darse fregazos** to beat up on one another (usually in a fistfight); **darse gusto** to have fun, have a good time; **dársela a alguien** to fool, deceive (used only in the negative): "Tú no me la das" 'You can't fool me'; **darse lija** to exalt oneself, praise oneself; **darse madera** (id. to **darse lija**); **darse paquete** to give oneself importance, boast of one's abilities; **darse topes/topetazos** to bump heads; to try to outdo each other (said of two or more persons); **darse trompa** to become aware of something; **darse trompazos** to beat up on one another; **darse una agarrada/darse un agarrón** to get into an argument; to get into a fistfight; **darse una chinguiza** to beat up on one another severely (usually in a fistfight); **darse una reatiza/riatiza** to give one another a severe beating; **darse un agarrón** (vulg.) to engage in copulation; **darse un calentón** to become sexually excited; to anger one another; **darse un fregadazo/darse un fregazo** to hit oneself on a object; **dando y dando** (said as a request for simultaneous exchange of objects, roughly equivalent to Eng. 'share and share alike')

de: de aburi many; **de a de veras** (var. of) *de veras*; **de agua** incomplete; weak, soft (said of persons); effeminate, faggy (slang); **de a madre** totally, completely; a great deal, a considerable amount; super, magnificent, swell; **de aquélla** very nice, super, neat, swell (etc.); **de (a) buena suerte** fortunately, luckily, it's a good thing: "De (a) buena suerte que vino temprano" 'It's a good thing

he came early'; **de aquella melaza**
terrific, super, swell (etc.); **de a
tiro** totally, completely; **de (a)
volada** fast, rapidly, quickly; **de
cada en cuando** from time to time,
once in a while (see also **cada vez
en cuando**); **de cincho** assuredly,
certainly (cf. **cincho**); **de cora**
enthusiastically; **¿de cuándo acá?**
since when? (used to indicate
disbelief and incredulity): "Ahora
ya no le tengo rencor a nadie
porque he cambiado — ¿De cuándo
acá?"; **de chaleco** free, gratis; **de
deveras** in truth, in earnest,
seriously; **de diario** daily, every
day; **de hilo** in a straight line,
directly; very fast; **de hoquis** in
vain; with no strings attached
(coll.), with no hidden compli-
cations; **de jilo** (var. of) *de hilo*; **de
malas** at least: "De malas ya mero
pagamos por la casa" 'At least
we've almost paid for the house';
de más antes of former days, of
yesteryear, of olden times; **de
oquis** (orthog. var. of) *de hoquis*;
de pasada on the way to; **de
patitas** feet first (i.e., to go out
feet first, be thrown out of a place
feet first in a prone position); **de
pilón** to make matters worse, on
top of all that (fig.): "Había
vomitado, y luego, de pilón le dio
calentura" 'He had vomited, and
then, on top of all that, he con-
tracted a fever' (see **fregar: para
acabarla de fregar**); **de por sí que**
as things now stand, as it is:
"No hables de él; de por sí que
no quiere venir a la fiesta"; **de
primero** at first, in the beginning;
de puerta nice, swell, good, excellent (etc.); **de rancho** from
the sticks, countrified, hickish,

farm-fresh (fig.): "Mi primo es
bien de rancho" 'My cousin is
straight from the farm' (fig.); **de
segundo -da** second-hand; **de
seguro** for sure, a certainty, a sure
thing; **de todo vuelo** beautiful,
enticing, shapely, sexy (etc.) (said
of women); **de un sopetón** in one
gulp; **de volada** (see **de a volada**);
de vuelta again; after returning;
del (contraction): **del otro lado**
(coll.) from Mexico; **del tiro**
totally, completely
deán (Ang.) m. dean (of a college)
debelidad (var. of) *debilidad*
debelitar (var. of) *debilitar*
decámada (var. of) *recámara*
decedir (var. of) *decidir*
decido (rus.) (var. of) *dicho*
(ppart. of *decir*)
decinueve (var. of) *diecinueve*
deciocho (var. of) *dieciocho*
**decir: a + (infinitive) + se ha
dicho**: "A comer se ha dicho"
'Let's eat'; **allí (ahi) es donde él le
dijo a ella** there's the rub, there's
the catch (Std. *allí está el busilis*);
decir bien to be right, to predict
accurately (Std. *tener razón*): "Te
dije que iba a venir.—Dijiste bien";
como quien dice so to speak, as
they say; **es como si dijera/dijiera
(dijeras/dijieras,   dijera/dijiera,
dijéramos/dijiéramos   dijeran/
dijieran) mi alma** It's as if I (you,
he/she, etc.) were talking to a
wall; **decir mal** to err in what one
has said, misspeak: "Ya se fue …
No, no, digo mal, todavía está
aquí" 'He went off already … No,
I'm wrong, he's still here'; **decir
pa'tras** (Ang.) to talk back to,
respond aggressively: "No te
dejes; dile pa'tras" 'Don't just

stand there and take it, talk back to him'; **decir un anuncio** to announce; **lo que se dice + adj.** very, what one calls + adj.: "Pedro es lo que se dice inteligente" 'Pete is what one calls intelligent' (Pete is very intelligent); **no decir ni mi alma** to say nary a word, keep absolute silence (esp. after a scolding); **no me lo diga(s) (digan)** interj.: You don't say, Really?, The devil you say (used when the speaker dares a braggart to make good a threat; also used to register surprise or incredulity); **¿no te digo?** or **¿no les digo?** interj. Well I'll be!, Son of a pup! (etc.); **que se diga** so to speak, to speak of: "Él no tiene muy buena voz, que se diga"; **¿quién dijo miedo?** (a set expression used by the speaker to try to convince the listener(s) that he is not afraid) Who's afraid?, Me, afraid?; **Tú dirás/Usted dirá/Ustedes dirán** It's up to you; you tell me; **Ellos dirán** It's up to them

deciséis (var. of) *dieciséis*

decisiete (var. of) *diecisiete*

Decora (Hispanization of) (North and South) Dakota

dedal (coll.) m. finger

dedo: apuntar el dedo to tell on someone, tattle on someone; **dedo chiquito** little finger (fifth finger on the hand); **dedo de los anillos** ring finger (fourth finger); **meter dedo** (slang, vulg.) to simulate copulation, insert the finger into a woman's vagina to simulate coition; **poner el dedo** (id. to **apuntar el dedo**)

defensa: defensa del carro bumper (automobile)

defensia (var. of) *defensa*

defícil (var. of) *difícil*

defoult (Eng.) m. default (in a sports competition)

defunto (var. of) *difunto*

degual (var. of) *desigual*

deit (Eng.) m. date, social appointment

dejado -da negligent in dress and personal hygiene, slovenly; lazy; meek

dejar: deja tú/deje Ud./dejen Uds. That's nothing, That's not the worse part (of the matter): "Deja tú; dicen que se robó el dinero también" 'That's nothing; they say he stole the money to boot'; **dejando de cosas** (set expression) all kidding aside, seriously speaking **dejar a la desidia** to procrastinate; **dejar la puerta abierta** to leave good feelings behind; **dejar plantado -da** to fail to keep a date or an appointment; **dejar saber** to inform, advise; **no dejarse** to take nothing from nobody (slang), refuse to accept insult, abuse, etc.; to fight back, return insult for insult; **(nomás) por no dejar** (just) to while the time away (to do something just to be doing something); **dejar por la paz** to quit, let something rest, leave something be, leave well enough alone; **dejarse (caer)** to yield to the seductive advances of the opposite sex; vr. (slang, vulg.) to put out, give freely of one's sexual favors: "¿Te dejas?" 'Do you do it?' 'Do you put out?'

dejón -jona person who lets others bully or manipulate him/her

delantar (var. of) *delantal* m.

delgado -da thin (ref. to persons only; *flaco -ca* apply to both animals and persons, though some insist that *flaco -ca* designate animal thinness only)

delincuente: delincuente juvenil mf. (Ang.) juvenile delinquent

demo(n)stración (Ang.) f. demonstration (ref. to political demonstration) (Std. *manifestación*)

demo(n)strar (Ang.) vn. to demonstrate (for a political cause, etc.)

den (Eng.) secluded room for studying or relaxing, den

dende (var. of) *desde*

dengue m. gesture (body or facial)

dentrar (var. of) *entrar*

denunciante m. cruel and ruthless policeman

deo (var. of) *dedo*

deodorante (Eng.) m. (var. of) *desodorante* m.

depachar (var. of) *despachar*

depender: depender en (Ang.) (var. of) *depender de*

deponer va. to vomit

depresión (Ang.) f. economic depression

depués (var. of) *después*

deputado -da (vars. of) *diputado -da*

derechazo hard blow with the right fist (usually in a boxing match)

derechero -ra straight shooter, person whose aim is consistently accurate

derechito adv. straight ahead (said in giving route directions)

derecho: decir por derecho to speak frankly, get to the point (coll.); **no haber derecho** to be unjust, unfair; to be inexcusable: "Los mismos ladrones nos volvieron a robar, y la policía no ha dado con ellos; hombre, no hay derecho" 'The same thieves robbed us again, and the police

haven't found them yet; man, that's inexcusable'

derrame: derrame del cerebro stroke, cerebral hemorrhage

derritir (var. of) *derretir*

desabrido -da wet blanket (coll.), killjoy, spoilsport (Std. *aguafiestas*): "No lo invites al pore (a la fiesta); es muy desabrido" 'Don't invite him to the party; he's a real wet blanket'

desabrochador m. clasp, fastener, clip

desacomedido -da unaccommodating, disobliging

desafanar vn. to get out of jail

desafisfecho -cha (Eng.) (vars. of) *desatisfecho -cha* (Eng.)

desahijar va. to prune (plants)

desahije m. act or effect of pruning (plants)

desaigrar (var. of) *desairar*

desanivelado -da (euph.) deceased, dead

desapartar (var. of) *apartar*

desarmador m. screwdriver

desatinar: hacer desatinar a alguien to make someone lose his cool (slang), cause someone to become very angry and quite disoriented

desatisfecho -cha mean, base, despicable (ref. to persons)

desayuno light breakfast taken during the early part of the morning

desbalagado -da dispersed, spread out; lost

desbaratar va. to change a larger monetary unit into smaller ones

desborrador m. (var. of) *borrador* eraser

desborrar va. (var. of) *borrar* to erase; to expunge

descadecimiento (var. of) *des-*

caecimiento weakness, lack of energy

descarapelar (var. of) *escarapelar*

descargador -ra freeloader (coll.), sponger, parasite (fig.)

descarrilado -da crazy, screwy (coll.), off one's rocker (fig.)

descípulo (var. of) *discípulo*

descoger (var. of) *escoger*

descolgar vn. to leave unannounced, take French leave (coll.)

descolorido -da (pej.) Anglo-Saxon, paleface

descompasar vr. to overstep the bounds of reasonable behavior or decorum

desconchi(n)flado -da in a state of disrepair, in poor working order

desconchinflar va. to put out of order, render unusable; vr. to break down, become inoperative

descontar (slang) vr. to beat it (slang), go away, leave; vr. to avenge oneself; to settle a financial debt

descontrolado -da out of control, uncontrolled

descontrolar vr. to lose control of oneself

descoser vr. (fig.) to shout it from the rooftops (coll.), open up and tell everything

descuacharrangado -da (slang) broken, shattered; in a bad state of disrepair

descuacharrangar (slang) va. to put out of order, render inoperable; vr. to break down, become inoperative

descualificar (Eng.) va. to disqualify

descuentar (var. of) *descontar*

descuidado -da: agarrar descuidado -da a alguien to take someone by surprise

descharchar (Eng.) va. to discharge (from the armed forces); (hum.) to break off an amorous relationship, give the gate to one's sweetheart (slang)

descharche or **descharchi** (Eng.) m. discharge from the armed forces (ref. to the act of discharge or the document certifying same); (hum.) dismissal given to the partner in an amorous relationship, walking papers (slang), the old heave-ho (slang)

desde: desde cuando adv. for a long time now: "Eso ya lo sé desde cuando" 'I've known that for a long time now'

desembarañador m. comb

desembarañar va. to comb hair

desenraice m. act and effect of uprooting (i.e., plants, shrubs, etc.)

desenraizado -da badly off (coll.), hopeless, incorrigible; **loco desenraizado** crazy old fool

desenraizar va. to uproot (plants)

desenrollar: desenrollar la calceta (slang) to dance

desepaquetar (var. of) *desempaquetar*

desfender (var. of) *defender*

desflechado -da disoriented

desfrozar (Eng.) va. to defrost

desganchar (var. of) *desenganchar*

desgarrado -da ragged, in rags

desgarranchado -da raggedy, torn, worn out (ref. to clothes and also to person wearing such clothes)

desgarranchar vr. to tear one's clothes to shreds

desgarrar (var. of) *esgarrar* to cough up phlegm

desgarreate or **desgarriate** m. heavy destruction of property; upheaval

desgasnatar vr. to yell, shout; to

talk too freely

desgotado -da (vars. of) *escotado -da* low neckline (i.e., dress which barely reaches above wearer's breast)

desgraciado -da (pej.) base, vile, mean, son-of-a-bitch

desgraciar va. to ruin; injure badly

desgranar va. to tear apart; **desgranarse la mazorca** vr. (hum.) to fall down (said of persons)

desgustar (var. of) *disgustar*

deshermanable unbrotherly, unsisterly (said of person who mistreats his/her sibling)

desiar (var. of) *desear*

desidioso -sa procrastinating; negligent

desimular (var. of) *disimular*

desinfestante (var. of) *desinfectante*

desinfestar (Ang.) va. to disinfect

desmadrar va. to beat up (in a fight); to destroy or deface maliciously; vr. to hurt oneself

desmanchar va. to remove spots

desmechar va. & vr. to pull at one another's hair in a fight

desnarizado -da (vars. of) *desnarigado -da*

desobligado -da irresponsible

desocupar va. to dismiss from a job, fire

despacientar vn. & vr. (var. of) *impacientar* vn. & vr.

despachador -ra store clerk

despagar va. to cut weeds

desparramar va. to broadcast news or gossip far and wide

despensa medicine cabinet

despercudido -da light-complexioned, light-skinned; pale

desperjuicio (var. of) *perjuicio*

despidir (var. of) *despedir*

despilfarrero (var. of) *despilfarro*

desplumar va. to defeat (in a contest)

después: después de (Ang.) in honor of, after: "Lo nombraron después de Benito Juárez" 'They named him after Benito Juárez'; **después de atole** (said of solution or assistance appearing too late to do any good)

despuesito adv. right after, immediately after: "Se fue despuesito de ti" 'He left just after you did'

despuesto -ta (vars. of) *dispuesto -ta*

despulmonar vr. to work hard (often to excess)

destapado -da hatless, without a head covering

destapador m. plunger (used to clean out clogged drains, etc.)

destapar vr. to obtain relief from constipation; vr. to remove one's headgear, uncover one's head

destender (var. of) *extender*; **destender la cama** to make the bed

destete m. weaning

destornudar (var. of) *estornudar*

destornudo (var. of) *estornudo*

destraído -da or **destraido -da** (vars. of) *distraído -da*

destribuidor (var. of) *distribuidor* m.

destruigo, destruigues, etc. (vars. of) *destruyo, destruyes,* etc. (pres. ind. forms of *destruir*)

detalle: allí (ahi) está el detalle there's the rub, there's the catch (Std. *allí está el busilis*)

detecta (Eng?) m. detective

detectiva mf. (var. of) *detective*

detenido -da freeloader (coll.); stingy person

detirar (var. of) *retirar*

detrás: andar detrás de alguien to

be making a play for a member of the opposite sex; to be harassing someone; to be pestering someone

detrato (var. of) *retrato*

detur m. (Eng.) detour

devalgar (var. of) *divulgar*

deveras (see **de deveras**)

devertir (var. of) *divertir*

devino (var. of) *divino*

devisar (var. of) *divisar*

devolver: devolver pa'tras (Ang.) va. to return, take back; vr. (var. of) *volverse* to turn back, return

devorcio (var. of) *divorcio*

día m.: **(el) día de finados** All Souls' Day (Nov. 2nd); **(el) día de la coneja** Easter, Easter Sunday; **el día del guajolote/el día del torque** (Eng.) Thanksgiving Day (Std. *Día de Acción de Gracias*); **(el) día de Valentín** (St.) Valentine's Day

di ay (var. of) *de ahí*: "Di ay se fueron a casa" 'From there they went on home' or 'And then they went on home'

diálago (var. of) *diálogo*

diamante (Ang.) m. baseball diamond (field, infield)

diame (Eng.) m. dime, ten-cent piece (cf. **daime, dime** et al.)

diantre mf. devil; **diantre de:** "Diantre de huerquito este!" 'You damnable mischievous little brat, you!'

¡diantres! interj. (var. of) *¡diantre!*

diavolada (see **de a volada**)

dibilidad f. (var. of) *debilidad* f.

dibilitar va. & vr. (var. of) *debilitar*

dicemos or **dicimos** (vars. of) *decimos* (1st pers. pl. pres. ind. of *decir*)

dicer or **dicir** (vars. of) *decir* (cf. **dijir**)

dicinueve (var. of) *diecinueve*

diciocho (var. of) *dieciocho*

dicipela (var. of) *ericipela* erysipelas (type of contagious skin disease)

dicisiete (var. of) *diecisiete*

diche (Eng.) m. irrigation canal; any type of ditch

Diego (de Rivera) (slang) m. dime, ten-cent piece

diente: diente picado tooth with a cavity or tooth decay; **pelar el diente** to smile; to show one's teeth (often in anger)

dientista (var. of) *dentista*

dientón -tona (vars. of) *dentudo -da*

diferiencia (var. of) *diferencia* (Std.)

diforme mf. (var. of) *deforme*

dignatario -ria (vars. of) *dignitario -ria*

dijía, dijías, etc. (vars. of) *decía, decías,* etc. (imperfect forms of *decir*)

dijiera, dijieras, etc. (vars. of) *dijera, dijeras,* etc. (past subj. of *decir*)

dijieron (var. of) *dijeron* (3rd pers. pl. pret. of *decir*)

dijir (var. of) *decir*

dijunto -ta (vars. of) *difunto -ta*

Dile (Hispanization of) Dilley, Texas

dilear or **diliar** (Eng.) vn. to deal or traffic in narcotic drugs

dilicado -da (vars. of) *delicado -da*

dima or **dimo** (Eng.) (slang) dime, ten-cent piece (cf. **daime, diame,** et al.)

dinero-oro United States currency (cf. **dinero-plata**)

dinero-plata Mexican currency

dino -na (vars. of) *digno -na*

dintista mf. (var. of) *dentista* mf.

dionde (var. of) *donde*

dioquis (see **oquis, de hoquis**)

Dios: Bendito sea Dios the Lord works in mysterious ways; **¡Dios me (te, lo, nos, los) libre!** Heaven (God) forbid!; **¡Dios nos (me) favorezca! ¡Dios no lo quiera!** Heaven forbid!; **en el nombre sea de Dios** Amen, So be it; **¡Ni lo mande Dios !** Heaven forbid!, Saints preserve us!; **Sea por Dios** Amen, So be it; (slang) That's the way the cookie crumbles (slang); **Si Dios es servido** God willing: "Buenas noches, hasta mañana. — Si Dios es servido"; **saber lo que es amar a Dios en tierra ajena** to know firsthand what trouble really is

dipa (Eng.) dipper, ladle

dipartamento (var. of) *departamento*

dipo (Eng.) depot, train station

diptonguizar (var. of) *diptongar*

diputado -da (Ang.?) deputy policeman (-woman)

dirección f. steering wheel (automobile)

dirretir or **dirritir** (vars. of) *derretir*

disabilidad f. (Ang.) physical disability (Std. *invalidez*)

discharchar (var. of) *descharchar* (Eng.)

disco: cambiar el disco to stop harping on the same theme, change the topic of conversation; **disco rayado** (fig.) said of a person who keeps harping on the same theme; the "harped-upon" conversational theme itself

disconfiado -da (vars. of) *desconfiado -da*

discuto (var. of) *discurso* discourse

disgustado -da hard to please

disinteresado -da (vars. of)

desinteresado -da

disiséis (var. of) *dieciséis*

disminuigo (var. of) *disminuyo* (1st pers. pres. ind. sg. of disminuir)

dispacio (var. of) *despacio*

dispedir (var. of) *despedir*

dispertar (var. of) *despertar*

dispierto, dispiertas, etc. (vars. of) *despierto, despiertas*, etc. (pres. ind. conjugations of *despertar*)

dispués (var. of) *después*

distancia: anteojos (antiojos) de larga distancia binoculars; telescope

distraido -da (vars. of) *distraído -da*

districto (var. of) *distrito*

distrital adj. mf. of or pertaining to a district

distruigo, distruigues, etc. (vars. of) *destruyo, destruyes*, etc. (pres. ind. conjugations of *destruir*) (cf. **destruigo** et al.)

disvariar va. (var. of) *desvariar*

ditado (var. of) *dictado*

ditecto (Eng?) detective

ditur (Eng.) detour

divirsión (var. of) *diversión*

divurcear or **divurciar** vr. (vars. of) *divorciar*

divurcio (var. of) *divorcio*

dizque (var. of) *dice que*

dobleplay (Eng.) m. double play (in baseball)

doce (see **dar las doce**)

doctor: visita de doctor very brief visit (expression usually in the form of a complaint voiced by a host when visitors depart after a stay the host feels was too brief; the complaint is common among members of the same family who feel they should "see" each other more frequently)

Doche (Eng.) m. Dodge (brand of automobile)

doler: doler la cintura to have a backache

dólor (var. of) *dólar* m. dollar

dolor: dolor de brazo spleen pain, stitch in the side (fig.); **dolor de cintura** backache (esp. in the lower back); **hacérsele dolor a alguien hacer algo** for it to hurt (fig.) someone to do something (ref. to ungenerous attitude): "Se te hizo dolor darme un pedacito de manzana" 'It hurt you to give me a little piece of the apple'

domás adv. (var. of) *nomás* adv.

domecilio (var. of) *domicilio*

dominguero suit of clothes reserved for formal occasions, 'Sunday best' (coll.); **dominguero -ra** n. & adj. (said of person who enjoys going out to have a good time or to visit on Sundays)

dompe (Eng.) m. garbage dump; dump truck; (fig.) house or room in a filthy condition

dompear or **dompiar** (Eng.) va. to dump, dispose of; to vomit; to dump, give someone the slip (fig.), get rid of someone

don: ay va con don (hum., vulg.) (said of a passing woman; double entendre: 'There she goes with Don' and also 'There she goes with a condom')

dona (Eng.) doughnut

doña Juanita (slang) marihuana

dormelón -lona (vars. of) *dormilón -lona*

dormiera, dormieras, etc. (past subj. forms of *dormir*) (vars. of) *durmiera, durmieras,* etc.

dormió, dormieron, dormiendo (vars. of) *durmió, durmieron, durmiendo* (resp. 3rd pers. sg. pret., 3rd pers. pl. pret., and ger. of *dormir*)

dormir: dormir como un tronco to sleep like a log (fig.), sleep very soundly; **dormir la borrachera** to sleep off an alcoholic binge; **dormir con alguien** (Ang.) to sleep with someone (coll.), have sexual intercourse with someone; **dormir la cruda** to sleep off a hangover; **dormírsele a alguien el gallo** to be caught napping, caught off guard (e.g., in a business deal or other competitive effort); to fail to take advantage of a favorable situation; to fail in the sex act (said of men who lose their erection); **poner a dormir** (Ang.?) to put to sleep (coll.), to knock out in a fist fight or boxing match

dormitorio (Ang.) dormitory (student residence) (Std. *residencia* the building)

dorreales or **dorriales** (vars. of) *dos reales*

dos: en un dos por tres in the twinkling of an eye (coll.), with extreme rapidity; **dos reales or dos riales** quarter, twenty-five cent piece

dostear or **dostiar** (Eng.) va. to dust, remove dust (as in cleaning a room)

dota (Eng?) m. doctor, physician

dotor m. (var. of) *doctor* m.

draivear or **draiviar** (Eng.) va. to drive (an automobile)

drenaje m. drain, catheter

driblear or **dribliar** (Eng.) va. to dribble (a ball, in basketball)

drinc or **drinque** (Eng.) m. drink (esp. an alcoholic drink)

droga (slang) debt

droma (Eng.) m. traveling salesman (<drummer [dated slang

expression for traveling salesman])

dropear or **dropiar** (Eng.) va. to drop, let fall

duérmamos (var. of) *durmamos* (1st pers. pl. subj. of *dormir*)

dulce: ser de dulce (slang, pej.) to be a pansy (slang, pej.), be a homosexual; **dulce con sal** m. hog skin crackling; **dulce de palito** m. (any sweet object embedded on a stick, e.g., an all-day sucker)

dulcero -ra candy vendor or maker

duque m. tobacco (loan metonymy, <Duke brand tobacco?)

durmir (var. of) *dormir*

duro -ra (slang) stiff (slang), dead; **traerla dura** to have a hard-on (vulg., slang), have an erection of the penis

E

ea (var. of) ella

echada f. boast; bluff, fib; brooding hen; **ser más las echadas que las culecas** (literally, for there to be more hens on the nest than the number that are actually laying eggs; said of persons who claim to have accomplished much but who actually have not)

echador -ra mf. braggart; bluffer

echar va.: **echar a cuestas** to throw someone on his/her back; **echar carnes** to curse; **echar de patitas a la calle** to fire, dismiss (from a job) in short order; to run off, tell to leave (e.g., a home, usually ref. to the manner in which one common-law partner tells the other to depart); **echar un aplastón/echar un tapón** to put someone in his/her place, put someone down (slang), tell someone where to get off (slang), reprimand; **echar a la bolsa / echar en la bolsa** to defeat; **echar al bote** to bewitch; **echar al pozo** to drive (send) to the grave: "Los hijos malos casi siempre echan a los padres al pozo de tantas penas que les dan" 'Bad children almost always drive their parents to the grave with the grief they cause them'; **echar a perder** to spoil,

pamper (esp. ref. to children); **echar de la madre** to curse at someone (the taboo word *madre* is usually included in the cursing); **echar el gato a retozar** to let out a secret, let the cat out of the bag (coll.); **echar en carrilla** to give chase to, chase away: "A Juan lo echaron en carrilla porque estaba molestando mucho"; **echar habladas** to insinuate; **echar (la) rifa** to read tarot cards to tell someone's fortune; **echar la sal** to jinx, bring bad luck; **echar la tranca** to latch (usually ref. to a screen door); **echar madres** to curse, cuss out (cf. **echar de la madre**); **echarle la ley a alguien** to get the law after someone; to bring a lawsuit against someone; **echar menos** (var. of) *echar de menos*; **echar mosca** to tease; **echar papas** to tell lies, lie; **echar un pedo** (vulg.) to expel wind; **echar piquete** to provoke, needle (coll.); **echar por la cabeza** to betray, tell the secrets of someone else: "Primitivo se enojó con Inocencio porque éste lo echó por la cabeza"; **echar tranca (a la puerta)** to lock (a door with a key), latch (a screen door); vn. **echár(se)las de lado** to brag, boast; **echar maromas** to do somersaults; **echar pulgas** to cause trouble; **echars(se) una polca** to dance a polka (or any other dance); **echar un palito** (slang) for a male to have sexual intercourse; vr. to lie down (said only of animals or, in anger or sarcastically, of humans); **echarle su lonche a alguien** to put someone in his/her place, tell someone where to get off (slang): "Pásale; papá te va a echar tu lonche" 'Come on in; daddy's going to give you what you've got coming' (usually said to a child who has misbehaved); **echarlo al juego** (var. of) *echarlo a juego* to tell as a joke, tell in fun; **echarse al plato/ echárselo** to get the best of someone, beat someone out; to seduce; to kill; **echársela** or **echarse al plato a una mujer** to possess a woman sexually; **echarse de ver** to be evident, show: "Es muy mezquino. — Se echa de ver." 'He's very stingy. — It shows.' **echarse el trompo en la uña** (usually said as a command): "¡Échate el trompo en la uña!" 'Put that in your pipe and smoke it!' (said as an admonishment or by way of revenge); **echarse encima** to jump on someone (fig.); **echarse trácala(s)** to fall into debt; **echarse un pedo** to expel wind; **echarse un pedo de aquéllos** (slang, vulg.) to let out a real stinker (ref. to a very bad smelling expulsion of bodily wind)

edeficio (var. of) *edificio*

editor (Ang.) m. newspaper editor (Std. *redactor*)

educación (Ang.) f. education (in all senses of the word in Eng., not solely 'upbringing' as per Std.)

educacional mf. (Ang.) educational, that which serves to enhance the learning process

¡eit! or **¡éitale!** (slang, used to call a person's attention): Hey you!

¡éjele! interj. (used to poke fun at someone): "¡Éjele, perdieron el juego!"

ejir (rus.) (var. of) *decir*

ejote msg. string beans, green beans

elante (var. of) *delante*

elástico rubber band

elba (slang) m. barber (<*el ba[rbero]*)

electar (Eng.) va. to elect, elect to office

electrecidad f. (var. of) *electricidad* f.

eléctrico -ca (slang) drunk

eligir (var. of) *elegir*

Eloisa (var. of) *Eloísa*

elote: ciertos elotes (verdes) certain (well-known) persons, certain so-and-sos (would-be oblique ref. to persons whom one coyly does not wish to name)

embachichar va. to con, dupe, swindle

embarado -da bloated (ref. to stomach bloated from indigestion)

embarazado -da (Ang.?) embarrassed

embarrada (var. of) *embarradura*

embarañado -da (var. of) *enmarañado -da*

embarrar va. to run over, crushing or flattening (e.g., a person with a vehicle); to spread (e.g., butter on a slice of bread)

embijar va. to paint; to smear, grease

embolar va. to confuse, mix up; vr. to get confused or mixed up

embolio (var. of) *embolia* stroke

embono (var. of) *abono*

emborucar va. to confuse, mix up; vr. to get confused or mixed up

emborrachar va. to make dizzy; vr. to become dizzy

embusteroso -sa liar

Emiterio (var. of) *Emeterio*

empacador -ra packer (person who works in a packing house)

empacar (slang) va. to eat; vr. to stuff oneself (coll.), eat to satiation

empachado -da fed up (fig.), extremely annoyed (with)

empachar va. to irritate, annoy

empalmado -da bundled up, wearing lots of clothes

empalmar va. to pile up items one on top of the other; vr. to bundle up, wear plenty of clothing (as for protection against the cold)

empalme: traer empalme to be heavily bundled up, be wearing many clothes

empanada semicircular jelly or roll or doughnut

empanal m. type of small bread roll

empanturrar va. to stuff (a person) with food; vr. to stuff oneself with food, eat to excess

empanzado -da stuffed, full (said of stomachs replete with food)

empanzar va. to stuff (a person) with food; vr. to stuff oneself with food, eat gluttonously

empaque (slang) m. chow (slang), food, meal, dinner; tooth packing (temporary filling for cavity)

emparejar vr. to tie the score in a game; to avenge

empedar vr. to get drunk (cf. **pedo**)

empelotado -da passionately in love

empelotar vr. to be passionately in love

empinado -da bent over

empinar va. to bend (usually ref. to persons); vr. to bend over

empistolado -da armed with a gun

empleado -da or **empliado -da** police officer, (esp.) immigration officer

emplumar vn. to become of age

emprestamista mf. (var. of) *prestamista* (Std.) moneylender

empuchar (Eng.) va. to push, shove

empuesto -ta (vars. of) *impuesto -ta*

en: en cas de (var. of) *en casa de*; **en el colorado** (Ang.) in the red (slang), in debt; **(de) en seguida de** alongside, next door: "Vive en la casa de en seguida de nosotros"; **en tanto que nada** in a jiffy, very quickly; **en un dos por cuatro/en un tres por cuatro** (vars. of) *en un dos por tres* in a jiffy, in a wink; **en veces** (var. of) *a veces* (Std.) at times; **en visitas** (var. of) *de visita* (Std.) on a visit

enamorar: enamorarse con (Ang.) (var. of) *enamorarse de* (Std.)

encá or **enca** prep. (vars. of) *en casa de*

encajar va. to blame; va. to stick with a pointed instrument; vr. to climb on someone's back; to get on top of one's partner to have sexual intercourse; vr. to stick a pointed object into oneself (usually through accident): "Julio se encajó un clavo en la mano derecha"

encalmado -da dying of thirst, extremely thirsty

encamorrado -da ill-tempered

encandilado -da tired

encandilar va. to tire; to lure, tempt; vr. to get tired, tire out

encanicado -da (slang) passionately in love

encanicar vr. to fall passionately in love

encantoneado -da or **encantoniado -da** (slang) married, hitched (slang)

encantonear or **encantoniar** (slang) vr. to get married, get hitched (slang)

encapuchado -da (slang) well-dressed

encaramado -da on top of

encaramar vr. to mount a horse; to mount someone to have sexual intercourse

encartado -da half-breed, of mixed racial background

encebar vr. to get grease on one's hands

encendido match (used for igniting)

encimar vr. to be where one is not wanted; to be or become a pest

encimón -mona (vars. of) *encimoso -sa*: **andar de encimón** or **ser encimón** to be a pest (fig.), be bothersome

encimoso -sa pest, annoying person

encontonear or **encontoniar** (vars. of) *encantonear, encantoniar*

encorralar va. to corner

encuerado -da naked

encuerar va. to strip, take the clothes off of; vr. to undress

encuetar va. to inebriate; vr. to get drunk

enchalecar (slang) va. to shoplift

enchaquetar va. to help (someone) put on a jacket; vr. to put on one's jacket

encharcado -da stuck in the mud; m. mistake

encharcar vr. to make a mistake; to get stuck in the mud

enchilada m. burned mouth or tongue (resulting from the ingestion of any type of food that contains hot chili)

enchilado -da infuriated, outraged

enchilar va. to burn someone's tongue with hot food; vr. to burn oneself (in the mouth) with hot food (esp. food containing hot chili)

enchinado -da in curls

enchinador m. hair curler

enchinar va. & vr. to curl hair; vr. **enchinársele el cuerpo a alguien** to get goosepimples (goosebumps)

enchinchado -da infested with chinch bugs

enchinchar va. to fill with bedbugs; vr. to become infested with bedbugs (usually said of mattresses)

enchuecar va. to twist; vr. to become twisted

endenantes adv. a little while ago

enderezar va. to straighten out (fig.), reform, rehabilitate; vr. to straighten oneself out, reform oneself

endeveras (var. of) *de veras*

endomingar vr. to dress up in style, dress up in one's 'Sunday best'

endrogar va. to get someone into debt; vr. to get into debt

enfajar va. to put a belt or sash on someone; vr. to put on one's belt or sash

enfatizar va. to emphasize

enferma (euph.) menstruating, having ones period; **enfermar** va. to hex, make sick through witchcraft; vr. to begin labor pains; to be in labor

enfermedad: enfermedad de andancia disease that is going around, mild epidemic (cf. **enfermedad que anda**); **enfermedad del carácter** character disorder, disease of social pathology (often considered innate); **enfermedad endañada** disease resulting from an act of witchcraft; **enfermedad que anda** disease that is going around, mild epidemic; **enfermedad secreta** venereal disease

enflacar va. to cause someone to become thin: "Lo inflacó de tantas penas"; vr. to become thin, lose weight; to diet (so as to lose weight)

enfriar: abanico de enfriar air conditioner

enfrifolar or **enfrijolar** vr. to eat an excessive amount of beans, stuff oneself with beans (usually pinto beans)

enganchado -da (Ang.?) hooked on drugs; (hum.) hooked or tricked into marriage

enganchar va. to hook or trick into marriage; va. (Angl.?) to get someone hooked on drugs; vr. (hum.) to become engaged to be married; to get married, get hooked (slang); vr. to get hooked on drugs

enganche m. engagement, promise to marry; downpayment; contract to obtain *bracero* laborers

enganchista m. (sometimes pej.) contractor of *bracero* labor

engarruñar vr. to get into a fight; to double up, shrink (esp. when extremely angry)

engartusar (var. of) *engatusar*

engrasada shoeshine; **dar una engrasada** to apply shoe paste to

shoes (so as to shine them)

engrasar va. to apply shoe paste to shoes (so as to shine them); va. (Ang.?) to grease the palm (or the hand), bribe

engrase m. applications of shoe paste to shoes for purposes of shining

engreír vr. to become attached to, fond of

engrido -da (vars. of) *engreído -da*

engrifar va. to administer marihuana to someone; vr. to take marihuana; to feel the effects of marihuana

engringolar va. to cause someone to become gringo-like, to gringoize; vr. to become like a gringo

enguaynar (Eng.) va. to get someone drunk on wine; vr. to get drunk on wine

engüerar vr. to become addled (ref. to people); to become rotten (ref. to eggs)

engusanar vr. to become wormy (ref. to animals and persons who fall prey to worms in their intestines)

enhuevar vr. to become stubborn

enjaulado -da jailed, in jail

enjaule (slang) m. jail

enjetado -da (said of person who is pouting; also said of person making a facial expression denoting anger)

enlistar (Eng.) or (var. of) *alistarse* (Std.) vr. to enlist in the armed forces

enmaizado -da: loco -ca enmaizado -da, resp. screwball (coll.), crazy old fool

enmantecar va. to dirty with grease or lard; vr. to become dirty with grease or lard

enmañado -da deceptive, fraudulent, tricky (ref. to persons)

enmarihuanar va. to administer marihuana to, cause to take marihuana; vr. to take marihuana

enmugrar va. & vr. (var. of) *enmugrecer* va. & vr.

enmugrentar va. & vr. to soil, dirty

enmular vr. to become obstinate, stubborn

enraizado -da: loco -ca enraizado -da, resp. screwball (coll.), crazy old fool (cf. **enmaizado**)

enredado -da (hum.) engaged to be married

enrodar vr. to become tangled, rolled up

enrollar vr. to become tangled

ensartar (vulg.) va. & vr. to insert one's penis into a vagina

enseñar: enseñar la oreja to show one's bad side, reveal one's defects; to reveal one's true colors; **enseñar una película** (Ang?) to show a movie

entabicar (slang) va. to jail, lock up in jail

entablazón f. obstruction, severe constipation

entacuachado -da (vars. of) *entacuchado -da*

entacuchado -da (slang) well-dressed, dressed up (coll.)

enteligir (var. of) *inteligir*

entender (see **hacer entender**)

enterrar va. to stick with a pointed instrument; vr. to stick a pointed object into oneself (usually through accident): "Me enterré una astilla en el pie"

entonado -da: andar entonado -da to be drunk

entoces (var. of) *entonces*

entonce (var. of) *entonces*

entosequido -da (Eng.) intox-

icated, drunk

entracalado -da in debt

entracalar va. to put into debt; vr. to become indebted, accumulate debts

entrada inning (in baseball); permission officially given by the father of a girl to a boy desirous of visiting her at home; **venir de entrada y salida** to visit or call upon someone briefly

entradera: entradera y salidera (ref. to person) gadabout

entradito -ta slightly drunk

entrado -da slighty drunk

entrador -ra daredevil, taker of risks

¡éntrale! interj. (used to encourage or stimulate) Go at it!, Do it!: "¡Éntrale; no le tengas miedo!"

entrar va. to tackle, take on (e.g. a job, a challenge, etc.); **entrarle a uno por una oreja (un oído) y salirle por otra (otro)** (Ang.?) (ref. to one who ignores sound advice or disobeys parents or elders); **éntrale chiquito -ta (chiquitito -ta)** Have a go at it, Go get'em tiger (slang) (an expr. used to encourage someone to accept a challenge)

entre: entre más...más the more... the more; **entre menos...menos** the less/the fewer...the less/the fewer

entresacar va. to thin hair (as done by barbers to customers so requesting)

entresemana sg. weekdays

entretener va. to delay; vr. to be delayed

entriego, entriegas, etc. (vars. of) *entrego, entregas*, etc. (pres. ind. of *entregar*)

entrincar: entrincar los dientes to

clench one's teeth

entro adv. (var. of) *adentro* adv.

entrón -trona daredevil, taker of risks, dreadnought

entumido -da (vars. of) *entumecido -da*

entumir vr. to get cold feet (fig.), shy away from something

envitado -da (vars. of) *invitado -da*

envitar (var. of) *invitar*

envoltijo (var. of) *envoltorio* bundle

envolver (Ang.) va. to involve (someone in something): "Querían envolverlo en ese problema"; (Ang.) vr. to become involved in: "Siempre se envuelve en mucho mugrero"

enyerbado -da bewitched, hexed

enyerbar va. to bewitch, hex

envueltos enchiladas

enzoquetar va. to muddy up, splatter with mud; vr. to get muddied up

¡epa! or **¡épale!** interj. Watch that!, Hey!, Careful!, etc.

epazote m. wormseed (Chenopodium embrosioides) (herbal tea used to treat stomachache or as a vermicide)

episodio (Ang.?) motion picture presented in serial form (e.g., in 15 parts, one each week)

erjostes (Eng.) fsg. flight attendant, stewardess, airline hostess (ant.) (Stds. *azafata, aeromoza*)

ero (rus.) (var. of) *soy* (1st pers. sg. pres. ind. of ser)

eroplano (var. of) *aeroplano*

erutar (var. of) *eructar*

ésa es de ay or **ése es de ay** (general expression of approval) (slang) Right on! (slang), That's right!

¡ésa(le)! (slang) (interj. used to call a female's attention) Hey you!; **¡ése(le)!** (slang) (interj. used to call a male's attention) Hey you!

escalera (hum.) tall person, daddy longlegs (coll.)

escame m. fear, terror

escamoso -sa fearful, frightened

escandaloso -sa squeamish

escansar (var. of) *descansar*

escante m. short while, moment: "Espérame un escante"

escarapelar va. to chip off; vr. to get chipped off

escarbar to dig, excavate deeply (not merely 'to scratch' as in Std.) (Std. *cavar*)

escarcha cold weather, cold season

escobón (slang, hum.) m. guitar

escoch (Eng.) m. Scotch whiskey; **escoch teip** (Eng.) m. Scotch tape

escondidas: jugar a las escondidas to play hide-and-seek (child's game)

escor (Eng.) m. score

escorcés (var. of) *escocés*

escrachar (Eng.) va. to scratch (slang), cancel, eliminate

escrebido -da (rus.) (vars. of) *escrito -ta* (ppart. of *escribir*)

escrebir (var. of) *escribir*

escrepón (Eng.) m. shoe with thick soles (scrape)

escrechar (Eng.) va. to scratch (cf. **escrachar**)

escribido -da (rus.) (vars. of) *escrito -ta* (ppart. of *escribir*)

éscrín or **escrín** (Eng.) m. ice cream

escrín (Eng.) m. movie screen

escuadra pistol (usually automatic); gun (in general); (fig.) square shooter, honest person; square deal, honest treatment

escuela (Ang.) classes, school day: "No hay escuela hoy" (Std. *no hay clases hoy*); **escuela alta** (Ang.) high school

escueto -ta quiet, tranquil

escuincle mf. child

esculcón -cona (pej.) snoop, person who enjoys searching through others' possessions without permission

escupe (slang) m. gun

escupida (slang) (fig.) gun blast

escupidera (slang) pistol, gun

escura (Eng.) motor scooter; child's (motorless) scooter

escurecer (var. of) *o(b)scurecer*

escúrer (Eng.) m. scooter, motorcycle; child's (motorless) scooter

escuro -ra (vars. of) *oscuro -ra*

esgado -da sideways, crossways: "El carro quedó esgado en medio de la calle" 'The car was left sideways in the middle of the street'

eslecs (Eng.) mpl. slacks, pants

eso: en eso at that moment, just then: "En eso llegó María" 'Just then María arrived'

espalda: espalda mojada (Ang.?) wetback (illegal immigrant from Mexico)

espaldar m. headboard; back of a chair

espatear or **espatiar** (Eng.) va. to spot, recognize

espauda or **espaura** (Eng.) (<yeast powder) baking powder

espelear or **espeliar** (Eng.) va. to spell (words)

espeletear or **espeletiar** (Eng.) (vars. of) *espelear, espeliar*

esperanza: ¡qué esperanza(s)! interj. (used to express strong doubt as to whether something will take place) That'll be the day!

espichadito -ta (Eng.<speech?) quiet, repressed, not talkative; subdued

espiche (Eng.) m. speech, discourse

espineche (Eng.) m. spinach

espiniento -ta or **espinillento -ta** pimpled, beset with facial pimples

espirina (var. of) *aspirina*

espírito (var. of) *espíritu*

esporte (Eng.) m. sport

esprín (Eng.) m. spring (Std. *resorte*); spring (Std. *primavera*)

espués (var. of) *después*

esquechar (Eng.) va. to sketch, draw, design

esqueche (Eng.) m. sketch, design

esquifa (var. of) *esquife* (Std.)

Esquilmo, el Skidmore, Texas

ésquimo mf (Eng.?) Eskimo (Std. *esquimal* mf.)

esquina: hacer esquina (slang) to (show) support (for)

esquinado -da or **esquiniado -da** adj. placed at an angle (usually ref. to a piece of furniture)

esquinar or **esquiniar** va. to place at an angle or in a corner of a room

esquinear or **esquiniar** (slang) vn. to go along with (fig.), assent to

esquipear or **esquipiar** (Eng.) va. to skip, to miss (e.g., a class, a lesson, an appointment); va. & vn to skip, jump, hop

esquite m. popcorn

estaca: pollito de estaca person approaching old age; adult or person approaching adulthood

estacar (Eng.) va. to stack, pile up

estación: estación de gasolina (Ang.?) f. gas(oline) station

estado: estado de la estrella solitaria (Ang.) Lone Star State

(Texas); **estado interesante** (euph.) pregnancy

estafeate or **estafiate** m. medicinal herb used for stomach disorders

estampa (Ang.) stamp, postage stamp

estaquita mumbletypeg (children's game played with a jackknife)

estar: **(a)hora sí (que) está(s) (están, estamos) curioso (curiosos)** this is a fine how-do-you-do, this is a fine state of affairs; **estar a manos** to owe nothing to anyone, be even; to have avenged oneself; **estar a toda madre** (for something to be) terrific, tremendous; **estar a una y un pedazo** to be penniless, stone broke (coll.); **estar bueno** to suffice, be enough: "¡Ya está bueno!" 'That's enough!'; **estar caliente** (Ang.) to be hot (said of the weather) (Std. *hacer calor*); **estar como la fregada** to be as _____ as can be (e.g., 'to be as ugly as sin', 'as mean as a junkyard dog', etc.) (ref. usually to any negative quality known both to speaker and listener) **estar como la jodida** to be as _____ as can be (usual ref. to a negative characteristic of which both speaker and listener are cognizant): "Ella está como la jodida" 'She's as ugly as sin'; **estar con el esposo/estar con la esposa** (euph.) to be having sexual intercourse; **estar con familia** to be pregnant; **estar curado -da de susto** fearless (ref. to person who does not frighten easily); **estar de aquea (aquélla)** (slang) to be tremendous, terrific, great, etc.; **estar de a tiro** to be incorrigible; **estar de lado** (coll.) to be in a good mood; **estar de la patada** (slang) to stink, smell bad;

to be incorrigible; to be very ugly, homely (usually ref. to women); **estar de muleta** (coll.) to be in a bad mood; **estar dioquis** (see **de hoquis**); **estar en la calle** to be destitute, in extreme poverty; **estar en la chilla** to be destitute, down and out, desperate; **estar en la línea/linia** to be drunk; **estar en que** to think, suppose, assume: "Yo estaba en que José ya se había graduado" 'I thought that Joe had already graduated'; **estar en su fuerza** to be at its greatest point of intensity (ref. to a series or progression of events or to emotions in general): "La depresión estaba en su fuerza entonces" 'The (economic) depression was at its apogee then'/"El amor de Juan y María estaba en su fuerza entonces" 'John and Mary's love was in full bloom then'/"A esa hora la música estaba en su fuerza" 'At that hour the música was going strong'; **estar en todo (menos en misa)** to mind everyone's business but one's own, attend to everyone's affairs but one's own; **estar febrero / estar marzo** or **estar febrero loco y marzo otro poco** to be crazy; **estar frío** (Ang.) to be cold (said of the weather) (Std. *hacer frío*); **estar hasta el copete** to be fed up, to have stood as much as possible; to be extremely drunk; **estar hasta las manitas** to be extremely drunk; **estar la patria muy pobre/estar la patria muy fregada** to be in a poor financial situation, be at the end of one's rope (fig.): "¿Vas a comprar el carro? — No puedo, está muy fregada la patria"; **estar madre** (slang) (for something to be) terrific, tremendous, super, great, etc.; **estar malo -la del apéndix** to have appendicitis; **estar malo el cuento** (for things to be in a bad state): "¡Está malo el cuento!" 'Things have come to a pretty pass!' (coll.); **estar padre (bato -ta)** (slang) (iron. expression used to indicate that one's feelings have been hurt; the implication is that revenge will be taken or poetic justice will prevail); **estar parejos** to be tied, end up in a tie; **estar poniéndosela a alguien** to be having sexual relations with someone; **estar que hasta / estar que nomás** to be very tense, fit to be tied, on pins and needles (fig.), at one's wits end (etc.); to be very ugly/beautiful/drunk, etc. (ref. to an extreme manifestation of an obvious quality known to both speaker and listener); **estar uno que se lo lleva el diablo/estar uno que se lo lleva judas/estar uno que se lo lleva el tren/estar uno que se lo lleva la chingada** to be very tense, fit to be tied, on pins and needles (as in anticipation of something to happen momentarily); **estar relajado -da** to have a hernia; **estar tirado -da** to be having a stroke of bad luck; to be jinxed, unlucky; to be abed, lying in bed (usual ref. to sick or lazy person); **estar tamañito -ta** to be edgy, be on pins and needles, (as in anticipation of something to happen momentarily); **estar torcidos** not to be on friendly terms (see also **torcerle la cara a alguien**); **estar tres piedras** to be terrific, tremendous, very beautiful, etc.; **estar uno que se lo lleva madre** to be very tense, be

overanxious; **estar volteado -da (voltiado -da) con alguien** to be at odds with someone, not to be on speaking terms with someone: "Ema y Eva están voltiadas" 'Emma and Eva are not on speaking terms'; **estarse haciendo** to be playing possum, be pretending, be playing dumb; **lo que está de tocar** (fixed expression) Whatever will be, will be

estara or **estare** or **estárer** (Eng.) m. starter (on an automobile)

estarear or **estariar** (Eng.) va. to start (an automobile)

este (used as a stalling device, i.e., inserted when the speaker cannot think of what to say next)

esteche hueguen (Eng.) m. station wagon (type of car)

Esteples (slang) (Hispanization of) Staples, Texas

estérico -ca (vars. of) *histérico -ca*

estijeras (var. of) *tijeras* (Std.)

estilacho (slang) style, fashion

estile (Eng.) m. a ball bearing used as a marble in a game of marbles

estilla (var. of) *astilla* (Std.)

estirada act or result of growing taller (usually said with ref. to teenagers): "No reconocí a tu hijo; se dio una estirada tremenda" 'I didn't recognize your son, he had grown so much'

estirar va. **estirar igual** to cooperate, pull together (coll.); **estirar la pata** (slang) to die; **estirarle al excusado** to flush the toilet; vr. to grow taller (usually said with ref. to teenagers)

estirón (slang) m.: **darse un estirón** to grow like a weed (fig.), grow considerably and suddenly (usually said with ref. to teenagers)

esto (see **a todo esto**)

estógamo (var. of) *estómago* (Std.)

estómago: estómago sucio indigestion, dyspepsia; 'infected stomach'; **volteársele** or **revolvérsele a alguien el estómago** to get an upset stomach

estóngamo (var. of) *estómago* (Std.)

estor (Eng.) m. store, shop

estraique (Eng.) m. strike, work stoppage; strike (in baseball)

estraiqueado -da or **estraiquiado -da** (Eng.) strike-out (in baseball); person who has struck out (in baseball)

estraiquear or **estraiquiar** (Eng.) va. to strike at and miss a pitched ball (in baseball); to strike someone out (baseball); vn. to strike, go on strike (Stds. *estar de huelga, ponerse de huelga*)

estrambólico -ca (vars. of) *estrambótico -ca* strange, unusual, eccentric, queer

estrellar vr. to faint, see stars (coll.); (Ang.) vr. to star, excel, shine (in a game, etc.)

estroc (Eng.) m. stroke, cerebral hemorrhage

estropojo (var. of) *estropajo*

estrujar va. to shake violently

estrujón m. violent shaking (usually administered to a person)

estuata or **estuatua** (vars. of) *estatua* (Std.)

estufa: ¡estufas California! (slang) Knock it off!, Quiet down!, Shut up!; **¡ya estufas!** (id.)

estufear or **estufiar** (slang) va. to

sniff the residue of powdered narcotic drugs

estule (Eng.) (slang) m. stoolie (slang), stool pigeon (slang), person who betrays one's companions by serving as a police informer

estulear or **estuliar** (Eng.) va. to stool on someone, serve as a police informer (cf. **estule**)

estuto -ta (vars. of) *astuto -ta* (Std.)

estuvo (3rd pers. sg. pret. of *estar*): **¡ya estuvo!** That's it!, We've got it made!, The job's done! (etc.)

examinación f. exam (in a school subject)

excluigo (var. of) *excluyo* (1st pers. pres. sg. ind. of *excluir*)

excusado: excusado de afuera/ excusado de pozo outhouse, outdoor toilet, privy

excusar (Ang.) va. to pardon, forgive

éxito (Ang.) exit, way out

experencia (var. of) *experiencia* (Std.)

explotar (Ang.) va. to explode, detonate; vn. (fig.) to explode with anger

exprés (Ang.) m. express (i.e., express train, express bus); carriage pulled by one or two horses

extra spare tire

extraordenario -ria (vars. of) *extraordinario -ria* (Std.)

extraviado -da half-crazy, slightly tetched (coll.)

extrordinario -ria (vars. of) *extraordinario -ria* (Std.)

F

fachas fpl. unkempt and messy appearance: "Andaba de unas fachas que daba lástima" 'He looked so messy that one felt sorry for him'

fachazo (slang) alcoholic drink; shot of liquor

facultoso -sa usurper of privileges, taker of rights one has not been authorized to enjoy

fain (Eng.) adj. fine, okay, all right

faja belt used for medicinal or therapeutic purposes; corset

fajar va. to spank; to beat (with a belt); to put a collar on someone (fig.), to control

fajazo blow administered with a belt

fajero wrapping or swaddling cloth for newborn babies; belt for medicinal or therapeutic purposes (esp. to hold in the navel of the newborn child)

falda shirttail (Std. *faldón*); part of a woman's slip accidentally showing: "Te sale la falda; métetela"

faldón m. fender (automobile)

faltar (slang): **faltarle a alguien un tornillo** to be daffy, have a screw loose (slang), be somewhat crazy

falsante mf calumniator, slanderer, maligner

falsario -ria (vars. of) *falsante* mf.

falsear or **falsiar: falseársele a alguien la rodilla** to sprain one's knee

falseo sprain

fallar: fallarle a alguien el coco to go or (to be) off one's rocker (slang), become slightly crazy

¡falláu! (Eng.) (slang) interj. Far out! (indicating approval of something)

fama: dar fama to praise, eulogize

familia: estar con familia to be pregnant

fanear or **faniar** (Eng.) va. to fan (baseball slang), strike out; **fanear el aire** to attempt and fail to hit the ball (baseball)

fantoche mf. presumptuous or pretentious

farmacético -ca (vars. of) *farmacéutico -ca* (Std.)

farmasista mf. (var. of) *farmacéutico -ca* (Std.)

farolazo: echarse un farolazo (slang) to drink down a shot of hard liquor

Farucas (slang) Falfurrias, Texas

faubol or **fáubol** (Eng.) m. foul ball (in ball sports, e.g., in baseball said of a ball hit to the left or the right out of the field of play)

faul (Eng.) m. foul (in sports

competitions)

favorecer: ¡Dios me (nos) favorezca! Heaven (God) forbid!

fe: a fe que yo (usually followed by a negative statement) as for me: "A fe que yo, nunca me portaría así" 'As for me, I would never behave in such a manner'

federal (<*feo*) (slang) ugly

federico -ca (<*feo*) (slang) ugly (cf. **federal**); crazy, insane, lunatic; fsg. federal police, federal troops

feilar or **feilear** or **feiliar** (Eng.) va. to fail, flunk (someone in a school subject); va. & vn. to fail (in a school subject)

Fela (dim. of) Felícitas

fenda (Eng.) fender (automobile); (slang, ant.) hair heavily greased and combed straight back on the sides; **da** haircut, fenders (slang, ant.)

fénder (Eng.) f. (var. of) *fenda* (Eng.) (Std. *guardabarros*)

fenómeno -na bigheaded, large-headed; m. monstrosity

feo: oler feo to stink (said of persons or things); **ponerse feo** to become dangerous, threatening, to turn bad (said of weather): "¿Trajiste tu capa? — ¿Por qué preguntas? — Porque se está poniendo feo el cielo"

feón -ona (vars. of) *feúcho -cha*

ferear or **feriar** va. & vn. to barter; make change for: "Por favor, feréame este dólar"

feria change, money due from a larger monetary unit; loose change, assortment of coins; **tener feria** to be flushed, have a great deal of money; to have more money than one customarily has on one's person

Ferni (nickname for) *Fernando*

feyo -ya (vars. of) *feo -a*

fiance m. (var. of) *fianza*

ficha bottle cap; slug; broke, without money; **andar ficha (lisa)** to be stone broke, completely without money; **ciertas fichas** certain so-and-so's

fichar va. to look for money

fichazo change, money returned from a larger monetary unit

fichera (slang) whore, prostitute

fiebre f.: **fiebre del valle** valley fever, coccidioidomycosis

fierrito hat pin

fierro (var. of) *hierro*; **fierros** tools of a barber's trade; **camino de fierro** (Ang./Gallicism?) railroad

fierrocarril (var. of) *ferrocarril* (Std.)

fiestero -ra fond of going to parties

fifí m. or **fifiriche** m. or **fifirucho** (slang) effeminate (male), faggot, pansy, swish, Miss Nancy, Miss Molly, nelly (etc.) (slang)

fijar vr.: interjs. **¡fíjese!** or **¡fíjese nomás!** Fancy that!, Can you imagine that! (expressions of surprise or incredulity)

fil (Eng.) m. field (ref. to both athletic and agricultural fields); field (ref. to one's academic field, academic major)

fila (slang) wife; (slang) knife; **cargar** or **traer fila** to carry a knife, a switchblade, etc.; **sacarle la fila a alguien** to pull a knife on someone

fildear or **fildiar** vn. to play the position of fielder (in baseball)

fildeo act or technique of fielding (in baseball)

fílder (Eng.) m. fielder (in baseball)

filera (slang) knife

filerear or **fileriar** (slang) va. to

knife, cut with a knife

filero (slang) knife

filetear or **filetiar** (slang) va. to knife, cut with a knife

filorazo (slang) knife wound (usually one inflicted in a knife fight)

filorear or **filoriar** (slang) (vars. of) *filerear, fileriar*

filosa (slang) knife

fina (dim. of) *Josefina* (see also **Pepa**)

finca building, edifice

fincar va. to construct a building

fisgadera act of snooping or peeping

fisgar vn. to observe a person of the opposite sex surreptitiously (as in the case of a Peeping Tom)

fisgón -gona Peeping Tom, person who snoops or peeps on others (observes them surreptitiously)

Fito (nickname for) *Adolfo*

fius (Eng.) m. fuse (electricity) (Std. *fusible*)

flaco -ca thin (usually ref. to animals)

flacón -cona somewhat thin (usually prefaced by *medio*: **medio flacón / media flacona**)

flanquear or **flanquiar** (Eng.) (vars. of) *flonquear, flonquiar*

fletear or **fletiar** (Eng.) va. to flatten (a tire, by letting the air out) (a person, by knocking him/her down with a blow of the fists); vr. to go flat: "La llanta se fletió"

flet (Eng.) m. flat, flat tire; **andar flet** to be flat broke (coll.), completely without money; adj. flat, out of tune (ref. to musical instruments)

flipear or **flipiar** (Eng.) va. to flip, flip over; vr. (slang) to go crazy, flip one's lid (slang)

flirtiar (var. of) *flirtear*

flochar (Eng.) va. to flush

flojón -jona somewhat lazy (often prefaced by *medio*: **medio flojón/ media flojona**)

flonquear or **flonquiar** (Eng.) va. to fail, flunk (someone in a school subject); v. & vn. to fail (in a school subject)

flor (slang) f. homosexual, pansy (pej.)

Flore (dim. of) *Florinda*

floriar (var. of) *florear*

floriando (slang) homosexual

flotar: flotarse una (slang) to drink a beer: "Se flotó una"

flout (Eng.) m. float (Std. *carro alegórico*)

flu (Eng.) mf. influenza

flunquear or **flunquiar** (Eng.) (vars. of) *flonquear, flonquiar*

focos eyeglasses

fodongo (Eng.<Ford) old battered-up car

fólder (Eng.) m. folder (envelope or filing apparatus) (Std. *carpeta*)

fonazo (slang) (Eng.) fun, enjoyment

fonchar (Eng.<fudge?) vn. to cheat in a marble game by placing or pushing the marble shooter closer to the target (see also **hacer fonche**)

fonche: hacer fonche (Eng.?) to cheat in a marble game by placing or pushing the marble shooter closer to the target (see **fonchar**)

fondongo (slang) buttocks, ass (vulg.)

fone (Eng.) mf. funny, amusing

fones or **fonis** (Eng.) mpl. comic strips, funnies (coll.)

fono (var. of) *teléfono*

forcito (Eng.) old battered-up car (cf. **fodongo**)

Forehués(t) or **Forohués(t)** (Hispanization of) Fort Worth, Texas

Forehuor (Hispanization of) Fort Worth, Texas

forihuán or **foritú** (slang) (Eng.) m. male homosexual (cf. **cuarent-aidós/cuarentaiuno**)

Foritos (slang) Fort Worth, Texas

forje (slang) m. female figure, woman's body

formal m. (Ang.?) formal (dance, gathering, etc.); **traje formal** m. formal evening wear (Std. *traje de etiquet*)

fornitura (Eng.) (infrequent) furniture

fortigo or **fortingo** (Eng.) old battered-up car (cf. **fodongo**)

forro (slang) good-looking person; pl. (said of two people who resemble each other): "Son forros" 'They're look-alikes'

frago (slang) cigar

frailecillo or **frailecío** blister bug, blister beetle (Meloidae)

frajear or **frajiar** (slang) va. to smoke; (slang) va. to smoke marihuana

frajo (slang) cigarette; **frajo de seda** (slang) marihuana cigarette

Franque (Eng.) (dim. of) Frank or *Francisco*

franque (Eng.) frank, honest

fregadal m. much, many, large quantity (of something): "Tiene un fregadal de huercos" 'He has a huge bunch of kids' (fig., i.e., a large family)

fregadazo blow with the fist or any other object; **agarrarse a fregadazos** (vulg.) to get into a scrap (slang), fight, get into a fight

fregadera action of washing dishes; harassment, annoyances; nagging; thingamagig (coll., said when one fails to remember the name of a

particular object); junk, trash

fregadito -ta m. deceitful (usually prefaced by *medio*: **medio fregadito**); mf. ruthless opportunist

fregadiza severe beating; hard time, difficult time

fregado -da penniless, down-and-out, destitute; (almost always adj.) (said of a woman who looks prematurely old as the result of excessive sexual activity); tricky, roguish, damned (fig.): **acá la fregada** or **acá la fregá** (vulg., slang) a long way, half way to hell and gone (slang), way the hell out there (slang); **¡a la fregada!** (vulg., slang) I'll be God-damned!; **caer como la fregada** to be repellent, repulsive; **estar como la fregada** to be as ____ as can be (e.g., 'to be as ugly as sin', 'as mean as a junkyard dog', etc.) (ref. usually to any negative quality known both to speaker and listener); **estar más + adj. + que la fregada** (coll.) to be more + adj. + than one could possibly be: "Ese bato está más loco que la fregada" 'That dude is crazier than a hoot owl'; **huerco fregado** damned little brat; m. shady dealer, sneaky person; f. hard time, difficult time; **irse a la fregada** (usually a command): "¡Vete a la fregada!" 'Go to hell!', 'Get the hell out of here!'; **llevárselo a alguien la fregada** to die; to fall onto hard times, be ruined (often financially): "Se lo llevó la fregada porque no hizo lo que debía"; **no importarle a alguien una fregada** not to give a damn (about something): "A mí no me importa una fregada" 'I don't give a damn about it'; **ser más + adj. + que la fregada** to be more + adj. + than hell: "Ese viejo es más pinche que la fregada" 'That old man is stinger than hell'

fregador -ra   deceiver, cheater; freeloader; opportunist

fregar   va. to cheat; to take advantage of; to break, put out of order: "Fernando fregó el televisor" 'Fernando broke the television set'; vn. to bear the brunt of, be forced to take the lion's share (of a job), have a real work out with; **de a tiro la friegas (friega/friegan,** etc.) (used to reprimand for abusive behavior) You're really something else, You're a real lulu, You're really just too much (all used ironically and with critical intent); **fregar la borrega** to bother, pester, annoy; **fregar la pac(i)encia** to nag the hell out of, pester the hell out of, bother, try one's patience; **para acabarla de fregar** to make matters worse, on top of all that (fig.); **te friegas que no** or **te friegas si no** (set expressions used by one to contradict emphatically a negative statement made by another) the hell it isn't, the hell you're not, the hell he's not, etc.: "Ya no voy a barrer más los escalones. — Te friegas si no." 'I'm not going to sweep the steps anymore. — The hell you're not.' (See also **chingar** and **joder**); **no la friegues (friegue/frieguen) / ya ni la friegas (friega, friegan,** etc.) (set expressions used to censure abusive behavior) (see also **chingar** and **joder**)

fregazo   blow with the fist or any other object; **agarrarse a fregazos** to get into a scrap (slang), fight, get into a fight; **darse fregazos** to beat each other up in a fistfight

fregón -gona   complainer, chronic bitcher (slang); bothersome, annoying; fraud, cheat, ruthless opportunist; (coll.) the boss, the big cheese

freguiza   (see **dar una freguiza, llevar una freguiza**)

freimiar   (Eng.) va. to frame (coll.), conspire to have convicted

friego: friegos de   (slang) many, a lot of: "Había friegos de hormigas en el zacate" 'There were a lot of ants on the grass'

frijol   m.: **se acabaron los frijoles** a derisive remark levelled at a person of Hispanic origin seen in public with a partner of the opposite sex who belongs to a different race or to a different ethnic affiliation

frejoles   mpl. (var. of) *frijoles* or *fréjoles* mpl. (Stds.)

frentazo   bumping together of two foreheads

frente: en frente de la gente (Eng.?) in public: "Lo regañaron en frente de la gente"

frentudo -da   big-browed; broad-faced

fresco   male homosexual

fría: jugarla fría   (Ang., slang) to play it cool (coll.)

friador -ra   refrigerator

friar   (var. of) *freír* to fry va. & vn. (*friar* is conjugated like *criar*)

frifol   m. (var. of) *frijol*

frifolero -ra   (vars. of) *frijolero -ra*

frijolero -ra   fond of eating beans

frío -a   (slang) dead; **frío de la matriz** cold womb, frigidity, lack of (feminine) sexual desire; female sterility; **tiempo de frío** winter, wintertime (the cold season)

frir   va. (var. of) *freír* (Std.)

frisa   (Eng.) freezer (type of refrigerator)

friscar (Eng.) va. to frisk, search a person for hidden objects

fríser (Eng.) m. & f. freezer (type of refrigerator) (cf. **frisa**)

friyar (var. of) *friar*

fruncir: fruncírsele a alguien (el culo) (slang, vulg.) to be afraid

fruta (Ang.?) (slang) f. fruit (slang), male homosexual

fuche or **fuchefuche** or **fuchi** or **fuchifuchi** interjs. Phew! (used to express disgust, repulsion, etc.); **tener fuchifuchi** to be afraid

fuego (var. of) *juego* game

fuera: andar con las nalgas de fuera to be wearing rags (coll.), be dressed in threadbare or tattered clothing; to be poverty stricken; **fuera de combate** unwell, out of sorts: "¿Cómo te sientes? — Fuera de combate" 'How do you feel? — Out of sorts'; **ir pa(ra) fuera** (euph.) to go to the rest room (water closet, toilet) (the expression may be a holdover from the days when a person had to go out of his house to the backyard privy (outhouse) to relieve himself

fuereño -ña stranger, someone not from the particular locality, outsider

fuerte m. influential person, someone with pull; male to whom all women are attracted; lucky person, someone who has it made; boss, strongman (fig.); **hacerse fuerte** to show great strength (often under emotional strain); to rise to the occasion

fuertísimo -ma (vars. of) *fortísimo -ma*

fuerza: a fuerza que sí most likely, in all likelihood, more likely than not: "¿Tendrán frío los gatos? — A fuerza que sí" 'Are the cats cold? — More likely than not'; **a toda fuerza** in full swing: "El baile estaba a toda fuerza" 'The dance was in full swing'; **estar en su fuerza** to be at its greatest point of intensity (ref. to a series or progression of events, or to emotions in general): "La guerra estaba en su fuerza entonces" 'The war was in its apogee then'; to be going strong: "A esa hora las polkas estaban en su fuerza" 'At that hour the polkas were going strong'; **hacer fuerza** to faze, affect: "Se murió su mamá y ni fuerza le hace" 'His mother died and it doesn't affect him in the least'

fulear or **fuliar** (Eng.) va. to fool, deceive

fultaim (Eng.) adv. full-time (Std. *horario completo, tiempo completo*)

fumada act of smoking a cigar or cigarette

fundillo or **fundío** (slang, vulg.) piece of ass (vulg.): "Tiene allí su fundillo cuando lo quiere" 'He's got a piece of ass [opportunity for sexual relations] right there whenever he wants it'

fundillón -llona or **fundillote -ta** big-bottomed (coll.) (said of person with a large buttocks)

fundilludo -da (ref. to person with a sexually-appetizing rear end)

funta (var. of) *junta*

furrias mf., pl. (pej.) (said of persons) base, mean, despicable; clumsy; lusterless, dull, uninteresting; sloppy, careless; (said of things) shoddily-made

futbolero (Eng.) football player

G

gaba (abbrev.) (var. of) *gabacho -cha*

gabachero -ra (pej.) gringoized, gringo-like; (pej.) gringo-lover, (person) obsequious to gringos

gabacho -cha (pej.) Anglo-Saxon, gringo

gabardino -na (pej.) (vars. of) *gabacho -cha*

gabinete m.: **gabinete (de cocina)** kitchen cabinet

gabo -ba (pej.) (vars. of) *gabacho -cha*

gacho (usually pej.) crude; mean, base; bad; ugly; ridiculous; ¡qué **gacho!** How humiliating!, How disgusting!; What a bummer! (slang); **torcer muy gacho** to die a horrible death

gai (Eng.) (slang) m. guy, fellow

gaita trick

gallazo (slang), shot, puff or fix of a narcotic drug

galleta cookie; **galleta de soda** saltine cracker

gallina: gallina porpujada (type of child's game)

gallo (slang) guy, fellow; hero; he-man, stud (coll.); street serenade; (slang) blood issuing from a wound received in a fight; pl. articles of hand-me-down or second-hand clothing; **dormírsele el gallo a alguien** to fail in the sex act, lose one's erection (said of a man); **sacar gallo** to show off a new possession (esp. an article of clothing)

gallón -llona brave; terrific, tremendous; m. he-man, stud (coll.)

gajo cotton

galgo -ga thin; sickly-looking

ganar vn. to go toward, head toward: "Ganó para el río" 'He headed off toward the river'

ganas: ganas tienes (y con ellas te mantienes) You'd like that, wouldn't you: "La maistra te va a flonquiar — Ganas tienes"

ganchar va. to hook onto (an object); to force commitment; to hook, trap (as into marriage); vr. to become engaged to be married; to get married

gancho (clothes) hanger

gandaya uneaten food that is thrown away after a meal

ganga (Eng.) gang, group of delinquent youths; circle of friends

gangoso -sa hare-lipped

gángster or **guénster** or **guénstor** (Eng.) m gangster, hoodlum

garabatos mpl. poor or unintelligible handwriting, scribblings

garache (Eng.) m. garage

garaje m. filling station, gasoline station

García: acá García (hum.) toilet: "Voy acá García" 'I'm going to the toilet' (play on words: *a cagar* + *[Gar] -cía*)

garganta: doña garganta aggressive, influential, powerful woman; shrew

garita customs house (on a border between two countries)

garnucho fillip (flip) with one's fingers against someone's head

garsolé (Gallicism?) m. sunbonnet

garra fsg. old cheap clothes; **estirar garra** or **sacar la garra** (slang) to gossip; to run someone down (slang), speak ill of someone; **andar con (en) la garra** or **estar mala de la garra** / **tener** or **traer la garra** to be on the rag (slang), be having one's menstrual period; **tirar garra** (slang) to dress up, dress elegantly

garranchar va. to slash, gash

gar(r)ar va. (var. of) *agarrar*

garraspera (var. of) *carraspera*

garrero vendor of second-hand clothing; dealer in second-hand clothing; piles of rags

garriento -ta ragged

garrote (slang) m. large male organ, big penis; (see also **limosnero y con garrote**)

garrotear or **garrotiar** va. to rout, defeat decisively in a sports match (usually in baseball); to batter, beat up; to collect many hits off a pitcher (in baseball)

garrotero -ra batter (baseball); slugger, batter successful in hitting

garrotiza severe beating (usually administered with a club); shellacking, decisive defeat in a game (usually baseball)

garruño scratch

gas m.: **acabársele a alguien el gas** (Ang.?) (fig.) to run out of gas, lose one's stamina; (see also **darle al gas**); **pedal de gas** accelerator

gaselín m. (var. of) *gasolina*

gaselina (var. of) *gasolina*

gasofa (slang) gasoline; **gasofa de la buena** (slang) premium gasoline

gasolín (Eng.) m. gasoline

gasolina: bicicleta de gasolina motorcycle

gata maid, female servant

gato (slang) fraidy-cat, fearful person; **corbata de gato** (slang) bow tie

gendarme m.: **hijo de gendarme** (var. of) *hijo de policía*

gente f.: **¡hasta dónde llega la gente!** (set expression) my, what some people are capable of!

gentecita (iron.) (var. of) *gentuza* (Std.), riffraff, rabble, bunch of lower-class persons

gentiazo or **gentillazo** multitude of people

giometría (var. of) *geometría*

gladiola (Eng.) (var. of) *gladíolo* (Std.)

globo (slang) (type of barbituate pill swallowed for narcotic effect)

glu or **glufa** (Eng.) f.: **hacer(se) a la glu(fa)** to sniff glue (for the mildly narcotic effect it produces)

glufo -fa high from sniffing glue (cf. **glu**); glue-sniffer

goce (var. of) *gozo*

godorniz f. (var. of) *codorniz* f.

gogote m. (var. of) *cogote* m.

golar (var. of) *volar*

golear or **goliar** (Eng.) vn. to make a goal (in an athletic contest, e.g. in soccer)

goler (var. of) *oler*

golfo (Eng.) golf (game of golf)

golpanazo severe, heavy blow

golpe m.: **darle el golpe al cigarro** /

darle el golpe al cigarrillo to inhale a cigarette or cigar

golpiar (var. of) *golpear*

golpiza series of blows; severe beating

goma paste (sticking paste)

gomitadera (var. of) *vomitadera*

gomitar (var. of) *vomitar*

gómito (var. of) *vómito*

gordo -da f. (coll.) pregnant; f. thick corn tortilla; **salir gorda** to get pregnant; **caer gordo -da** to be repugnant, repellent: "Ese tipo me cae gordo"

gorila or **gorrrila** f. (cf. Std. m.)

gorilón -lona or **gorrilón -lona** gorilla-like resembling a gorilla; large and ponderous person

goriludo -da or **gorriludo -da** (vars. of) *gorilón -lona, gorrilón -lona*

gorupero place infested with *gorupos* (chicken fleas)

gorupiento -ta infested with *gorupos* (chicken fleas)

gorupo chicken flea

gorra (slang) heroin capsule

gota (slang) gasoline; (see also **sudar**)

goteador or **gotiador** m. eye-dropper, medicine dropper

Goyo -ya (dims. for) *Gregorio -ria*

grábol (Eng.) m. gravel

gracias: para esas gracias if that's the way it's going to be, if that's how it is: "Mañana vamos a tu casa a celebrar la fiesta. — Muy bien, traigan su guajolote. — Újule, para esas gracias mejor nos lo comemos en casa."

gracia(s): ¡qué gracia(s)! Thanks a lot! (iron.), Thanks for nothing

gradación f. (var. of) *graduación* f.

gradar (var. of) *graduar*

grado (Ang.) grade, mark in a school subject; **hacer grados** to receive grades, make a certain grade: "Hice puras A's el semestre pasado" 'I made straight A's last semester'; year or level in school: "Pedro está en el segundo grado"

graduante mf. postgraduate student

grajea sleet

grajear vn. to sleet

gramo (slang) packet of heroin

grampa (var. of) *grapa*

grande mf. advanced in years, old; grown-up, adult; **creerse muy grande** to consider oneself superior; **más grande** older (Std. *mayor*); m. (slang) (Ang<one grand?) a thousand dollars; **casa grande** (Ang.) (slang) the big house (slang), penitentiary

grandotote or **grandotototo** mf. extremely large, immense, gargantuan

graniento -ta full of sores

granizazo major hailstorm

granjear or **granjiar** to fawn, flatter, do favors so as to ingratiate oneself or receive favors in return

grano sore, open skin lesion; ulcer; wound

grasa shoe paste; **dar grasa** to apply shoe paste (in order to shine shoes)

greñero -ra disheveled and unkempt hair: "Trae un greñero de la mierda" (vulg.) 'He's got a messy head of hair'

greve or **greive** or **greivi** (Eng.) m. gravy

grifa (slang) marihuana

grifo -fa marihuana user; kinky (ref. to hair)

gringada action or behavior typifying a gringo; a group of gringos

gripa (var. of) *gripe* f.

gritadera or **gritadero** (vars. of) *gritería*

grocería (Eng.) grocery store

grocería (Eng.) groceries, food, provisions

grulla cold air; police, police force; ugly: "¡Tu madre! — ¡La tuya, que está más grulla!" (exchange of insults among children)

guacha (Eng.) wrist watch; washer (used in plumbing) (Std. *arandela*)

guachar (Eng.) va. to watch

guachatería (Eng.) washateria, laundromat

guache m. (var. of) *guacha* (Eng.) f.

guachimán (Eng.) m. watchman, guard

guaflera (Eng.) waffle maker, machine for making waffles

guáfol (Eng.) m. waffle

guaifa (Eng.) (slang, hum.) wife

guain (Eng.) (slang) m. wine

guaino -na (Eng.) wino (slang), person habitually drunk (esp.) on wine

guainero -ra (Eng.) (cf. **guain**) habitual drinker of wine; heavy drinker (of any alcoholic beverage)

guáiper (Eng.) m. windshield wiper

guajolote mf. (fig.) fool, idiot; **el Día del Guajolote** Thanksgiving Day (Std. *Día de Acción de Gracias*)

guamazo hard blow (with the fist or other object) (see also **güemazo, huamazo, huemazo**)

guango -ga loose-fitting; flabby; **caerle** or **venirle a alguien guango -ga** to compare unfavorably: "Ese tipo me viene guango" 'That guy is a pushover for me' (i.e., it will be easy for me to defeat him in physical combat or in games that call for mental agility)

guantada blow, slap

guapo -pa industrious; intelligent; talented

guardavacas m. (var. of) *guardavaca*

guardia: ángel de la guardia (var. of) *ángel de la guarda*

guarear or **guariar** (slang) va. to say hello to; to plan to meet; **ay te (lo, los) guareo** (slang) See you (later), See ya 'round, So long, Be seeing ya (coll.) (See **ay: ay nos vemos / ay te guacho/ay te guacho cucaracho/ay te miro/ay te miro casimiro**)

guariche m. (slang) coffee

guato festivity; commotion

guataso -sa noisy (ref. to persons)

guayín (Eng.) m. wagon drawn by horses

güelar (var. of) *volar*

güeldear or **güeldiar** (vars. of) *hueldear* or *hueldiar*

güelito -ta (vars. of) *abuelito -ta*

güelo, güeles, etc. (vars. of) *huelo, hueles*, etc. (pres. ind. conjugation of *oler*)

güelta (var. of) *vuelta*

güelva, güelvas, etc. (vars. of) *huela, huelas*, etc. (pres. subj. conjugation of *oler*)

güelvo, güelves, etc. (vars. of) *vuelvo, vuelves*, etc. (pres. ind. conjugation of *volver*)

güemazo hard blow, slap (cf. **guamazo**)

güeno -na (vars. of) *bueno -na*

guengsta (Eng.) m. (cf. **gánsgter**)

güerco -ca (vars. of) *huerco -ca*

güergüenza (var. of) *vergüenza*

güerinche mf. or **güerinchi** mf. (pej.) blond, fair-complexioned (cf. **güero**)

güero -ra blond, fair-complexioned; mf. Anglo-Saxon

güerta (var. of) *huerta*

guerra (see **dar guerra**)

güeso (var. of) *hueso*

güete (var. of) *cuete* m. gun

güetear or **güetiar** va. to shoot

güey mf. (var. of) *buey* mf.

guía steering wheel (automobile)

güichol (var. of) *huichol* m.

güila (var. of) *huila*

Güile (Eng.) Willie ([dim. of] William)

güínchil (Eng.) m. windshield (automobile)

guindo dark red color

güine (Eng.) m. wienie, wiener sausage; **comer güines** (slang, tag question equivalent to Eng. '... or something?'): "Estás loco o comiste güines?" 'Are you crazy or something?'; (vulg.) m. penis, male member (euph.)

guirafa (var. of) *jirafa* giraffe; very tall person

guisar va. to fry

güiza (var. of) *huiza*

gusgo -ga (slang) glutton, chow hound (coll.) (cf. **busgo -ga**)

gusjear or **gusjiar** (slang) va. to eat, chow down (slang)

gusto: darse gusto to have a ball (coll.), enjoy oneself royally, have a very good time; **hacerle los gustos a alguien** to indulge, pamper or humor someone **tener** or **traer gusto** to be (feel) happy: "Pedro tiene mucho gusto porque ganó la apuesta" 'Peter is very happy because he won the bet'

H

ha, hamos (vars. of) *he, hemos* (1st pers. sg. and pl. of pres. ind. *haber*)

haber: hay: "Y ¿qué hay con eso?" 'So?', 'So what?', 'What about it?'; ¡bien haiga! 'Good for you!' (expression of approbation); no haber derecho or no haber razón to be inexcusable, (ref. to the repeated bad behavior of a person); to not be right (fitting, proper): "Pepe se emborrachó otra vez con el dinero que le prestaste — Ya lo sé, y, hombre, no hay derecho" 'Joey got drunk again with the money you lent him — I know that already, and, man, that's inexcusable'

hablada f. offensive word; innuendo, insinuation; bluff; puras habladas nothing but talk; pure unadulterated bullshit (vulg.); echar habladas to make sarcastic remarks; to offend

habladería (var. of) *habladuría*

habladero -ra m. chatter, excessive talk; mf., boastful, bragging

hablador -ra liar; gossiper

hablantino (var. of) *hablantín*

hablar va. to call, telephone: "Te hablan por teléfono" 'Someone's calling you on the phone'; vn. to gossip; to speak ill of someone;

hablar con taco to speak in a pompous manner; hablar (hasta) por los codos to talk a blue streak, talk excessively; hablarle a una mujer to ask a woman to go steady; to tell a woman how one feels about her (romantically); hablar nomás por no dejar to talk just to be talking (for no particular reason); hablar pa' tras (Ang.) to talk back to, answer in a sassy manner: "No le hables pa' tras a tu papá" 'Don't talk back to your dad'; hablar recio to speak loudly

hacer va. to figure, imagine, assume: "Yo te hacía en el centro" 'I figured you were downtown'; hacer agua to urinate (Std. *hacer aguas menores*); ¡bien hecho! 'Good for you!' (expression of approbation); estarse haciendo to be playing possum, be pretending, be playing dumb; hacer a alguien ver su fortuna to give someone a hard time; hacer a la ley to win over (to a particular way of thinking): "Tú no le puedes decir nada. Él ya la hizo a su ley." 'You can't tell her anything. He already won her over.'; hacer a(l) trochemoche to do a half-assed job (slang), do poorly, do with a lick and a promise (coll.); hacer aprecio to pay attention; **hacer atole** (see **atole**); **hacer barranqueña** to assemble and carry along a large quantity of items; **hacer bola** to fluster, confuse; **hacer boruca** to fluster, confuse; **hacer bueno** (Ang.) to replace, make good (ref. to replacement of belongings lost or destroyed); **hacer** or **poner cara de hacha** to make (put on) an expression of intense displeasure; **hacer cargos** to place charges against, sue; **hacer caquis/hacer caquis maquis** (euph.) to go potty (euph.), do number two (euph.), defecate (said of infants or small children); **hacer como agua** to do effortlessly; **hacer chicharrón** to burn to a crisp; **hacer chillar** to cause to cry; to anger; **hacer (de) menos** to scorn; to belittle; to ignore; to snub, slight; **hacer entender** to get through after repeated efforts (coll.), succeed in getting (someone) to listen to reason; **hacer garras** to tear to shreds; **hacer jale** (slang) to steal; to cheat; to work; to make advances to a member of the opposite sex; **hacer jalón** (slang) to make advances to a member of the opposite sex; **hacer jamberga / jamborga / jambórguer de** (slang) to make mincemeat of (coll.), beat up soundly (in a fight); **hacer la barba** to flatter; **hacer la lucha** to try to convince, try to get someone to change his/her mind; to give it a try; **hacer la pala** to accompany; **hacer la parada** to humor, go along with, tolerate, put up with; **hacer la vida** (Ang.?) to make a living; **hacer las paces** to make up (coll.), resolve (settle) a personal difference; **hacer los**

tamales de chivo to cheat on one's spouse, commit adultery; **hacer maje** to fool, deceive; **hacer mandados** to run errands (Std. *hacer recados*); **hacer ojo** to cast a spell upon, cast the evil eye upon; **hacer pedo** (slang) to make trouble; to harass; to make advances to a member of the opposite sex; to make a scene, an uproar: "Jorge estaba haciendo pedo en la cantina"; **hacer picadillo** to grind; to make mincemeat of; to squash; **hacer placer** to be courteous and attentive; to humor, go along with: "Mejor es que le hagas placer al jefe para que no te desocupe"; **hacer por** (var. of) *hacer el esfuerzo por*; **hacer topillo** (slang) to make a fool of; **hacer (un) batidero** to botch, mess up a job or other commitments; to mess up a place (coll.), make it dirty, soiled or untidy; **hacer un batidero y medio** to mess up and then some (ref. to a place or a job); **hacer (un) mugrero** to botch, mess up a job or other commitments; to mess up a place (coll.), make it dirty, soiled or untidy; **hacer (un) mugrero y medio** to mess up and then some (ref. to a place or a job); **hacer una (mala) parada** to do someone a bad turn, play a dirty trick on; **hacer a la glu(fa)** vn. to sniff glue (for mildly narcotic effect); **hacer bien** (Ang.) to do well, earn money in copious amounts; to be wise, act prudently: "Haces bien en no decírselo"; **hacer borlote** (slang) to make trouble; to make noise; make a scene (slang), cause an uproar; to make advances to a member of the opposite sex; **hacer buches (de sal)** to fill one's mouth with warm salt water so as to kill germs and lessen the pain of a toothache; **hacer (la) caca** (vulg.) to defecate (Std. *cagar*); **hacer carrito** to harp on the same subject, talk incessantly about the same topic; **hacer(le) chapuza a alguien** to cheat someone; **hacer como que** to pretend, act as if, feign: "Haz como que te pegué muy recio" 'Act as if I struck you real hard'; **hacer coraje(s)** to throw fits of anger, throw a tantrum; **hacer cositas** (euph.) to have sexual relations; **hacer cuacha** (vulg., slang) to defecate; to make mincemeat of (fig.), beat up soundly (in a fight); **hacer de las suyas** to blunder as usual; to misbehave as always; **hacer desatinar a alguien** to make someone lose his cool (slang), cause someone to become very angry and quite disoriented; **hacer dinero** (Ang.) to make money, get rich; **hacer dinero a manos llenas** to make money hand over fist (fig.), make large quantities of money, get very rich quick; **hacer el cáliz** to try, make an effort: "No sabe si puede ganar, pero quiere hacer el cáliz"; **hacer el cuerpo** to defecate; **hacer fuerza** to faze, affect: "Se murió su mamá y ni fuerza le hace" 'His mother died and it doesn't affect him in the least'; **hacer gastos** to spend money (usually unexpectedly and at times unnecessarily); **hacer gente a alguien** to treat an undeserving person decently; **hacer grados** (Ang.) to receive grades, make a certain grade (Std. *sacar notas*): "Esteban está haciendo muy malos grados";

hacer hambre to work up an appetite; **hacer la cruz** to make one's first sale of the day (ref. to storekeepers); **hacer la chi(s)** (euph.) to urinate, make "wee-wee" (euph., also baby talk) (Std. *hacer chis*); **hacer la perra** (slang) to loaf, while away the time; **hacer mal modo** to slight, be rude to; **hacer pantominas** to create a scene, make trouble, make a spectacle of oneself: "No te contentaste hasta que hiciste tus pantominas" 'You just weren't happy until you could make an idiot of yourself'; **hacer papeles** (id. to **hacer pantominas** supra); **hacer pedo** (vulg.) to make a fuss, raise a stink, create trouble; **hacer pendejo -ja a alguien** to cheat on someone, deceive (e.g., one's spouse, fiancé (e), etc.); **hacer pininos** (for a baby to make amusing and endearing little gestures); (for a baby to begin to take his/her first steps); **hacer (la) pipi** (slightly euph.) to urinate, "make water" (euph.) (esp. said of and to children) **hacer por** to try to; **hacer roncha** to run up one's winnings in a game of chance after starting out with a very small amount of money; **hacer suertes** to do magical tricks; **hacer tiempo** (Ang.) to do time in jail, comply with one's jail term; (Ang.) to "make time" with the object of one's affections, engage in a display of affection toward; **hacer tonto -ta** to cheat, deceive; **hacer tracalada** to make much noise, raise a ruckus; **hacer trampa** to resort to crooked tactics (e.g., in a business deal); **hacer trompas** to put on a sad or annoyed facial expression; to pout; **hacer un batidero** to botch, mess up a job or other commitments; to mess up a place (coll.), make it dirty or untidy; **hacer vaca** to run up one's winnings in a game of chance after starting out with a very small amount of money (cf. **hacer roncha**); **¿qué hace qué?** it seems like only yesterday that: "¿Qué hace que era niño?" 'It seems like only yesterday that he was a child'; **hacerla de** vr. to play the role of: "Luis Aguilar la hace de trampe" 'Luis Aguilar plays the role of the villain'; **hacer(le) la lucha** to give it a try, make an effort; **hacerle pedo a alguien** (vulg.) to make a play for someone (with amorous intentions); to harass, bother, needle, pick on; **hacerle plática a alguien** to strike up a conversation with someone; **hacerse boca cerrada** to pretend to be quiet and reserved; **hacerse boca chiquita** to pretend to be a small eater; **hacerse cachetón -tona** to ignore an assignment; to conveniently forget a debt or a commitment (see also **hacerse chato**); **hacerse circo** to make a fool of oneself; **hacerse chato -ta** to ignore an assignment; to conveniently forget a debt or a commitment; **hacerse chinche** to act stingy, miserly; to overstay one's welcome; **hacerse de: ¿qué se hizo de _____ ?** (fixed expression) Whatever became of _____ ? **hacerse del rogar** (var. of) *hacerse de rogar* to want to be coaxed; **hacerse (el/la) tonto -ta** to act dumb, play dumb; **hacerse fuerte** to arm oneself with fortitude and patience to face difficult times, be strong enough to ward

off difficult situations; **hacerse gacho** to be unpleasant; **hacerse grande** to act big, act superior, give oneself airs; **hacerse la casqueta** to masturbate; **hacerse la gran caca** (vulg., offensive) to act like a big shit (vulg.), put on airs; **hacerse la gran cosa** to put on airs, act presumptuously; **hacerse la puñeta** (vulg., slang) to do a hand job (coll.), masturbate; **hacerse (la) mosquito muerta** to give the (false) impression that one is reticent, quiet and full of oneself; **hacerse pato** to retract (a statement), renege, back down; **hacerse pa' tras** (Ang.) to back out, renege; to take back, apologize for; **hacerse pesado el bulto** (fig., coll.) (for one's responsibilities to become burdensome); **hacérsela** (vulg., slang) to pull on it (coll.), masturbate; **hacérsele a uno** to have it made (coll.), have one's dreams come true, triumph: "Ya se me hizo" 'I've got it made now'; **hacérsele dolor a alguien hacer algo** for it to hurt (fig.) someone to do something (ref. to ungenerous attitude): "Se te hizo dolor darme un pedacito de manzana" 'It hurt you to give me a little piece of the apple'; **hacérsele el cuerpo chinito** to get goose-pimples (goosebumps)
hacer: (miscellaneous fixed expressions); **hacerla** (Ang.?) to make it, arrive (fig.), be successful: "El bato ése ya la hizo" 'That guy has it made'; **no le hace** It doesn't matter; **no le haga(s) (hagan)** leave well enough alone, Don't stir things up (coll.); **¿qué le hace?** 'What does it matter?' 'So what?'; **que mandado hacer** (set expres-

sion used to indicate any quality in excess): "Está más loco que mandado hacer" 'He's crazier than a hoot owl'; **¡qué suave (le haces/ hace/hacen)!** 'Nice going!' (iron.), 'That's a fine howdy do!'; **tenerla hecha** (Ang?) to have it made (to have achieved a level of accomplishment sufficient to insure future success)

hacha: hacer or **poner cara de hacha** to make (put on) an expression of intense displeasure; **¡hijo del hacha!** interj. (mildly euph. though considered lowerclass)

haiga (var. of) *haya* (3rd pers. subj. of *haber*); **¡bien haiga!** 'Good for you!' (expression of approbation); **ya te lo haiga/ya se lo haiga/ya se los haiga** (set expression of admonition, warning, etc.): "¿Estudiaron? — No — Ya se los haiga"

hallar: hallarse en la calle to be broke, penniless; **no hallarse** to be ill at ease, uncomfortable, not to feel at home (fig.): "Estoy impuesto a la ciudad; no me hallo en los pueblos chiquitos"

hamborguesa (var. of) *hamburguesa* (Eng.)

hambre: muerto -ta de hambre (fig., iron., said with ref. to a greedy, selfish person); f. strong or intense desire to have sexual intercourse with a member of the opposite sex; **hacer hambre** to work up an appetite; **pasar hambres** to go hungry, experience hunger frequently

hambriado -da famished, very hungry

harina: ser harina del mismo costal to share the same characteristics, be cut from the same cloth (fig.)

hambreado -da or **hambriado -da** hungry; starving; strongly desirous of having sex

hambriento -ta stingy; mean

hartada act and effect of overeating: "Se murió de la gran hartada que se dio"

harto -ta glutton

hartón -tona glutton

hasta: salir hasta bien to turn out for the best, be a blessing in disguise: "Salió hasta bien que no te invitaran a la fiesta del jefe; mataron a un empleado allí anoche" 'It turned out for the best that they didn't invite you to the boss's party; they killed an employee there last night'; **adj. + hasta (d)onde pisa(s) (pisan)** extremely, to the nth degree: "Julián es huevón hasta (d)onde pisa" 'Julián is extremely lazy'; **(y) hasta eso** (fixed expression) and the funny (strange, curious) thing about it: "Y hasta eso, no tengo sueño" 'And the funny thing about it is that I'm not sleepy'; **hasta pa'ventar (tirar) pa' riba** (*hasta para aventar para arriba*) with much to spare, with many to spare, in excess; **hasta que no** until (the no is superfluous): "No nos vamos a ir hasta que no lo hagas" 'We won't go until you do it'; **hasta que se le/te/nos/les hizo** or **hasta que se le** (etc.) **cumplió** he/she (etc.) finally got what he/she had wanted, finally realized his/her goals

hecho -cha: hecho -cha bola very flustered, very confused; **hecho -cha madre / hecho -cha máquina** adv. quite rapidly; **tenerla hecha** (Ang.) to have it made (coll.), be very successful: "Ya la tienes hecha"

helada beer (in cans or bottles) (cold or at room temperature)

helado popsicle

herviendo (var. of) *hirviendo* (ger. of *hervir*)

hespital m. (var. of) *hospital*

hesta (var. of) *hasta*

hestérico -ca (var. of) *histérico -ca*

hestoria (var. of) *historia*

hielera refrigerator; icebox (ant.)

hielería ice plant (place where ice is made and sold), ice house (id.)

hielero ice man (vendor and deliverer of ice) (ant.)

hierba (slang) marihuana; (slang) mf. & adj. mean, base, low; **hierba anís** (var. of) *anís*; **hierba colorada** dock herb (Rumex crispus) (prepared as a solution and gargled to treat tonsilitis); **hierba del burro** bush herb (Hymenoclea sp.) (prepared as a solution and applied to arthritic areas and infected cuts); **hierba del indio** desert milkweed (Asclepias sp.) (prepared as a tea and used to treat kidney ailments); **hierba del manzo** swamp root (Anemopsis californica) (prepared as a tea and used to treat stomachache); **hierba del pasmo** spasm herb (Haplopappus larincofolius) (prepared as a tea and either drunk or inhaled in the treatment of *pasmo*); **hierba mala** (var. of) *mala hierba*; **y demás hierbas** (fixed expression) and so on and so forth (Std. *y así sucesivamente*)

hierbajal or **hierbajar** or **hierbazal** m. (vars. of) *herbazal* m.

hierbero grassland (Std. *herbazal*); herbalist

hijo: ¡hijo! interj. (varies in meaning according to intensity and type of articulation, from mild ["Damn!"] through strong ["Son of a bitch"], esp. when followed by a prep. phrase, e.g.: *¡hijo de cabrón!, ¡hijo de la chingada!*) (this last is esp. strong); **hijo del hacha** (see **hacha**); **hijo de policía** or **de gendarme** person to whom no attention has been paid or who has not received any share of something: "¿Acaso soy hijo de policía?" (ref. to traditional popular antipathy towards the police); **hijo de la guayaba** (see **guayaba**); **¡híjola!** or **¡híjole!** (see also **¡jíjole!**) interjs. (vary in meaning according to intensity and situation, from a mild 'Damn!' through something much stronger)

hinchar: hinchársele a alguien (slang) to do what one damn well pleases: "¿Cuándo te vas a ir? — Cuando se me hinche"

hindidura (var. of) *hendidura*

hindura (var. of) *hendedura*

hipo: dar hipo to scare, frighten

hiprocresía (var. of) *hipocresía*

Hiuto or **Hiuta** Utah

hito -ta (vars. of) *hijito -ta*

hocicón -cona loud-mouthed; foul-mouthed

hociquiento -ta (vars. of) *hocicón -cona*

hogado -da (vars. of) *ahogado -da*

hogar (var. of) *ahogar* va.

hojarasca type of sweetroll

hojelata (var. of) *hojalata*

hombrazo he-man, stud (slang)

hombre (can also be used as vocative when addressing a woman): "No hombre, ni siquiera sabía que estabas enferma"; **el hombre de la hora** (Ang.) the man of the hour (coll.), the person currently held in highest regard

hombrecito baby boy (Std. *varón*): "Mi prima tuvo un hombrecito" 'My cousin had a baby boy'

hombrera woman strongly attracted to men

hombro: meter hombro (slang) to lend a helping hand, put one's shoulder to the wheel (fig., coll.)

hombrona (var. of) *hombruna* (Std.)

hoquis (orthog. var. of) *oquis*

hora (var. of) *ahora*

hora: a la hora de la hora / a l'ora de l'ora at the moment of truth, at the time of crisis, when all is said and done (coll.)

hórale interj. Knock it off!; Move it!, Hurry up!, (etc.); That's it!, You're right!; (with interrogative intonation): How about it?, What do you say to that?, And … ?

horcado -da (vars. of) *ahorcado -da*

horcar (var. of) *ahorcar*

horita or **horitita** or **horititita** (etc.) (vars. of) *ahorita, ahoritita,* etc.

hormiga (Eng.?, expansion disguise of the Eng. army) (slang) army, the armed forces

horongo (var. of) *jorongo*

horqueta slingshot

horquía or **horquilla** clothespin

hotel: hotel municipal (hum.) country or city jail

hoy: hoy en la noche tonight (Std. *esta noche*)

hoyito: hoyito de la chi urinary opening (female)

huacha (var. of) *guacha*

huachar (Eng.) va. to watch, observe, watch out; ¡**huáchalo!** or ¡**huáchate!** (slang) Watch out!, Be careful!

huachetería (Eng.) washeteria, self-service automatic laundry

huachimán (var. of) *guachimán*

huaflera (var. of) *guaflera*

huaino -na (vars. of) *guaino -na*

huamazo (Eng?) (var. of) *güemazo* et al.

huango (var. of) *guango*

huarachazo (slang) dance

huarache (slang) mf. Mexican citizen

huarear or **huariar** (vars. of) *guarear, guariar*

¿huasumara? (Eng.) What's the matter?

huato (var. of) *guato*

huatoso -sa (vars. of) *guatoso -sa*

huayín (Eng.) (var. of) *guayín* m.

huayo (dim. of) *Eduardo* (see also *Yayo*)

huehuo (var. of) *huevo*

hueldeador -ra or **hueldiador -ra** (Eng.) welder

hueldear or **hueldiar** (Eng.) va. to weld, solder

huelva, huelvas, etc. (vars. of) *güelva, güelvas,* etc. (in turn vars. of) *vuelva, vuelvas,* etc. (pres. subj. of *volver*)

huemazo (var. of) *güemazo* (see also **guamazo** et al.)

hueno -na (vars. of) *bueno -na*

huerco -ca kid, brat, young child

huerfanato or **huerfanatorio** (vars. of) *orfanato* orphanage

huerte (var. of) *fuerte*

hueso: huesos pl. (slang) dice; **hueso sabroso** funny bone (coll.) (point near the elbow where the nerve may be pressed against the bone to produce a tingling sensation)

huevo: a huevo forcibly, by force; **huevo huero** (coll.) rotten egg; ¡**huevos!** interj. Hell no! (strong negative); **huevos rancheros** Mexican-style scrambled eggs with peppers, onions, tomatoes, etc.; **tener huevos** (vulg.) to have balls (semi-vulg. & slang), possess considerable strength of character, intestinal fortitude

huevón -vona (pej.) lazy, no account (coll.), good-for-nothing

huevonada laziness

huevonear or **huevoniar** (coll.) vn. to loaf, be idle

huevudo male with large testicles

huey (var. of) *buey* m.

hichaca billiard pocket

huichol m. wide-brimmed straw hat

huifa (Eng.) (slang) wife (see also **guifa**)

húiga, húigas, etc. (vars. of) *huya, huyas*, etc. (pres. subj. of *huir*)

¡huije! interj. (expression used to make fun of someone or to provoke to anger) (see also **ije, iji**)

huila or **huilacha** (slang, pej.) prostitute, whore; two-dimensional quadrangular kite

Huimble (Hispanization of) Winmberly, Texas

huine (Eng.) (var. of) *güine* m.

huiquén (Eng.) m. weekend

huirihuiri (slang) gossip, idle talk

huirlocha (slang) jalopy, old car

huiscle m. (var. of) *whiski* (Eng.)

huívora (child language var. of) *víbora*

huiza (slang, pej.) whore, prostitute; (non-pej.) girlfriend; fiancée

hule m. inner tube; floor linoleum; shoe sole; (slang) condom, rubber (slang); **quemar hule** (slang, Ang.) to burn rubber (slang), accelerate a car rapidly from a standing position

humadera (var. of) *humareda* (Std.)

humado -da (vars. of) *ahumado -da*

húngaro -ra gypsy

hurgonear or **hurgoniar** va. to shake violently

huyar (var. of) *aullar* vn.

huyir (var. of) *huir* vn.

I

icir (var. of) *decir*

idear or **idiar** vn. to idle the time away by daydreaming about things beyond one's means to acquire or achieve

ideoma (var. of) *idioma* mf. (Std. m.)

ideoso -sa or **idioso -sa** daydreamer (cf. **idear, idiar**)

idioma (often f. *la idioma*)

idioso -sa fancier, aficionado (of something)

ido -da or **media ido/medio ida** nuts (slang), crazy, cuckoo (slang)

Igle (Pas) (coll., Hispanization of) Eagle Pass, Texas

ignorar (Ang.) va. to ignore, not to pay attention to (Std. *no hacer caso*)

igualado -da social climber (ref. to person, often overbearing, who tries to achieve a superior social level)

igualar vr. to social climb (coll.), try to achieve a superior social level

iluminado -da: andar iluminado -da to be lit up like a Christmas tree (slang), be very drunk

ilumino (var. of) *aluminio*

imperial f. type of bleached cotton cloth

impidir (var. of) *impedir*

implemento (Ang.) tool, implement

impliado -da (vars. of) *empleado -da*

imponer va. to accustom, train, get (someone) used to: "No lo impusiste a trabajar, por eso es tan huevón"; vr. to get used to, accustomed to; to be dependent on (someone)

impruvear or **impruviar** (Eng.) va. & vn. to improve

impuesto -ta accustomed, used to

Inacio -cia (vars. of) *Ignacio -cia*

incenso (Eng.?) incense (Std. *incienso*)

incomtax (Eng.) m. income tax

incontrar (var. of) *encontrar*

inconviniente (var. of) *inconveniente* (Std.)

incordio (slang) chicken's egg

indección f. (var. of) *inyección* f.

indiada (pej.) disorderly mob; illbread persons belonging to the same clan, etc.

indigesto -ta: sentirse indigesto -ta to feel bloated; to feel one has a stomach disorder

individo -da (vars. of) *individuo -dua*

infante mf. (Ang.?) infant, baby

infección: infección de la sangre (euph.) syphilis

infilda or **infílder** (Eng.) m. in-
fielder (baseball)
inflencia (var. of) *influencia*
influencia (var. of) *influenza*
infriar (var. of) *enfriar*
inglesado -da (non-pej.) Anglo-
ized, Anglo-like
inocente (euph.) (ref. to various
degrees of mental retardation):
"Los niños inocentes no pueden
asistir a la escuela con los demás
niños"
inorante (var. of) *ignorante*
inorar (var. of) *ignorar*
inspectar (Ang.) to inspect (Std.
inspeccionar)
instructar (Eng.) va. to instruct,
teach
instructear or **instructiar** (vars.
of) *instructar* (Eng.)
instrumento (Ang.?) tool (slang),
penis
insultativo -va (vars. of) *insultador
-dora*
insulto digestive indisposition (upset stomach, etc.)
inteligir vn. (for someone to be
good at something): "Le intelige a
las matemáticas" 'He's very good
at math'; **inteligirse con** to be in
charge of: "¿Quién se intelige con
este negocito?" 'Who's in charge
of this business?'
intero -ra (var. of) *entero -ra*
intiligente (var. of) *inteligente*
intonado -da up on (coll.), tuned
in (slang), abreast of the latest
news and happenings
introducido -da outgoing; friendly;
sociable; extroverted
introducir (Ang.) va. to introduce,
present (two people previously
unacquainted with each other)
(Std. *presentar*)
ir: ir acá García (slang) to go to
the toilet (see discussion of
García); **ir a Dalas** (<Dallas)
(slang) to have sexual intercourse,
come across (slang), put out
(slang) (play on words: *Dalas
<Dallas<darlas* 'to give out with
one's sexual favors, come across
with') (in the expression *ir a Dalas*,
the last two words represent a
rough Hispanization of the name
of the Texas city, Dallas); **ir a dar
a** to end up (in a place): "Fueron a
dar a la playa" 'They ended up on
the beach'; **ir a patín / ir a patina**
(slang) to go on foot; **ir al bai bai/
ir al ba bai** to go bye-bye (coll.),
go out for a walk or a car ride; go
out to enjoy oneself; **ir cayendo
poco a poquito** to come around bit
by bit, yield (cease to resist) little
by little; **ir chisqueado -da** or
chisquiado -da to run at top
speed, go like a bat out of hell
(coll.); **ir de jilo** (slang) to run
rapidly, go like a bat out of hell
(coll.); to go directly (without
stopping) to one's destination; **ir
de perla** to have a good time; to
have good luck: "Le dieron el
primer premio—¡Caray, le fue de
perla!"; **ir dioquis** (see **dioquis, de
hoquis**); **ir hecho chile** (slang) to
run rapidly, go like a bat out of
hell (coll.); **ir hecho máquina** to be
going very rapidly; **ir pa(ra) fuera**
(euph.) to go to the rest room
(water closet, toilet) (the expression may be a holdover from the
days when a person had to go out
of his house to the backyard privy
[outhouse] to relieve himself); **ir
pa' tras** (Ang.) to go back, fail to
keep (i.e., one's word, a promise,
etc.); vn. to return: "Se fue pa' tras
pa' México"; **irle a** (coll.) to bet

on: "¿Quién va a ganar?—Pues yo le voy al campeón" 'Who's going to win?—Well I bet on the champ'; **irle a alguien a la mano** to discipline a child by spanking him/her; **irse a las greñas** to go at one another in a fight which involves pulling hair (usually said of two women); **irse pa(para) (ar) riba** to climb the ladder of success, go to the top (of one's trade or profession); **írsele a alguien el sueño** to lose one's sleepiness, get over one's tiredness; **írsele a alguien la mano** to slip up, lose control; to miscalculate; **írsele a alguien la voz** to hit a sour note while singing; **írsele la onda a alguien** to go off on a tangent; **írsele a alguien las patas** (slang) to slip up, lose control of oneself, lose one's head; to throw caution to the wind (often used in a sexual context, e.g., "Mírala, está gorda, se le fueron las patas"); **írsele a uno la mente** to lose one's trend of thought; to have a mental lapse; **írsele uno a alguien** to give someone the slip, elude someone: "Lo seguimos hasta la esquina, pero se nos fue" 'We followed him up to the corner, but he gave us the slip'; **si a ésas vamos** if that's the case, if that's how things stack up: "Si a ésas vamos, yo también puedo usar dos camisas por día"; **vámonos a la fregada** Beat it!, Scram!; **¿vamos llegando...?** how's about stopping off...?: "¿Vamos llegando a ca Pedro?" 'How's about stopping off at Pedro's house?'; **y que aquí y que allá y que fue y que vino** (coll.) etcetera, etcetera, and so on and so forth; **y vamos que** even though: "Y no terminó su tesis el pendejo ése, y vamos que le dimos dos años" 'And that dummy didn't finish his thesis, even though we gave him two years'

irrigar   (Eng.) va. to irrigate

istafiate   (var. of) *estafeate, esta-fiate*

ivierno   (var. of) *invierno* (Std.)

ixtle   m. fiber of the century plant (used to make lariats, etc.)

izquierdista   mf., adj. left-handed person (Std. *izquierdo -da*)

J

jabalín m. (ref. to person whose hair stands straight on end, as in a crewcut)

jabla (var. of) *jaula*

jacalear or **jacaliar** vn. to habitually go around visiting one home after another in order to bear tales and gossip

jacalera woman who goes from house to house bearing tales and gossip; busybody (coll.)

jai: andar uno en su jai (Eng.) to be on one's high horse, be disdainful or conceited, be putting on airs of superiority

jaibol (m.; pl. **jaiboles**) or **jaibola** (f.) (Eng.) highball (cocktail)

jaiboleada or **jaiboliada** (Eng.) cocktail party

jaic (Eng.) m. hike, long walk in the countryside

jaigüey or **jaihuey** or **jaíhuey** (Eng.) m. highway

jainiar (slang) vn. to make love, engage in the sexual act; to engage in sexual foreplay; make out (slang)

jaino -na (slang) m. boyfriend; fiancé; f. girlfriend; fiancée

jaipo -pa (Eng.) (slang) m. needle used to inject narcotic drugs into the veins of the human body; mf. person who mainlines narcotic drugs into his/her veins

jáiscul or **jaiscul** (Eng.) high school

jaitón -tona (Eng.) high-toned (coll.), snobbish; stylish; elegant

jalado -da (slang) drunk; f. pull, jerk (cf. **jalar**)

jalador -ra hard-working, diligent, industrious

jalar va. (slang) to steal; vn. (coll.) to work, to toil; to function, work; vr. **jalársela** (vulg., slang) to masturbate: "Lo pescaron jalándosela" 'They caught him pulling away at it!; **¡jálale!** or **¡jálele!** interjs. (slang) Hurry up!, Move it!

jale (coll.) m. work, job; **hacer jale**; (coll.) to work; (slang) to steal

jalea (slang) adj. very elegant, dressed to kill (usually with *andar*): "Anda muy jalea" (poss. Ang? <jelly bean, ant. slang for elegant, well dressed)

jaletina (var. of) *gelatina*

jaló (Eng.) hello

jalón: andar de jalón (slang) to be on the make (slang), be out looking for a date or a sexual partner; **de un jalón** once and for all; all at once: "Se tomó todo el vino de un jalón" 'He drank the wine down in a single gulp'; **hacer**

jalones to flirt, make passes at a member of the opposite sex; **hacerle jalón a alguien** to make passes at someone (with amorous intentions)

jalonear or **jaloniar** va. to jerk; to pull

jallar (var. of) *hallar*

jambado -da (slang) stolen, ripped off (slang)

jambar (slang) to steal

jamberga (hum.) m. & f. or **jamborga** m. & f. or **jamborgue** m. or **jambórguer** m. (Eng.) hamburger; **hacer jamberga de** (et al.) (slang) to make mincemeat of (someone), beat up soundly (in a fight)

jambo -ba (slang) m., f. thief; adj. thieving

jambón -bona (slang) thief; thieving

jamón m. bacon; **jamón tortilla** (slang) straightforward and honest person

jando (slang) money

jaqueta (Eng.?, Ang.?) jacket, coat

jardín infantil m. kindergarten

jaria (slang) hunger

jaripeo (type of rodeo)

jarocha or **jarucha** lively and alert (said of women)

jaspe (slang) m. meal (dinner, supper, etc.)

jaspear or **jaspiar** (slang) va. to eat

jaspia (slang) hunger

jatana (slang) guitar

jaula (slang) jail, cage (coll.)

jaule (slang) m. burglary

jeder (var. of) *heder*

jediondez f. (var. of) *hediondez* f.

jediondo -da (vars. of) *hediondo -da*

jefa (slang) wife; mother

jefe (slang) m. father

jervir va. (var. of) *hervir*

jeta: colgar jeta(s)/colgar chica(s) jeta (s)/colgar tamaña(s) jeta(s) (slang) to pout

jetear or **jetiar** vn. to pout

jey fíver (Eng.) m. or f. hay fever

ji interj. (slightly euph.) (<*jijo* <*hijo*, q.v.)

jicotera: armarse la jicotera to start, break out (ref. to a quarrel, trouble, scandal, etc.)

jiedo, jiedes, jiede, jedemos/ jíedemos, jieden (vars. of) *hiedo, hiedes*, etc. (pres. ind. of *heder*)

jijo (var. of) *hijo*; interjs.: **¡jijo!** (varies in intensity according to degree of emphasis, type of intonation, etc.); **¡jijo del hacha!** or **¡jijo de la chapel!** (<*LaChapelle*, the name of a San Antonio street found in the central part of the city); **¡jijo de la mañana¡** or **¡jijo de la guayaba!** (all vary in intensity, though all tend to be fairly euphemistic — 'Golly Moses!' is an average gloss for most); **¡jíjole!** interj. (varies in meaning according to intensity and situation, from a mild 'Damn!' through something much stronger)

jilo: andar de jilo to be in a hurry; **ir de jilo** to pass by in a hurry; interj. **¡jilo!** (rather euph.) Gosh!, Gee!; **¡jilo de la chingada!** (not quite as strong as the correspondent ¡*hijo de la chingada*!); **¡jijo de la mañana!** (var. of) ¡*hijo de la mañana*!

jincar (var. of) *hincar*

jiorge (var. of) *Jorge*

jipe or **jipi** mf. (Eng.) hippie

jipicano -na (a blend of *hippie* and *chicano*) a Chicano hippie

jipo -pa (Eng.) hippopotamus; n. & adj. obese; m. "Hippo Size" (soft drink manufactured in San Antonio, Texas)

jira (Eng.) m. & f. heater, heating device

jiricua pie baldness, vitiglio

jirimiquear or **jirimiquiar** vn. to whimper

jiriola: ir(se) de jiriola (slang) vn. to cut classes, not to attend school

jit (Eng.) m. hit, musical success, successful musical composition; base hit (baseball)

jitazo (Eng.) (slang) tremendous hit, extremely popular musical composition

¡jito! interj. (euph.) Golly!, Gosh!

jocoque m. curdled milk; yogurt

joda: arrimarle a alguien una joda to give someone a rough time, make it hard for someone; **llevar una joda** to have a terrible time, go through trying times

jodarria (slang) harassment

jodedera (slang) harassment; nagging

jodedor -ra hard, backbreaking: "El trabajo de la construcción es jodedor" 'Road construction work is backbreaking'; ruthless, opportunistic; deceptive; bothersome, annoying (ref. to persons or things)

joder va. to deceive, cheat; to take sexual possession through deception; va. to break, put out of order: "Linda jodió el radio" 'Linda broke the radio'; **de a tiro la jode(s)/joden**, etc. (a set expression used to reprimand someone for aggressive behavior) You're something else, You're a mess, You're a real lulu (all used ironically and with a critical intent);

joder la paciencia to nag the hell out of, pester the hell out of, bother, try one's patience; **para acabarla de joder** (set expression) to make matters worse, as if that were not enough; **te jodes que no** or **te jodes si no** (set expressions used by one to contradict emphatically a negative statement made by another) the hell it isn't, the hell you're not, the hell he's not, etc.: "Su hermana ya no te quiere — Te jodes que no" 'His sister doesn't love you anymore — The hell she doesn't' (see also **chingar** and **fregar**)

jodido -da down-and-out, destitute; in poor health; (coll.) out of one's gourd (slang), crazy: "Pues ese tipo está jodido si cree que vamos a hacer todo esto en quince minutos"; **¡A la jodida!** (vulg., slang) I'll be God-damned!; **acá la jodida** (vulg., slang) a long way away, half way to hell and gone (slang), way the shit out there (vulg., slang); **estar como la jodida** to be as ____ as can be (usual ref. to a negative characteristic of which both speaker and listener are cognizant, e.g.): "Ella está como la jodida" 'She's as ugly as sin'; **no la jodas (joda/jodan)/ya ni la jodes (jode/joden)** (set expression used to censure abusive behavior) (see also **chingar** and **fregar**); **ser más + adj. + que la jodida** to be + adj. + than hell: "María es más gorda que la jodida" 'Mary is fatter than hell'

jodón -dona ruthless, opportunistic; deceptive; **el mero jodón** (slang) the big boss, the head honcho (slang)

jogar (rus.) (var. of) *jugar*

jol (Eng.) m. hall, corridor

jola (slang) money

jolino -na short, not tall, not long

jom (Eng.) m. home base (baseball)

jomrón (Eng.) m. home run (baseball)

jonchar (Eng.? < to hunch?) va. & vn. to cheat in a game of marbles by moving the marble shooter closer to the target

jonche: hacer jonche (id. to **jonchar**)

Jondo (local rendition of) Hondo, Texas

jondo -da (vars. of) *hondo -da*

jone or **joni** (Eng.) (vocative, term of endearment) honey

jonqui (Eng.) (pej.) mf. hunky, honky (both pej.), Anglo-Saxon

jonrón m. (Eng.) (var. of) *jomrón* m.

jorobas msg., fsg., adj. (var. of) *jorobado -da*

joronche (slang) mf. hunchback

josco -ca (vars. of) *hosco -ca*; m. (fig.) bad boy

josla (Eng.?<hustler) keen; neat, terrific, swell, etc.

joslear or **josliar** (Eng.?) (cf. **josla**) va. & vr. to steal: "Se joslió dos dulces" 'He stole two bars of candy'

jotinche m. or **jotinchón -chona** (slang) (vars. of) *jotingo -ga*

jotingo -ga (slang) m. faggot, male homosexual; f. lesbian; m. sissy, effeminate boy or man; m. milksop

jotito (slang) young male homosexual

joto -ta (slang) m. fag, male homosexual; f., dike, lesbian

jotquey (Eng.) m. hot cake (type of pancake)

joventud f. (var. of) *juventud* f.

Juan (slang) m. cockroach (see also **Taltascuán** et. al.)

Juani (dim. of) *Juan* (blend of *Juan* and *Johnny*? or apocope of the dim. *Juanito*?), *Juanito*

Juanita (slang) marihuana

Juaquín (var. of) *Joaquín*

Juariles m. (also orthog. var. of *Juarílez* m.) (slang) *Ciudad Juárez, México*

judas: estar uno que se lo lleva judas to be very angry, very hot under the collar (coll.); **me lleva judas** (set expression) Well I'll be, Well I'll be darned

juegar (rus.) (var. of) *jugar*

juego (var. of) *fuego*

juerte mf. (var. of) *fuerte* mf.

juerza (var. of) *fuerza*

juerzudo -da (vars. of) *forzudo -da*

juez de (la) paz (Ang.) m. justice of the peace

jugada (ref. to a woman who has frequently indulged her carnal appetites, who has played around a lot)

jugar: jugarla fría (Ang., slang) to play it cool (coll.); **jugarse plancha** to be slow to react (because of lack of preparation, laziness, etc.)

juguetón -tona (Ang.?<one who plays around [coll.]) (hum.) m. adulteror; f. adultress

jui, jui(s)te(s), jue, juimos, jueron (vars. of) *fui, fuiste*, etc. (pret. of *ser/ir*)

juila (Eng.?<wheeler) bicycle

juisque (Eng.) m. whiskey

juiza (var. of) *huiza*

julia (slang, underw.) police wagon, paddy wagon (coll.); ambulance

jum m. (Eng.) (var. of) *jomrón* m.

jumadera (var. of) *humadera, humareda*

jumar   (var. of) *fumar*
jumarada   (var. of) *humarada*
jumedad   f. (var. of) *humedad* f.
jumo   (var. of) *humo*
jumrón   m. (Eng.) (var. of) *jomrón* m.
Júnior   (Eng.) m., adj. junior (see also **yúnier** et al.)
junrón   m. (Eng.) (var. of) *jomrón* m.
juntar   vr. to become reconciled (usually ref. to lovers, husbands and wives, etc., who have separated)
junto: andar juntos   to go steady (coll.) (ref. to boy and girl who date each other exclusively); **junto**

de (var. of) *junto a*: "Vive junto de su hermano"
juquear or **juquiar**   (Eng.) vn. to play hookey, absent oneself from school (see also **juqui**)
juqui   (Eng.) m. hookey, unexcused absence from school.; **jugar juqui** (Ang., Eng., resp.) to play hookey, absent oneself from school without permission
jura   (slang)   sg. policeman; pl. police force
jurgonear or **jurgoniar**   (vars. of) *hungonear, hurgoniar*, resp.
justicia   (slang) fsg. police force
jut   m. (Eng.) hood (aut.)

K

Kanses   (Eng.) (var. of) Kansas
karmesa   (orthog. var. of) *carmesa*

L

laberinto scandal; noise; intrigue

laberintoso -sa squeamish; exaggerating; rabble rouser

labio: labio cucho harelip

labioso -sa flatterer; smooth talker (coll.)

labor f. cultivated field; field used for farming

la: la de malas (coll.) bad luck: "Le tocó la de malas" 'He had some bad luck'

lado: buscarle a alguien por su lado to approach someone from his good side (fig.), get someone in a good moment; **dar a uno por su lado** to humor someone, side with someone, indulge someone; **el mejor lado** (Ang.) some one's best side, most appealing personality traits; **el otro lado** (coll.) Mexico; **estar de lado** (coll.) to be in a good mood

ladrería barking of dogs

largatizo (var. of) *lagartijo*

lagarto -ta alligator

laira (Eng.) lighter, cigarette lighter

Lalo -la (dims. of) *Eulalio -lia*

lambeache or **lambiache** (vulg.) ass kisser (vulg.), flatterer, obsequious person (mf.)

lambeculos (vulg.) mfsg., pl. (var. of) *iameculos* mfsg., pl.

lambehuevos (vulg.) mfsg., pl. apple-polisher, ass kisser (vulg.)

lamber (var. of) *lamer*

lambiche mf. (var. of) *lambeache, lambiache, lambiachi* mf.

lambida (var. of) *lamida*

lambión -biona flatterer, apple-polisher, ass kisser (vulg.)

lambizque mf. (coll.) freeloader, person who avoids paying

lambizquiar (var. of) *lambuzquiar*

lambuzco -ca hollow leg (coll.), person perpetually looking for something to eat; person perpetually eating

lambuzquear or **lambuzquiar** va. to nibble at food in between mealtimes; to go around looking for food to eat in between mealtimes; vn. to be obsequiously and hypocritically courteous

lameache mf. or **lamiache** mf. (vars. of) *lambeache, lambiache, lambiachi* mf.

lameculos (vulg.) mfsg., pl. flatterer, apple-polisher, ass kisser (vulg.)

lamer (vulg.) va. to kiss ass (vulg.), ingratiate oneself (with someone)

lamparear or **lampariar** (slang) va. to look at: "Está lampariando a las batas que pasan"

lampreado -da or **lampriado -da** roasted; roasted with a beaten egg covering

lamprear or **lampriar** va. to roast meat; to cover a roast with beaten eggs

lana (slang) money; **andar lana morado -da** (slang) to be in love with (play on words: *lana morado -da* < *enamorado -da*)

lanero -ra wool worker; person who gathers the sheep's wool from the ground and places it on a platform where it is bundled

lángara mf. sly, astute, cunning: "Pedro es un lángara"

lanudo -da flushed with money (ref. to person carrying around an unaccustomed amount of money or to a person suddenly much richer than before)

lao (var. of) *lado*

lápiz msg. & mpl. (word wrongly interpreted as already bearing the plural maker): "Traigo un lápiz... no, parece que traigo dos lápiz"

laquiar (Eng.) va. to lock shut

largado -da estranged, abandoned (by a spouse): "Pobre María está largada, ¡y con tanta familia!"

largar va. to abandon (leave) one's spouse, run away from one's mate: "Juan largó a su esposa"

lástico (var. of) *elástico*

lastimada action and effect of injuring or hurting (physically or emotionally)

lastimón m. (var. of) *lastimada*

lata (see **dar (la) lata**)

latido stomach spasms or palpitations

lavadero act of washing clothes

lavado douche

lazazo blow with a rope

lazo clothesline

leacho (var. of) *liacho*

lección f. (var. of) *lección* f.

lectricidad f. (var. of) *electricidad* f.

leche f. (vulg.) (male) semen, sperm; **leche agria** sour milk, curdled milk; **mosca en leche** dark-complexioned person married to (or associating with) a fair-skinned person

lechudo -da (slang) lucky

lechuza bat

leer: leer las cartas/ leer la(s) baraja (s) (vars. of) *echar las cartas*

leido -da (vars. of) *leído -da* (ppart. of *leer*)

lejecitos (iron.) adv. quite far away, quite a distance

lencho -cha (dims. of) *Lorenzo -za*

lengón -gona (vars. of) *lenguón -guona*

lengonear or **lengoniar** (slang) vn. to gossip; to chat, converse

lengua (slang) necktie; **bullir la lengua** to gossip; to talk excessively; **echar lengua** to work excessively; to walk a long distance on a wild goose chase (coll.), walk a long distance in vain; **lengua de zapato** shoe's tongue (Std. *lengüeta de zapato*); **lengua grande** big-mouthed (coll.), talkative, garrulous; **lengua, lengua pa' Lorenza** (set expression used to poke fun at someone who has walked a long distance on a wild goose chase, i.e., without accomplishing his objective); **tener lengua mocha** to talk very little; **tener lengua suelta** to talk frequently; to be garrulous; **tirar lengua** (slang) to talk too much, be very garrulous

lenguón -guona liar; malicious gossiper; foul-mouthed, filthy-mouthed

lentodos (slang) eyeglasses

leña (slang) marihuana

leñito (slang) marihuana cigarette

león, -ona greedy; ambitious; unrelenting in the pursuit of something: "Ella es una leona para las estampillas; nunca deja de pedírnoslas cuando viene de compras"; **tirar a león** to ignore, not pay attention to

lepe (coll.) mf. brat, squirt, annoying young child; short-legged, heavy-set person

ler (var. of) *leer*

les: jugar a la les to play tag; **traer la les** (also **traerla**) to be "it" in a game of tag (*les*<Eng. last, i.e., 'Last one in is the loser'?, or perhaps <*lass* young girl?)

letrato (var. of) *retrato*

levantada pick-up, woman who allows herself to be solicited for sexual activity: "Tú eres pura levantada" 'You're nothing but a pick-up'

levantar: levantar aceite (slang) to blow off steam (coll.), get angry; **lavantar chancla/levantar chancle** (slang) to move rapidly, really "pick up one's feet" (coll.); **levantar el alarme/levantar la alarma** (Ang.?) to raise an alarm, give warning; **levantar la bandera** (Ang.) to raise the flag (i.e., run the flag up the flagpole) (Std. *izar la bandera*); **levantar la casa** to clean the house, tidy up the house; **levantarse con las gallinas** (Ang.?) to get up with the chickens (fig.), arise very early in the morning

levante (slang) mf. pick-up, person picked up (usually in an anonymous fashion) by another

for subsequent sexual activity; act of picking up for subsequent sexual activity

levantón m. boost in one's morale: "Hay que darle un levantón, está muy triste"

ley (slang) fsg. police force; **meter a la ley/meter en la ley** to bring suit against (someone)

leyer (var. of) *leer*

liacho badly-tied bundle (e.g., of clothes)

lial (var. of) *leal*

librar: ¡Dios me (te, lo, nos, los) libre! Heaven (God) forbid!

libroteca (var. of) *biblioteca*

licar (slang) va. to look at, observe: "Está licando la tienda que piensa robar"; to see

Lico (dim. of) *Federico*

licorear or **licoriar** (slang) va. to look at, observe; to see (cf. **licar**)

licuador m. blender, machine used to blend food

Licha (dim. of) *Alicia*

liebre (slang) f. odd job

liendroso -sa or **liendrudo -da** (vars. of) *lendroso -sa*

lima (slang) shirt

limar (slang) va. to degrade, humiliate

Limburgo (slang) Edinburg, Texas

limosnero -ra pej. moocher, sponger (coll.), parasite (fig.); **limosnero y con garrote** (ref. to person who wants to have his/her cake and eat it too, one who wants a mile when offered an inch, etc.)

limpio -pia (slang) cleaned-out, stone-broke, penniless

linar (var. of) *alinear*

linda (slang) vagina; **quitar la linda** to cause to lose one's virginity, to deflower (said of women): "Si no te cuidas te van a quitar la linda"

línea   penny pitching (mild type of gambling game); (Ang.) line, falsehood used to convince: "Le estaba dando una línea" 'He was handing (feeding) her a line'; **andar en la línea/estar en la línea** (coll.) to be drunk; **tirar línea** (slang) to flatter, hand someone a line (slang)

linia   (var. of) *línea*

linolio   (var. of) *linóleo*

linterna   small store or business; (slang) eye; (coll.) firefly

Lío   (Eng.) *Leo* (proper name)

lión   m. (var. of) *león* m.

liona   (slang) jail

lipestic or **lipestique** or **lipistic** or **lipistique**   (Eng.) m. lipstick

liquear or **liquiar**   (Eng.) va. to lick; vn. to leak

liquellar   (slang) va. to see; to look

lira   (slang) guitar

lírico -ca   self-taught (ref. to persons who play instruments by ear or to persons who recite poems, etc., from memory without having learned them from a script); a born ____ (ref. to someone who is said to have inherent talent for something, e.g.): "un músico lírico" 'a born musician'

lis   m. (Eng.) lease, rental contract

lisa   (slang) shirt

listerina   (Eng.) mouthwash (in general) (loan metonymy Listerine)

listones   mpl. children's game in which the children divide into two bands; band one decides upon a particular color, which band two then tries to guess by knocking on an imaginary "door" and participating in the following dialogue: "Tan tan—¿Quién es? (response

from band two)—La vieja Inés—¿Qué quería?—Un listón—¿De qué color?" At this point the second band names a color. If named correctly, band two receives a point; if not then it is the turn of band one to guess the color

Lito -ta   (dims. of) *Carmen* (mf.), *Carmelito* (m.), *Carmelita* (f.)

liviano -na   adj. (ref. to persons with a bad reputation); f. woman of ill repute

lobatismo   (Ang.) cub scouting

lobi   (Eng.) m. lobby, hall, vestibule

Lobica   (slang, Hispanization of) Lubbock, Texas

Lobo   (hum. slang, Hispanization of) Lubbock, Texas

lobo   (fig.) astute and clever person

locario -ria   (slang) crazy

Lócat   (slang, Hispanization of) Lockhart, Texas

loco -ca   (slang) drunk; m. (slang) dollar bill; **andar loco -ca** (slang) to be high on narcotic drugs; **bato loco** (slang) cool dude (slang); **loco de atiro** crazy through and through; **loco -ca enmaizado -da** (coll.) crazy old fool, doddering old idiot; **tirar a(l) loco** (slang) to ignore: "Se enojaron porque los tiraron al loco"; **¡qué loco!** or **¡qué locote!** (slang) (set expression used to praise an accomplishment): "Gané el primer premio—¡Qué loco!"

locote: andar locote   (slang) to be high on narcotic drugs

logo   adv. (var. of) *luego* adv.

lonas   overalls, coveralls (type of men's work clothes)

lonchar   (Eng.) vn. to eat lunch

(see also **lonchear**)

lonche (Eng.) m. lunch (light midday meal); sandwich (Std. *emparedado*): "¿Cuántos lonches quieres hoy?"; **echarle a alguien su lonche** (slang) to tell someone off, bawl someone out (slang): "¡Qué bueno que le echó su lonche; lo merecía!"; **echarse a alguien de lonche** to defeat someone in a sports competition; to beat someone up in a fight

lonchear (Eng.) vn. to eat lunch (see also **lonchar**)

lonchera (Eng.) (cf. **lonche**) lunch pail, lunch bucket (container used to carry one's lunch to work)

lonchería (Eng.) (cf. **lonche**) lunch-room; small café

londre or **londri** (Eng.) m. laundry, place where clothes are cleaned; laundry, dirty clothes to be cleaned

lonjonudo -da very fat and flabby

lore: ¡ji lore! (Eng. Lordy, dim. of Lord) interj. (euph.) Lordy me! (cf. other interjs. with **jijo**)

Los (slang) Los Angeles, California: "Ese bato es de Los" 'That guy is from Los Angeles'

los (var. of) *nos* (1st pers. pl. object pron.): "El siempre que los ve los pide que véngamos a casa" 'Every time he sees us he asks us to come over to his house'

losotros -tras (vars. of) *nosotros -tras*

lucario -ria (vars. of) *locario -ria*

lucas (slang) mfsg. crazy, foolish; **tirar a lucas** (slang) to ignore

Luce or **Luci** (dims. of) *Lucía*

lucir vr. to show off, act ostentatiously

Lucha (dim. of) *Lucía, Luz*

lucha: hacer la lucha to try, make

an effort, give it a try; **hacerle la lucha a alguien** to try to convince someone (usually against his/her will), try to get someone to change his/her mind

luchista mf. go-getter (coll.), aggressive person

luchón -chona (id. to **luchista** supra)

luego: luego luego or **luego lueguito** adv. right away, immediately; **pos luego/pues luego** of course, without doubt, certainly

luenga (var. of) *lengua*

Luli (Hispanization of) Luling, Texas

Luis Morales (hum.) m. man with low moral standards (bilingual play on words: 'loose morals')

Luisa Morales (hum.) f. woman with low moral standards (bilingual wordplay, cf. **Luis Morales** supra)

lumbre: ser muy lumbre (said of a person who wears things out, i.e., clothes, or who puts them in a state of disrepair in a short time); **sacar lumbre** to harp on the same subject, talk incessantly about the same topic

lumbre f. light, match (for lighting cigarettes, etc.) (Angl.?): "Dame lumbre" 'Give me a light'; **andar uno que toca lumbre** to be hard up, be in dire need (usually said of a person who stands ready to resort to any means to resolve his economic situtation)

lumbrero -ra firefighter, fireman

lumbriz (fig.) mf. thin (person) (var. of *lombriz*, a form which is seldom heard in Texas)

luna menstruation period; **bajarle la luna a alguien** to flow (said of menstrual fluid), have one's period; **estar mala de la luna** to be having one's (menstruation) period

lunada moonlight party

lup (Eng.) m. loop

Lupe (dim. of) *Guadalupe* m., f.

luquimia (Eng.) *leukemia* (Std. *leucemia*)

luquis (slang) mf. crazy person

lurio -ria or **lurias** mfsg. (slang) crazy: "Ese bato está lurias" 'That guy is crazy'

luto: traer luto (fig.) to have dirty fingernails

luz: apagarle las luces a alguien (Ang.) to turn out the lights on someone (slang), knock someone out, render him/her unconscious; **bil de la luz** (Ang.) electric light bill

LL

llamar vr. to go back on one's word, retract a promise: "Carlos se llamó, por eso estoy enojado"

llamarada: llamarada de petate flash in the pan (coll.), person who promises to be a great success, but fails

lamón -mona person who goes back on his/her word, fails to carry out a promise

llanta (fig., hum.) doughnut; (fig., slang) spare tire (slang), role of fat around a person's waist; pl. gifts given at a wedding

lantón -tona (slang, pej.) African American

llegar: llegarle a alguien to get to someone, get the best of someone; **llegarle (darle) a uno la (el) agua a la cabeza (al pescuezo)** (fig.) to have a hard time keeping one's head above water (fig.), be in a tight spot (slang), be in trouble, be in a predicament; **¿vamos llegando...?** 'How's about stopping off...?': "¿Vamos llegando a ca Pedro?" 'How's about stopping off at Pedro's house?'

llenar va. & vr. to soil, dirty, stain (esp. clothes): "Le llenaste la camisa de jugo" 'You stained his shirt with juice'; vn. **llenar de ____** to have enough ____, e.g.,

llenar de sueño to have enough sleep

llevar va.: **llevar los libros** to keep the books, record the accounts and transactions of a business; **llevar pa'tras** (Ang.) to return, take back; to retract (e.g., a promise), go back on (one's word); vn. **llevar una freguiza** or **llevar una joda** to have a hard time of (something); vr. to kid around (slang), direct humor towards (someone) with apparent offensive intent though never with genuine malice; **llevarla** to pay for, be given the responsibility for, have to shoulder the blame for: "Cuando el hogar se desbarata la mujer es la que la lleva" 'When a home breaks up it's the woman who pays for it'; to take out on: "Todo el día el profesor mira a las muchachas bonitas y después cuando llega a casa es la mujer la que la lleva" 'All day the professor is looking at pretty girls and then when he gets home he takes it out on his wife'; **llevarse a alguien el tren/ llevarse a alguien la chingada/llevarse a alguien la fregada/llevarse a alguien la jodida** (vulg.) (fixed expressions): "¡Me lleva la chingada!" 'Well I'll be doubled damned!'; (also used in the sense of 'to find oneself in a tight spot': "¡Ya me llevaba el tren!" 'I was really in trouble then!'); **llevarse a alguien** to get the best of one in a business deal, take someone (slang): "Ese chico sí que te llevó" 'That boy really got the best of you'; (slang) to knife (someone); **llevarse de encuentro** to run over (someone)

llorada act of crying: "Tuvo su buena llorada" 'She had a real good cry'

llorar: ya ni llorar es bueno No use crying over spilled milk

lloretas mfsg. crybaby, whimperer

llorido cries, act of crying: "Nos despertaron sus lloridos" 'His crying woke us up'

llorona (slang) patrol car (police); fire engine; siren (of a fire engine or a police car); **la llorona** ghost-woman who, according to folk legend, killed her baby and afterwards threw it into the water; when she died she was forced to atone for her crime by wandering along the banks of the river, mourning the child; many towns and villages are said to have their own local *lloronas* who haunt the banks of the local stream

llovedero -ra heavy rainfall, cloudburst; continuous rainfall

M

maca (var. of) *hamaca*

Macalen (Hispanization of) McAllen, Texas

macalililiá children's game in which the participants form two human chains facing each other; a type of sung dialogue transpires, during which one child and then another asks something of a child from the other group

macanazo blow with a blackjack

macanear or **macaniar** va. to strike over the head with a blackjack or other heavy instrument

macánico -a (vars. of) *mecánico -ca*

macano -na cheap, common, ordinary; f. cheapskate, parsimonious person; blackjack (weapon)

maceta (slang) head; (slang) hand; slowpoke, person who acts or learns slowly

macita (var. of) *mamacita* beautiful and desirable woman; (slang, often vocative) sweet mamma

macizar va. to secure something for oneself, appropriate

macizo (slang) boyfriend; gang leader; favorite son (ref. to local or regional politicians who enjoy considerable popularity)

macuache mf. useless person

macuco -ca old person

macueco -ca left-handed

machacar: machacar la muela (slang) to eat

machete (var. of) *machetón -tona;* m. (slang) tomboy; **kid machetes** mfpl. (Eng. kid + *machetes*) (ref. to person who does everything wrong)

machetear or **machetiar** va. to do a job clumsily, leave a job half done

machetón -tona lazy; clumsy, awkward

machín -china strong; outstanding, excellent

machito type of Mexican food prepared in the same way as the chittling and consisting of the same ingredients (pig entrails)

macho very masculine, studly (slang); m. type of roast dish of liver, sweetbreads and other meat; adv. **a lo macho** in a manly manner: "Pórtate a lo macho" 'Act like a man' ; **no apearse de su macho/no bajarse de su macho** to be unyielding, stubborn (in an opinion or on a stand one has taken)

machón -chona (vars. of) *amachón -chona* stubborn; f. woman who acts like a man, tomboy

madama (Eng.) madame (title of

address which maids give to the women they work for)

madera flattery; **madera gacha** flattery, adulation; falsehood, lie; interj. ¡**madera (gacha)!** Hog wash!, Bull roar!; (see also **dar madera**)

maderear or **maderiar** va. to flatter; to lie, deceive; vr. to pass the time; to boast, brag

maderera or **madería** lumber yard

maderista mf. braggart; liar; flatterer

madre f. (slang) shapely and sexy woman; **acá la madre de los burros/acá la madre de los caballos** adv. very far away; **dar en la mera madre/dar en toda la madre** (slang) to beat up severely (usually in a fistfight); **echarle a alguien de la madre/ mentarle a alguien la madre** to insult someone by referring to his/her mother (in however veiled or cryptic a fashion); **echar madres** to curse, speak obscenities; **en la madre** where it hurts (coll.), in a vulnerable spot (physical or emotional): "Le van a dar en la madre"; **estar uno que se lo lleva madre** to be very tense, be overanxious; ¡**madre santa!** interj. (fairly euph.) Good Lord!, Heavens!; **no importarle a alguien madre** not to give a damn about anything; **no tener madre** (expression used as mild or hum. criticism of someone's boldness or bad behavior); **no valer madre** not to be worth a damn; ¡**pura madre!** interj. Hell no!, The hell (you say)!; ¡**qué padre madre!** (slang) What a gorgeous hunk of woman!; (see also **a toda madre, dar en la madre, de a madre**)

madrecita (slang) beautiful and sexy woman (see also **macita** and **mamacita**)

madruguero -ra early riser

magacín (orthog. var. of) *magazín*

magazín (Eng.) magazine, periodical

magazina (var. of) *magazín*

Mague (dim. of) *Margarita* (Eng. Maggie?)

Maique (Eng.) (dim.) Mike (<Michael)

Maique pron. I; me; mine (probable hum. substitution of *Maique* (Mike) for my/mine)

maistro -tra (vars. of) *maestro -tra*

maiz m. (var. of) *maíz* m.

maje mf. (slang) dumb, ignorant; **hacerle maje a alguien** to make a fool of someone

majadero -ra loudmouth (coll.) (ref. to boisterous and aggressive talker)

mal adv., adj.: **agarrarla (agarrarlo) mal** to take it (a remark, gesture, attitude, etc.) the wrong way, take offense, take exception to: "No lo vayas a agarrar mal, pero tengo que decirte lo que andan diciendo de ti" 'Don't go taking it the wrong way, but I have to tell you what they are going around saying about you'; **mal averiguado -da** hot-tempered, easily provoked; **mal dado -da** damaging (ref. to a hard blow to the body's more vulnerable parts); **mal de hiel** gall bladder disease; **mal de la sangre** (euph.) syphilis; **poner a alguien en mal** to speak ill of someone, discredit, run down (fig.), badmouth

malajos interj. (used to express impatience) Dammit to hell!; ¡**malajos seas!** Damm you!

malamé m. corn, maize; chicken feed

malanco **-ca** somewhat rotten (fruit); sick; slightly under the weather (coll., ref. to persons who are mildly sick); mean, base, vile; **salir malanco -ca** to turn out to be bad (ref. to persons, e.g., a bad spouse, a bad son, etc.)

malancón **-cona** sick, ill; disreputable (ref. to persons); **salir malancón -cona** (id. to **salir malanco -ca**)

malaveriguado **-da** pugnacious, quarrelsome

malcreadar or **malcriadar** to talk back to, be insolent with: "No le malcriades a tus mayores" 'Don't talk back to your elders'

malcriado -da sassy, impudent

maldiciento -ta (vars. of) *maldiciente* (Std.)

maldito -ta superior: "Ella se cree muy maldita" 'She thinks she's really some big deal' (coll.)

Male (Eng.) Molly (personal name)

malecito slight but bothersome cold in the head; cold on the verge of becoming flu

males mpl. (var. of) *malas enfermedades*; **¿cómo sigue de males?** (set expression) How are things with you?; **para colmo de mis males** (set expression) To make things worse, As if that weren't enough

maleta baby's excrement found on a diaper

maletudo -da baggy (ref. to person wearing baggy pants)

malhaya or **malhaya sea** interjs. Cursed be ... !: "!Malhaya sea el día en que naciste!"

Mali (Eng.) (var. of) *Male* Molly

malía or **malilla** m. male actor who plays the heavy (villain) in movies; cruel

malición f. (rus.) (var. of) *maldición* f.

malinche mf. bad, evil; turncoat, betrayer

malo **-la:** **mala (in)digestíon** (pleonasm for) indigestion; **mal genio** bad-tempered; **mal hablado -da** foul-mouthed, given to insults; **mala reata/mala riata** m. tough guy (coll.), mean bastard: "No hay que negarlo, es mala riata"; **mala yerba** (fig.) bad seed, person marked for tragedy or bad deeds from birth onward; untrustworthy person; **andar de malas** to be in a bad mood; **de malas** at least: "De malas no perdí todo el dinero"; **la de malas** bad luck: "Le tocó la de malas" 'He had some bad luck'

malora mf. perverse, malevolent: "Pedro es un malora"; f. evil deed

malpasado **-da** ill-nourshed; irregularly fed

malpasar vr. not to eat regularly

maltratado -da beat, beaten down (ref. to someone who shows all the signs of having lived a hard life); f. reprimand, scolding

malva astute, clever

mallate mf. (orthog. var. of) *mayate* mf.

mallugado -da (vars. of) *magullado -da*

mallugar (var. of) *magullar*

mallugón m. (var. of) *magullón* m. / *magullarrdura* / *magullamiento*

mama (var. of) *mamá* (both Stds.)

mamacita (slang) pretty girl

mamada act of sponging off of someone (coll.), living at someone else's expense

mamadera sinecure

mamador -ra sponger (coll.), parasite (fig.), person who lives off a sinecure; cocksucker (vulg.), cuntlapper (vulg.), person who performs oral sex

mamá grande grandmother (Std. *abuela*)

mamaleche f. hopscotch (children's game) (see also **bebeleche**)

mamalón -lona (slang) m. male homosexual; f. lesbian

mamar va. & vn. to sponge (coll.), live off of someone else's work or income; **mamar chiche** to nourish oneself through the breast (said of babies): "El bebé mama chiche, no necesita botella"; to sponge (coll.) (id. to **mamar**); **mamar y dar tope** to have one's cake and eat it too (coll., ref. to the desire to receive the maximum possible)

mamases (var. of) *mamás* (pl. Std. of *mamá*) fpl.

mamasota (slang) beautiful woman (see also **macita, mamacita**)

mami (Eng.) f. mommy, mamma

mamis fsg. (var. of) *mami*

mamón m. baby's pacifier

mana (var. of) *hermana;* (often used in the vocative and then not necessarily to one's own sister): "Oye, mana" 'Listen woman'

mancilla (var. of) *manecilla*

mancornía/mancornilla or **mancuernía** (usually fpl.) cufflink(s)

mancha negra black sheep (fig.), member of a family who brings disgrace upon the rest

manda religious wow; **pagar una manda** to fulfill a religious vow

mandadero -ra errand boy/girl; messenger; **agarrar a alguien de mandadero -ra** to use someone as an errand boy/girl repeatedly (he/she usually complains by saying:

"Ya me agarraste de mandadero -ra")

mandado errand; order (i.e., of groceries, at or from a store); groceries, foodstuffs; **hacer mandados** to run errands

mandador-ra (vars. of) *mandón -dona* bossy

mandar: **mandar a la chingada/ mandar al diablo/mandar a la fregada/mandar a la porra** to tell (someone) to go to hell (coll.), dismiss someone in extreme anger; **mandar a la chinita por tu amor** (euph. var. of) *mandar a la chingada (a la fregada, a la jodida)* to tell someone to go to hell (see also **a pasear(se), a paseo**); **mandar muy lejos** to tell someone to go fly a kite (fig.), tell someone off, get angry at someone; **¡ni lo mande Dios!** Heaven (God) forbid!; **¿quién te manda?** Who told you to get involved in this business?

manea brake (on a vehicle); **echar la(s) manea(s)** to apply the brakes, put the brakes on (lit. and fig.)

maneado -da or **maniado -da** limited in talent, with limited competency

manear or **maniar** va. to brake

manejador -ra (Ang.) manager; **manejador -ra de la ciudad** (Ang.) city manager

manejar or **manijar: rueda de manejar (manijar)** steering wheel (of a car)

manejera or **manijera** handlebars (on a bicycle); steering wheel (on a car); any type of handle; **írsele a alguien la manejera** to lose control of the steering wheel

manflor -flora m. male homosexual; f. lesbian

manga (slang) attractive (adj. ref. to persons); sharp dresser (coll.), person who dresses stylishly; **ariscar mangas** to roll up one's sleeves (for any reason, but esp. in preparation for a fistfight); **buscarle mangas al chaleco** to complicate matters

mangaza (slang) girl with an attractive figure

mango -ga handle (of a kitchen utensil or of any apparatus); m. (slang) penis; **pajuelearle el mango a alguien** to be good at something, excel: "A Godofredo le pajuelea el mango pa' jugar béisbol"

manijar (var. of) *manejar*

manijera (var. of) *manejera*

manil (slang) m. money

manita: dar (una) manita to lend a helping hand; **andar hasta las manitas** to be very drunk

manito (var. of) *hermanito*; **andar manitos** to be real buddy-buddy (slang), be on very friendly terms

mano (var. of) *hermano*; (coll.) friend, buddy, pal; (also used as a verbal stalling device, i.e., inserted when the speaker cannot think of what to say next); fpl. **chocar (las) manos** to shake hands; **estar a manos/ponerse a manos/quedar(se) a manos** to owe nothing to anyone, be even (coll.); to have avenged oneself; **irle (venirle) a alguien a la mano** to discipline a child by spanking him / her; **írsele a alguien la mano** to slip, lose control; to miscalculate; **mano a mano** on equal terms, even, tied; **meter mano** (vulg.) to engage in manual coitus, insert one's finger into a vagina to simulate copulation; to engage in

enthusiastic and vigorous sexual foreplay; **pasársele a alguien la mano** (var. of) *írsele a alguien la mano* (supra); **salir a manos** to break even in a game of chance; **sobar la mano** (fig., coll.) (var. of) *untar (la mano)* (Std.), to bribe, grease the palm (or hand) of (slang); **zafársele a alguien la mano** to slip up, lose control; miscalculate

manopla (slang) hand

manoseada or **manosiada** (ref. to a woman who has indulged her carnal appetites frequently, a woman who has been "handled" frequently)

manoseadera or **manosiadera** act of "handling" a woman; sexual foreplay

manoseador or **manosiador** m. (ref. to man who "handles" or engages in sexual foreplay with a woman)

manosear or **manosiar** va. to handle, pet, paw (etc., i.e., engage in vigorous sexual foreplay)

manoseo (id. to **manoseadera**, supra)

manque conj. (var. of) *aunque*

mantelito table napkin

mantenido -da m. gigolo; f. kept woman, mistress; mf. sponger

mantequía (var. of) *mantequilla*

mantía (var. of) *mantilla*

Manuela or **doña Manuela** or **doña Manuelita** (hum., slang) masturbation (Std. *masturbación*); **hacerse la manuela** (hum., slang) to masturbate, jack off (vulg., slang), pull it (vulg., slang) (Std. *masturbarse*)

manzanear or **manzaniar** va. to seek to gain favor through gifts

mañanear or **mañaniar** (slang) va.

to steal

mañanitas early morning serenade on the occasion of someone's birthday, typically sung outside the house of the celebrant

mapa or (more frequently) **mape** (both m.) (Eng.) mop (cf. **mope** et al.)

mapeada or **mapiada** action and effect of mopping (Eng.) (cf. **mapa, mape** et al.)

mapeador or **mapiador** (Eng.) m. mop; person who mops floors, mopper (see also *mapero -ra*)

mapear or **mapiar** (Eng.) va. to mop (see also **mopear** et al.)

mapero -ra (Eng.) person who mops floors, mopper (see also **mapeador** et al.)

máquina car, automobile; (coll.) fire engine; locomotive; **hecho -cha máquina** (coll.) adv. very rapidly (see also **a toda máquina**); **máquina de (cortar) zacate** lawn mower

maquinita barber's clippers

Maquis or **Maquishuel** (slang) (Hispanization of) Maxwell, Texas

maraca (slang) dollar, dollar bill

maravioso -sa (vars. of) *maravilloso -sa*

marca person ostracized by his/ her own peers or compatriots

marcado (var. of) *mercado*

marcado -da scar-faced

marcar va. to brand, scar

marchanta woman customer

marcho (slang) convict, prisoner

margayates mpl. confusion, disorder

María Juanita (slang) marihuana

maricocaimorfi (slang) mf. person who habitually uses marihuana, cocaine and morphine

mariguana (var. of) *marihuana*

mariguano -na or **marihuano -na** habitual marihuana user

marijuana (var. of) *marihuana*

mariola (slang) marihuana

mariposa (slang) prostitute

maritata mf. street vendor, peddler

marmaja (slang) money

maroma sommersault (see also **marometa**)

maromear or **maromiar** va. to set a trap for, seek to entrap; vn. to turn sommersaults; (fig.) to betray

maromeo act of betrayal

marometa sommersault (see also **maroma**)

marota tomboy, slightly masculine girl

marqueta (Eng.) market; meat market

marquetero -ra (Eng.) (cf. **marqueta**) clerk in a store or market; butcher

martiar or **martillar** (slang) to eat

martillo or **martío** (slang) food

marzo (slang) daffy, screwy, slightly crazy; **febrero loco y marzo otro poco** a little bit crazier with each passing day

marrana (pej.) bitch (term of insult); **marrana cuina** (pej.) fat and ugly old bitch (insult directed at a woman)

marrano: marrano de agua hippopotamus

marrar (var. of) *amarrar*

marroquiano -na (vars. of) *parroquiano -na*

marrullero -ra lazy, sluggish

más: de más antes of former days, of yesteryear, of older times; **más al rato** (pleonasm) (var. of) *al rato*; **más antes** (pleonastic var. of) *antes* before, beforehand; **más después** (pleonasm) (var. of) *después;* **más mejor** (pleonastic var. of) *mejor* better; **más que quién sabe qué** a lot, a great amount: "Ahora la ama más que quién sabe qué"; **más nada** (var. of) *nada más*: "No tengo más nada acá conmigo" 'I don't have anything else with me here'; **más ____ que quién sabe qué** (coll.) more ____ than you could possibly imagine; **entre más ____ más** the more ____ the more

masa (slang) mf. slowpoke, lethargic person; flabby, blubber-bellied (coll.)

masacota or **masacote** f. disorganized mixture, jumble of various items

mascada scarf

máscara (coll.) woman with an ugly face

masacudo -da doughy, having the appearance or consistency of dough

masero -ra vendor of ready-made dough for tortillas

Mases (Hispanization of) Mathis, Texas

masota beautiful and sexy woman, red hot mamma (slang) (see also **macita, mamacita, mamasota**)

masudo -da doughy, not well-baked (ref. to pastry or other dough product)

mata plant (any plant in general); **mata de sol** sunflower; **la mera mata** the real McCoy (coll.), the genuine article

mataburros msg. (coll.) dictionary, lexicon; cheap grade of whiskey

matagusanos msg. worm-killer, medicine used for purposes of deworming people or animals; any deworming agent

matolote m. type of spine-backed fish

matamosca m. (var. of) *matamoscas* msg., pl. flyswatter

matanza slaughterhouse

matatena children's game in which stones are thrown in the air

matauñas (slang) msg., pl. nail clipper(s)

mate: darle a alguien en el mero mate to hit someone right where it hurts

matón -tona m. (slang) gangster; self-styled lady-killer, Don Juan type; f. wicked and evil woman; mf. killer, assassin, murderer

matraca mf. chatterbox (coll.), person who talks incessantly

matralladora (var. of) *amatralladora* (in turn var. of) *ametralladora*

matrimoniar (slang) vr. to get married

matriz (slang) f. prostitute

matutena (var. of) *matatena*

maula clever, astute; **traer maula** (coll.) to be up to something, have something up one's sleeve (coll.)

mayate (pej.) mf. African American

mayestro -tra (vars. of) *maestro -tra*

mayor (Ang.) m. mayor (of a city) (Std. *alcalde*)

mayote m. nag, old horse

mayugar (orthog. var. of) *magullar*

mazorca (slang) teeth, set of teeth

mazuma (slang) money (<mazuma, ant. English <Yiddish, slang of the 1930's)

meadera frequent urinating

meadero (var. of) *meadera*

mear: mearse fuera de la borcelana (fig.) to miss the mark; (fig.) fail to resolve a problem; (fig.) to mess up a job (coll.), bungle, botch

mecanear or **mecaniar** vn. to do mechanical work, work as a mechanic

mecatazo whiplash, lash of a whip

mecate: andar como burro sin mecate to run wild and free, do as one pleases; **cada chango a su mecate y a darse vuelo** (lit. 'each monkey to his rope and start swinging') every man for himself, let each person do his own thing (slang)

meceta (var. of) *maceta*

meco -ca lower-class person; person in a bad mood; **mecos** (vulg.) semen, seminal fluid

mecha (Eng.) match (for lighting fire) (Std. *cerilla, fósforo*)

mechachito -ta (vars. of) *muchachito -ta*

mechar (Eng.) va. to match, compare (one thing with another); to match, harmonize (attempt to make two items harmonize with each other)

mechas disheveled hair, mop of hair (coll.); **agarrarse a las mechas/agarrarse de las mechas** to pull one another's hair in a fight; **irse a las mechas/irse de las mechas** to pass from a verbal to a physical battle (esp. one in which hair is pulled)

mechudo -da person with long and unkempt hair; hippie

medecina (var. of) *medicina*

mediagua: estar mediagua to be drunk

medicina: medicina de la botica / medicina de la farmacia / medicina de patente (Ang.) patent medicine (Std. *específico*)

mediero -ra sharecropper (unequal partner on a ranch or farm)

medio nickel, five-cent piece

Mejicle (slang) Mexico

mejicanada or **mexicanada** action or behavior typifying a Mexican; a group of Mexicans

mejor: a la mejor (Std. *a lo mejor*); **más mejor** (pleonasm) better (Std. *mejor*); **mejor mitad** (Ang.) f. better half (coll.), wife

Mela (nickname for) *Carmela*

mela (slang) human head

Mele (nickname for) *Guillermo*

melena (slang) head (body from the neck upward)

melitar m. (var. of) *militar* m. soldier

melón m. hornless or dehorned bull; **melona** f. (slang) human head

membrecía membership

membresía (orth. var. of) *membrecía*

Meme (Eng.) Mamie (woman's name)

Memo (nickname for) *Guillermo*

Menarde or **Menarve** (Hispanization of) Menard, Texas

menazar (var. of) *amenazar*

méndigo -ga (vars. of) *mendigo -ga* (latter is infrequently used in Texas); m. rogue, trickster; cheap, stingy; mean, base, wicked

meneada or **meniada** or **meneadero -ra** or **meniadero -ra** the act of stirring (esp. a liquid in a container): "Dale una meniada al caldo" 'Stir up the soup'

menear: menearlas or **menear las nalgas** to wiggle one's hindquarters

menijar (var. of) *manejar*

meniu (Eng.) m. menu

menjurge m. (var. of) *mejunge* m. disorderly pile of objects jumbled together

menorar (var. of) *minorar*

menos: de menos at least (Std. *a lo menos, por lo menos*); **entre menos burros, más olotes/mientras menos burros, más olotes** the fewer people, the more there is to go around (often said with ref. to food); **estar en todo menos en misa** be minding everybody's business except one's own; **entre menos ____, menos ____** the fewer ____, the fewer ____; **hacer (de) menos** to slight: "Mi mamá se enojó con sus vecinos porque la hicieron (de) menos en la fiesta" 'My mom got angry with her neighbors because they slighted her at the party'

menso -sa ignorant; foolish; dummy (fig.)

mensual (slang) (hum. var. of) *menso -sa*

mente: írsele a uno la mente to lose one's train of thought; to have a mental lapse

mentidera (coll.) several lies at once, string of lies

mentir vn. to be wrong, be in error: "Pues, vino a las ocho... No, miento, vino a las ocho y media"

mentira: una bola de mentiras a pack of lies (Std. *una sarta de mentiras*)

mentiritas: de mentiritas in make-believe fashion

mentolato (Eng.?) mentholatum

menudo soup or stew made with various types of tripe and well seasoned, esp. with salt; *menudo* is popularly known as an efficacious hangover cure

meón, -ona person who urinates frequently, weak-bladdered (coll.)

mero himself/herself (intensifer): "Él mero, lo dijo" 'He himself said it'; very: "La pusiste a(l) mero último" 'You put her at the very end'; **el mero bebé** the one and only (coll.); **el mero mero/el mero petatero** (slang) the big boss, the big cheese, the head honcho (slang); the real McCoy, the genuine article (slang); **el mero jodón/el mero chingón (chingonón)** (slang) the big boss, the head honcho (slang); **ya mero/ya merito** almost, nearly

mes m. menstrual period; **tener el mes** to have one's (menstrual) period

mesa: salir por debajo de la mesa to always come out on the short end of the stick (fig.), always fail in whatever one attempts

mesmo -ma (vars. of) *mismo -ma*

mestro -tra (vars. of) *maestro -tra*

¡métele! (var. of) *¡arrémétele!* interj. Hit 'em!; Hurry up!; Get to work! (etc.)

meter va. to stick, sting (slang), charge excessively for: "Le metieron quinientos dólares por esa carrucha" 'They stung him $500 for that old heap'; **en la que me metí** a fine mess I got myself into; **a todo meter** full speed ahead, very rapidly; stupendous, exceptional, marvelous (etc.); **meter a alguien en bola** to get someone into trouble, involve someone in a conflict; **meter a alguien en la ley** to bring a lawsuit against someone; **meter a alguien en un trabajo** to use one's influence to obtain a job for someone; **meterle a alguien una paliza/reatiza/porriza** (etc.) to give someone a severe beating; **meter caballo** vn. (slang) (fig.) to put in a bad word (about someone), speak ill of; **meter el**

codo (slang) to put in a good word for someone, speak well of; **meter el cloche** to step on the clutch (of a vehicle); **meter hombro** (fig.) to help out, lend a helping hand; (fig.) to put in a good word for someone, speak well of; **meter mano** (vulg) to engage in manual coitus, insert one's finger into a vagina to simulate copulation; to engage in enthusiastic and vigorous sexual foreplay; **meterle duro/ meterle mucho** to do something to excess (esp. the drinking of alcohol): "Le mete duro a la tomada" 'He really drinks heavily'; vr. to consume, eat up: "Me metí dos platos de frijoles"; to cover territory, travel: "Me metí 20 millas en una hora"; **meterse en el ejército/cuerpo aéreo/la marina** (etc.) to enlist in the army, air force, navy (etc.); **metérsela doblada a alguien** to get the best of someone in a business deal, a sports competition, etc. "A Pedro se la metieron doblada en ese juego"; **metérsele a alguien en la cabeza** (coll.) to get (something) into one's head, for an idea to occur to someone; to be bullheaded about something

metiche or **metichi** mf. busybody, meddler

metido -da: metida del sol sunset (Std. *puesta del sol*, less common); **estar muy metido -da con alguien** to be very involved with someone (esp. in a love affair); **estar muy metido -da en algo** to be very absorbed in something; f. (vulg.) act of fornication (see also **dar una metida**)

metralladora (var. of) *ametralladora*

mexicano-americano (Ang.) Mexican-American (Std. *mexicoamericano*)

México: México ven por tu gente (expression of disapproval directed at Mexican-Americans who are making a spectacle of themselves); **México viejo** (Old) Mexico (as distinct from New Mexico, U.S. state)

mezquino wart

mezquite (slang) m. month

mí (personal pron.): **¿a mí qué?/ ¿a mí qué me da?** What's that to me?, What concern's that of mine? (expresses indifference)

miadera (var. of) *meadera*

miar (var. of) *mear*

Micaila (var. of) *Micaela* (woman's name)

miedo: cagarse de miedo (vulg.) to be frightened out of one's skull (slang), be extremely frightened; **¿quién dijo miedo?** who's afraid?, me, afraid? (not I);

miembrecía (var. of) *membrecía*

mentras: mientras menos at the very least (Std. *cuanto menos*); **por mientras** for the time being, meanwhile

miércoles (euph.) msg. feces, "number two" (euph.; the word that *miércoles* avoids is *mierda*); **!miércoles!** interj. (mildly euph.) Damn!, Hell!

mierda (vulg.) excrement, feces (also with ref. to persons:) (vulg.) son-of-a-bitch, no-good bastard (etc.); **acá la mierda** (vulg., slang) a long way away, half way to hell and gone (slang), way the shit out there (vulg., slang); **no valer mierda** (vulg.) not to be worth a shit (vulg.), not to be worth a damn

migra (slang) or **migración** immigration service (U.S.); U.S. immigration office; U.S. immigration
officer(s); U.S. border patrol
(patrolman)

Miguel (slang) (personal pron.) I;
me (hum. identification between
mí and *Miguel*)

milagro: ¡qué milagro! What a
pleasant surprise!

militario (var. of) *militar* n. & adj.

Milo -la (dims. of) *Emilio -lia*

milque (Eng.) f. milk

mimela (slang.) (personal pron.) I
(Std. *yo*) (cf. **Miguel**, supra)

Mine (Eng. Minnie or dim. of)
Minerva, Herminia

Mingo (dim. of) *Domingo*

mión, miona (vars. of) *meón,
meona*

mira (Eng.) f. meter (e.g., parking, water [etc.])

miramonte (slang) (3rd pers. sg.
pres. ind. of *mirar*)

mirar: mirar adelante para (Ang.)
to look forward to, anticipate;
estar de mírame y déjame (pej.,
said with ref. to a homely woman):
"Esa mujer está de mírame y
déjame"; **¡mira nomás!** (interj. of
surprise): Well I'll be damned!,
Will you look at that!

mireles (slang) (personal pron.) I
(Std. *yo*) (1st pers. sg. subject
pron.) (cf. **Miguel, mimela** et al.)

mirojear or **mirojiar** va. to peep,
sneak a look at, glance at covertly
and often with lust aforethought

Misa: La Misa (hum. or else
mock Eng. for) La Mesa, Texas

misa: misa de gallo (var. of) *misa
del gallo*; **estar en todo menos en
misa** to mind everyone else's
business but one's own

Misión (re-Hispanization of) Mis-
sion, Texas

misiricordia (var. of) *misericordia*

míspero (var. of) *níspero* Japanese plum tree

mistear or **mistiar** (Eng.) va. to
miss; to fail to attend (e.g. a class);
to feel the absence of: "Te misteo
mucho, vuelve pronto"; to fail to
hit (e.g. a target): "Le mistié al
pajarito con mi rifle"

míster (Eng.) m. mister, Mr.

mita y mita (var. of) *mitá y mitá*
(*mitad y mitad*) half-and-half (as
when one person shares something with another)

mito: cortar el mito (slang) to
silence, shut up: "Le cortaron el
mito" 'They shut him up'

mitote m. uproar, din; distur-
bance; trouble; noisy party, loud
festivity

mitotear or **mitotiar** va. to stir up,
incite; vn. to make trouble, raise
hell (coll.), to go on a wild spree

mitotero -ra rowdy, noisy; trouble-
some, hard to handle; instigator,
rabble-rouser, troublemaker

mixear or **mixiar** (Eng.) va. to mix
(see also **mixtear** et al.) (note: of
the four variants, *mixiar* is the
most prevalent)

mixtear or **mixtiar** (Eng.) va. to
mix

moca (Eng.?) mug (e.g. for
drinking coffee)

moco: tirar moco (slang) to cry;
(see also **dar en el moco**)

mocha switch-engine (locomotive
used to shuffle cars in a trainyard)

mochacho -cha (vars. of) *muchacho -cha*

mochar (Eng.?) va. & vn. to
mooch off of (slang), sponge
(coll.), live off the earnings of
others; **¡móchate!** (slang) Bug off!,

Get out of here!, Cut out! (slang)

mochera camp-follower (woman who resides near a military base so as to be proximate to the amorous attentions of military personnel, who often pay her for services rendered)

mocho -cha (said of someone missing an extremity, i.e., one-handed, one-armed, one-legged); m. soldier (usually of low rank); m. broken, spoken imperfectly (ref. to language): "Juanito habla (el) inglés mocho" 'Johnny speaks a broken English'; impudent, sassy

mofla or **mofle** (Eng.) m. muffler (aut.) (Std. *silenciador* m.)

mogote m. brush land, brush country

mojado -da illegal immigrant to the U.S. from Mexico, wetback (pej.)

mojarra mf. illegal immigrant to the U.S. from Mexico, wetback (pej.)

mojo (var. of) *moho* rust

mojón m. solid drenching, thorough soaking

mojoso -sa (vars. of) *mohoso -sa* rusty

molcajete: cara de molcajete (slang) (pej.) (insult used to indicate a very ugly face)

molcas (var. of) *molcajete*; **ciertas molcas** (used to ref. to person whose name one wishes to avoid mentioning; cf. **ciertos elotes**)

moler: moler gente to bother (someone), make a nuisance of oneself: "¡Cómo te gusta moler gente!"

molón -lona pest, bothersome person; complainer

molote m. burn of hair, topknot

molleja pocket watch

mollera: mollera caída fallen fontanelle (the soft part of a baby's skull which sometimes "falls" or retracts before becoming fully hardened); **mollera cerrada** (fig.) (ref. to person who is slow to learn)

mollete m. cake baked in the shape of a loaf

momio -mia dunderhead, blockhead, dolt

momio (var. of) *momia*

mompes (Eng.) mpl. mumps

Mona (dim. of) *Ramona*

monarco movie theater, cinema (<?, perhaps *mono*, q.v., or, through metonymy *Monarco*, name of a particular theater)

moneada or **moniada** or **moneadera** or **moniadera** act of being or attempting to be cute or amusing

monesterio (var. of) *monasterio*

moni msg. or **monis** mpl. (Eng.) money

monito -ta (rus.) (vars. of) *bonito -ta*

monita paper doll, cartoon cutout doll

mono (slang) movie theater, cinema; movie, film; **apretarle a alguien el mono** to bewitch, hex someone; **mono de agua** fireplug; **ser muy mono -na** to be a very elegant dresser

mononteros (var. of) *monotoneros* gang of attackers

monquiar (Eng.) (slang) vn. to monkey around with (slang), engage in often meaningless activities for the sake of killing time

monstro -tra (vars. of) *monstruo -trua*

mope (Eng.) m. (infrequently used var. of *mape*)

mopeada or **mopiada** (Eng.) (vars.

of) *mapeada, mapiada* (Eng.), resp.

mopeador -ra or **mopiador -ra** (Eng.) (vars. of) *mapeador -dora, mapiador -dora* (Eng.), resp.

mopear or **mopiar** (Eng.) (vars. of) *mapear, mapiar* (Eng.), resp.

moqueadera or **moquiadera** act of crying; nasal drip

moquear or **moquiar** (slang) vn. to cry; to drip (said of noses)

moquera or **moquería** act of crying; nasal drip

moquetazo punch in the nose

moquiento -ta (vars. of) *mocoso -sa*

mora (slang) juvenile detention home, house of correction for boys or girls; pl. **pescar en las moras** to catch (someone) red-handed, catch in the act

Moras: Las Moras (Spanish name for) Brackettville, Texas

mordelón -lona (pej.) m. policeman, f. policewoman (usually ref. to corrupt policemen, i.e., those who accept *mordidas*)

mordida bribe; payoff, kickback

More (Hispanization of) Moran, Texas

moreteado -da or **moretiado -da** bruised, covered with bruises

moretear or **moretiar** va. to bruise; vr. to bruise oneself

morfa (var. of) *morfina*

morfiniento -ta user of narcotic drugs (esp. morphine)

morido -da (vars. of) *muerto -ta* (ppart. of *morir*)

moriendo (var. of) *muriendo* (ger. of *morir*)

moriera, morieras, etc. (vars. of) *muriera, murieras*, etc. (past subj. conjugation of *morir*)

morieron (var. of) *murieron* (3rd

pers. pl. pret. of *morir*)

morió (var. of) *murió* (3rd pers. sg. pret. of *morir*)

mormación f. nasal obstruction

mormado -da nasal (ref. to sound of the voice of a person with a temporary articulatory defect resulting from a stopped-up nose, a throat inflammation, etc.)

mormar vr. to contract an inflammation of the nasal passages, the throat, etc. (and which serves to nasalize or otherwise distort the vocal quality)

mormullo (var. of) *murmullo*

mormurar (var. of) *murmurar*

Moro or **Morondel** (slang) (Hispanization of) Martindale, Texas

morosaico -ca (Eng.) motorcycle

morragia (var. of) *hemorragia*

morraludo (ref. to man wearing baggy pants)

morro -rra short and chubby; f. squeeze (slang), girlfriend

morrocoyo (slang) any type of insect

mortificación f. worry, preoccupation

mortificar va. & vr. to worry

mosca (fig.) pest, bothersome person; **mosca en leche** dark-complexion person married to (or associating with) a fair-skinned person; **por si las moscas** just in case

mosquerío swarm of flies

mosquiento -ta fly-ridden, abounding in flies

mosquita muerta person who pretends to be timid and reserved but is not; wolf in sheep's clothing (fig.), person pretending to be harmless

mostrar: mostrar la oreja to show one's bad side, reveal one's defects; to reveal one's true colors

mota f. moss balls on trees (type of tree fungus); (slang) marihuana

Mota, (La) Spanish name for Hunter, Texas

motea or **motella** (rus.) (vars. of) *botella*

moteado -da or **motiado -da** (vars. of) *goteado -da* or *gotiado -da*; (slang) **andar moteado -da** to be high from using marihuana

motear or **motiar** (slang) vn. to smoke pot (slang), smoke marihuana

motel (Eng.) m. motel

moto -ta (slang) marihuana freak, habitual user of marihuana; **andar moto -ta** to be high on marihuana

motor: bicicleta de motor motorcycle

motorcicleta (var. of) *motocicleta*

motosaica m. (Eng.) motorcycle

mover: mover la jicotera to stir things up, get things moving (coll.); **moverse de casa** vr. (Ang.) to move, change residences (Std. *mudarse de casa*); **no le muevas** leave well enough alone

movida: movida chueca (slang) crooked move, unsavory deal; illicit love affair; **tener movida** (slang) to have plans for a sexual assignation

moyote m. mosquito

mu (var. of) *muy*

muchachón -chona m. boyish; f. girlish: "Se ve muy muchachón" 'He looks very boyish'

muchar (var. of) *mochar* to cut (off)

muchito -ta (vars. of) *muchachito -ta*

mueble (rus.) m. automobile, car

muela: contar las muelas pl. to pull the wool over one's eyes (fig.), deceive: "A mí no me cuentes las muelas: tú me robaste ese dinero"

muelón -lona bothersome person, pest

muerto -ta: caer(se) muerto to drop dead; (slang) to pay up, pay, cough up (slang); **estar muerto -ta** to be unaware of a fraud or a deception; to be adamant, stubborn, hard to convince; **muerto -ta de hambre** (fig.) (said of a greedy and selfish person); **no tener en qué caerse muerto** to be totally broke, penniless

mugrar (rus.) va. to dirty, make dirty; vr. to get dirty, dirty oneself (see also **enmugrar**)

mugre f. (word used to name something the speaker has forgotten) what-chamacallit, thing-amagig, gizmo, etc.); prostitute; tramp; scum (of society) (fig.), worthless individual

mugrero junkyard (fig.), place filled up with with useless and dirty objects; botch-job, work badly done; **hacer (un) mugrero** to botch, mess up a job or other commitments; to mess up a place (coll.), make it dirty, soiled or unitidy; **hacer (un) mugrero y medio** to mess up and then some (coll.) (ref. to a place or a job)

mujer: mujer de la calle (pej.) streetwalker, prostitute; **mujer jugada** or **mujer paseada/pasiada** or **mujer pateada/patiada** woman with a lot of mileage on her (coll.), woman with considerable sexual experience

mujercita baby girl: "Mi tía tuvo una mujercita" 'My aunt had a baby girl'

mujerero (var. of) *mujeriego*

mujeringo (pej.) effeminate, sissy,

fruity (slang)

mulo -la: ser mulo -la (fig.) to be stubborn; f. (Eng.) (slang) money, moola (slang)

muleta: aguantar muleta (see **aguantar**); **estar de muleta** (coll.) to be in a bad mood

muncho -cha (vars. of) *mucho -cha*

munincipal mf. (var. of) *municipal*

mf.

murir (var. of) *morir*

música; tener or **llevar la música por dentro** (said of an introverted person) to have one's real self hidden; **música de boca** harmonica, mouth organ

musiquero -ra musician

mustio -tia ill-humored; dull, lusterless

N

na (var. of) *nada* nothing

nacional mf. Mexican, Mexican national, someone from Mexico; mpl. (coll.) beans, frijoles

Nacho -cha (dims. of) *Anastasio -sia*

nacho (Eng.<natch<naturally) (slang) naturally, sure thing (coll.), you bet (coll.)

nada: nada vale there's nothing to, the ____ is insignificant .... (expression used to indicate that one thing is of little importance compared to something else, which is worse): "Nada vale la borrachera, lo peor es la cruda" 'Being drunk is nothing, the worse part is the hangover'; **por nada** (var. of) *de nada*: "Muchas gracias — Por nada" 'Thanks a lot — You're welcome'

naday (slang) adv. no (usually a negative response to a question)

nadien (var. of) *nadie* pron.

nadís f. (var. of) *nariz* f.

nagua or **nahua** (vars. of) *naguas* fpl. petticoat; skirt

nagualón -lona fat and flabby; said of one whose clothes hang loosely and unevenly

nagualudo -da (vars. of) *nagualón -lona*

naguas (var. of) *enaguas*; **ama-rrarse las naguas** (fig.) to act resolutely

naidie(n) (vars. of) *nadie* pron.

naifa (Eng.) knife

nailón (Eng.) m. nylon

nalgas: (slang) adv. no (usually a negative response to a question); **andar con las nalgas de fuera** to be wearing rags (coll.), be dressed in threadbare or tattered clothing; (fig.) to be poverty stricken; **nalgas pelonas** (vulg.) (hum.) bare-assed: "Él anda con las nalgas pelonas" 'He's going around bare-assed'; (see **dar las nalgas**)

nalgatorio (hum.) big buttocks

nalgón -gona (vars. of) *nalgudo -da*

nalgueada or **nalguiada** spanking

nalguear or **nalguiar** va. to spank; to pat someone on the buttocks

nana baby-sitter

nanay (slang) adv. no (usually a negative response to a question)

Nando -da (dims. of) *Fernando -da*

napquetín (Eng.) m. napkin (Std. *servilleta*)

naqueado -da or **naquiado -da** (Eng.) knocked out, unconscious (see also **noqueado** et al.)

naquear or **naquiar** (Eng.) va. to

knock out, render unconscious; vn. to knock on a door

naquin (Eng.) m. napkin

naranjado -da (vars. of) *ana-ranjado -da*

naranjales (slang) adv. (var. of) *naranjiles* adv.

naranjas or **naranjas chinas** or **naranjas de la China (trajo el cartero)** (slang) no (negative response to a question): "¿Vienes conmigo? — ¡Naranjas!"

naranjiles (slang) adv. no (negative response to a question) (cf. **naranjas**)

Naranjo (Hispanization of) Orange Grove, Texas

narco (slang) member of the narcotics squad of the police force; detective (in general) (Eng.? <nark)

nariz fsg. or fpl. (slang) adv. no (usually a negative response to a question); **ser nariz** to be nosy, be a busybody (coll.), be overly interested in the affairs of others (see also **narizón -zona**); pl. **sorber con (por) las narices** to sniff, inhale through the nose; fpl. **narices de tísico** good sense of smell: "Tienes unas narices de tísico" (often said in exasperation, as by a mother to a child who has succeeded in smelling out a cake that was to be kept whole until dinnertime)

naranja dulce f. children's game in which the following verse is sung by a moving circle of participants: "Naranja dulce, limón partido / Dame un abrazo que yo te pido"; one child is stationed inside the circle, and when he/she succeeds in embracing one of those forming part of the circle,

that child enters the center and is replaced by its former occupant

Nato -ta (dims. of) *Natividad* or *Natalio -lia*

natural m. "regular" haircut, however defined (traditionally a cut in which the hair does not cover the ears or descend below the collar line

nayotas (slang) fpl. nose

navaja: navaja de bolsa (Ang.? or var. of?) *navaja de bolsillo* (Std. *cortaplumas, navaja*) pocketknife, penknife; **sacarle la navaja a alguien** to pull a knife on someone

navajear or **navajiar** va. to cut with a knife

navajero -ra flatterer; knife wielder (person whose favorite weapon is a knife)

ne (slang) adv. no (usually a negative response to a question)

necedera (var. of) *necedad* foolishness

necesidad: hacer las necesidades (euph.) to go to the bathroom (for purposes of fecal or urinary evacuation)

necio -cia annoying, bothersome; fussy, fidgety, irritable: "Yo creo que el niño tiene calentura porque está muy necio" 'I think the child has a temperature because he's very fussy'

necitar (var. of) *necesitar*

negrada large group of African Americans

negrete (slang) adv. no (usually a negative response to a question)

negrita elderberry (Sambucus mexicana) (prepared as a tea and used to treat colic)

negro(s) (slang) adv. no (usually a negative response to a question); (pej.) mpl. **cena de negros** any disorderly gathering; a shambles

Nei mf. *Inéz* mf.

nejo -ja dirty; yellowed (ref. to old tortillas)

nel or **nela** or **nela canela** (slang) no (negative response to a question)

Nelo -la (dims. of) *Manuel -la*

Nelsen or **Nelson** or **Nelson dijo Wilson, préstame tu llave Stilson** (slang) adv. no (usually a negative response to a question)

nene or **nenel** (slang) adv. no (usually a negative response to a question)

nequin (Eng.) mf. napkin

nerel (slang) adv. no (usually a negative response to a question)

neta (Eng.) net (tennis or volley-ball net)

Neto (dim. of) *Ernesto*

ni: ¡ni lo mande Dios! Heaven (God) forbid! God, I hope not! **ni madre** (coll.) not a thing, not a single mother-lovin' thing (slang): "¿Qué hay en la hielera? — Ni madre"; **ni peligro** not a chance, fat chance (slang); **ni por ahi te pudres** (said to a friend or close relative who has not visited you in a while) 'What's become of you?'; **ni soca** (slang) not a bit, not at all

nicanor (slang) adv. no (usually a negative response to a question)

nicle (Ang.) m. five-cent piece; (slang) adv. no (usually a negative response to a question)

nicolás (slang) no (usually a negative response to a question)

niervo (var. of) *nervio*

nieve f. ice cream (Std. *helado*); cocaine; **nieve de palito** eskimo pie, ice cream on a stick

nievería (var. of) *nevería*

nievero -ra (vars. of) *nevero -ra*

ice-cream vendor; a person fond of eating ice cream

nigachura or **nigasura** or **niguesura** (Eng.) slingshot, nigger's shooter (ant. slang)

niguas (slang) no (negative response to a question)

nil (slang) adv. no (usually a negative response to a question)

ningunear or **ninguniar** (slang) va. to kill, wipe out (slang), off (slang)

Nino -na (dims. of) *Bernardino -na*

niño: el niño más (ref. to person whose name one wishes to avoid mentioning) (cf. **ciertos elotes [verdes], [molcas]**); **niño del ojo** pupil (of eye)

niunca (var. of) *nunca*

Niuquis (slang) New Braunfels, Texas (see also **Nuquis**)

no: ¡no digo! interj. I told you so!, Didn't I tell you?!; How about that? (indicates admiration for a thing, a feat, etc.); **no haber derecho** to be inexcusable, not be right (fitting, proper): "Pepe se emborrachó otra vez con el dinero que le prestaste — Ya lo sé, y, hombre, no hay derecho" 'Joey got drunk again with the money you lent him — I already know that, and, man, that's inexcusable'; **no parar(le) la cola a alguien** (a set expression applied to one who is constantly on the go): "A Juan no le para la cola aun cuando está enfermo" 'John is constantly on the go even when he's sick'; **¿no que no _____ ?** Didn't you say that _____?: "¿No que no te casabas?" 'I thought you said you were never going to get married!'; **¿no que no chiquito -ta?** I thought you told me you weren't (going to do whatever you said); **ya si no** after all, when everything is considered: "La muerte de su hermana lo acongojó mucho — Ya si no" 'His sister's death hit him very hard — After all'

noblado -da   (vars. of) *nublado -da*

nocaut   (Eng.) m. knockout (in boxing) (see also **nacaut**)

noche   late at night, late hours of the night: "Vino muy noche" 'He came very late last night'

nochebuena   poinsetta plant (Euphorbia pulcherrima)

nochecita   adv. fairly late at night

nodriza   nurse (in general) (Std. *enfermera*)

nojado -da   (rus.) (vars. of) *enojado -da*

nojar   (rus.) (var. of) *enojar*

nojotros -tras   (rus.) (vars. of) *nosotros -tras*

nomás   adv. just; only; no sooner; **aquí nomás/ay nomás** just so-so: "¿Cómo le va? — Ay nomás"; How about that?, What do you think of that? (often a slightly self-congratulatory response to a compliment); **no nomás** not just; not only; **nomás en cuanto** (var. of) *en cuanto* as soon as; **nomás no** (resolute negative reply to a request or a suggestion): "¿Nos puedes hacer ese favor? — ¡Nomás no!"; (iron.) Yes indeed, Yes sirree: "¿Se lo llevaron a la cárcel? — Nomás no"; **nomás por no dejar** to do something just to while the time away or just for the hell of it

nones   (slang) adv. no (usually a negative response to a question)

nopalero -ra   person employed to cut *nopales* or to clear land

covered with *nopales*; very fond of eating *nopales (nopalitos)* (prickly pears); (pej.) common laborer, peon

noquear or **noquiar**   (Eng.) va. to knock out (in boxing); vn. to knock on a door (see also **naquear** et al.)

noria   well (in general, e.g., **noria de agua** water well, **noria de aceite** oil well); drain

norteado -da or **nortiado -da**   crazy, nutty, cracked (coll.), disoriented (fig.)

nortear or **nortiar**   va. to drive crazy; vr. to go crazy

nortecito   cold front accompanied by strong winds from the north

novela   (var. of) *telenovela*

noviero -ra   easily enamored, quick fo fall in love (ref. to person who flits from *novio -via* to *novio -via*)

nublazón   f. (var. of) *nublado* storm cloud; cloudiness

nublina   (var. of) *neblina*

nuecera   a woman who works in a pecan factory as a processor, packager, etc.

nuecería   pecan factory, pecan processing plant

nuevas   news (i.e., information forming part of a newspaper account or media broadcast)

nuevecísimo -ma   (vars. of) *novísimo -ma* very new, brand new

nuevecito -ta   very new, brand new

nuiquis   (slang) New Braunfels, Texas (see also **niuquis**)

ñango -ga   thin, scrawny

ñublado -da   (ant. Std.) (vars. of) *nublado -dao*

ñudo   (ant. Std.) (var. of) *nudo*

O

obedencia (var. of) *obediencia*

oceano or **ociano** (vars. of) *océano*

odioso -sa incorrigible; overbearing

ofecina (var. of) *oficina*

ofendor -ra (Eng.) offender; juvenile delinquent

oficina (Ang.) political office, elective office (e.g., mayor, congressman, etc.): "¿Pa' qué oficina estás corriendo?" 'What office are you running for?'

ofrecido -da apple-polisher, flatterer; f. woman who is prone to throwing herself at a man's feet, putting herself thereby at his mercy

oido -da (vars. of) *oído -da*

ójala y (var. of) *ojalá (que)*: "Ójala y vengas pronto" 'I hope you come soon'

ojete (vulg.) anus; stingy, cheap, parsimonious

ojo: ojos capotudos bulging eyes, pop eyes (slang); drooping eyelids; **ojo de botón** buttonhole; **ojo de chícharo** (slang) alert, sharp; **ojo de venado** deer's eye (Muzuna sloani) (used as an amulet for protection against *El Ojo* — the Evil Eye); **hacer ojo** to cast a spell on someone, give someone the *mal de ojo*; **quedarle a alguien el ojo:** "¿Cómo le quedó el ojo?" 'How does that grab you?' (slang), 'How do you like that as a result?'; **traer a alguien entre ojos** to have one's eye on someone, be watching someone for any little slip (misbehavior)

olo, oles, ole, etc. (vars., chiefly rus., of) *huelo, hueles, huele*, etc. (pres. ind. conjugation of *oler*)

olote m. corncob (ear of corn with husk and grains removed); **entre menos burros más olotes** the less you eat the more there'll be for someone else (often said as a reprimand to a child who refuses to eat)

olla (slang) buttocks, ass; **pata-learle (pataliarle) a alguien la olla** to kick someone in the ass; to beat someone up in a fight

ombligón -gona ponderous, heavyset (ref. to persons); (said of a person with a large navel)

onda trend of the moment (in style, thought, speech, etc.), latest fad; **estar en la onda** to be up-to-date, with it (slang); **en onda** turned on, with it, up-to-date

onde (var. of) *donde*

onque (rus.) (var. of) *aunque*

¿ontá? (rus.) (var. of) *¿dónde está?*

¡opa! or ¡ópale! Hey!, Hey you! Watch out!; Uff! (grunt issued when lifting a heavy object)

oquis (var. of) *de oquis, dioquis* advs. (see also **andar dioquis, estar dioquis**)

ora (var. of) *ahora*

¡órale! interj. Hurry up!; That's it!, That's right!; fine by me, okay, sure; Throw it!, Let's have it!, Over here!; Stop it!, Knock it off! (coll.); ¡**órale, órale!** Do it right now!

oralia (slang) (var. of) *órale*

orden m. (Ang.) any request for merchandise (Std. *pedido*)

ordenar (Ang.) va. to order, request merchandise (Std. *pedir*)

oreja handle (on a pitcher, a mug, etc.); telephone receiver and mouthpiece; hearing aid; pl. (slang) yes (affirmative response to a question); **apachurrar oreja/ planchar oreja/trampar oreja** (slang) to sleep; **enseñar la oreja/ mostrar la oreja** to show one's bad side, reveal one's defects; to reveal one's true colors; **parar la(s) oreja(s)** to perk up one's ear(s), listen attentively (usually so as to hear what one should not); **tirar oreja** (slang) to listen

orgullecer (var. of) *enorgullecer*

orilla: **estar de orilla** to be in a good mood; **ser de orilla** to be temperamental, mercurial

orillar vr. to pull over to the curb of the street (when driving a car)

orinada act of urinating

orita (var. of) *ahorita* right now

ormi (Eng.) m. army

orquestra (var. of) *orquesta*

orutar (var. of) *eru(c)tar*

oruto (var. of) *eru(c)to*

otate m. bamboo pole or stick (Bambu arundinacea)

otro mf.: msg. **el otro cahete (de la cara)** or **el otro lado (del charco)** Mexico; mpl. **ser de los otros** (slang) to be a (male) homosexual; fpl. **ser de las otras** to be a lesbian

ovaroles (Eng.) mpl. overalls (type of work pants) (see also **overoles**)

oven (Eng.) m. oven (Std. *horno*)

overoles (Eng.) overalls (type of work pants)

óvulos vaginal suppositories (which may be used as contraceptives)

oyí, oyiste, oyimos (vars. of) *oí, oíste, oímos* (1st and 2nd pers. sg and 1st pers. pl. pret. forms of *oír*)

oyido -da (vars. of) *oído -da*

P

pa' (var. of) *para* (prep.)

paca bale; pack

pacá (var. of) *para acá*: "Ven pacá" 'Come here'

pacencia (var. of) *paciencia*

pachanga (coll.) party, festivity

pachocha (slang) money

pachorras mf. slowpoke

pachorrudo -da slowpoke

pachucano (var. of) *pachuco* the dialect of the Pachuco

pachuco -ca Chicano "zoot-suiter" of the 1940's; m. boy or f. girl from El Paso, Texas; m. the dialect of the Pachuco; **El Pachuco** (slang) El Paso, Texas (There are several possible explanations of the word's origin: that it is a deliberate deformation of *Paso* with probable support from the Mexican city of Pachuca, or that the deformation of *Paso* may form part of the well-known process whereby nicknames beginning with *c* derive from syllables whose initial consonant is s, thus: *Chente <Vicente*)

pachuquismo linguistic oddity said to be typical of *pachucos*

paciencia: chingar (fregar, joder) la paciencia (vulg.) to try one's patience, nag the hell out of (vulg.), pester the hell out of (vulg.), bother

pacienta (var. of) *paciente* f.: "El paciente y la pacienta tenían mucha paciencia"

pacito (var. of the dim. of) *papacito* daddy (term of endearment in child language)

Paco -ca (dims. of) *Francisco -ca*

pacoima (slang) square (slang), person not up-to-date, not "with" whichever current trends

pacón (Eng.) m. popcorn

paded f. (child language var. of) *pared*

pader f. (var. of) *pared* f.

padrasto (var. of) *padrastro*

padre (slang) keen, terrific, neat, etc.; **está padre, (bato -ta)** (slang) (iron. expression used to indicate that one's feelings have been hurt; the implication is that revenge will be taken or poetic justice will prevail); **¡qué padre madre!** (slang) What a broad!, What a doll! (ref. to a very attractive woman); **padre de más de cuatro** (slang) he-man, stud, macho

padrote (slang) m. pimp; gigolo

paentro or **pa'entro** (vars. of) *para adentro*

pafuela (var. of) *pajuela*

pafuelazo (var. of) *pajuelazo*

pafueleada or **pafueliada** (vars. of) *pajueleada* or *pajueliada*, resp.

pafuelear or **pafueliar** (vars. of) *pajuelear* or *pajueliar*, resp.

pa' fuera (see **dar pa'fuera**)

pagador -ra person who settles debts promptly

pago pay, wages

pagre (rus.) (var. of) *padre*

pagrecito (rus.) (var. of) *padrecito*

pagulear or **paguliar** (slang) to pay (see also **paulear** or **pauliar**)

pai (Eng.) m. pie

paimentado -da (vars. of) *pavimentado -da*

paimentar (var. of) *pavimentar*

paimento (var. of) *pavimento*

paine m. (rus.) (var. of) *peine* m.

paipa (Eng.) pipe, smoking pipe; waterpipe

pais m. (var. of) *país* m.

paisa mf. (var. of) *paisano -na*

pajarear or **pajariar** (slang) va. to look; to see; to watch, keep an eye on (coll.)

pájaro (slang) jailbird, prison inmate; **pájaro -ra nalgón -gona** (slang) person with a large posterior, fat ass (vulg.); (pej.) weakling, effeminate person, wimp

pajuela woman of easy virtue, whore

pajuelazo whipping, (physical) blow; shot or gulp of liquor

pajueleada or **pajueliada** whipping

pajuelear or **pajueliar** va. to whip; **pajuelearle a alguien (el mango) (aparato) para hacer algo** to excel at doing something: "A Roberto le pajuelea el mango pa' enseñar idiomas"; **pajuelearle el callo a alguien** (said of feet which smell badly): "A Primitivo le pajuela el callo"

pal (var. [contraction] of) *para el*: "¡Vámonos pal centro!"

palabra: palabra mala swearword, dirty word (Std. *palabrota*)

palabrota very erudite and learned word

palagar m. (var. of) *paladar* m. (hard) palate, roof of the mouth

pale (Eng.) m. pal, friend

paledar m. (var. of) *paladar* m.

palero -ra (coll.) cover, cover-up agent, person who covers up the unintentional or deliberate mistakes of others

paleta popsicle; ice cream on a stick

palío (var. of) *palillo* toothpick

palito game resembling cricket; (euph.) penis; **echar un palito** to have sexual intercourse; **dulce de palito** lollipop; (usually) pl. clothes-pins

paliza (see **dar una paliza**)

palo tree; (slang) penis; interj. Wham!, Crash!; **palo blanco** aspen tree; **ser de palo** to be insensitive, hard as a rock (coll.)

paloma butterfly

palomía (var. of) *palomilla*

palomilla gang, street corner gang; circle of friends

palomita moth

palotazo blow with a rolling pin

palote m. rolling pin; (vulg.) large penis

pallá or **pa' allá** (vars. of) *para allá*: "¿Ónta Jorge? — Se jue pallá" 'Where's Jorge? — He went over there'

pallamas (orthog. var. of) *pa-yama(s)* (see also **pijama**)

pamita tansy mustard herb (Descurainia pinnata) (prepared as a tea for the treatment of *empacho*)

pan (vulg., slang) vagina (see also **panocha, panocho**); **pan (de) dulce** Mexican pastry; **pan de huevo**

type of Mexican pastry in semi-spherical form; **pan de maíz** or **pan de maiz** cornbread; type of old-fashioned dance

pana lint, fluff

panasco -ca fat

pancá (var. of) *para la casa de:* "¿Ónta Chente — Se jue pancá su buelita"

Pancho -cha (dims. of) *Francisco -ca*

pancho -cha: pancho riata tough guy, mean bastard: "Ése es muy pancho riata de verdad"; **ser muy pancho -cha** to be lacking in good taste, esp. with ref. to clothes: "Ése es muy pancho pa vestirse" 'That guy's got lousy taste in clothing'; (in general) to be lusterless, plain, dull, colorless; to be unsophisticated

pandeado -da or **pandiado -da** (vars. of) *pando -da*

pandear or **pandiar** vr. to retract, take back: "Cuando se lo reclamaron, se pandió" 'When they confronted him with what he had said, he took it back'

pando -da tilted, lopsided; (slang) drunk, looped

panecío (var. of) *panecillo*

pánel (Eng.) m. panel van (type of small truck similar to a delivery van)

panita lint, fluff

panocha or **panocho** (slang) vulva

panochuda (vulg.) ref. to woman with a large vagina

panqueque (Eng.) m. pancake

pantaletas woman's panties

pantalón m. (usually mpl.); **pantalones aguados** baggy trousers; **pantalones cortos** shorts, short pants; **pantalones de cuchilla** bell-bottom(ed) trousers; **pantalones**

de pechera bib overalls; **pantalones de plits** (Eng.) pleated trousers (Std. *pantalones de pliegue*); **pantalones pegados** overalls (work trousers); **pantalones de ranchero** overalls; (blue) jeans

pantalonudo -da (ref. to person with baggy pants)

pantas (Eng.) pants, trousers

pantasma (var. of) *fantasma*

pantera elegant, groovy (slang) (said. esp. of attractive and noticeable woman): "¡Qué pantera!"

pantión (var. of) *panteón* cemetery

pantomina (var. of) *pantomima;* **hacer pantominas** to make a scene (coll.), make a public spectacle of oneself, make a fool of oneself: "No te asilenciaste hasta que hiciste tus pantominas" 'You didn't shut up until you could make a scene in public'

panzazo (var. of) *panzada* push or shove with one's belly

panzona (vulg.) knocked up (vulg.), pregnant

panzoncita (hum.) (ref. to a chubby woman who is pregnant)

panzonzota (ref. to woman who is enormously pregnant)

paño handkerchief

papa: ¡la papa! interj. Great!, Terrific!, Swell!; **papa maceada** or **papa maciada** or **papa molida** mashed potatoes; pl. **echar papas** to lie, tell lies

papachado -da (vars. of) *apapachado -da*

papachador -ra (vars. of) *apapachador -ra*

papachar (var. of) *apapachar*

papachos (usually pl.) fondling, pampering, indulging; **hacer papachos** to pamper, fondle, spoil (said of children), indulge

papa grande or **papá grande** m. grandfather

papalote m. paper kite; windmill; propeller

papalotearle (papalotiarle) a alguien para hacer algo to excel at doing something: "A Nino le papalotea para pichar"

papases (var. of) *papás* (Std.) mpl.

papasote (slang) m. handsome man; sexy male; sugar daddy; daddy-o (slang)

papel (Ang.) m. newspaper; **papel de china** tissue paper (used for packing gifts); mpl. **hacer papeles** to make a spectacle of oneself or play the fool in public, create a scene in public; **papel picado** confetti

papelería establishment that buys used papers and magazines for recycling

papelero -ra m. newsboy, newspaper seller; mf. show-off; braggart; fraud; person prone to making scenes in public or to making a fool of him/herself; exhibitionist; mess of papers, scattered papers

papero -ra liar; pretender

papi (Eng.) m. pappy, daddy

papiro paper (in general); newspaper, periodical; **papiro de cíticen** (Ang.) citizenship paper, document attesting to citizenship

papis (Eng.) msg. (var. of) *papi*

papita little white lie, falsehood of generally minor proportions

papular (Eng.) (var. of) *popular* adj.

paquete m. the best part of anything; first prize; mf. opportunist

paquetudo -da (slang) excellent, topnotch

para: pa(ra) (a)cabarla de chingar (fregar, joder) to make matters worse, on top of all that (fig.); **pa(ra) esas gracias** in that case: "Vete por el perro — ¿Dónde está y qué hago con él cuando lo encuentre? — Bueno, pa' esas gracias yo voy mejor"; **para que vea(s) (vean)** that just goes to show (that one can not judge a book by its cover); let that be a lesson to you

parada dirty deal, unfair bargain; **hacerle a alguien una (mala) parada** to play a diry trick on someone; give someone a dirty deal; **hacerle la parada a alguien** to go along with someone's stand (position on an issue) or joke

parado -da m. on foot; standing; **dejar a alguien parado -da** (in baseball) to strike someone out without a chance (i.e., with pitches so aimed that the batter has no chance to even swing at the ball); to stand someone up, fail to keep an appointment or show up for a date; f. **traerla parada** to have a hard-on (slang, vulg.), have an erection

paralis (var. of) *parálisis* msg.

parar vr. to leave a sick bed upon getting well; **¡páre(n)le ahi!** interj. (coll.): Knock it off!, That's enough of that!; va. to stand something up perpendicularly; **pararle el alto a alguien/pararle los pedos a alguien** to put a stop to someone's abusive behavior, put someone down (slang); **pararse en una boda** to stand up for (the bride/the groom) at a wedding, participate as one of the nuptual couple's sponsors; **no parar(le) la cola a alguien**: "Llámale por teléfono a ver si está en casa, porque a ése nunca le para la cola" 'Call him up to see if he's at home, because he's constantly on the go'

parche mf. disagreeable person; leech, sponge, person who lives off of others; a close family member

parde m. (rus.) (var. of) *padre* m.

pardi (Eng.) m. (var. of) *pare/pore* party

pare: ponerle pare a algo to put an end to something (usually excesses, abusive or unfair behavior, injustices, etc.)

pare m. (Eng.) (var. of) *pore* party

pared f.: **pared verde** (Ang.) (slang) Walgreen's drug store (national chain of stores)

parejo -ja: estar or **quedar parejos -jas con alguien** to be even with someone, owe nothing to someone: "Aquí está lo último que te debo; quedamos parejos ahora"; to be tied, end up in a tie (with someone); to be even with someone after having exacted full revenge; **ser parejo -ja** to be honest, honorable

parentro (var. of) *para adentro* inside

parián m. large market; marketplace

pariente (Ang.) m. (usually mpl.) parent(s)

parna (Eng.) m. partner (usually term of non-pej. address towards an African American)

parparear or **parpariar** (vars. of) *parpadear*

párparo (var. of) *párpado* (Std.)

parque m. role of tape used as ammunition for cap guns; **parque de animales** zoo; **parque de pelota**

(Ang.) baseball stadium, baseball park

parqueadero or **parquiadero** (Eng.) parking place; parking lot; act of parking a car

parqueado -da or **parquiado -da** (Eng.) parked (ref. to cars or hum. to persons, e.g., "parked" or seemingly immobile in a chair)

parquear or **parquiar** (Eng.) va. to park; vr. (slang) to sit down, "park" oneself in a chair; to remain seated at great length, thus overstaying one's welcome

parquete m. (var. of) *paquete* m.

parte f.: pl. **partes de carro** (Ang.) auto parts

partido -da m.: **ser buen partido** to be a good partner (esp. in a sports competition); f. part (in one's hair); (vulg.) vagina

parto: segundo parto afterbirth (placenta and membranes)

parranda group of drunken revelers

parrandear or **parrandiar** vn. to go on a drunk, go on a drinking spree

parriba or **pa'(a)rriba** (vars. of) *para arriba*

particular (Ang.?) mf. particular, demanding, picky, choosy (Std. *exigente*); discriminating

pasada: de pasada in passing: "Dale el libro de pasada" 'Give him the book as you go by'

pasadero -ra or **pasador -ra** passable (ref. to a job accomplished, commitments fulfilled, the physical attributes of persons, etc.)

pasar va.: **pasar braca** (Ang.?) to give someone a break (opportunity); **pasar algo** to be able to eat food without vomiting after an attack of stomach disorder: "El enfermo ya está pasando la comida"; vn. **pasarla** to be getting along in a so-so fashion, just getting by: "¿Cómo le va?—Pasándola"; **pasarla bien** to be doing well; **pasarla mal** to be doing poorly; **pasar un buen tiempo** (Ang.) to have a good time (Std. *divertirse*); **pasársele a alguien el caballo** to lose one's opportunity to do something on one's behalf; **pasársele a alguien la mano** (var. of) *írsele a alguien la mano*

paseado -da or **pasiado -da**: f. **estar muy paseada (pasiada)** (ref. to women) to have a lot of mileage, to have indulged oneself freely in sexual relationships: "Esa mujer está muy pasiada"

paseador -ra or **pasiador -ra** (said of someone fond of doing the town, going out on a spree)

paseando or **pasiando** (see **andar: ándate pasiando**)

pasear or **pasiar** vr. to go out on the town; to take a leisure trip or outing

paseño -ña person from El Paso, Texas

paseo parade, procession

pasguato -ta idiot, numbskull

pasiar (var. of) *pasear*

pasión f.: pl. (slang) **¿qué pasiones?** What happened?, What's up? (deformation of *¿Qué pasó?*)

pasito adv. (said of rivers sufficiently empty of water to allow crossing without having to take one's clothes off)

paso: andar dando malos pasos or **andar en malos pasos** to be up to no good (i.e., to be having an affair or to be involved in shady deals)

paso: El Paso del Águila (Hispanization of) Eagle Pass, Texas

pasote (slang) m. handsome man, sexy male; sugar daddy; daddy-o; **¿qué pasotes (con los zapatotes)?** (slang) What's wrong?, What happened? (deformation of *¿Qué pasó?*) (cf. **pasión**)

pasta hay, feed for livestock

pastero cowboy who rides the boundaries of a ranch to check whether everything is running smoothly

pastilla or **pastía** (slang) money; money traditionally thrown to children by godparents at a baptism

pastor -ra stupid; discourteous; countrified, hickish, farm-fresh (coll.)

pastorella traditional theatrical representation of the birth of Christ performed around Christmas time

pastores: Los Pastores traditional Christmas pastoral play which depicts the visit of the shepherds to the stable at Bethlehem

pastura (slang) tobacco

pata f.: pl. **echar a alguien de patas (a la calle)** to throw someone out feet first; **írsele a uno las patas** to slip, fall into an error or fault, lose control of oneself, lose one's head; to throw caution to the wind (often used in sexual context, e.g.: "Está embarazada porque se le fueron las patas")

patada (Ang.) kick (of a firearm), recoil; kick (obtained from alcohol or drugs), thrill; (see also **agarrar patada, dar la patada, dar patadas de ahogado, estar de la patada**)

patalear or **pataliar: patalearle la olla a alguien** (slang) to kick someone in the ass

patero -ra smuggler (esp. one using small rafts—*patos*—to smuggle goods across the Rio Grande)

Pati (dim. of) *Patricia*

patín m. wooden scooter used by children (see also **a patín**)

patinar: patinarle a alguien el coco to be daffy, screwy (slang), flighty

patitas (see **de patitas**)

pato bedpan; small raft with canvas sails used in fording rivers (esp. the Rio Grande/Río Bravo, by illegal immigrants from Mexico to the U.S.); (slang, vulg.) homosexual, faggot (slang); **pato del agua** weakling, effeminate male; homosexual; wimp

patón (slang) m. policeman, flatfoot (slang)

pa'tras (var. of) *para atrás* again adv.: "¡Entra pa' tras!" 'Come on back in again!' (see also **dar pa'trás, hacerse pa'trás, ir pa'trás, llevar pa'trás, pasar pa'trás, venir pa'trás**)

paulear or **pauliar** (slang) va. to pay

pavico diaper

payamas (Eng.) mpl. pajamas

pedal: pedal de gas accelerator

pediche or **pedichi** mf. persistent, demanding, bothersome

pedidera repeated asking, tiresomely constant requests for something

pedíorico (var. of) *periódico*

pedir: pedir emprestado -da (var. of) *pedir prestado -da*; **pedir la entrada** (see **entrada**); **pedir un ojo y la mitad del otro** to ask for an excessive amount of something

pedo fight; uproar; drunkenness, inebriation; **pedo -da** adj. drunk; **echarle un pedo a alguien** to scold: "Le echó un pedo porque llegó tarde"; **pararle a alguien los pedos** to put a stop to someone's abusive behavior; to put someone in his/her place; **¡puro pedo!** (slang, vulg.) pure unadulterated bullshit! (vulg.), Bull roar! (vulg.), The hell you say!; **¿que pedo te cargas?** (slang) What are you trying to prove?, What are you up to?; **traer (le) a alguien al puro pedo** to harass someone; (see also **andar pedo, hacer pedo**)

pedorra: chinche pedorra stinkbug (any insect of the Pentatomidae family)

pedorrear or **pedorriar** (slang) va. to scold, give a warning to; vr. (vulg.) to fart continuously

pedorrera (vulg.) continuous breaking of wind: "Le agarró una pedorrera de la fregada" 'He really farted up a storm' (slang)

pedrada innuendo, insinuation: "Esa pedrada no curvió" (lit.) 'That (intended) curve ball didn't curve' = 'Your attempted insinuation was actually a direct accusation'

pegar: andar pegando to get along well together (ref. to persons); **pegarle (de más) (al cuento/al relato)** to add something (usually a mendacious element) to a story or a narration; **pegar(le) a uno el sueño** to get sleepy: "Al niño le pegó el sueño como a las doce"

pegasoso -sa (vars. of) *pegajoso -sa*

pegoistia or **pegoites** mf. pest (ref. to person who imposes his/her presence upon others against their wishes) (see also **pegoste**)

pegoste mf. pest (id. to **pegoistia**)

pegostear or **pegostiar** va. & vr. to smear with a sticky substance

peinador m. vanity table (low table with a mirror, piece of bedroom or bathroom furniture also serving as a dressing table)

peladaje m. crowd of *pelados*, group of lower-class people (who are usually acting in an ill-bred fashion)

peladero a place frequented or inhabited by vile, worthless persons; scum, rabble, a group of persons regarded with contempt: "No sé por qué te gusta andar entre el peladero" "I don't know why you like to be around scum"

pelado -da lower-class person; ruffian, bully

peladora gold digger (fig.), woman in search of a wealthy husband or boyfriend

pelar va. to give a haircut to; vr. to get a haircut; **pélamela/pélame la verga** interjs. (vulg., slang) (very strong expressions of unwillingness or defiance): "Kiss my ass" (vulg., slang), "Suck my dick" (vulg., slang); vr. to flee, leave in a great hurry; to peel off, flake; **pelársela** to pull back the foreskin of one's penis; **pelar gallo** (slang) to die; **pelar (el) ojo** to open one's eyes wide so as to stare fixedly at something; **pelar el diente/pelar (los) dientes** to smile mockingly; to bare one's teeth (as in anger)

pelea boxing; boxing match

peleonero -ra or **pelionero -ra** pugnacious

pelerío pile of hair, great abundance of hair: "Barre ese pelerío que dejaste en el piso"

peliar (var. of) *pelear*

película (var. of) *película*

pelitos hair of the genital zone; soft hair on the human body

pelizcada (var. of) *pellizcada*

pelizcar (var. of) *pellizcar*

pelizco (var. of) *pellizco*

pelizcón (var. of) *pellizcón*

pelmas mfsg pl. slowpoke

pelo stature, height (of person): "Juan y Jorge son del mismo pelo"; **alzársele a alguien el pelo/alzársele a alguien los pelos** to stand on end (said of one's hair): "Se le alzaron los pelos"; **pelo alborotado** unkempt (uncombed, tousled, disarranged) hair; **pelo chino** curly hair; **pelo derecho** (Ang.) or **pelo liso** straight hair (as opposed to kinky or curly hair); **pelo parado** hair standing on end, standing straight up (as in a crew cut); **pelo quebrado** naturally curly or wavy hair

pelón: pelón pelacas/pelón pelacas, cuida las vacas/pelón pelacas, cuida las vacas, yo las engordo y tú las enflacas (expression used to poke fun at persons — usually boys — who wear crew cuts)

pelón -lona skinhead, person with hair cut close to the scalp (as in a crew cut); difficult, hard to resolve; **nalgas pelonas** (vulg.) (hum.) bare-assed: "Él anda con las nalgas pelonas" 'He's going around bare-assed' (see also **andar con las nalgas pelonas**)

pelota: cargar pelota por/traer pelota por (slang) to really have the hots for, be passionately in love with: "Se ve que ese bato carga pelota por su chava" 'You can see that that guy really has the

hots for his chick'; **en pelotas**
(vulg.) naked; mpl. guts, intestinal
fortitude: "Ese bato tiene pelotas"
'That dude has guts'

pelotazo m. (ref. to both men and
women as adj.) astute, sly, sharp

peluca (hum.) hair; pl. **andar** or
estar pelucas (slang) to be cleaned
out, broke (usually as a result of
having lost one's money in a game
of chance)

pelucar (slang) va. to clean someone out in a game of chance

peludo -da physically mature;
large in size; difficult, hard to
resolve

peluquero -ra habitual winner in a
game of chance

pelusa riffraff, ill-behaved lower-
class types

pellín m. buttocks

penar: andar penando (said of a
soul clothed as a ghost which
roams the earth, fulfilling an
unfinished commitment or right-
ing a wrong which circumstances
did not permit it to right during its
lifetime)

penco -ca child born out of
wedlock

pendejada foolish or stupid act

pendejiar (var. of) *pendejear*

**pendejo -ja: hacerse (el) pendejo/
(la) pendeja** to play dumb, pretend not to know or understand;
hacer pendejo -ja a alguien to fool
someone; to cheat, defraud

pendejón -jona (pej.) stupid idiot,
ignoramus

**pendiente: estar con el pendiente
de alguien o de algo** to be worried
about someone or something:
"Estoy con el pendiente de María
porque todavía no ha llegado";
tener(le) a alguien con el pen-

diente to have someone worried
(about someone or something):
"¿Ya llegó María? — No, me tiene
con el pendiente" 'Did María
arrive? — No, I'm worried about
her'; **tener pendiente de alguien** or
de algo to be worried about
someone or something: "Tengo
pendiente de Jorge, porque llora
tanto"

pene or **peni** (Eng.) m. penny, one
cent piece; f. (slang) penitentiary
(reduction of *penitenciaría* or
hispanization of the Eng. pen
(slang) = prison)

penitencia (var. of) *penitenciaría*
(Std.)

penqueque (Eng.) m. pancake
(see also **panqué** et al.)

pepa (slang) clitoris: "La pepa es
donde la mujer siente más
sensación sexual"

Pepe -pa m. (dim. of) *José*; f. (dim.
of) *Josefa* and *Josefina* (see also
Fina)

**pepenar: pepenarle a alguien
unos golpes** to hit someone

pepetoria or **pepitoria** (vars. of)
pipitoria

pepeyendo breaking wind (ger.)
(The ger. is the only form used of
the consequently hypothetical verb
pepeyer)

percurar (var. of) *procurar*

perder: perder la camisa (Ang.) to
lose one's shirt (coll.), lose a
considerable amount of money

perfilado unravelled sewing

perico -ca talkative person, chatterbox (coll.), gossip; f. (slang)
radio

periórico (var. of) *periódico*

periquear or **periquiar** (slang) vn.
to talk incessantly, chatter

periquera (slang) upper gallery of

a movie theater

perla   (see **ir de perla**)

persinar(se)   (vars. of) *persignar(se)*

personal m. poll tax

perra   (see **hacer la perra**)

perrilla or **perría**   sty, inflamation on the eyelid

perro -rra f.: **la perra de cuatro llantas** (hum.) Greyhound bus; **perro caliente** (Ang.) m. hot dog (type of sausage); **perro chato** bulldog; mf. **ser como el perro (la perra) que no tiene ni deja tener** to have a dog-in-the-manger attitude (ref. to a selfish person); f. **suerte perra** very bad luck; mf. **trabajar como perro -rra** to work quite hard

perroda   (var. of) *pedorra* (see also **chinche pedorra**)

perrón -rrona m., f. bully; malicious person

perrusquillo -lla or **perrusquío -a** drunk; lower-class person

pesado -da (Ang.) (slang) adj. (ref. to the very latest in extravagant and far-out popular music = Eng. slang expression 'heavy music'); **ponerse pesado -da** to get nasty (coll.), act in an unpleasant manner (see also **caer pesado**)

pésamo   (var. of) *pésame*

pesar: pesarle a alguien las bolas/ el buche/las pelotas (vulg.) to be (very) lazy; **pesarle a alguien el buche** (said of a person who has a big buttocks)

pescado   fish in general (cf. Std. *pez* live, uncaught fish)

pescar: pescar a alguien en la mentira/pescar a alguien en las moras to catch someone redhanded (coll.), discover someone's involvement in a criminal act, in a falsehood, etc.; **pescarle a alguien**

la noche to be overtaken by nightfall

pescuezo: tener el pezcuezo torcido to have a crick in one's neck; **darle (llegarle) a uno la (el) agua al pescuezo (a la cabeza)** (fig.) to have a hard time keeping one's head above water (fig.), be in a tight spot (slang), be in trouble, be in a predicament

pescuezón -zona or **pescuezudo -da** (vars. of) *pescozudo -da*

peseta   twenty-five cent piece; repugnant and repellent person (see also **caer peseta**)

pesetudo -da   repugnant, repellent; rich, well-to-do

peso   dollar; **tener buenos pesos** to have a great deal of money, be flushed (coll.)

pespunte   (see **a pespunte**)

pestaña: tirar pestaña (slang) to sleep

peste: echar pestes to raise a stink (fig.), make trouble

pesudo -da   rich, well-to-do (see also **pesetudo -da**)

pesuña: gran pesuña (slang) foot; toenail

petaca   automobile trunk

petacona   large and shapely woman

petate m. small rug, mat; **liar el petate** to die, kick the bucket (slang) (see also **petatear**); **sombrero de petate** straw hat

petatear or **petatiar**   (slang) vr. to die, kick the bucket (slang) (see also **liar el petate**)

petatero -ra: el mero petatero/la mera patatera the boss, the big cheese (coll.)

petatón -tona: el mero petatón/la mera petatona the boss, the big cheese

petatús (var. of) m. *patatús* (Std.)

peticout (Eng.) m. petticoat

Petra (dim. of) *Petrona*

peyer vn. (var. of) *peer* vn.

pezón: pezón enlechado engorged nipple, caked breast

piatón -tona (vars. of) *peatón -tona*

picadillo confetti (see also **hacer picadillo**)

picado -da adj. ready for more, stimulated, excited (ref. to person whose appetite has been whetted by something); **diente picado** tooth with a cavity; **¡qué picado!** (fixed expression) You'd like that, wouldn't you? (used ironically)

pícap (Eng.) m. (var. of) *pícop*

picar va. to provoke, incite, needle (fig.); to bug (slang), annoy, bother: "¿Qué te pica?" 'What's bugging you?'; vr. to become addicted, get hooked (slang): "Pepe se picó con la cocaína" 'Joey got hooked on cocaine'; **pa'que se pique(n)/pa'que te piques** (slang) Eat your heart out! (slang), Put that in your pipe and smoke it (slang); **picarle a alguien los ojos** to make a fool out of someone; vr. to become excited by something and to want more of it, get a taste of something and go to extremes to satisfy the appetite (cf. **picado**); to get angry; to inject oneself with drugs; to hurry, move quickly; **¡pícale!** interj. Move it!, Hurry up!; **¡pícate!** interj. (an incitement to envy, approximately) Put that in your pipe and smoke it!

picle (Eng.) m. pickle

pico: cerrar el pico to keep silent; to become silent, shut up (coll.)

picón -cona m. act of provoking someone to anger; barb, cutting or bitting remark; (see also **piquete**); mpl. **dar picones** to tease, make jealous, pique, needle (coll.); adj. mf. (ref. to instigator, i.e., person who enjoys needling or inciting to anger; also ref. to person easily aroused to anger or otherwise incited)

pícop (Eng.) m. pickup truck (see also **pícap**)

picoreta wind-up metal top which makes a winding noise when spinning

picoso -sa spicy (ref. to food which burns the inside of the mouth)

picote mf. chatterbox (coll.), excessive talker

picudo -da card shark (person expert and somewhat unscrupulous at playing cards)

picha (vulg.) penis; (Eng.) m. pitcher (baseball) (see also **píchar**); **picha-quecha-naca** (composite ref. to game of baseball) (Eng.) (cf. **quecha**)

pichada (Eng.) pitch (in baseball)

pichar (Eng.) va. & vn. to pitch (baseball)

picheo (Eng.) act of pitching (baseball)

pícher (Eng.) m. pitcher (baseball)

pichicato -ta stingy, miserly

pichicuate m. water snake (Qenus natrix)

pichón -chona m., f. born loser (coll.), person who always loses or comes out last; easy to defeat; easy to deceive; m. (vulg.) penis

pichoneada/pichoniada: dar una pichoneada/pichoniada to pet heavily (the male usually being the aggressor) (see also **pichonear**)

pichonear or **pichoniar** va. to

effortlessly defeat a novice in a sports competition; vn. to engage in active sexual foreplay (see also **dar una pichoneada/pichoniada**)

pichudo (slang) cocksman (vulg., hum.) (ref. to man with a large penis)

pidemos (var. of) *pedimos* (1st pers. pl. pres. ind. of *pedir*)

pidiche or **pidichi** (vars. of) *pediche, pedichi,* resp.

pidir (var. of) *pedir*

pildoriento -ta (slang) user of narcotic pills

piedra: pl. gallstones; **piedras en la vejiga** gallstones (Std. *cálculo biliar*); **esa piedra no curveó** (id. to **esa pedrada no curveó**, q.v. supra); **estar tres piedras** (slang) to be tremendous, terrific, very nice (ref. to persons and things)

piedrada (var. of) *pedrada* (Std.)

piedrería (var. of) *pedrería* (Std.)

piedriza stoning, act of throwing stones

pierda (var. of) *piedra*

pierdada (var. of) *pedrada*

pierna: más pueden las piernas que los brazos (v.s. **brazo**)

piernudo -da large-legged; f. woman with attractive legs

pieses mpl. (var. of) *pies* (mpl. of *pie* foot)

pieza: agarrar algo de una pieza (v.s. **agarrar**); **cambiar la pieza** to stop harping on the same topic, cease to talk about the same thing: "Por fin cambió la pieza y comenzó a hablar de algo diferente"

pildorear or **pildoriar** vr. to ingest narcotic pills: "Ese bato se pildorea" 'That guy is a pill-popper'

píldoro -ra (slang) person high on narcotic pills

piliar (var. of) *pelear* (Std.)

pilícula (var. of) *película* (Std.)

pilingo -ga small child; child small for his/her age, pee-wee (slang) (see also **pilinguache** et al., **pirrongo -ga**); f. (vulg) penis

pilinguache or **pilinguachi** or **pilingüe** mf. (vars. of) *pilingo -ga*

pilmama baby-sitter; wet nurse; nurse maid

pilón m. additional amount, premium (a little extra given to someone who has made a purchase); **de pilón** free, gratis; **de pilón** to make matters worse, on top of all that (fig.): "Lo insultaron, y de pilón, le dieron una paliza" 'They insulted him, and on top of all that, they gave him a thrashing' (see **fregar: para acabarla de fregar**)

pilonga (slang, vulg.) male sex organ, penis (cf. **pilinga**)

pilotear or **pilotiar** va. & vn. to drive a car

pillido sharp cry

pimientito -ta (hum.) half-pint (coll.), person of very short stature

pimpo (Eng.) pimp, whoremaster

pimpón (Eng.) m. ping-pong, table tennis

pincel (see **a pincel**)

pinche mf. mean, base, despicable; m. punk, hoodlum; mpl. clothespins

pinchi (slang) (var. of) *pinche* (slang)

pinchurriento -ta weak-willed, easily swayed

pinga (vulg.) penis (cf. **pringa**); mf. tricky person

pingo mischievous person; little devil (coll.), imp

pinguas (usually pl.) narcotic pills; **llevar pinguas** (slang) to behave mischievously

pinguito -ta malicious; mischievous, impish

pininos (usually mpl.) baby's first steps (when just learning to walk)

pinta (slang) jail, penitentiary

pintar va. to dye one's hair; vr. to escape, run off, leave rapidly

pintero -ra painter (Stds. *pintor -ra*)

pinto -ta very dark-skinned though without negroid facial features; **pinto -ta viejo -ja** jailbird (coll.), person often jailed; **poner pinto a alguien** to heap with insults, tear to pieces (fig.), tell someone off in no uncertain terms

pintorregear or **pintorregiar** vr. to use cosmetics to excess

pintote m. type of yellow catfish

pintura: pintura pa' las uñas nail polish; **no poder ver a alguien ni en pintura** not to be able to stand the sight of someone, hate someone intensely, to hate someone with a purple passion (fig.)

piocha pointed beard; (slang) nice-looking, attractive; swell, great, keen, excellent (etc.)

piojero or **piojera** swarm of lice

pión, piona (vars. of) *peón* m., *peona* f.

pionillo croton (Croton coresianus) (herb prepared as a tea and used in treating colic)

pior (var. of) *peor*

Piosol (Hispanization of) Pearsall, Texas

pi(p) pi(p) (Eng.?) peep! peep! (onomatopoeia), the sound of an auto horn

pipa (Ang.) pipe for conducting gases or fluids (Std. *tubo*) (cf. **paipa**)

pipi or **pipí** (euph.) f. penis; **hacer**

(la) pipi/pipí (mildly euph.) to urinate, "go pee-pee" (euph., said esp. of and to children)

pipián (slang) m. food (in general)

pipilín m. (var. of) *pipirín* m.

pipilisco -ca near-sighted

pípilo (slang) gigolo; effeminate man; male homosexual

pipirín (slang) m. food (in general) (cf. **pipilín**)

pipitoria (used only in the following fixed expression): **raza pipitoria** (pej.) (ref. to Mexicans or Mexican-Americans); type of candy make with brown sugar and pumpkin seeds

piquenique (Eng.) m. picnic

piquetazo (var. of) *picotazo*

piquete m. provocation, insult; barb, cutting or biting remark; (see **picón**); **darse un piquete** (slang) to inject narcotic drugs; **dar(se) piquetes** to incite, goad, provoke, insult, needle (one another); **echar piquetes** to insult; **estar de piquete** to be on unfriendly terms; **piquete de aguja** (hum.) fornication; **ser de piquete** to have a hot temper; to enjoy inciting others to anger; to be easily offended, quick to take offense; (slang) to be a drug addict

piquetear or **piquetiar** (Eng.) va. to picket (as a factory, by workers on strike); to boycott

piquinique m. (var. of) *piquenique* m.

piquito kiss; small mouth

pirata (slang) drunk, soused; mf. thief

piratón -tona (slang) very drunk, smashed (slang)

pirfantear or **pirfantiar** va. & vr. to dress up, dress elegantly

pirinola top (child's toy); penis

pirujo -ja sly, astute, clever

pirulero -ra vendor of *pirulí* (type of caramel candy); **Juan Pirulero** (type of children's game)

pirringo -ga small child (see pilongo et al.)

pisar (slang) va. to couple (slang), fornicate (with); (Ang.?) to step on the gas (coll.), accelerate a car; **adj. + hasta (d)onde pisa** extremely, to the nth degree: "Pepe es malo hasta (d)onde pisa" "Joey is extremely bad'

pisón m. (var. of?) *pisotón* step, heavy tread, heavy footstep

pisoteada or pisotiada trampling

pispís m.: **tener pispís** to be afraid

pisporra or pisporria bump on the head

piste m. alcohol

pisteadera or pistiadera act of drinking alcohol

pistear or pistiar va. & vn. to drink alcohol, take nips of alcoholic liquor

pisto -ta drunk, inebriated; m. alcohol; **echarse un pisto** to take a drink of alcohol; m. money; small quantity of anything

pistola (hypodermic) syringe

pistón -tona very drunk, ploughed (slang)

pistudo -da wealthy

pita dagger

pitar va. & vn. to honk (the horn of a car); to blow on a whistle, blow on any wind instrument

pitazo mf. clever, shrewd; wise, intelligent

pito mf. (id. to **pitazo**)

pizarro asbestos siding (used in the construction of buildings)

pizca harvest (usually ref. to cotton crop harvest)

pizcador -ra cotton picker

pizcar va. to pick cotton; to pick up, collect, glean

plancha: ser or jugarse plancha to be slow to react (because of lack of preparation, laziness, etc.)

plata (see a plata limpia)

pelotazo astute, clever, alert: "Juanita es un pelotazo; cuidado con ella"

placa pl. false teeth, dental plate; plaque (substance that accumulates between teeth); **placas (de carro)** car license plates; sg. (slang) police force, cops, "the badge"

placer: hacerle placer a alguien to treat someone well, be very courteous toward someone; to humor someone

plancha wallflower (fig.), shy and retiring person; person who fails to take advantage of opportunities; **hacerse plancha** to overstay one's welcome; **tirar plancha** to be left holding the bag (fig.), be abandoned (as by one's boyfriend or girlfriend)

planchada sg. (var. of) *planchado* sg. clothes to be ironed (Std.)

planchar: planchar oreja (slang) to sleep

planfleto (Eng.) pamphlet (Std. *folleto*)

planiar (var. of) *planear*

planta: planta de huevos (Ang.) eggplant

plantado -da stood up, jilted; dressed elegantly; f. hard slap on the face

plántano (var. of) *plátano*

plantar va. (slang) to inter, bury; to strike, hit, slap; vr. to dress elegantly; to overstay one's welcome, visit for longer than one should (see also **hacerse plancha**

hacer rancho, etc.); **plantársela a alguien** to hit someone with one's fist or with the palm of one's hand

plantía or **plantilla** first baseman's glove (baseball)

plasta lazy person; slow-moving person; hair oil; greasy

plátano or **plántano** (vulg.) penis

platicada chat, conversation

platicadera lively conversation

platicador **-ra** chatterbox, excessive talker

platicar va. to tell a story

platicón -cona fond of talking

plato phonograph record, platter (slang); base (in baseball); **colmarle a alguien el plato** to exhaust someone's patience; **echarse al plato** to take advantage of someone; to seduce sexually; to kill

plebe f. mob of lower-class people; lower-class people in general; gang of children; children in general; f. hecklers, harassers

plegón: echarle a alguien un plegón to tell someone off

pleit (Eng.) m. home plate (baseball)

pleito boxing; boxing match

plit (Eng.) m. (usually mpl. *plits*) pleat

plocha (var. of) *piocha*

ploga f. or **plogue** mf. (Eng.) plug (e.g., electric plug); (vulg.) f. mistress, kept woman, bed-mate

ploguear or **ploguiar** (Eng.) va. to plug, plug in (Std. *enchufar*); (Eng.) (vulg.) va. to fornicate

plomazo pistol shot

plomear or **plomiar** (slang) va. & vn. to shoot with a pistol

plomo -ma gray (color); m., f. slow-moving person who dislikes work; **ser (muy) plomo -ma** to be (very) slow to react to a given situation

plujear or **plujiar** (Eng.) va. & vn. to plunge

pluma prostitute; woman of easy virtue, run-around (coll.)

pobrar (var. of) *probar* va.

poca or **pócar** (Eng.) m. poker (card game) (see also **póquer**)

pocito (hum.) vagina

poco: ¡a poco! (fixed expression of surprise): You don't say!, Really?!; (expression of doubt): "¡A poco crees que me vas a engañar!" 'So you think you're going to cheat me!'; **poco a poquito** (var. of) *poco a poco*

pochismo Spanish word or construction reflecting English influence (cf. **pocho -cha**)

pocho **-cha** (pej.) gringoized Mexican; (pej.) Mexican-American, Chicano

poder: poderlas to be influential; to be a favorite (e.g., in political circles, among members of the opposite sex, etc.): "Él es de los que las puede"; **poderle a alguien** to wound (fig.), hurt (fig.); to displease, annoy: "Le pudo lo que le dije" 'What I said hurt him'; **puede que** perhaps, maybe

podo (slang) marihuana

poeta (slang, ant.) jitterbug (person who enjoys dancing the jitterbug, a popular dance of the 1940's)

polecía (var. of) *policía*

poli f. police

policía: hijo de policía (see also **hijo**)

polis f. insurance policy

polís (Eng.) m. policeman; f. police force

politiquiar (var. of) *politiquear*

póliza (Ang.) policy, course of

action

Polo -la (dims. of) *Hipolito, -ta Apolonio, -nia Leopoldo -da*

polquear or **polquiar** (vars. of) *polcar*

polquero -ra person who enjoys polkas

polvadera (var. of) *polvareda* dust cloud

polveado -da or **polviado -da** all powdered up, covered with powder

polvear or **polviar** vr. to powder oneself, cover oneself with powder (e.g., to powder one's nose)

polvero -ra (vars. of) *polvareda*; f. powder puff

polvito: echar polvitos to hex, bewitch (see also **polvo**)

polvo: echar polvos to hex, bewitch

polvoso -sa (var. of) *polvoroso -sa*

pollito: pollito de estaca (id. to **pollo -lla**, q.v. infra)

pollo spit, phlegm

pollo -lla or **pollón -llona** person entering a subsequent stage in his/her life, e.g., an adolescent about to become an adult; can also ref. to someone whose physique is advanced for his/her chronological age, e.g., an adolescent with a body that is already adult

pompa (Eng.) faucet (Std. *grifo*); pump (Std. *bomba*)

pompañero -ra (rus.) (vars. of) *compañero -ra*

Pompe or **Pompi** (dims. of) *Pomposa*

pompeador -ra or **pompiador -ra** (slang) swinger (person who enjoys a very active and adventuresome sex life) (cf. **pompear**)

pompear or **pompiar** (Eng.) va. to pump; (vulg.) to fornicate

pompiado -da (slang) tired, exhausted

ponchar (Eng.) va. to puncture; to punch; vr. to go flat (said of an aut. tire)

ponche mf.: **estar ponche** (slang, Eng.) to be punchy, punch-drunk (analogy with behavior of a groggy boxer); (slang) to be crazy

ponche or **ponchi** (Eng.) m. punch, blow with the fist

ponchi (var. of) *ponche* adj.

pone (Eng.) m. pony (see also **poni**)

poner vr. (var. of) *oponerse*

poner va. to supply, provide, furnish: "El padrino va a poner el salón" 'The best man is going to furnish the dance hall'; **estar poniéndosela a alguien** (see **estar**); **pon** (var. of) *supon* (<*suponer*); **pon cuidado** watch and see, keep your eyes and ears open; just (you) wait and see: "A Juan lo van a arrestar; pon cuidado" 'They're going to arrest John; just you wait and see'; **poner (hacer) cara de hacha** to make (put on) an expression of intense displeasure; **poner de patitas en la calle** to fire, dismiss (from a job) in short order; to run off, tell to leave (usually ref. to the manner in which one common-law partner tells the other to depart); **poner el carro en reverso** to shift into reverse gear; **poner cuidado** to pay attention; **poner a alguien al alba** (slang) to alert somone, put someone on guard; **poner a alguien del asco** to heap insults upon someone: "Pobrecito, lo pusieron del asco"; **poner a alguien en mal** to bad mouth, speak ill of someone, discredit, run down (fig.); **poner a**

alguien pinto to heap insults on someone; **poner cola** (slang) to tail someone (coll.), have someone followed; **poner de la basura** to heap with insults, shout insults at: "Se metió a la casa porque la estaban poniendo de la basura"; **poner (el) dedo** to accuse, point the finger at; **poner gorro** to harass: **ponerle el ojo morado a alguien** to give someone a black eye; **poner nombre** to name, give a name to: "¿Cómo le pusieron?" 'What name did they give him?'; **poner pa'tras** (Ang.) to put back, fail to promote (as a child in school); to put back, return to a place (as a glass to a cupboard); **poner un hasta aquí** to draw the line (fig.), indicate the limits beyond which a particular form of behavior is unacceptable; **ponerle pare a algo** to put an end to something (usually excesses, abusive or unfair behavior, injustices, etc.) vr. **ponerse águila** (slang) to become alert, be on the alert; **ponerse agusado -da** (slang) to become alert, be on the alert; **ponerse bruto -ta** to get stupid drunk (coll.); to get high on drugs; **ponerse caballón -llona** (slang) to get high on alcohol or narcotic drugs; **ponerse (con)** to challenge, mess around with: "No te pongas con él" 'Don't mess around with him'; **ponerse con uno del tamaño de uno** to pick on someone one's own size; **ponerse cuete** to get drunk; **ponerse chango** to become alert; **ponerse del asco** to get extremely dirty; **ponerse el aire pesado** for a situation to become tense; **ponerse en el avispero** to become alert; **ponerse en la línea/**linia to get drunk; **ponérsela a alguien** to hit someone (fig.), succeed in obtaining money through pressure or artful persuasion; "Si no te cuidas, te la van a poner"; **ponérselas** to get drunk: "Anoche se las puso, por eso todavía no se levanta"; **ponerse las botas** to have a ball (fig.), have a field day (coll.), have a good time; **ponerse pesado -da** to get tough with, act insultingly towards: "Hórale, no te pongas tan pesado" 'Don't get so tough'; **ponerse trucha/ponerse truche** (slang) to become alert, get wise (slang)

poni (Eng.) m. pony

poní, poniste(s), ponió, ponimos, ponieron (vars. of) *puse, pusiste*, etc. (pret. conjugation of *poner*)

¡pónele! or **¡pónga(n)le!** interj. Get to work!, Get busy!, Get with it!, Hurry up! (etc.); **¡pónele Jorge al niño!** interj. Get to work, Get busy! (etc.)

pope (Eng.) m. puppy, infant dog

populacíon (Ang.) f. population, number of inhabitants within a given area

poquear or **poquiar** (Eng.) vn. to play poker

póquer (Eng.) m. poker (card game) (see also **poca** et al.)

por: de por sí It's bad enough as it is (without you making it worse): "De por sí que hace frío y tú dejas la puerta abierta" 'It's cold enough as it is, and you have to go and leave the door open'; **por allí** or **por ahi le va** more or less, thereabouts: "¿Así debo hacer el trabajo? — Por ahi le va"; **por la buena** willingly; **por la mala** by force; **por mientras** meanwhile, for the time being, for now; **por**

nada (var. of) *de nada*; **por si las moscas** just in case; **por sí o por no** just in case: "Vamos a cerrar la puerta por sí o por no" 'We're going to shut the door, just in case'

pora m. man encharged with maintaining sheep-shearing equipment

porazo (Eng.) (cf. **pore**) blowout (slang), large noisy party

pore (Eng.) m. party

poro (var. of) *pero* conj.

porque: porque sí just because

portable (Eng.) adj. portable (Std. *portátil*)

portamoneda fsg. (var. of) *portamonedas* fpl.

portemener msg. (var. of) *portamonedas* fpl.

pos (var. of) *pues* conj.; **pos luego/ pues luego** of course, without any doubt, certainly

posta ball bearing; pellet; railroad tie; post, a stake of wood or other material driven into the ground to serve as a support or marker

poste tall; skinny; (vulg.) m. rod (slang, vulg.), large penis; (var. of) *posta*

postemilla or **postemía** abscess in the mouth

postero -ra (pej.) cedar chopper (lower- or working-class central Texas Anglo-Saxon); poor white (in general)

postotes (Eng.) mpl. Post Toasties (brand name of type of breakfast cereal); dry breakfast cereal (in general)

pozo (slang) (Ang.?<hole) solitary confinement cell in a jail; **echar al pozo** to drive (send) to the grave: "Echó a su madre al pozo con sus borracheras" 'He drove his mother to the grave with his

drinking sprees'

pozol(e) m. drink made from corn and sugar

practical (Eng.) mf. practical (Std. *práctico -ca*)

Prai: La Prai (Hispanization of) La Pryor, Texas

praiticar (Eng.?) (var. of?) *practicar* to practice

prática (var. of) *práctica*

preba (var. of) *prueba*

prebar (var. of) *probar*

precincto or **precinto** (Eng.) precinct (electoral)

precula (Eng.) precooling system in vegetable cannery, used to keep vegetables fresh and unspoiled

precupar (var. of) *preocupar*

preguntar: preguntar una pregunta or **preguntar una cuestión** (Ang.) to ask a question (Std. *hacer una pregunta*)

prencepal (var. of) *principal*

prencipio (var. of) *principio*

prender va. to hook on (= cause to be addicted to) narcotic drugs

prendido -da hooked on (addicted to) narcotic drugs

presa lake

previlegio (var. of) *privilegio*

pricula (Eng.) (var. of) *precula*

priculero -ra (Eng.) (see **precula/ pricula**) worker in the precooling section of a vegetable processing plant

prieto -ta (Ang.?) dark (refers to an African American)

primero: de primero at the beginning (Std. *al principio*)

principal (Ang.) m. principal of a school (Std. *director de escuela*)

probe or **probre** (vars. of) *pobre* poor

procurar va. to look after, watch over: "Juan procura mucho a su hermanita"; to make a play for, seek to gain the affections of: "Jorge anda procurando a esa chavala"; to seek out the company of, go look for

producí, produciste, etc. (vars. of) *produje, produjiste*, etc. (pret. forms of *producir*)

profesionista mf. (var. of) *profesional*

pronta adj. (sole ref. to women) (said of a very young adolescent girl who begins to "run around with" men)

pronto: ahora pronto recently

pronunciar (Ang.) va. to declare that something is so (Std. *declarar*): "Yo los pronuncio casados" 'I now pronounce you man and wife'

propetario -ria (vars. of) *propietario -ria*

protestante -ta m., f. Protestant (Std. *protestante* mf.)

provisión fsg. groceries

pucha: ¡la pucha! interj. Oh yeah?! (simultaneous indication of doubt and defiance)

puchar (Eng.) va. to push, shove

puche (Eng.) m. push, shove

¡puchi! interj. Whew! (expresses distaste towards an awful smell)

pueblo downtown, business section of a city

puela frying pan

puerta interj. (vulg.) (used to indicate that a woman is revealing, whether inentionally or not, those parts of her body which should not be shown, esp. the vaginal region); **dar puerta** to show off something new; (said of women) to show (uncover) the vaginal region, whether intentionally or not; **de puerta** nice, good, super (express-

ion of approval)

puertazo (var. of) *portazo*

puertero -ra (vars. of) *portero -ra*

puertón m. (var. of) *portón* m.

pues: pues luego/pos luego of course, without doubt, certainly

pujar vn. to grunt

pujido grunt; **hacer pujidos** to grunt (see also **pujar**)

pul (Eng.) m. pool, billiards; (Eng.) pull, influence (usually political)

pulga flea market; pl. **¡újule, pa' mis pulgas!** (fixed expression of annoyance) That's the last thing I needed!

pulgiento -ta flea-ridden, lousy (in the literal sense)

puliar (Eng.) va. to pull

pulman (Eng.) m. pullman

puntada very appropiate joke or story; pl. **¡qué puntadas!** What crazy ideas!

puntía (var. of) *puntilla*

punto -ta: ser punto -ta to be cooperative, accommodating; to to be game, willing to try something; mpl. **andar de puntos** (v.s. **andar**)

puñeta masturbation; **hacerse la puñeta** (vulg.) to masturbate

puñeteada or **puñetiada** (vulg.) masturbation

puñetear or **puñetiar** (vulg.) va. to masturbate; vr. to masturbate, jack off (vulg., slang) (see also **puñeta: hacerse la puñeta**)

puñetero -ra (vulg.) fond of masturbation

purgación f. gonorrhea, clap (slang)

puro -ra utter, absolutely; only, nothing but (e.g.,: "¡Puras habladas!" 'Nothing but talk!' or "¡Pura perica!" 'Pure unadulterated bullshit!')

putear or **putiar**   vn. to solicit customers (said of prostitutes)

puto   (slang) male homosexual, fag (slang)

Q

qué: **¡qué cabeza!** (fixed expression directed at a stubborn or dense person); **¡qué esperanza(s)!** interj. (used to express strong doubt as to whether something will take place) That'll be the day!; **¡qué bonito!, ¿no?** (iron.) That's a fine howdy do!; **que + (the thing requested) + ni que + (the thing requested) / que + (the thing requested) + ni que + mis patas (tus patas) / que + (the thing requested) + ni que nada** an expression with which one refuses another's request emphatically: "Papá, quiero que me compres un carro—Que carro ni que mis patas" 'Papá, I want you to buy me a car—A car, my foot (ass)'; **¡qué casualidad!** That'll be the day! (general expression of incredulity); **¡qué gracia!** (iron.) Why, that's nothing!; **¿qué hace que?** it seems like only yesterday that: "¿Qué hace que andaba jugando a las escondidas?" 'It seems like only yesterday that he was playing hide-and-seek'; **¿qué húbole?** or **¿qui úbole?** (slang) What's up?, What's happening? (phrases often used in greeting); **¿que le hace?** What's the difference?, What does it matter?, So what? (fixed expressions); **que ni qué** for sure, certainly, without doubt: "Ese niño se va a enfermar, que ni qué"; **que no ni que no** (set expression) used by the speaker when he/she refuses to take no for an answer: "Hijo, lávate los pies—Ahorita no mamá—Que no ni que no"; **¿que qué?** Huh?, Whatcha say? (discourteous); **¡qué sí!** (stress on *qué*) I should say so! Absolutely!: "¿La besó el novio? —¡Qué si!"; **¿qué tal?** (indication of pleasant surprise upon hearing good news) How about that?, Imagine that!; **¿qué tanto?** how much? (Std. *¿cuánto?*); **¿qué es Ud. de____?** How are you related to____?; **que quien sabe qué** (coll.) (fixed expression) many, a lot, an exorbitant number: "Ese ranchero tiene más caballos que quien sabe qué" 'That rancher has more horses than you can shake a stick at' (coll.); **yo que tú (yo que él,** etc.**)** If I were you (him, etc.); **y que aquí y que allá y que fue y que vino** etcetera, etcetera, and so on and so forth

quebrado -da (Ang.) broke, pennilesss; (Ang.) f. break, opportunity; first shot in a game of pool; **dar quebrada** to give someone an

opportunity: "¡Dame una quebrada momás!" 'Just give me a break!';
hablar un inglés (francés, español,
etc.) **quebrado** (Ang.?) to speak
broken English (French, Spanish,
etc.)
quebranzas   pl. (hum.) taxes
quebrar: ser de esos (esas) que no
quiebran ni una taza/ni un plato
to be the type of person who is not
able to hurt a fly (coll.), be extremely gentle
quecha   (Eng.) m. catcher (baseball) (see also **queche** et al.)
quechar   (Eng.) va. to catch (a
ball, in baseball); vn. to play the
position of catcher (in baseball)
queche or **quécher** (Eng.) m.
catcher (in baseball) (see also
quecha)
quedar   va. to fit, match, harmonize with, go well with: "Este traje
le queda bien" 'This suit fits him
well'; vn. to match, harmonize:
"¿Le queda ese pantalón a ese
saco?" 'Do those pants match that
coat?'; to matter, concern, involve:
"¿A mí qué me queda de eso?"
'What's that to me?/How does
that involve me?'; vn. to die: "Allá
quedó" 'He died then and there'
'That was the end of him'; vr. to
end, terminate: "La vista se quedó
donde se besaron" 'The movie
ended where they kissed each
other'; vr. to flunk, fail a course; to
not pass (not be promoted) to the
next higher grade (ref. to elementary and secondary schools); **ay**
que quede let it rest, let it be
(etc.); **¿cómo te (le, les) quedó el**
ojo? (slang) How does that grab
you?, How do you like them
apples? (slang); **quedar a la**
medida (for clothes) to fit to a T:

"El sombrero le quedó a la
medida" 'The hat fit him to a T';
quedar al pelo to fit to a T: "La
chaqueta le quedó al pelo" 'The
jacket fit him to a T'; **quedar en**
donde mismo to make no
progress, make little headway; to
not better oneself, not improve;
quedar en nada to amount to
nothing, turn out to be a failure; to
fail to reach an agreement or
solution; to be abandoned: "¿Qué
pasó con el programa? — Quedó
en nada"; **quedar hecho pedazos/**
quedar como trapo mojado to be
dead tired, end up dead tired (as
after vigorous activity); **quedar**
parejos to be tied, end up in a tie;
quedarle a alguien vn. to be
someone's business, be of interest
to someone: "¿A ti qué te queda
de eso?" 'What business is that of
yours?'; vr. **quedar(se) en la calle**
(fig.) to be left penniless, lose
everything, be left on the street
penniless; vr. **quedarse en las uvas**
(fig.) not to understand a thing, be
left completely in the dark (Std.
quedarse en ayunas, fig.); vr.
quedarse súpito -ta to fall fast
asleep as soon as one lies down;
vr. **quedar(se) tieso -sa** to die; vr.
quedarse limpio -pia to become
broke (penniless), get cleaned out
(slang); **quedarse tamañito -ta** to
be left on pins and needles,
become nervous in anticipation of;
quedársele to retain (a thought):
"Eso no se me queda a mí, por
más que lo estudie" 'I can never
remember that, no matter how
much I study it'; **sin que me (te,**
etc.) **quede nada** all modesty aside,
if I say so myself: "Qué bien
escribí esta carta, sin que me

quede nada"; vr. **tú, ¿dónde te quedas?** or **tú no te quedas muy atrás** you're no better, you're just as bad; **y allí se quedó** (fixed expression) And that's where it ended (ref. to a story, novel, movie, etc.)

quedo: dar más quedo (quedito) to turn down the volume of a radio receptor (a television set, etc.)

quedré, quedrás, etc. (vars. of) *querré, querrás,* etc. (future conjugation of *querer*)

quedría, quedrías, etc. (vars. of) *querría,* etc. (conditional conjugation of *querer*)

quehacerosa or **quihacerosa** adj. woman who enjoys doing housework

quejón -jona plaintive, complaining; querulous

Quela mf. (Eng.) Keller (surname)

Quela (dim. of) *Ángela* or *Micaela*

quelista mf. (Eng.) Kelly Field employee (Kelly Field is a military installation found on the south side of San Antonio, Texas)

quemado -da suntanned; f. burn, scald; (Ang.?) burned out (coll.), used up, pooped (out) (coll.) (ref. to persons)

quemadora incinerator

quemar vr. to be close to the solution of, be near to a hidden object one is seeking (usually in a game); to get a suntan; **quemar hule** (Ang.) (slang) to burn rubber (slang), drive a vehicle at great speed, put the pedal to the metal (slang); **traer que quemar** (slang) to have cigarettes in one's possession

quemazón f. fire (Std. *incendio*); an object that has been burned; **venta de quemazón** fire sale (sale of merchandise minimally damaged by a fire in the store)

quemón m. burn; (fig.) burn, insult; **dar quemones** (slang) to attempt to anger, to taunt, to needle (coll.)

quémpar or **quémper** (Eng.) m. camper (recreational vehicle)

quen (rus.) (var. of) *quien*

Quénede (Hispanization of) Kenedy, Texas

Queno -na (dims. of) *Eugenio, Eugenia*

quenque adv. piggyback; m. piggyback ride; **subir al quenque** to climb on (someone's back) for a piggyback ride

queque or **queique** (Eng.) m. cake; **¡aire al queque!** interj. Beat it!, Scram!, Get out of here!; **andar hasta el queque** (slang) to be lit up like a birthday cake (fig.), be very drunk

quequito (Eng.) cupcake

querendón -dona loving, affectionate (ref. to person who forms close attachments easily)

querer: ¡Dios no lo quiera! Heaven (God) forbid!

quermes (var. of) *quermés* or *quermese* m. church bazaar

quero, queres etc. (vars. of) *quiero, quieres,* etc. (pres. ind. conjugation of *querer*)

quescuezo (var. of) *pescuezo*

quescuezudo -da (vars. of) *pescuezudo -da*

queso (slang) smegma that collects around the lower part of the head of an uncircumcised child's penis

Queta (dim. of) *Enriqueta*

quien: ¿a quién y a cuántos?

What concern is that of anyone's?;
¿quién te (lo) manda? I told you
so!

quihacer   m. (var. of) *quehacer* m.

quimona   (var. of) *quimono* (Std.)

quinceañera or **quinciañera** girl
who is just turning fifteen and in
whose honor a coming-out party is
traditionally given

quinda or **quínder** (Eng. <Ger-
man) m. kindergarten

Quinesvil   (Hispanization   of)
Kingsville, Texas

quinientas: a las quinientas or
allá a las quinientas after a long
period of time (often ref. to delayed reaction; also ref. to solutions or assistance coming too late
to be of any good)

Quinipa (Hispanization of) Knip-
pa, Texas

Quino -na   (dims. of) *Joaquín
-quina*

quinta small park-like area containing a gazebo, a band platform,
etc., in the center, which is used
for meetings or recreational purposes

Quique   (dim. of) *Enrique*

quire   (Eng.) mf. kitty, kitten

quiro -ra   (Eng.) kiddo, bud, bub
(slang) (terms of endearment, also
vocatives)

quit (Eng.) kid (used, at times
maliciously, as a prefix to a series
of sobriquets denoting physical
attributes, e.g., *quit jorobas* [said to
a hunchback])

quitar va.: **quitar la linda** (slang)
to deflower (euph.), cause to lose
one's virginity (said of women):
"Si no te cuidas te van a quitar la
linda"; vr. to stop, cease, subside
(esp. with ref. to weather phe-
nomena): "Ya se quitó l' agua"
'It's stopped raining now'; **quien
quite y** perhaps: "Quien quite y
vengan temprano" 'Perhaps they'll
come early'; **no se le quita** You
can't take that away from him
(fig.), You've got to give him his
due: "No se le quita, de veeras
saaabe sus cosas" 'You've got to
hand it to him, he really knows his
stuff'

R

rabo: viejo rabo verde (see **verde**)

rabón -bona (hum.) short-statured; overly short (ref. to articles of clothing shorter than is appropriate): "Ese vestido le queda muy rabón" 'That dress is too short for you'; **pantalones robones** highwater pants (hum.), pants not reaching the ankle

rachar (Eng.) va. to rush, crowd up upon (esp. in sports)

radiodería (var. of) *radiador* m. (aut.)

Rafa or **Rafe** or **Rafel** (dims. of) *Rafael*

raid (Eng.) m. ride (in a car)

Raihuot (Hispanization of) Redwood, Texas

raitar or **raitear** or **raitiar** (Eng.) vn. to ride (in a car), go for a ride, go riding

raitón (Eng.) m. ride (in a car)

raiz f. (var. of) *raíz* f.

rajada (vulg.) vulva

rajada (var. of) *rajadura*

rajar vr.: **rajarse con** to denounce, squeal (slang), betray: "Ya no tengo nada que ver con él porque se rajó con la policía" 'I don't have anything to do with him anymore because he squealed to the cops'

rajeta(s) mfsg., pl. (most often used as an adjective) tattletale, betrayer, denouncer, squealer (slang); breaker of promises: "Todo el mundo sabe que ella (él) es muy rajetas"

rajolear or **rajoliar** vr. to back down, take back (a promise)

rajón -jona coward; tattletale, betrayer, stool pigeon (slang); breaker of promises

ralea bunch of disorderly and ill-bred persons

ralo -la weak, flavorless (commonly ref. to coffee or other beverage)

ramada (var. of) *enramada*

ramas pl. bushes

ramfla (slang) jalopy, old battered-up car

ranchero -ra shy, bashful, countrified; country; regional: **música ranchera** country music (the Mexican and Chicano equivalent of Anglo-American country and western music); **pantalones de ranchero** overalls; (blue) jeans

rancho small rural farming community; (Eng.) ranch (Std. *hacienda*); **hacer rancho** to overstay one's welcome, continue to visit for too long; adj. **de rancho** countrified, cornfed (coll.), farmfresh, hickish, from the sticks: "Tu primo es muy de rancho" 'Your cousin is quite farm-fresh'; **ser puro rancho** to be very countrified, straight from the farm (fig.), a hick from the sticks (coll.)

ranfla (orthog. var. of) *ramfla*

ranquear or **ranquiar** (Eng.) va. to rank, arrange, classify

raptar (Ang.) va. to rape (Std. *violar*)

rapto (Ang.) rape (Std. *violación*)

raqueta (Eng.?) racket, illegal business operation

rascada or **rascadera** act or effect of scratching

rascarrabias mfsg., pl. irritable and easily annoyed persons

rascón m. (id. to **rascada** supra)

rascuache mf. punk, worthless person

rasguñada (id. to **rascada** supra)

rasguñon m. scratch

raspa adj. & n. riff-raff, ill-bred person: "Había mucha gente raspa ahí"; stingy, parsimonious; f. snow cone (shaved ice, to which is added a sweet fruit flavoring)

raspada act and effect of scraping

raspadora apparatus used to make scraped ice (esp. for snow cones) (see **raspa**)

rasposo -sa scratchy, uneven (ref. to surfaces), bumpy

rasquera itching sensation

rastrillar vr.: **rastrillarse (la greña)** (slang) to comb one's hair

rastrillazo blow delivered with a rake

rastrillo (slang) comb

rasurada (var. of) *rasura, rasuración* or *rasurado* act or effect of shaving

rato: a poco rato shortly, soon thereafter; **más al rato** (pleonasm) (var. of) *al rato*

ratón: ser ratón de un agujero to be a one-woman man or a one-man woman (i.e., to be completely uninterested in any member of the opposite sex except one's spouse)

ratonera (fig.) old and decrepit house, squalid or depressing dwelling; swarm of mice or rats; den of thieves, hang-out for criminal or other low-life elements

ratonero (var. of) *ratonera* mouse hole, rat hole (also fig. old house)

raun(d) (Eng.) m. round (period of time into which a boxing match is divided); **dar un raund** to go for a whole round, be able to last for a whole round (boxing)

raya pay, wages, paycheck; penny-pitching (game won by the person who pitches a penny closest to a designated line)

rayado -da (said of person carrying large sums of money or various other valuable possessions); scratched: "Ese disco está rayado" 'That record is scratched'

rayar (rus.) va. to write; to pay wages; vr. to come into money or property; to hit a streak of good luck; **rayarse el disco (la pieza)** to sound like a broken record (said of any conversation in which the speaker wears out the listeners by harping on the same subject) "¡Cállate, ese disco ya se rayó!"

raza (collective ref. to persons of Hispanic background in general; also ref. esp. to Mexican-Americans) (note: the word may have negative or pej. connotations to older Mexican-Americans): "En esa escuela había pura raza" 'There were nothing but Mexican-Americans in that school'

razón: con razón no wonder

(coll.), that's reason enough: "Se enfermó ayer. Con razón no vino"; **no hay razón** there's no excuse (for abusive behavior), that's uncalled for

reajuste m. period of adjustment

real m. unit of currency equal to twelve and a half cents, hence only used in multiples of two or more, with ref. to U.S. currency; thus *dos reales* = $0.25, *cuatro reales* = $0.50, *ocho reales* = $1.00

realizar (Ang.) va. to realize, become aware of (Std. *darse cuenta de*)

reata or **riata** (vulg.) penis; interj. Pow! (accompanies the administration or simulation of a blow, usually with the fist); **ser buena reata/riata** (coll.) to be a good Joe (coll.), be considered a good fellow by others; (see also **Pancho Riata**)

reatal or **riatal** m. large quantity of something

reatazo or **riatazo** blow with the fist; pl. severe beating, whipping, thrashing (see also **dar(se) reatazos**)

reatiza or **riatiza** severe beating (see also **dar(se) una reatiza**)

rebajar va. to belittle, disparage; humiliate; to reduce in price; **rebajar de peso** to lose weight, reduce

rebaje or **rebajo** reduction of price, discount

rebaloso -sa (rus.) (vars. of) *resbaloso -sa*

rebatar (var. of) *arrebatar*

reborujo noise; confusion, commotion, melee

rebotazo big bounce

rebusto -ta (vars. of) *robusto -ta*

reca (Eng.) wrecker (Stds. *ca-mión, grúa*)

recámada (var. of) *recámara* (Std. *alcoba*)

recar (Eng.) va. to wreck (usually a car); vr. to have a wreck

recargado -da arrogant, presumptuous

recargar vr. to brag, boast; **recargárselas** to brag, boast

recarguista mf. braggart

recebir (var. of) *recibir* (Std.)

reclamar va. to confront (i.e., confront someone with the truth): "Voy a reclamarle la verdad", "No dijo nada cuando se lo reclamé"

recle: al recle (slang) in a while

recogido -da adopted child; foster child; put away (coll.) in a penal or mental institution; retired, in for the night

reconociencia recognition; acknowledgment; gratitude, appreciation

recordar va. to keep or bear in mind; to awaken

recortado -da low on funds (see also **andar recortado -da de dinero**)

recortar va. to denigrate, put down (a person), speak ill of; to trim a small amount (of hair); to lay off, disemploy

recorte m. newspaper clipping; slight hair trim

recreción f. (var. of) *recreación* f.

reculón m. sudden jerk made by a car when the accelerator is depressed rapidly

rechancho -cha selfish, egocentric; chubby

rechinar vr.: **rechinársele a alguien el cuerpo** to get goose pimples (goose bumps)

rechinche mf. stingy, parsimonious (cf. **chinche**)

rede f. (var. of) *red* f.

redepente (var. of) (metathesis of) *de repente*

redetir or **reditir** (vars. of) *derretir*

rediculeza or **ridiculeza** (vars. of) *ridiculez* f.

redículo (var. of) *ridículo*

réferi (Eng.) m. referee

referir va. to recall a favor one has done (for someone): "A mí no me gusta que me refieran nada" 'I don't like for people to recall the favors they've done me'

refín (slang) m. food

refinar (slang) va. to eat

refuega wild and volatile woman

regadera shower-bath; (ref. to any messy room full of misplaced objects)

regador -ra (vars. of) *regadera*

reganchar (var. of) *reenganchar* va. to contract for work (often for agricultural work, field work, etc.)

reganche m. (var. of) *reenganche* m. (used with the following variant meaning): bonus given to a (farm) worker in advance of the start of the job

reganchista mf. payer of the *reganche* (q.v.) bonus

regañada bawling-out, scolding

regar: regarla to make a mess of things, foul things up, do a poor job; to create problems; to be foolish; **regársela** to make trouble

regla: bajarle la regla a la mujer to flow (said of menstrual fluid), have one's period

regresar va. to return an object to its owner (Std. *devolver*); to return a person to loved ones, friends, enemies, etc., or to the place from which he/she came

regüelto -ta (vars. of) *revuelto -ta*

Reimundo (var. of) *Raimundo*

reir (var. of) *reír*

reja (slang) (synecdoche) jail

relación f. buried treasure

relajado -da: estar relajado -da to have a hernia

relajar va. to ridicule, make a fool of; vr. to ridicule oneself

relaje m. trick, joke; cruel teasing, humiliation

relativo -va (Ang.) relative (person one is related to by blood or other kinship ties)

relís m. sharp cliff, precipice; (Eng.) m. release (from a job, from prison, from responsibility, etc.)

reló m. (orthog. var. of) *reloj* m.

reloj de alarma (Ang.) m. alarm clock (Std. *despertador*)

remodelación f. remodeling (of a house or other edifice)

remover vr.: **remover(se)le a alguien la conciencia** to be bothered by one's conscience: "Se le removió la conciencia"

remple (slang) m. car, automobile

remuda herd of horses

remudera lead horse, horse which wears a bell in a herd of horses

remudero cowboy in charge of watching the horses at night

remueques mpl. excessive and tasteless adornments

rendir vn. to suffice, be enough (usually used in the negative): "Veinte tortillas no rinden aquí; debes hacer más"

renegar vn. to protest, complain, grumble

renegón -gona m., f. constant complainer

rentar (Ang.?) va. to lease, rent, offer for rent: "Voy a rentar esta casa el mes que viene porque me hace falta el dinero" (Std. *alquilar*)

rentero -ra (Ang.?) renter, person

who pays money for the privilege
of using or occupying (Std. *inqui-
lino -na*); m. landlord, f. landlady
repegón -gona pest, annoying
person
repelar vn. to complain, grumble
repelido act of complaining, grum-
bling
repelón -lona complainer, grum-
bler
repetir vn. to belch, burp (esp.
said of babies)
repiocha mf. extremely beautiful;
terrific, swell (coll.)
repitir (var. of) *repetir*
repuñoso -sa selfish
reque (Eng.) m. wreck (of an
automobile)
requear or **requiar** (Eng.) va. to
wreck (a car); vr. to have a wreck
(see also **recar**)
réquer (Eng.) m. wrecker (Stds.
camión, grúa)
requintado -da (vars. of) *arrequintado -da*
res f. numbskull; **caer la res** (ref.
to someone who has been fooled,
taken in, deceived): "¿Sabes que
Samuel se casó con ésa de quien
te hablé antes? — ¡Uh, pues cayó
la res!"
resaca artificial lake or reservoir
resarmador m. (var. of) *desarmador* m. (Std. *destornillador* m.)
resbalón m. affair (amorous);
andar en el resbalón to be having
an affair; **resbalón -lona** shrewd,
clever, slippery (fig.); teasing
resedá (var. of) *reseda* (Std.)
resequedad f. dryness
resongar to talk back rudely (esp.
to one's elders); vn. to complain;
to kick (as a burro); to blow one's
top (slang), get angry
resortes mpl. suspenders (for

trousers)
respingar vn. to complain; to kick
(as a burro); to blow one's top
(slang), get angry
respingón -gona m., f. habitual
complainer; m. act of complaining
or blowing one's top (slang)
responsablidad f. (var. of) *respon-
sabilidad*
responsalidad f. (var. of) *respon-
sabilidad* f.
resta (slang) restaurant
resurada (var. of) *rasurada* (cf.
resurar)
resurar (Eng.?, phonetic crossing
of the 1st syllable of 'razor' with
Std. *rasurar*?) va. to shave; vr. to
shave oneself
resurección f. (var. of) *resur-
rección* f.
Resvil (Hispanization of) Reed-
ville, Texas
retacar va. to fill a container
tightly up to the very top; vr. to
stuff oneself (said of someone who
overeats)
retejilado -da very rapid: "La
chota lo paró porque iba retejilado"; in quick succession:
"Perdieron cinco juegos rete-
jilados" 'They lost five games in
quick succession'
retesuave (slang) mf. great, super,
keen, tremendous
retinto -ta very dark-skinned
(though without other specifically
Negroid features)
retobar or **retobear** or **retobiar** vn.
to talk back impudently (esp. to
older persons, to one's parents,
etc.)
retobón -bona m., f. sassy back-
talker (ref., esp., to young person
who consistently talks back to
older people)

retra (slang) m. (var. of) *retrato* (Std.)

reversa (Ang.) reverse gear (vehicle); **darle de reversa (a un vehículo)** to back up (reverse) (a vehicle); (fig.) to back up (backtrack) when one has made a mistake

revolver va. to confuse, muddle; vr. to become confused, muddled: "No digas nada ahorita; me voy a revolver si no te callas"; **revolvérsele a alguien el estómago** to get an upset stomach

revuelto -ta upset (said of stomach)

rezar: rezar rezos/rezar oraciones (pleonasm) to pray

rezumbar: rezumbarle a alguien (el aparato/el mango) para hacer algo (slang) to excel at doing something: "A Chente le rezumba (el mango) para jugar al pimpón"

riaclo (slang): **al riaclo** in a while (see also **al recle**)

rial (var. of) *real*

riata (var. of) *reata*

riatazo (var. of) *reatazo*

riatiza (see **reatiza, dar(se) una reatiza**)

ricés (Eng.) m. recess (play period during the school day)

Riche (Eng.) Richie (dim. of) Richard

ridetir or **riditir** (vars. of) *derretir* (see also **dirretir, redetir** et al.)

ridícolo -la (vars. of) *ridículo -la*

rieles (slang) mpl. woman's legs (hum.)

rielotes (slang, hum.) mpl. woman's legs

rieso (var. of) *recio*

rifa card reading (form of fortune telling); **echar rifas** to read the cards, to tell someone's fortune

rifar vr. to excel at something; to find a bargain; to have it made (coll.)

rifle m.: **estar como rifle** to be in superb physical condition for any undertaking (esp. for the sex act)

riley or **ríley** (Eng.) m. relay (race)

rillo (var. of) *río* river

rin (Eng.) m. ring; rim

rinconar (var. of) *arrinconar*

rinconera quack midwife

rinche (Eng.) m. Texas Ranger (paramilitary state police corps member)

ring (Eng.) m. ring (boxing) (Std. *cuadrilátero*)

ringuear or **ringuiar** (Eng.) va. to ring (a bell)

rir (var. of) *reír* (see also **reir**)

risa: cagarse de risa (vulg.) to laugh uncontrollably

risión -siona m., f. ridiculous; brunt of jokes, one who makes a fool of himself

risionada anything that provokes laughter

ritmo (Ang.) rhythm method (of birth control)

riuma (var. of) *reúma* mf. (Stds.), *reuma* mf.

riumático -ca (vars. of) *reumático -ca*

riumatismo (var. of) *reumatismo*

riyo, riyes, riye, riyemos/ reyimos, riyen (vars. of) *río, ríes,* etc. (pres. ind. of *reír*)

Robe or **Róbete** (vars. of) *Roberto* (man's name)

Robestán or **Robestáun** (Hispanization of) Robstown, Texas

robón -bona m., f. thief; thieving, larcenous

roche or **rocho** m. (Eng.<roach< Sp. *cucaracha*) roach , cockroach (see also **rucho**)

rodadillo caster, small wheel on a swivel inserted in or attached to the bottom of a piece of furniture or other heavy apparatus to make it easier to move

rodiado -da (vars. of) *rodeado -da*

rodiar (var. of) *rodear*

rogón -gona m., f. person who constantly begs for favors; person who enjoys being coaxed to do things; f. brazen hussy (coll.), woman who does not hesitate to make advances at men

rogar: hacerse del rogar (var. of) *hacerse de rogar* to want to be coaxed

rol (Eng.) m. bread roll; hair roll, hair roller

rol m. or **rola** f. (slang) automobile

rola (slang) phonograph record; song

rolado -da (slang) asleep; lying down

rolante (slang) m. automobile

rolar (slang) vn. to sleep; vr. to go to bed, go to sleep

role (slang) (Eng.?) m. hair roller; automobile (see also **rol, rola**); sleep (state or act of sleeping)

roleta (var. of) *ruleta*

roliar (slang) (Eng.) va. to roll someone (slang), steal from someone while he/she is asleep or drunk

romance (Eng.) m. romance, love

romo -ma short-statured

romper va. to tear (note: verb does not mean 'to break' as in Std.; for the Texas equivalent of 'to break' see **quebrar**); vr. **romperse la cabeza** to hurt oneself in the head (Std. *descalabrarse*)

rompido -da (vars. of) *roto -ta* (pparts. of *romper*)

roncadera loud snoring; combined snoring of many persons

roncón -cona m., f. person who snores frequently

roncha: hacer roncha to run up one's winnings in a game of chance after starting out with very little money

ropa: ropa de abajo underwear, underclothes; **ropa de salir** dress clothes, "Sunday best" (coll.)

roquirol (Eng.) m. rock 'n' roll (the music; the dancing appropiate thereunto)

rosa: rosa de castilla herb rose (Rosa sp.) (its petals are prepared as a tea and taken as a mild purge)

rosado -da irritated (skin): "Traigo la piel rosada aquí en el pescuezo"; chapped (lips); **andar rosado -da** to have a skin irritation in a "certain place" (euph.; when the irritated part of the body is not mentioned it is assumed to be the anal region)

rosar m. (var. of) *dorsal* m.

rosas (var. of?) *rosetas* popcorn

rosca washer (a flat dish or ring of metal, rubber or plastic, used in plumbing to prevent leakage, to relieve friction or distribute pressure)

rosquita (var. of?) *rosquilla* ring-shaped pastry

rost (Eng.) m. roast (roasted meat); roasting pan

rosticería (Eng.<roast) place where roast meat is sold; restaurant which specializes in roast meat

rotado -da (ppart. of *rotar*, q.v. infra) ruptured (with a hernia)

rotadura rupture (with a hernia) (see also **rotura**)

rotar va. & vr. (var. of) *romper*

(apparently a back formation from the Std. ppart. of *romper*, i.e., *roto*) (note: *rotar* is used in all the expected tenses and modes and is fully regular in its conjugation: *rotan, rotaron, rotaban, rotarán, rotarían, que roten, que rotaran*, etc.)

rotura   rupture (with a hernia)

royer   (var. of) *roer* va.

rozar vr.   to chap one's skin (esp. the lips)

rozón   m. slight scratch, break, or irritation of the skin; flaying of the skin

Rube   (dim. of) *Rubén*

rucaiba   (slang) mother, ole lady (slang)

rucailo -la   old person

ruco -ca   (slang) m. old man; husband; boyfriend; boy (in general); f. old woman; wife; girlfriend; girl

rucho   (Eng.<roach<*cucaracha*) roach, cockroach (see also **roche, rocho**)

rueda: rueda de manejar (manijar) steering wheel (of a vehicle) (Std. *volante*); **rueda de la fortuna** Ferris wheel; **rueda de San Miguel** type of children's game

rufiano -na   overly-familiar, overbearing

ruido: buscarle ruido al chicharrón (see **chicharrón**)

rula   (Eng.) ruler (measuring instrument)

Rumaldo   (var. of) *Romualdo*

rumbado -da   strewn, scattered (often with ref. to possessions such as toys, clothes, etc., left all over a room)

rumbar   va. to carelessly strew or scatter things about

rumia   (var. of) *riuma* (Stds. *reuma* mf., *reúma* mf.)

runrún   m. gossip

ruñir   va. to gnaw; to eat away at

Rure or **Ruri**   (Eng.) Rudy (dim. of) Rudolph

rusco -ca   stingy, parsimonious

rústico -ca   lusterless, dull, uninteresting (ref. to persons)

rutero -ra   newspaper deliverer; m. paperboy

S

sábanas: ya sábanas (slang) (expansion-disguise of *sabes*) you already know

saber: no saber dar santo y seña de alguien to be unable to tell where someone is; **no saber en donde está uno** not to know whether one is coming or going (fig.), to be highly confused; **para que sepas** (**sepan**, etc.) (set expression of defiance) So there!; **que quién sabe qué** very/extremely ____-er than a ____ (used in comparative expressions): "Está más loco que quién sabe qué" 'He's crazier than a loon'; **saber a que atenerse** to know the score (slang), know in advance what the situation is; **saber lo que es amar a Dios en tierra ajena** to know firsthand what trouble really is; **saber los secretos de alguien** (said, hum., when drinking from someone else's glass); **sepa Dios** or **sepa el burro de los mecates** (expressions indicating incredulity) God only knows!, Who can say?!

sablista mf. bum (coll.); freeloader

sabo (rus.) (var. of) *sé* (1st pers. ind. of *saber*)

sabroso -sa superior to others, hot stuff (slang): "Él se cree muy sabroso" 'He thinks he's really something'

sacar va. to throw in someone's face (fig.) the favors one has done for that person: "Vete, a mí no me gusta que me saquen los favores que me hacen"; to inherit (as physical or personal traits); "María sacó la nariz de su mamá" 'María inherited her mother's nose'; to make (money), earn: "Con esta chamba no vamos a sacar ni para pagar por los frijoles" 'With this job we're not even going to make enough to pay for the beans'; vr. to get (what one deserves): "Eso es lo que se sacan por andar molestando gente" 'That's what they get for going around bothering people'; vr. to weasel out (slang), cleverly find a way out of a responsibility or commitment; to move quickly aside to avoid a blow; **de ahí no te sacan** (**de ahí no lo [etc.] sacan**) (set expression) no one can make you yield on that point (ref. to stubborn person unwilling to be convinced); **sacar aire** to burp (a baby); **sacar daga con** to show off something new (esp. an article of clothing); **sacar la garra** to gossip; **sacar lumbre** to harp on the same subject, talk incessantly about the same topic; **sacarle a alguien la colorada** to give someone a bloody nose (see also **colorada**); **sacarle (la vuelta) a algo/ alguien** to dodge, avoid something/someone: "El jefe siempre nos da mucho trabajo y por eso le sacamos (la vuelta) cuando lo vemos venir"; **sacarle a alguien los trapos/ trapitos al sol** or **sacarle a alguien los trapos/trapitos a remojar** to hang out someone's dirty linen (fig.), bring the skeleton(s) out of someone's closet (fig.); **sacarle canas a alguien** to give someone gray hairs; **sacarle la navaja a alguien** to pull a knife on someone; **sacar patada** (Ang.) (slang) to get a kick out of (something): "Él es de los que sacan su patada de las drogas" 'He get his kicks from drugs'; **¡sácate!** interj. Pow!; **¡sácate la daga!** Get to work!; Get with it!; Your turn to pay!

sacate m. (orthog. var. of) *zacate* m.

sacateada or **sacatiada** evasive act, avoidance

sacatear or **sacatiar** va. to avoid, evade, sidestep, duck, dodge

sacatón -tona (coll.) m., f. freeloader

sacón -cona m., f. shirker, avoider of responsibilites

¡sácote! (var. of) *¡sácate!* (q.v.)

sacudir vr. to try to shake off the blame from oneself, attempt to exculpate oneself

safado -da (orthog. vars. of) *zafado -da*

safar (orthog. var. of) *zafar*

safo(s) (orthog. var. of) *zafo(s)*

saico -ca n. (Eng.) psycho (slang), a psychopath; adj. psychopathic, crazy; insane

sain (Eng.) m. sign, placard, poster

sainar or **sainear** or **sainiar** (Eng.) va. to sign (Std. *firmar*)

saine (Eng.) (var. of) *sain*

sal: echarle a alguien la sal to jinx, bring bad luck to

salado -da jinxed, cursed with bad luck

salamanquezco salamander

Salamónicos (slang) San Marcos, Texas

salarete m. bicarbonate of soda; baking powder

salida: salida de los dientes teething; **venir de entrada y salida** to call on someone briefly, stop by for a brief visit

salidera y entradera constant leaving and entering, coming and going

salidero -ra gadabout, person who is always out on the town

salidor -ra m., f. person who enjoys going out on the town (coll.), frequent seeker of nightlife entertainment

salir vn. to come to, cost: "El viaje completo me salió a cien dólares" 'The round trip (ticket) came to a hundred dollars'; **salir a luz** (Ang.?) to come to light, become apparent; **salir a manos** to break even in a game of chance; **salir canuto** to attempt to defer payment on merchandise or services after these have been delivered or performed: "Le corté el sacate y me salió canuto" 'I cut his grass and then he promised to pay me some other day'; **salir de su cuidado** to give birth: "Tu tía ya salió de su cuidado"; **salir dioquis**

(see **de hoquis, dioquis**); **salir gorda** to get pregnant; **salir pa' fuera** (euph.) to go to the bathroom (euph., to urinate or defecate) (see also **ir pa' fuera**); **salir hasta bien** to turn out for the best, be a blessing in disguise: "Salió hasta bien que no te dieron el primer trabajo; acaban de llamar para ofrecerte otro mejor" 'It turned out for the best that they didn't give you the first job; they've just called to offer you a better one'; **salir por debajo de la mesa** to always come out on the short end of the stick (fig.), always fail in whatever one attempts; **salir sobrando** to be superfluous, redundant; to be academic; to be useless or of little or no importance (often said with ref. to help offered after a problem has been solved); **salirse** to spill one's seed (coll.), for the man to withdraw the penis before ejaculation so as to avoid pregnancy; **salirse (de la casa)** to elope (Std. *huirse*); **salírsele a uno** to let slip, say without intending to (Std. *irse* or *írsele* a uno la lengua, fig. and coll.)

salubidad f. (var. of) *salubridad* f.

saludes mpl. (var. of) *saludos* (Std.)

salvar (Ang.) va. to save (money) (Std. *ahorrar*)

sanababiche or **sanababichi** (Eng.) (vulg.) m. son-of-a-bitch

San Anton (slang) San Antonio, Texas

San Antoño (var. of) San Antonio, Texas

San Cuilmas (hum.) San Antonio, Texas; (hum.) (any town one wishes to burlesque)

sanar (euph.) vn. to give birth, deliver

sanchar va. to cheat on one's spouse, commit adultery

Sánchez m. the third person in an amorous triangle (ref. to the male lover of the other man's wife)

sancho -cha adj. adulterous; m. adulteror; f. adultress; mf. animal raised as bottle-fed (in the absence of or rejection by the animal's mother)

San Felipe Del Río (original Spanish name of) Del Rio, Texas

sangre (slang) adv. no (negative response); **calentársele a uno la sangre** (var. of) *encendérsele a uno la sangre* to get boiling mad (coll.), become infuriated; **sangre débil** anemia (coll.); **sangre de chango** mercurochrome; **sangre de chinche** unpleasant, repulsive (ref. to persons); **sangre pobre** anemia; **tener la sangre liviana** to be pleasant, agreeable, well-liked

sangriar (var. of) *sangrar*

sangrón -grona m., f. disagreeable, repugnant (ref. to persons); conceited

sángüich(e) or **sángüichi** or **sánhuich(e)** (Eng.) m. sandwich

Santa Clos (Eng.) m. Santa Claus (Std. *Padre Noel*)

santo: mpl. **darse uno de santos** to be grateful, to thank one's lucky stars; **no saber dar santo y seña de alguien** to be unable to say what became of someone who is unaccountably absent

sapo frog; (orthog. var. of) *zapo*

sapoltura (var. of) *sepultura*

sarampión: sarampión de tres días German measles, rubella

sardera camp-follower (prostitute who establishes herself near a military base); woman very fond of soldiers

sardina (fig.) low man on the totem pole, person whose job is of minimal importance

sardo (slang) soldier; sergeant

sarmador m. (var. of) *desarmador* screwdriver (Std. *destornillador* m.)

sarsa (var. of) *salsa*

sartén m. (var. in gender of) *sartén* f.

sarruchar (var. of) *serruchar*

sarruche m. (var. of) *serrucho*

sarrucho (var. of) *serrucho*

sastrería dry cleaners (Std. *tintorería*)

sastrero -ra tailor (Std. *sastre*)

satín m. (var. of) *satén* satin

sátiro -ra senile old person

saurino -na (var. of) *zahorí* fortune teller, soothsayer

saxofón m. (var. of) *saxófono* m.

secador m. napkin; small cloth used to dry the dishes

seción f. (var. of) *sección* f.

seco: venirse en seco to engage in coitus interruptus, have an ejaculation elsewhere than inside the woman's vagina

secondaria (var. of) *secundaria* (most typically *escuela secondaria*)

sectiembre (var. of) *septiembre*

sedal m. type of strong string (used in fishing line, for flying kites, etc.)

sedazo screen door; window screen

sedol m. morphine

seguida: en seguida (de) alongside, next door (to): "Vive en la casa de en seguida" 'He lives in the house next door'

seguir: seguir en las mismas to continue living the same style of life (usually negative and unproductive)

seguido adv. frequently, often

segundo (see **de segundo** secondhand)

seguranza insurance (Std. *seguro*)

seguro safety pin (Std. *imperdible*); **seguro que sí** of course, naturally (see also **de seguro** for sure); **seguro que no** of course not, by no means

segurola interj. (slang) Yes sir, Yes indeed

semáfaro (var. of) *semáforo*

semásforo (var. of) *semáforo*

sembrar (slang) va. to bury a corpse

semía (var. of) *semilla*

semos (var. of) *somos* (1st pers. pl. pres. ind. of *ser*)

sencío -cía (vars. of) *sencillo -cilla*

sense or **sensén** m. game of marbles; the ring in that game (played in essentially the same fashion as the game of marbles, i.e., the object is to knock out marbles from the center of the ring)

sentaderas fpl. (var. of) *asentaderas* fpl.

sentador -ra m., f. (Ang.) babysitter

sentencia (Ang.) sentence, combination of words constituting a complete utterance (Stds. *oración, frase*)

sentenciada: tenérsela sentenciada a alguien to place someone under warning, indicating that revenge will be carried out at some future time: "Mira, Concha, cuídate que ya te la tengo sentenciada" 'Watch out, Concha. The day you're least expecting it I'm going to get my revenge on you'

sentenciar: sentenciársela a alguien (id. to *tenérsela sentenciada*, see **sentenciada**)

sentido outer ear (Std. *oreja*)

sentir: sentir bascas to gag, feel nauseated

sentón m. hard flop experienced when one sits down abruptly

señorita virgin: "Ella todavía es señorita, gracias a Dios"

sepo (var. of) *sé* (1st pers. sg. pres. ind. of *saber*) (see also **sabo**)

sepulgro (var. of) *sepulcro*

ser: aunque sea at least: "Ayúdale hasta las seis aunque sea" 'Help him until six at least'; **bendito sea Dios** the Lord works in mysterious ways; **es como si dijera/dijiera (dijeras/dijieras, dijera/dijiera, dijéramos/dijiéramos, dijeran/dijieran) mi alma** It's as if I (you, he/she, etc.) were talking to a wall; **¡no vaya a ser (tan de repente)!** That'll be the day! (general expression of incredulity); **ser algo de alguien** to be related to someone: "¿Qué es Carlos de Jorge?" 'How is Carlos related to Jorge?'; **ser caliente** to be hot, sexually excitable by nature; **ser de agua** (v.s. **agua**); **ser de dulce** (v.s. **dulce**); **ser de los otros** (v.s. **otro**); **ser de orilla** (v.s. **orilla**); **ser de palo** (v.s. **palo**); **ser lumbre** (v.s. **lumbre**); **ser de vida** to be safe, be in the clear (slang): "Ya somos de vida" 'We're safe now'; **ser más + (adj.) + que la chingada (fregada, jodida)** (vulg.) to be more + adj. + than hell: "Esa ruca es más fea que la chingada" 'That broad is uglier than hell'; **ser por de más** to be useless, be in vain: "Es por de más tratar de darle consejos" 'It's useless to try to give him advice';

sea por Dios so be it (fixed expression indicating resignation); **si es de que** if: "Iremos si es de que viene temprano" 'We'll go if he comes early'; **tú lo serás (Ud. lo será**, etc.) The same to you! (expression used to return an insult)

serenatear or **serenatiar** va. to serenade

serenatero -ra serenader, person who serenades

serenito -ta on an even kilter, smoothly: "El mecánico compuso el carro, y ahora corre serenito" 'The mechanic fixed the car, and now it runs smoothly'

servicio (euph.) chamber pot; (Ang.?) or (var. of?) *servicio militar* or *servicio activo*

serviente -ta m., f. (vars. of) *sirviente* m., *sirvienta* f.

sésgale interj. Stop that!; Cut it out!, Stop bothering me!

seso: mpl. **tener (buenos) sesos** to be intelligent

sesonar (slang) to sniff glue (for a mildly narcotic effect)

setear or **setiar** (Eng) va. to set (esp. with ref. to hair)

severito -ta (pej.) numbskull, blockhead

seya, seyas etc. (vars. of) *sea, seas*, etc. (pres. subj. of *ser*)

sexudo -da sexy

shainear or **shainiar** (Eng.) (vars. of) *chainear* or *chainiar* (note: digraph "sh" pronounced as palatal sibilant [š])

sho (Eng.) (var. of) *cho* (Eng.)

sí: (no) dar de sí (used more in the negative) (not) to be reasonable, yield, be compromising, easy to convince; to budge (door, window, etc.): "Quise abrir la puerta con el martillo, pero no dio de sí" 'I tried to open the door with the hammer, but it wouldn't budge'; **de por sí que** as it is, as things (now) stand: "No hables de él ; de por sí que no quiere venir a la fiesta" 'Don't talk about him; as things now stand he surely won't want to come to the party'; **porque sí** just because; **traer de por sí** to be born with: "Ese talento lo trae de por sí" 'He was born with that talent'; **¡(sí) (a)horita!** That'll be the day! (general expression of incredulity) (see **ser: ¡no vaya a ser tan de repente!**); **y tú (ella,** etc.) **sí** (iron.) Yeah, I'll bet, That'll be the day: "Me voy a casar mañana — Y tú sí"

si: ya si no well, after all, when all else is considered: "Después de que le pegó la pelota, le dolió mucho la cabeza — Ya si no." 'After the ball hit him, his head hurt a lot — Well, after all.'

sía (var. of) *silla*

siempre after all, anyway, still: "¿Siempre te vas?" 'Are you still going to go?'/'Are you going, after all?'

sietecueros msg. watery blister on the sole of the foot (caused, according to popular tradition, by stepping barefoot in horse urine)

siguir (var. of) *seguir*

silabario (slang) (expansion-disguise of *sí*) adv. yes (affirmative response)

silencito -ta quiet; taciturn

silindro (slang) (expansion-disguise of *sí*) adv. yes (affirmative response)

símbulo (var. of) *símbolo*

simón or **símon león** or **simonacho** (all slang) (expansion-disguises of

sí) adv. yes (affirmative response)

simple mf. adj. (euph.) mentally retarded (cf. **inocente**)

simpletón -tona (Eng.?) m., f. simpleton, idiot, fool

sinc (Eng.) m. sink, washbasin (see also *sinque*) (Std. *fregadero*)

singlista mf. player of a singles match in tennis

sinó (var. of) *sino* but, but rather

siñor -ñora (rus.) (vars. of) *señor, señora*

sinque (Eng.) m. sink, washbasin (see also **sinc**)

sinsoncle or **sinsontle** or **sinsonte** m. mockingbird (see also **cenzoncle** et al.)

sintar (var. of) *sentar*

sintarazos (slang) (expansion-disguise of *sí*) adv. yes (affirmative response)

sintemos (var. of) *sentimos* (1st pers. pl. pres. ind. of *sentir*)

sintir (var. of) *sentir*

sinvergüenzo (var. of) *sinvergüenza*

síquele (Eng.) (interj.) Sic 'em! (expression of encouragment said to dogs)

siranda spanking (neologism used as a pseudo-noun solely within a specific context: "Bueno, si quiere siranda" 'Well, if you want a spanking... ') (derived from the phrase "Bueno, si quieres ir, anda," said to a child who asks permission to go somewhere knowing in advance that his/her parents have already denied that permission; in a sense *siranda* is a form of disguised speech to prevent the child from losing face in front of a playmate)

sirol or **sirol sirolacho** (slang) (expansion-disguise of *sí*) adv. yes

(affirmative response)

sirvir (var. of) *servir*

sirre m. (var. of) *sirle* or *sirria* dung, manure (esp. of cows, sheep, goats)

sisote m. boil (skin inflamation); sore; ringworm

sista (Eng.) sister (female sibling); Sister (nun)

so (rus.) (var. of) *soy* (1st pers. sg. pres ind. of *ser*)

so (Eng.) conj. so, therefore, (Std. *así que*)

sobador **-ra** m. masseur; f. masseuse

sobajar va. to humiliate, shame

sobar: sobar la mano (var. of) *untar la mano* (Std.), to bride, grease the palm (or hand) of (slang)

sobita mf. son-of-a-bitch (Eng.< S.O.B. + -*ita*)

sobrando (see **salir sobrando**)

sobrepelo fur coat

sobrepiso linoleum

sobres (usually mpl.) overshoes; (slang) adv. yes (affirmative response)

soca (Eng.) f. sucker, all-day sucker (type of hard candy mounted on a stick and ingested through sucking); **ni soca** (slang) not a bit, not at all

socado -da (Eng.) soaked, cleaned out (in a game of chance) (cf. **socar**); see also **andar socado -da**)

socar (Eng.) va. to soak (slang), clean out (slang), win all of someone's money in a game of chance

socas (see **andar socas**)

¡sócate! (Eng.?) interj. Socko!, Wham!, Pow!

socroso -sa (metathesis of?) *costroso -sa* dirty, filthy

sodería soft drink; bottling plant

sodero **-ra** person who bottles soda (soft drinks) in a bottling plant; person who sells or delivers soft drinks; person fond of consuming soft drinks

sodonga (slang) soda water, soft drink

sofacear or **sofaciar** vn. to lie on a sofa

sofbol or **sófbol** (Eng.) m. softball (baseball played with a larger, softer ball); f. softball (the ball itself)

soflamero **-ra** finicky; oversensitive, touchy

sofoque mf. heckler

sol: mata de sol sunflower; **metida del sol** sunset (Std. *puesta del sol*, less common)

solano **-na** (slang) alone, unaccompanied

solar m. patio; yard (either front or back yard or else both considered as a single space)

soldadera camp-follower

solecitar (var. of) *solicitar*

solecito intense heat

solimas (slang) (expansion-disguise of *sólo* or *a solas*) alone

sololoy or **celuloy** m. (vars. of) *celuloide*

soltar va. to let out, expand (the size of clothes); vn. to fade (clothes), come off (color on utensils)

soltura diarrhea, loose bowels

sombra carpet, rug

sombrear or **sombriar** vr. to move into or stay in the shade

sombrero: sombrero de petate straw hat

sombrerón **-rona** or **sombrerudo** **-da** person (usually male) who habitually wears a large hat; (pej.)

kicker, this term is usually applied to the present-day rancher or cowboy type (used less often to refer to the female counterpart)

sombría (var. of) *sombrilla* parasol or umbrella

sonado -da (slang) turned on (slang), under the influence of narcotic drugs

sonajear or **sonajiar** va. to spank or whip a child

sonar va. to spank: "Le sonaron fuerte" 'They gave him a sound spanking'; to pay; vr. to beat up; to spank: "Al niño se lo sonaron"

soncear or **sonciar** (orthog. vars. of) *zoncear* or *zonciar*

soncera (orthog. var. of) *zoncera* or *zonzera*

songa (Eng.) (slang) song

sonsera (orthog. var. of) *zoncera* or *zonzera*

sonsear or **sonsiar** (orthog. vars. of) *zoncear* or *zonciar*

sonso -sa (orthog. var. of) *zonso -za* or *zonzo -za*

soñaliento -ta (vars. of) *soñoliento -ta*

soñar (slang) vr. to put oneself under the influence of marihuana

sopa mf. convict, jailbird (coll.); ¡sopa! interj. Pow!, Wham!; **sopas** adv. yes (affirmative response) (slang)

sopear or **sopiar** vn. to use tortillas or pieces of bread (rather than forks and spoons) as eating utensils

sopera soup bowl; bowl for any purpose

sopetón (see **de un sopetón** in one gulp)

sopitas fpl. pieces of cornmeal tortillas mixed with scrambled eggs and bits of onion

soplado -da bloated; heavy, fat

soplar va. to punish with a whipping or with blows

soplete m. harsh scolding

sopletón or **soplón** m. punishment through a severe beating or whipping

soplo heart murmur

soponcio uneasiness; despair

sopora (Eng.) mf. supporter (Std. *partidario -ria*)

soportar (Ang.) to support, back up, be a partisan of (Std. *apoyar*); to sustain, maintain; to finance

soporte (Ang.) m. support, backing, partisanship (Std. *apoyo*)

sopresa (var. of) *sorpresa*

soqueado -da or **soquiado -da** (Eng.) (vars. of) *socado -da* (see also **andar soqueado -da** et al.)

soquear or **soquiar** (Eng.) (vars. of) *socar* (Eng.)

soquete (orthog. var. of) *zoquete* m.

sorber: sorber (con las narices) (Std. *sorbir por las narices*) to sniff, inhale through the nose

sordeque m., **sordeca** f. (slang) (disguise of *sordo*) deaf person

sorprendiente mf. (var. of) *sorprendente* mf.

sorrastro -tra dissipated; degenerate

sospirar (var. of) *suspirar*

sospresa (var. of) *sorpresa*

spich (Eng.) m. speech, discourse, oration (see also **espiche**)

star (var. of) *estar* to be (resultant conjugation): *stoy, stas, sta*, etc. (pres. ind.) and *ste, stes, ste*, etc. (pres. subj.)(see also **tar**)

stepiar (Eng.) vn. to step (Std. *plantar el pie*)

stimrola (Eng.) steamroller

storia (rus.) (var. of) *historia* or

hestoria

straique (Eng.) m. (var. of) *estraique* (Eng.)

straiquiar (Eng.) (var. of) *estraiquear, estraiquiar*

suadero (var. of) *sudadero*

suato -ta foolish, stupid

suave (slang) easy, unconcernedly (see **agarrarla suave**); (slang) nice, cool (slang), okay: "(Es)tá suave, bato" 'Cool, man'; **darle a alguien la suave** to humor someone; to flatter someone, give someone a snow job (slang); **¡que suave (le haces/hace/hacen)!** Nice going! (iron.), That's a fine howdy do!

suavizar vr. to regain one's composure, to cool it (slang)

subajar va. to discredit, run someone down (coll.)

sube y baja or **subeibaja** m. teeter-totter

subir: subir pa(ra) (ar)riba (pleonasm) to go up, ascend; **subírsele a alguien el/lo indio** to lose one's temper; to get very angry; **subírsele la tomada a alguien** to get tipsy, high on alcohol

sudada act and effect of sweating

sudar: sudar la gota gruesa (var. of) *sudar la gota gorda* to sweat blood, overtax oneself

sudón -dona m., f. person who sweats easily, profusely, and often; m. act and effect of sweating

sueño: llenar de sueño to have enough sleep

sueñal m. considerable tiredness or sleepiness

suera (Eng.) sweater (see also **suéter**)

suerte fsg.: **de (a) buena suerte** fortunately, luckily, it's a good thing; **suerte chaparra/suerte perra** very bad luck; **suerte loca** good luck; fpl. magic tricks; **hacer suertes** to do magic tricks

suertero -ra lucky, fortunate

suertudo -da lucky, fortunate

sufrido -da said of a person who conceals his pain or grief from others, of one who endures it in silence

sufrir: sufrir de la cintura to have back trouble, have a bad back

suich or **suiche** (Eng.) (electrical) switch

suichi (Eng.) m. switch (electrical) (Std. *interruptor* m.)

suídá or **suidad** f. (vars. of) *ciudad*

suidadanía (var. of) *ciudadanía*

suidadano -na (vars. of) *ciudadano -na*

suimear or **suimiar** (Eng.) vn. to swim

suimimpul (Eng.) m. swimming pool

sumbar (orthog. var. of) *zumbar*

sumir vr. to get into debt

supcio -cia (vars. of) *sucio -cia*

supido (ppart.) (var. of) *sabido*

súpito -ta fast-asleep

suprentendente or **suprintendente** mf. (vars. of) *superintendente* mf. (Std.)

sura quarter, twenty-five cent piece; **caerle sura a alguien** not to be liked by, be disagreeable or distasteful to (said of persons): "Ese tipo me cae sura" 'I can't stand that guy'

sure (Eng.) m. sewer

suroto -ta (slang) unpleasant, annoying; f. petty thief

sur(r)umato -ta (vars. of) *zurumbato -ta* (see also **zurum-bático -ca**)

susirio (var. of) *susidio*

sustituigo (var. of) *sustituyo* (1st pers. sg. pres. ind. of *sustituir*)

sustituyir   (var. of) *sustituir* (Std.)

susto   (an illness which, according to popular belief, is caused by a traumatic experience, resulting in symptoms of nervous tension, loss of appetite, etc.); **curar de susto** to cure (by sorcery) the after-effects of *susto* or any frightening experience; **estar curado -da de susto**

(said of a person who doesn't scare easily)

sut   (Eng.) m. suit (Std. *traje*)

swinguear or **swinguiar**   (Eng.) to swing (slang), enjoy oneself as the jet set does (frequent connotation: to participate actively in sex of an often exotic variety)

T

ta, tamos, tan (see **toy**)

tabaceado -da or **tabaciado -da**
weak; tired, played-out (see also
tabaquiado -da)

tabaquiado -da (slang) weak, etc.
(id. to **tabaceado -da**)

tabique (slang) m. jail

tabiro (slang) jail

tabla: **tabla marina** surfboard;
estar/quedar/salir tablas to be
tied (esp. in a sports competition);
to be even, break even

tablita shoe with a pointed toe

taco gall, impudence; effrontery:
"Tú sí que tienes taco diciendo
eso" 'You've really got a lot of gall
saying that'; **hablar con taco** to
speak in a pompous manner

tacotillo tumor; boil (skin irritation)

tacuache m. (var. of) *tlacuache*;
mf. drunk, inebriated

tacuachita or **tacuachito** (type of
polka)

tacuche m. (slang) suit of clothes;
clothes (in general), wardrobe;
(slang) worthless bum, good-
for-nothing person

tacucho (slang) (var. of) *tacuche*
suit of clothes

Tacho -cha (dims. of) *Anastasio
-sia*

tadre (var. of) *tarde* adv. and f.

tafetán m. adhesive tape

taipear or **taipiar** (Eng.) va. to type,
typewrite

taipiador -ra (Eng.) (cf. **taipear**)
m., f. typist; f. typewriter

taipista (Eng.) mf. typist

talache m. (var. of) *talacho* pick
axe

tal: tal por cual mf. (pej.) a substitute expression for the stronger
'son-of-a-bitch', 'no good bastard':
"Nunca me ha gustado ese tal por
cual"

talaraña (var. of) *telaraña*

talón -lona m., f. (slang) thief,
hustler (coll.); m. fifty-cent piece,
half-dollar

talonear or **taloniar** (slang) va. to
steal; to hustle (slang); to walk
hurriedly

taltascuán m. cockroach (see also
**Juan, Tapajuán, Tapascuán,
tascalcuán** et al.)

tallador m. washboard

talla joke, witty anecdote; (Eng.)
tire (aut.); (Eng.) tie, necktie;
(Eng.) railroad tie

tallar va. to scrub, wash (e.g.
clothes); **tallarse los ojos** to rub
one's eyes

tallarín -rina (Eng. <tired?) (slang)
tired

talle (slang) m. work; job

talludo **-da** stubborn; tough, resistant; old, aged; flexible as regards the truth, moderately mendacious

tamalada tamale bake (social event at which tamales are the main dish)

tamalero -ra very fond of tamales; maker and/or vendor of tamales; (pej.) common laborer, peon

tamales mpl.: **hacerle a alguien los tamales de chivo** to deceive one's spouse in an adulterous affair

tamañito -ta (see **estar tamañito -ta, quedarse tamañito -ta**)

tamaño **-ña: colgar tamaña(s) jeta(s)** (slang) to pout

tambo (slang) jail

tamborero **-ra** (vars. of) *tamborilero -ra* drummer

tamboreteado -da or **tamboretiado -da** tired, worn-out; beaten up (in a fight)

tamboretear or **tamboretiar** va. to beat up (in a fight)

tamboriza: darle a alguien una tamboriza to beat someone to a pulp in a fight

tamién (var. of) *también*

tanates mfsg. strong-willed person

tando (slang) hat

tanque mf. (fig.) fat person; (Ang.) m. tank (slang), jail

tan-tan (onomatopoetic) knock-knock (sound made when knocking at a door)

tanteada or **tantiada** estimate, calculation

tantito -ta (dims. of) *tanto -ta*: "Échale tantita sal" 'Just throw in a little bit of salt'; a moment, a second: "Espérate tantito" 'Wait a second'

tanto -ta: en tanto que nada in the twinkling of an eye: "Lo hizo en tanto que nada"; **¿qué tanto?** How much? (Std. *¿cuánto?*); **un tanto** a little bit, a fixed amount: "Le podemos dar un tanto ahora y mañana lo demás"

tapa (slang) hat; hubcap (var. of) *tapacubos* (Std.); (see also **volarse la tapa**)

tapado -da constipated; narrow-minded; unyielding, uncompromising; naive

tapajuán m. cockroach (see **taltascuán** et al.)

tapar va. to constipate: "El pan me tapó" 'The bread constipated me'; vr. to become constipated

tapascuán **m.** cockroach (see **taltascuán** et al.)

tapón -pona m., f. short, stocky person; m. **echarle a alguien un tapón** to tell someone off

taquero -ra person who prepares and sells tacos

tar (var. of) *estar* (see also **star**)

tarántula (fig.) mf. hairy person

tardeada or **tardiada** late afternoon party (usually held out-of-doors)

tardecito -ta adv. a little bit late; very late (iron.)

tarecua (slang) shoe

taris (slang) m. jail

tarlango (slang) hat

tartana old car, jalopy

tarugada foolish action

tarugo -ga fool, idiot

¡tas! or **¡tas tas!** interj. Pow! Wham!, Bang! (imitation of sound of bullets)

tasajear or **tasajiar** va. to slice (esp. meat)

tasajillo or **tasajío** type of cactus plant with very prickly leaves

tascalcuán m. cockroach (see

taltascuán et al.)

tasinque m. sheep-shearer (person who shears sheep for a living)

tatajuán m. cockroach (see taltascuán et al.)

tatema meat roasted in the hot embers of a fire (esp. ref. to heads of animals cooked in this fashion)

tatú (Eng.?) or (var. of?) tattoo (Std. *tatuaje*)

taun (Eng.) m. town; downtown, city center

taúr m. (var. of) *ataúd*

taurería funeral home

tavía (var. of) *todavía*

taxa (Eng.) tax (esp. income tax)

taxación (Eng.) f. taxation

taya (orthog. var. of) *talla* (Eng.)

té (slang) m. marihuana

tecato -ta (slang) junkie, heroin user, drug addict

tecla (slang) cigarette butt

tecol m. (slang) (abbrev. of) *tecolote* m.

tecolota (slang) cigarette butt

tecolote (slang) m. policeman; owl; night watchman

tecorucho old tumble-down house

tecurucho (var. of) *tecorucho*

teip (Eng.) m. tape

teipiar (Eng.) va. to tape

tejabán- bana m., f. small old house, often in disrepair, covered with a tile roof

tejón -jona m., f. (hum.) short-statured; (euph.) **tejones si no hay liebres** (*tejones* is euph. for "Te jodes ..." and the last four words constitute nonsense syllables; the literal translation is 'Badgers if there are no hares')

Tela (dim. of) *Estela*

tele (abbrev. of) *televisor* and *televisión* f. television; woman's breast; baby bottle, nursing bottle

telefón (auditory adoption from Eng.) m. telephone (Std. *teléfono*)

telefonazo: echar un telefonazo to make a telephone call, to phone someone

telefoneada or telefoniada telephone call

telele m. convulsion, fit; tantrum

telenovela soap opera

telefoniar (var. of) *telefonear*

televí f. (abbrev. of) *televisión*

televigente m. (var. of) *televidente*

tembeleque mf. (var. of) *tembleque* mf. adj.

temolote m. (var. of) *tejolote* stone pestle

templete m. badly-built construction armature (scaffolding)

temponear or temponiar va. to be accustomed to

Tencha (dim. of) *Hortensia, Cresencia*

tendajero -ra storekeeper (esp. ref. to owner of a small grocery store)

tendajo small store (esp. small grocery store)

tendedero or tendedera act of hanging out clothes to dry on a clothesline

tender: tender la cama (Std. *hacer la cama*)

tendido -da: estar tendido -da to be lying in state (said of a dead person in a funeral parlor) (Std. *estar expuesto -ta en capilla ardiente*)

tendida act of hanging out clothes to dry on a clothesline (cf. tendedero et al.); clothes hung out to dry

tener: con eso tuve (tuvo, tuvimos, tuvieron) That was the last straw, That's all I (he, she, you, we, they) needed; no tener en qué caerse

muerto -ta to be destitute, dirt-poor; **tener bien agarradito -ta a alguien** to have someone wrapped around one's little finger (slang), have someone eating out of one's hand (usually makes ref. to the woman who dominates her husband, boyfriend or fiancé, utterly and effortlessly); **tener boca chica** to be taciturn, speak infrequently; **tener (un) buen tiempo** (Ang.) to have a good time, enjoy oneself; **tener buenos pesos** to have a great deal of noney, be flushed (coll.); **tener carrito** to harp on the same subject, talk constantly about the same thing; **tener cuerpo de tentación y cara de arrepentimiento** to have a beautiful body and a homely face (ref. to women); **tener el alma en el cuerpo** to wear one's heart on one's sleeve (fig.), allow one's emotional state to be very noticeable; **tener fon/tener un fonazo** (Eng.) to have fun, have a good time; **tener gusto** to be (feel) happy: "José tiene mucho gusto porque le dieron un regalo" 'Joe is very happy because they gave him a present'; **tener huevos** (vulg.) to have a lot of guts (coll.), have sufficient bravery for; **tener la cara de hacer algo** to have (sufficient) audacity to do something; **tener la sangre de chinche** to be repugnant to, be repellent to; **tener mala la tomada:** "Tiene mala la tomada" 'When he drinks he really gets his Irish up' (ref. to person—Irish or not—who habitually becomes belligerent or pugnacious after having had a few alcoholic drinks); **tenerla hecha** (Ang.?) to have it made (to have achieved a level of accomplish-ment sufficient to insure future success); **tener a alguien de su cuenta** to have someone on a string (fig.), have someone in a position of dependency: "Ya déjalo, ya lo tuviste bastante de tu cuenta"; **tener (la) lengua suelta** to be garrulous, speak frequently; **tener (un) mal tiempo** (Ang.) to have a bad time, not to enjoy oneself; **tener mucha lengua** to be very talkative; **tener pelotas** (vulg., slang) to have guts (coll.), intestinal fortitude; **tener que darle a alguien en el codo** to have to make someone pay for something (ref. to difficulties in getting a stingy person to pay) (cf. **codo**); **tener un tornillo suelto** (Ang.?) to have a screw loose, to be slightly crazy

tenis mpl.   (Eng.?<tennis, slang for tennis shoes) tennis shoes; **colgar los tenis** (slang) to die

tentadera   repeated act of touch-ing, feeling, pawing (excessive handling by one person of an-other)

tentón -tona   m., f. person given to excessive and repeated touch-ing, feeling, fondling, etc. (cf. **tentadera**)

teórica   (slang) talk, chatter

teoricar   (slang) va. & vn. to talk, chatter, jabber

tepalcates   mpl. odds and ends of little value

tepascuán   m.   cockroach   (see **taltascuán** et al.)

tepocate   m. (coll.) kid, runt (small child of unprepossessing appear-ance)

tequilero -ra   seller of tequila; person fond of drinking tequila

teralaña   (metathesis of) *telaraña*

Tere   (dim. of) *Teresa*

terregal   m. dust cloud

terrero   dust cloud

terroso -sa   dusty

tesón: agarrar tesón con   to harp on (a subject); to use or wear (repeatedly): "Agarró tesón con la corbata nueva" 'He kept on wearing the new tie'

testal   m. round ball of dough constituting the proper amount of *masa* (q.v.) needed to make a single tortilla

testear or **testiar**   (Eng.) va. to test, examine

testo -ta   full, stuffed

tetera   (var. of) *tetero* baby bottle; sinecure; act of drinking alcohol; **agarrar la tetera** to take to the bottle (coll.), become an alcoholic

tiachingada: acá   tiachingada (tiachingá)   (vulg., slang) a long way away, half way to hell and gone (slang), way the shit out there (vulg., slang)

tiatro   (var. of) *teatro*

tibón   m. (Eng.) T-bone steak

ticha   (var. of) *tícher* (Eng.) mf.

tichar   (Eng.) va. & vn. to teach

tícher   (Eng.) mf. teacher

tiempal   m. long period of time, coon's age (slang): "Hace un tiempal que no lo veo" 'I haven't seen you in a coon's age' (coll.)

tiempecito   bad weather; plenty of time, time to spare

tiempo   (Ang.) time, clock time (Std. *hora*): "Ya es tiempo de ir" 'It's time to go'; (see also **buen tiempo, mal tiempo**)

ticurucho   (var. of) *tecorucho*

tienda   fly (of trousers); **andar con la tienda abierta/traer la tienda abierta** to have one's fly open; **tienda de cinco y diez** (Ang.) five-and-ten-cent store

tiendero -ra   (vars. of) *tendero -ra*

tiernísimo -ma   (vars. of) *ternísimo -ma*

tierra: caerle tierra a alguien   to be taken by surprise: "Estaban jugando a los dados cuando les cayó tierra. Fue la policía" 'They were playing dice when they were taken by surprise. It was the cops'; **saber lo que es amar a Dios en tierra ajena** (see **saber**)

tierral   m. large cloud of dust; large amount of dust

tierregal   m. (var. of) *terregal* m.

tierroso -sa   (vars. of) *terroso -sa*

tieso -sa   (Ang.?) stiff (slang), cold stone dead (coll.), dead; (fig.) **dejar tieso -sa** to kill, assassinate; (fig.) **quedar(se) tieso -sa** to die

tíguere -ra   m., f. (vars. of) *tigre* mf.

tijera: ser cortados -das por la misma tijera   (said of persons having the same characteristics) to be cut from the same cloth (fig.)

Tila   (dim. of) *Otilia*

tiliches mpl.   stuff, junk, old bits of odds and ends; personal effects

timba   (slang) capsule of heroin

timona   (var. of) *quimono* (Std.)

tina   pail (usually one of galvanized iron)

tinaco   large elevated tank for the storage of drinking water (often the water supply for an entire municipality)

tiniado -da   (Eng.) (slang) high from sniffing paint thinner (which produces a slightly narcotic effect)

tinto -ta   (slang) African American

tío: Tío Samuel   (Ang.) Uncle Sam (symbolic representation of the United States); **tío taco** (pej.) Mexican-American who has sold out (slang) to Anglo society, accepts its values, and generally opposes militant Chicano politics

tipazo Adonis, extremely handsome man

tipo -pa elegantly dressed; **andar (muy) tipo -pa** to be elegantly dressed

tíquete (Eng.) m. ticket (entrance pass), receipt, etc.; ticket (list of political candidates); traffic ticket; **la casita de los tíquetes** box office (theater), ticket office (railroad depot) (Std. *taquilla*)

tiquetería (Eng.) (cf. **tíquete**) large number of tickets

tiquetero -ra (Eng.) (cf. **tíquete**) ticket-seller

tiracho -cha (slang) African American

tiradero disorderly collection of items left scattered about a room

tirado -da disorderly, helterskelter, unkempt; f. hunting (with a firearm); (vulg.) fornication, sexual intercourse; f. (vulg., slang) screwed, (vulg., slang) sexually possessed (ref. to a female); **dar una tirada** (vulg.) to fornicate; **estar tirado -da** to be abed, lying in bed (usual ref. to sick or lazy person)

tirador -ra spendthrift, squanderer, wastrel (Std. *derrochador -ra, gastador -ra*); m. sex friend, satyr; f. nymphomaniac

tirante adj. mf. stiff (slang), dead

tirantitas fpl: **levárselas tirantitas a alguien** to keep a tight rein on someone: "A sus hijas se las lleva tirantitas"

tirar va. (slang) to use, come out with (coll.): "Está tirando mucho totacho" 'He's using a lot of English'; to waste money, squander; **hasta pa' tirar pa' riba (hasta para tirar para arriba**) with much to spare, in great abundance, in excess: "Tiene dinero hasta para tirar para arriba" 'He's got money to burn'; **tirar a león/lión** to pay no attention to, ignore; **tirar a lucas** (slang) to ignore; to ditch (slang), leave unaccompanied; **tirar alto** to aspire to a lucrative or prestigious position or career, to shoot for the stars (fig.); **tirar besos** to throw kisses (usually at an audience or at children, as along a parade route); **tirar flores** to compliment; **tirar línea** (Ang.?) to feed someone a line, tell someone an embellished version of the truth; vn. **tirar (la) basura** (mildly euph., slang) to take a dump (slang), defecate; **tirar bonque** (slang) to sleep; **tirar chancla/ tirar chancle** (slang) to dance; **tirar (el) agua** (slang) to urinate; **tirar garra** (slang) to dress well; **tirar gritos** to shout, yell; **tirar pestaña** (slang) to sleep; **tirar plancha** (slang) to be left holding the bag (slang), be abandoned (e.g., a woman waiting in vain for her fiancé at the church on their putative wedding day); **tirar zoquete** (mildly euph., slang) to defecate; **tirarla pa'** (slang) to head for, go toward a destination: "Ése, ¿pa' ónde la tira?" 'Hey you, where ya goin?'; **tirarle a todo** to try one's hand at everything; **tirarle a todo y no darle a nada** to be a Jack of all trades and a master of none (coll.), be able to do many things but none well; **tirar moco** (slang) to cry; **tirar nailon** (slang) to dance; **tirar playa** (slang) to take a bath; to take a shower bath; **tirar rollo**

(slang) to talk; **tirar saliva** (hum.) to talk; vr. **tirarse a la calle/ tirarse a la perdición** to go wrong, take the road to perdition; to become a prostitute; **tirarse la manteca** (slang) to let the cat out of the bag (coll.), tell a secret; **tirarse uno** or **tirarse un pedo** (vulg.) to expel anal gas

tiricia sadness

tirilí mf. (slang) juvenile delinquent (see also **tirilón, tirilongo**)

tirilón -lona (slang) juvenile delinquent

tirilongo -ga (slang) (id. to **tirilí, tirilón -lona**)

tiringüitingüi, tiringüitingüi rock-a-baby

tiro shooting marble used in the game of marbles; cue ball (in pool or billiards); (see also **a tiro de que, a todos tiros, de a tiro/del tiro**)

tirón: vivir a(l) tirón to have a hard time making ends meet, barely eke out a living

tironear or **tironiar** (slang) to make love; to pull at each other's limbs and clothes in a fight or in fun

tis f. (var. of) *tisis* (q.v.)

tísico: narices de tísico (said of a person having an) extra-keen sense of smell

tisis adj. (var. of) *tísico -ca* tubercular

Tita (pet name for) *Jesusita*

titiritear or **titiritiar** (vars. of) *tiritar* (Std.)

tiví (Eng.) m. television, T.V. (abbrev.)

tizón -zona dark-complexioned person

tlachichinole m. type of herb (Kohleria deppeana) prepared in solution and used as a vaginal douche

to or **too** (vars. of) *todo* all

toalla napkin, table napkin

toallita protective cover for furniture surfaces (tables, chests of drawers, etc.), antimacassar

toavía (var. of) *todavía*

tocador m. large cloth draped over chest of drawers for decorative effect

tocar: andar uno que toca lumbre to be hard up financially, be in dire need (usually said of a person who stands ready to resort to any means to resolve his econcomic situation); **lo que está de tocar** whatever will be, will be; **ya le tocaba** his number was up, he was destined to die

tocino ham

tochar (Eng.) va. to touch

tochdaun or **touchdáun** (Eng.) m. touchdown (in football)

todo (see **tirarle a todo y no darle a nada**); (see also **estar en todo** and **a todo vuelo**)

tofudo -da (Eng.) (slang) tough, rough (ref. to aggressive persons)

toíto -ta (vars. of) *todito -ta*

tolaco or **toleco** (slang) fifty-cent piece, half-dollar

tolido or **toliro** (slang) toilet

Tolido or **Toliro** (vars. of) Toledo (influence of Eng. pronunciation)

tololoche m. string bass, bass viol, cello (Std. *contrabajo*)

tolón (slang) m. fifty-cent piece, half-dollar

tomada or **tomadera** act of drinking alcohol; **agarrar la tomada** to take to drink, develop drinking as a habit; **tener mala (la) tomada:** "Tiene mala la tomada" 'When he drinks he really gets his Irish up'

(ref. to person — Irish or not —
who habitually becomes belligerent or pugnacious after having
had a few alcoholic drinks)

tomador **-ra** m., f. habitual
drinker; alcoholic

tomar va. & vn. to drink alcoholic
beverages; **tomar al cabo** to carry
out, execute (Std. *llevar a cabo*);
tomarle sabor a algo to enjoy
something, develop a taste for

tomate (slang) m. eye, eyeball;
tomate de fresadilla small-sized
tomato which remains green when
ripe

tomatear or **tomatiar** (slang) va.
& vn. to see; to look

tomatera tomato-packing factory

tonadita singsong intonation

tonces (var. of) *entonces*

Tone (Eng.?<Tony) (dim. of)
Antonionia

tontarreaje or **tontarriaje** m.
bunch of idiots, aggrupation of
foolish persons

tontiar vn. (var. of) *tontear* vn. to
talk nonsense, act foolishly

tonino -na heavy-set person

Toño -ña (dims. of) *Antonio -nia*

tope: mpl. **darse topes** to bump
heads; to try to outdo each other
(said of two persons)

topillo or **topío: hacer topillo**
(slang) to make a fool of someone

toque (slang) m. puff on a cigarette (esp. on a marihuana
cigarette)

torcadiscos (var. of) *tocadiscos*

torcer va. (slang) to draft into the
army; (slang) to jail, put in jail;
torcerle la cara a alguien to snub
someone; vn. (slang) to die; **torcer
muy feo** or **torcer muy gacho** to
die a horrible death; vr. to have a
falling out with someone: "Jorge y

Julio se torcieron, pero ya se
conformaron"; **torcerse el pescuezo** vr. to twist one's neck; to
sprain one's neck

torcido -da angry; (slang) jailed

torcha (var. of?) *antorcha* (slang)
match (for lighting fire to an
object)

torearla or **toriarla** (slang) to defy
the law; (slang) to do the town, go
out on a spree; vr. to make the
attempt

tórica (var. of) *teórica*

torito: torito de la virgen horned
toad

tornillo or **tornío: andar de tornillo**
to be in a bad mood; **tener un
tornillo suelto** (Ang.?) to have a
screw loose (slang), be slightly
crazy

torque or **torqui** (Eng.) m. turkey

torta: torta de pan loaf of bread

tortear or **tortiar** va. to applaud;
vn. to slap one's hands back and
forth while making tortillas

tortilla: tortilla de azúcar flour
tortilla prepared with sugar and
cinnamon; **tortilla de harina** flour
tortilla; **tortilla de maíz/maiz**
cornmeal tortilla; **tortilla de masa**
cornmeal tortilla; (see also **hacer
tortilla**)

tortillería place where tortillas are
made and sold

tortillero -ra very fond of tortillas
(thin unleavened pancakes made
of cornmeal); maker and/or vendor of tortillas; (pej.) common
laborer, peon

torón -rona m., f. adj. strong and
heavy-set, bull-like (usually applied to male persons)

torzón m. sharp internal pains (in
person's intestine, etc.)

torre: darle a alguien en la torre

(slang) to hit someone where it hurts (coll.); to beat someone up in a fight; (var. of?) *tostón*

tosta (slang) fifty-cent piece, half-dollar

tostón (slang) fifty-cent piece, half-dollar; **caerle tostón a alguien** not to be liked by, to be repugnant to: "Ese bato me cae tostón" 'I don't like that guy'

totacha (slang) the English language; Pachuco speech style (the Spanish typically spoken by Pachucos); Chicano slang (in general)

totachar (slang) vn. to speak using Chicano slang (cf. **totocha**); to switch codes, speak in a mixture of Spanish and English, alternate between Spanish and English

totacho (var. of) *totacha*

totorusco -ca awkward, graceless; coarse-featured

tovieron (var. of) *tuvieron* (3rd pers. pl. pret. of *tener*)

toxido (Eng.) tuxedo

toy, tas, ta, tamos, tan (vars. of) *estoy, estás, está*, etc. (pres. ind. forms of *estar*)

toy (var. of) *todo*; **con toy todo** ____ and all: "Se lo comió con toy todo" 'He ate it, ____ and all' (____ = whichever item of food)

trabajanta baby-sitter

trabajar va. to bewitch, hex: "Parece que te están trabajando desde que volviste del viaje, pues te estás portando muy mal"

trabajo: trabajo cochino (Ang.?) (slang) dirty work (slang), criminal undertaking

trácala debt

tracalada uproar, din

tracalero -ra person frequently in debt

traco shoe

traducí, traduciste, etc. (vars. of) *traduje, tradujiste*, etc. (pret. conjugation of *traducir*)

traer va. to have (ref. to physical condition or part of the body): "Traes los ojos chinitos" 'You have sleepy eyes'; **¿qué chingadera (s) traes?** (vulg.) What the hell are you up to?; **traer carga** (slang) to be carrying narcotic drugs; **traer (mucho) empalme** to be (heavily) bundled up, be wearing (a considerable amount of) heavy clothing; **traer de por sí** to be born with: "Ese talento lo trae de por sí" He was born with that talent'; "Es malo de por sí" 'He was born bad'; **traer entre ojos** to have one's eye on someone (fig.), keep a watch out for someone, observe someone with interest; **traer la educación en las patas/traer la educación en los pies** not to behave like an educated person (said of any ill-mannered recipient of a higher academic degree); **traer a alguien al puro pedo** (slang) to harass, annoy someone; **traer gusto** to be (feel) happy "María trae mucho gusto porque se va a casar mañana" 'Mary feels very happy because she is going to get married tomorrow'; **traer la tienda abierta** to have one's fly open; **traer pelota** (vulg.) to be passionately in love with someone, have the hots for someone (slang); to be carrying the torch for someone; **traer puro clavo** (slang) to be loaded with money, be in the money; **traer que quemar** (slang) to have cigarettes in one's possession; **traer tiempo** (see **tiempo**); **traer trago** to have a few drinks under one's belt (slang), to have been drinking alcohol for quite a while: "Ese ya trae trago" 'He's already had a few'; **traer trote** (coll.) to have something up one's sleeve, be up to something: "¿Qué trote traes?" 'What are you up to?'; **traerla** to be "it" in the game of tag; vr. **¿qué (te) traes?** (fixed expression) What's with you?, What are you up to? (coll.); **traérsela a alguien muy cerquita** to keep a tight rein on someone, keep someone on a short leash (fig.)

tragadero -ra act of eating heavily

tragante m. esophagus

tragar: tragarse los años to look younger than one's years

trago alcohol in general; **agarrar el trago** to take to drink, develop drinking as a habit

traiba, traibas, etc. (vars. of) *traía, traías,* etc. (imperfect conjugation of *traer*)

traido -da (vars. of) *traído -da* (ppart. of *traer*)

traidré, traidrás, etc. (vars. of) *traeré, traerás,* etc. (future conjugation of *traer*)

traidría, traidrías, etc. (vars. of) *traería, traerías,* etc. (conditional conjugation of *traer*)

traila (Eng.) trailer (Std. *remolque*)

trailero -ra or **treilero -ra** truckdriver, one who drives a large truck (esp. an eighteen-wheeler); person who dwells in a mobile home

trailón m. (var. of) *treilón* m.

trailona (Eng.) (var. of) *treilona*

trair (var. of) *traer*

trajeado -da or **trajiado -da** elegantly dressed

trajiar (var. of) *trajear*

trajiera, trajieras, etc. (vars. of) *trajera, trajeras,* etc. (past subj. conjugation of *traer*)

trama wheat flour bread

tramados mpl. (slang) pants, trousers

tramos mpl. (slang) pants; **tramo fregón** (slang) zoot suit (type of clothing worn by hoodlum elements in the 1930's and 1940's)

trampa: llevarse a alguien la trampa: "¡Me lleva la trampa!" 'Well I'll be damned!'; (also used in the sense of 'to find oneself in a tight spot'): "¡Ya me llevaba la trampa!" 'I was really in trouble then!'

trampa or **trampe** (Eng.) m. tramp, bum; villain in a movie

trampar oreja (slang) to sleep

trampear or **trampiar** va. to hunt animals; to trap animals; vn. to enter without paying (as into a movie theater)

tranca: echar la tranca (see **echar**)

trancalero -ra (vars. of) *tracalero -ra*

tranví m. (var. of) *tranvía* m.

trapeada or **trapiada** sponge bath

trapear or **trapiar** (Eng.) va. to trap (see also **trepear**); va. to give a spong bath; vr. to take a sponge bath

traque (Eng.) m. railroad track

¡tras! interj. Bang!, Crash!

tras(h)ambriado -da undernourished

trasculcar (var. of) *esculcar* to search (a person), search through (boxes, etc.)

trastear or **trastiar** va. to wash dishes, do the dishes

trasterío pile of dirty dishes

(waiting to be washed)

trastero　closet; storage room; attic

trastes mpl. (var. of) *trastos* dishes; furniture

travesía shortcut; **echar/hacer/ tomar una travesía** to take a shortcut

trayer (var. of) *traer*

treato (var. of) *teatro*

treila f. or **tréiler** m. (Eng.) trailer (Std. *remolque*)

treilero -ra (vars. of) *trailero -ra* driver of large truck (esp. of an eighteen-wheeler)

treilón (Eng.) m. (var. of) *trailón* large tractor-trailer attached to a truck

treilona (Eng.) truck (esp. eighteen-wheeler)

treintatreinta m. thirty-thirty (type of firearm)

tremprano (rus.) (var. of) *temprano*

tren (see **a todo tren**)

trer (var. of) *traer*

tres: las tres three puffs (on a cigarette); **¡dame las tres!** Let me have a puff!; **tres piedras** (slang) keen, excellent, great, super (etc.); "El cho estuvo tres piedras" 'The show was terrific'

Tres Ríos (Hispanization of) Three Rivers, Texas

treúnfo (var. of) *triunfo*

triato or **triatro** (vars. of) *teatro, treato*

tribo m. (var. of) *tribu* f.

trilazo (Eng.) big thrill

trimeada or **trimiada** (Eng.) trimming (of hair)

trimear or **trimiar** (Eng.) va. to trim (hair)

Trine or **Trini** mf. (dims. of) *Trinidad* mf.

tripa water hose; (hum.) thin

person; **amarrarse la tripa** to tighten one's belt (fig.), economize; to endure hunger; **tripa ida** blocked intestine; (folk medicine) belief that fear can serve to lock or block intestines

tripón -pona m., f. small child under the age of ten

triqui-triqui interj. (Eng.) m. trick-or-treat! (said by children on Halloween as they go from house to house asking for candy or other treats)

triste: fpl. **las tristes** (slang) three puffs on a cigarette (cf. **tres**)

tritear or **tritiar** (Eng.) va. to treat, entertain at one's own expense

troca (Eng.) truck (see also **troque**); **troca de dompe** dump truck

trocón -cona (Eng.) m., f. large truck (esp. eighteen-wheeler)

trochemoche: hacer algo a(l) trochemoche to do a half-assed job (coll.), do something poorly

trola (slang) match (for igniting); cigarette

trole (slang) mf. crazy; drunk

trompa (slang) mouth; fpl. thick-lipped person; mf., pl. sourpuss (coll.), person having a grouchy dispositon often accompanied by an unhapppy facial expression; **hacer trompas/poner trompas** to put on a sad facial expression; to be grouchy; (see also **darse trompa**)

trompadas fpl. fistfight

trompazos (see **darse trompazos**)

trompezar va., vn. & vr. (var. of) *tropezar* va., vn. & vr.

trompezón m. (var. of) *tropezón* m. trip, stumble

trompón -pona m., f. thick-lipped

tronadera thunderstorm; repeated cracks of thunder; volley of shots from a firearm; volley of bangs from firecrackers

tronado -da drunk

tronador m. (vulg.) male fond of engaging with frequency in amorous activities

tronar va. to smoke (esp. marihuana); **tronar cohetes (cuetes)** to pop firecrackers; **tronar las manos** to applaud, clap; **tronar truenos** (pleonasm) to thunder (used only in the impersonal); vn. **tronar los huesos** to crack (ref. to bones): "Al sentarse le truenan los huesos" 'When he sits down his bones crack'; vr. to kill: "Se tronaron a González" 'They killed González'; (vulg.) to copulate; to seduce; to spank; to beat up (in a fight); to shoot

tronco (fig. & vulg.) male sexual organ (esp. one of larger than average dimensions); (fig.) short and chubby person; **caer como un tronco** to drop off to sleep, fall asleep rapidly; **dormir como un tronco** (Ang.?) to sleep like a log

troque (Eng.) m. truck

troquero -ra (Eng.) truckdriver

trostear or **trostiar** (Eng.) va. to trust

trote: agarrar trote con to keep harping on (a theme); to wear or do (something) unceasingly (i.e.,

to fail to change one's clothes): "Ya agarraste trote con esa camisa"; **andar al trote con** to be all wrapped up in (fig.), completely involved with: "El niño anda al trote con el juguete que le compramos"; **hacerle trote a alguien** to make advances at someone; **traer trote** (coll.) to have something up one's sleeve, be up to something: "¿Qué trote traes?" 'What are you up to?'

truenar va. (var. of) *tronar*

truje, trujiste, trujo, trujimos, truj-(i)eron (vars. of) *traje, trajiste*, etc. (pret. conjugation of *traer*)

trunco -ca (Eng.) drunk

trunquis (Eng.) adj. mf. drunk

tualla (var. of) *toalla*

tubo (slang) sock, stocking; inner tube; **tubo de plástico** intrauterine device, coil, loop (contraceptive device)

tuerca: (llave de) tuerca monkey wrench

tuétaro (var. of) *tuétano*

tuist (Eng.) m. twist (the dance)

tuna (Eng.) tuna, tuna fish (Std. *atún* m.)

tupido -da abundant; dense; filled to the brim; **de barba tupida** heavy-bearded

turrón m. block, bar: "Cómprame un turrón de magnesia" 'Buy me a bar of magnesia'

U

uju or **újule** shucks (interj. of disappointment, annoyance, or disgust varying in intensity according to intonation, emphasis, etc.)

Ugenio -nia (vars. of) *Eugenio -nia*

Ulalio -lia (vars. of) *Eulalio -lia*

ultimadamente (var. of) *última-mente*

último: al último finally, at last (Std. *por fin, al fin*)

umbligo (var. of) *ombligo*

unde (var. of) *donde*

unión (Ang.) f. (labor) union; fpl. long underwear (Eng.?<union suit)

uno: uno tras otro (slang) (euph.) sausage: "Le dieron uno tras otro pal refín" 'They gave him sausages for dinner'

unque (var. of) *aunque*

untada (var. of) *untadura*

uña: uña de gato type of prickly shrub

uñera (var. of) *uñero* ingrown toenail, hangnail

¡úpale! (interj. used when lifting up a child) Up you go!

Uropa (var. of) *Europa*

urutar (var. of) *eructar*

urzuela split hair (tip of hair which has split in two)

úrzula (var. of) *úlcera*

urraca (fig.) (pej.) non-black person with a very dark complexion

Usebio -bia (vars. of) *Eusebio -bia*

uvas: quedarse en las uvas not to understand a thing, be completely in the dark (Std. *quedarse en ayunas*)

V

vaca (fig.) adj. stupid, unintelligent (said of persons); **hacer vaca** to run up one's winnings in a game of chance after starting with a very small amount of money

vacear or **vaciar** vr. to bleed to death

vacil m. fun, amusement (cf. **vacilada**); act of flirting; **agarrar a alguien de vacil** to pick on someone to bear the brunt of one's kidding (teasing)

vacilada (slang) kidding, joking; fooling around, having a good time; **andar en la vacilada** to be having a good time, be fooling around

vacilador -dora m., f. joker, kidder; flirt

vacilar: vacilar(se) a alguien to make a fool of someone; to play a joke on someone; to kid or tease someone; to toy with someone, amuse oneself idly with someone; to trifle with someone; **a vacilar a ca Chapa (a vacilar en casa de Chapa):** "Vete a vacilar a ca Chapa" 'Go tell it to the marines' (Std. *a otro perro con ese hueso*) (note: this saying may be be peculiar to San Antonio, Texas, as it involves a local ref. to a well-known drugstore on the west side of that city; the store was torn down in the 1960's)

vacilón -lona m., f. flirt, person who flirts; person who serves as comic relief, joker; movie cartoon; **agarrar a alguien de vacilón** to pick on someone to bear the brunt of one's kidding (teasing) (see **vacilar a alguien, agarrar a alguien de vacil**)

vacota (fig.) clumsy, awkward

vagonero man who loads railroad cars

vaisa (orthog. var. of) *baisa*

vala, valas, etc. (vars. of) *valga, valgas*, etc. (pres. subj. of *valer*)

valer: no valer caca (cuacha, mierda) (vulg.) not to be worth shit, be very worthless; **no valer tres cominos** (coll.) (var. of) *no valer un comino* to be worthless; **no valer tres cacahuates** to be worthless, not to be worth a darn (coll.); **valer madre** to be worthless

valsear or **valsiar** (vars. of) *valsar*

vampiro -ra bloodthirsty person (fig.), mercenary

vanela (var. of) *vainilla*

varaña (orthog. var. of) *baraña*

varo dollar (U.S. currency); peso (Mexican currency et. al)

várvula (var. of) *válvula*

vasija set of dishes

vedera (var. of) *vereda*

vegetable (Eng.) m. vegetable (Std. *verdura*)

vejarano -na or **vejerano -na** (blend of *viejo* and *veterano?*) (pej.) old person

vejiga balloon

veladora large votive light

veliz (orthog. var. of) *velís* m.

venado -da square, person not attuned to the latest fads (slang); **sangre de venado (que se vaya por un lado)** (this expression is said to a person aiming at a target when one wishes to throw his aim off)

vendido -da (pej.) Uncle Tom, race traitor (very pej. ref. to Mexican-American who has sold out to Anglo interests or who always sides with Anglos in ethnic conflicts)

venir va.: **venirle a alguien muy aguado (guango)** to be no match for someone: "Ese tipo me viene muy aguado" 'That guy is no match for me'; **venirle (irle) a alguien a la mano** to spank someone; **venir a la medida** to fit to a T (coll.): "El sombrero le vino a la medida" 'The hat fit him to a T' (coll.); **venir al pelo** (for clothes) to fit to a T (coll.): "La chaqueta le vino al pelo" 'The coat fit him to a T' (coll.); **venir de entrada y salida** to visit or call upon someone briefly; vn. **venir pa' tras** (Ang.) to return, come back (Std. *volver*); vr. (vulg.) for a man to have an orgasm; **venirse en seco** (vulg.) for a man to have an orgasm outside the woman's vagina; **¿a qué viene (todo) eso?** What are you implying?, Why are you bringing that matter up?;

viene saliendo la misma gata It's all the same in the end, It comes to the same thing, same difference; **ya vengo** I'll be back soon, I'll see you shortly; **y qué aquí y que allá y que fue y que vino** (coll.) etcetera, etcetera, and so on and so forth

venta: venta de garaje (Ang.) garage sale, sale of miscellaneous objects; **venta de quemazón** fire sale, sale of merchandise minimally damaged by a fire in the store

ventajoso -sa opportunistic

Vento (dim. of) *Ventura*

ventosa (folk medicine) cure for pains in the side of the abdomen supposedly caused by contact with cold air; the cure consists in placing the mouth of a glass over the affected region; the cold air is then supposed to be sucked out by the glass and the patient is cured

ver va. to opine, think about: "¿Cómo la ve?" 'What do you think (about it)?'; **ahora (lo) verás (verán,** etc.) Now you're in for it, Now you're going to get it (phrases of warning); **estar de verse** to be acceptable; **no poder ver a alguien ni en pintura** not to be able to stand the sight of someone, hate someone with extreme intensity; **para que vea(s) (vean)** that just goes to show (that one can not judge a book by its cover); let that be a lesson to you; **verle la cara a alguien** to seek out humbly, to ask for forgiveness or reconciliation, to eat crow (fig.); to face someone reluctantly in order to ask for a favor (expression most often used in the negative); **verle la cara de pendejo a alguien**

(slang) to see someone approaching (fig.); to think that someone looks and is a fool or a dummy (fig.); **ya lo verás (verá,** etc.**)** Now you're in for it, Now you're going to get it (phrases of warning): "Te dije que limpiaras el carro y no lo hiciste. Ya lo verás" 'I told you to clean the car and you didn't do it. Now you're in for it'; **(ya) ves (ve, ven)** You see?, Didn't I tell you (so)?

verdad f.: **¿pa(ra) qué más que la verdad?** Let's tell it like it is, Why tell anything but the truth?

verde mf. greenhorn, inexperienced person

verdelaga(s) or **verdolaga(s)** (slang) mf. greenhorn, inexperienced person

verga: pélame la verga or **pélamela** interj. (very strong and vulgar slang) (expression of unwillingness or defiance): Kiss my ass (vulgar, slang), Suck my dick (vulgar, slang)

vergüenzoso -sa (vars. of) *vergonzoso -sa*

veriguar va. & vn. (var. of) *averiguar* va. & vn.

veriguata (var. of) *averiguata* dispute, argument, din, noise

verijón -jona m., f. wide-hipped; clumsy; f. adverse to doing housework

Verne (Hispanization of) Vernon, Texas

vesitar va. & vr. (var. of) *visitar* va. & vr.

Veva (dim. of) *Genoveva*

vevir va. & vn. (var. of) *vivir* va. & vn.

veya, veyas, etc. (vars. of) *vea, veas,* etc. (pres. subj. conjugation of *ver*)

veyo (var. of) *veo* (1st pers. sg. pres. ind. of *ver*)

vez f.: **cada vez en cuando** from time to time, once in a while (see also **(de) cada en cuando**); **una vez al (por) año** once in a blue moon (coll.), seldom, rarely, infrequently

vía, vías, etc. (vars. of) *veía, veías,* etc. (imperfect conjugation of *ver*)

viajear or **viajiar** vn. (vars. of) *viajar* vn.

viancico (var. of) *villancico*

víboda (var. of) *víbora*

víbora (slang) penis; **picar la víbora** (slang): "Cuídate, no te vaya a picar la víbora" 'Watch out, don't let them get into your pants' (euph.) (said to a girl about to go out on a date, warning her not to let the male persuade her to become engaged in copulative activities)

vica (orthog. var. of) *bica*

viceprincipal (Ang.) m. vice principal, assistant director of a school

víceras (slang) fpl. sunglasses

vici- (var. of) *vice-* (prefix indicating subordinate position, e.g., *vici-presidente = vice-presidente*)

vicoca (orthog. var. of) *bicoca*

victrola (Eng.) (var. of) *vitrola* (Eng.)

vida: ser de vida to be safe, be in the clear (slang): "Ahora sí son de vida" 'Now they're really in the clear'

vide (var. of) *vi* (1st pers. sg. pret. of *ver*)

vido (var. of) *vio* (3rd pers. sg. pret. of *ver*)

vidriera (de carro) windshield (of a car)

vidrios mpl. (slang) eyeglasses; **ay nos vidrios** (slang) Catch ya later (slang), See you later; **¡por vidrios!**

interj. (euph.) (var. of) ¡*Por vida de Dios*!

vieja (pej.) old hag (slang); old biddy (slang); **vieja chingada/vieja cabróna/vieja jodida** (pej.) (vulg.) old bitch (vulg.), damned old bitch (vulg.); **vieja** or **viejota** broad; a sexually attractive woman, a hunk of a woman

viejero -ra m. man who chases around after women; f. woman who chases around after men

viejez f. (var. of) *vejez* f.

viejito -ta (slang) f. cigarette butt; **casa de (los) viejitos** nursing home, old folks' home

viejo -ja (slang) m. husband; father; f. wife; mother; whore; attractive woman (in general); cigarette butt (see also **viejita**); **viejo -ja rabo verde** (var. of *viejo -ja verde*)

vien (orthog. var. of) *bien*

viernes m.: **cuchara de viernes** meddler, meddlesome person

vígora or **vígura** (vars. of) *víbora*

vinagrón m. scorpion (Scorpionida)

vinir vn. (var. of) *venir* vn.

virdio (var. of) *vidrio*

vigüela (var. of) *viruela*

virol (slang) m. bean (usually mpl.)

vironguear or **vironguiar** vn. (orthog. vars. of) *bironguear, bironguiar*, resp.

vironguero -ra (orthog. var. of) *bironguero -ra*

viruela: viruela loca chicken pox

virul mf. or **virulo -la** one-eyed

virula bicycle

vis- (var. of) *vice-* (id. to **vici-**, q.v.)

visita: en visita on a visit, visiting (Std. *de visita*); **visita de doctor** (var. of) *visita de médico* very brief

visit

visitar: visitar con (Ang.) visit with (coll.)

vista (coll.) film, movie; fpl. (more frequent than fsg.) motion-picture show, movies: "Anoche fuimos a las vistas" 'Last night we went to the movies'

vistero -ra movie fan, avid movie-goer, cinéaste

vistir va. & vr. (var. of) *vestir* va. & vr.

Vítor (var. of) *Víctor*

Vitorio -ria (vars. of) *Victorio -ria*

Vitoriano -na (vars. of) *Victoriano -na*

vitrola (Eng.) victrola, phonograph, record player

vividor -ra m., f. opportunist

vivir: vivir a(l) tirón to have a hard time making ends meet, barely eke out a living

vodeviles (Eng.) mpl. vaudeville

volado -da (said of a person who reacts quickly and positively to advances or flattery); very much in love; **andar volado -da con alguien** to be very much in love with someone, have a crush on

volada: de (a) volada or **diavolada** fast, rapidly, quickly

volando right away, right this minute; "Traime el papel volando"

volantín m. merry-go-round

volar va. (slang) to steal; vr. to fall in love; to blow one's brains out, shoot oneself in the head; vr. to become giddy; to become infatuated; **volarle a alguien la cabeza** to give someone a swelled head (fig.), an exaggerated sense of importance; to make someone feel dizzy, lightheaded, giddy; **volársela** or **volarse la tapa de los sesos** to blow one's brains out, shoot oneself in the head (see also **levantarse** or **saltarse la tapa de los sesos**); **volársele a alguien la cabeza** to become dizzy, giddy, lightheaded; to get dizzy spells; to become confused; **volársele a alguien la tapa** to blow one's top, get angry: "A Rubén se le voló la tapa de deveras" 'Rubén really blew his top'; (see also **a volar**)

volcánico -ca vulcanized; m. patent medicine, in liquid form, applied to sore muscles

volcanizar va. to vulcanize

volcano (Ang.) volcano (Std. *volcán*)

voler (var. of) *oler*

volteado -da or **voltiado -da** m., f. homosexual; **estar volteado -da con alguien** to be at odds with someone, not to be on speaking or friendly terms with someone: "Fueron amigos por muchos años, pero ahora están volteados" 'They were friends for many years, but now they are not on speaking terms'

voltear or **voltiar: voltear(le) el estómago a alguien** to turn one's stomach (fig.), be repugnant to; **voltearle a alguien la cabeza** (Ang.?<to turn one's head) to give someone a swelled head (fig.), cause someone to assume an exaggerated sense of importance; **voltearle** or **torcerle la cara a**

alguien to give someone the cold shoulder (coll.); to snub; to slight; vr. to have a falling out, have a disagreement that ends in a broken or cool relationship; **volteársele a alguien el estómago** to get an upset stomach (see also **revolvérsele a alguien el estómago**)

volver: vn. **volver pa' tras** (Ang.) to return, go back (Std. *volver*); va. **volverle a alguien el alma al cuerpo** to regain one's composure after being scared; **ya vuelvo** I'll be right back, I'll see you shortly

volvido -da (vars. of) *vuelto -ta* (ppart. of *volver*)

vomitadera vomiting spell, serial regurgitation

vorrado (orthog. var. of) *borrado*

voz f. (Ang.) voice (lessons) (Std. *canto*): "Estoy estudiando voz" 'I'm taking voice lessons'

vrigen f. (var. of) *virgen* f.

vuelo: agarrar vuelo to get a running start; (see **de todo vuelo**); **a todo vuelo** very good, excellent, super (etc.): "Esa película estuvo a todo vuelo" 'That movie was super'

vuelta: dar la vuelta to drop by (a place), drop over (for a visit): "Mañana no dejes de dar la vuelta" 'Don't forget to come by tomorrow for a visit'; **de vuelta** again; after returning

vuevo (var. of) *huevo*

W

waxear or **waxiar** (Eng.) va. to wax (a floor)

wexear or **wexiar** (vars. of) *waxear* and *waxiar*, resp.

Y

y: *¿y diay (qué)?* or *¿y de ahí (qué)?* So?, So what?; **y que pa(ra) (a)llá y pa(ra) (a)cá** (fixed expression) and so on and so forth, etc., etc. (see also **y que aquí y que allá y que fue y que vino**); **y ¿qué hay con eso?** So what about it? (coll.)

ya: **ya está** or **ya estuvo** That's it!, consider it done (consider the job finished); **ya estuvo** I've got it made, there's no way I can fail; **ya lo hubo** or **ya lubo** (id. to **ya está**); **ya ni yo** (**ya ni ella,** etc.) (expression used to shame someone into doing something that another person of lesser ability can do): "*¿No puedes hacer esto? ¡Qué vergüenza! Ya ni Linda que es tan joven*" 'Can't you do this? That's absurd! Linda can do it and she's much younger than you'; **¿ya si no?** Well after all, what did you expect (would happen)?; **ya te lo haiga** or **ya te lo haya** You'll be sorry!; **¿(ya) ves (ve, ven)?** You see?, Didn't I tell you (this would happen)?; **ya, ya** (expression of sympathy usually directed at children) There, there, that's all right

yanitoría (Eng.) janitorial service

yaque (Eng.) m. jack (aut.) (Std. *gato*)

yarda (Ang.) yard, lawn, plot of grass in front of, on the side(s) of or behind a house; **yarda de madera** (Ang.) lumberyard

Yayo (dim. of) *Eduardo* (see also **Huayo**)

yec (Eng.) m. jack (Std. *gato*) (see also **yaque**)

yedo (slang) marihuana

yequear or **yequiar** (Eng.) va. to jack up (a car, a structure, etc.)

yerse (Eng.) m. jersey, sweater

yes (Eng.) m. jazz

yesco -ca (slang) marihuana smoker; drug addict; f. marihuana

yet (Eng.) m. jet, jet airplane

yido (var. of) *ido* (ppart. of *ir*)

yin (Eng.) m. gin (alcohol); **yin de algodón** cotton gin

yip(e) (Eng.) m. jeep

yir (var. of) *ir* to go

yira or **yiri** (Eng.) mf. jitterbug (dance); jitterbugger (person fond of dancing the jitterbug)

Yoche (Eng.) (dim. of) George; (Hispanization of) George West, Texas

yoga f. or **yogue** m. (Eng.) jug (see also **yoque**)

yogas or **yogas el cantinero** (slang) I (1st pers. sg. pron.) (disguise-expansion of Std. *yo*)

Yole (dim. of) *Yolanda*

Yoli (dim. of) *Yolanda*

yompa (Eng.?) jumper (type of hunting jacket worn by men)

yómper (Eng.?) m. jumper (type of combination blouse and skirt worn by women)

yonca (Eng.?<junker) bicycle

yonque (Eng.) m. junk; junkyard

yonquear or **yonquiar** (Eng.) va. to junk

yoque (Eng.) m. jug (see also **yoga** et al.)

yoyo (Eng.) yoyo, type of toy top which is raised or lowered by spinning it from a string

yudar va. (rus.) (var. of) *ayudar*

Yula (Hispanization of) Beulah, Texas

yúnier or **yúnior** (Eng.) m. younger; youngest of several; Junior (e.g., "Éste es Juan yúnier" 'This is Juan, Jr.', said by a father in ref. to his identically-named son)

Yuta (Hispanization of) Utah (U.S. state)

Yuyo (dim. of) *Jesús* (se also **Chuy**)

Z

zacatal m. tall dense grass in great abundance

zacate (slang) m. low-grade marihuana

zacateada or **zacatiada** (orthog. vars. of) *sacateada* or *sacatiada*, resp.

zacatear or **zacatiar** (orthog. vars. of) *sacatear* or *sacatiar*; resp.

zafar vr.: **zafársele a alguien la mano** to slip, lose control; to miscalculate **zafarse un hueso** to dislocate a bone from the socket or the joint

zafo: can zafos (slang) The same to you!, Take your words and eat them (fig., said to take revenge for any derogatory remarks initially directed toward you by someone else)

zambo -ba bowlegged

zambutir va. & vr. (var. of) *zambullir* va. & vr.

zancuderío or **zancudería** or **zancudero** swarm of mosquitos

zanoria (var. of) *zanahoria*

zapeta diaper

zapo (slang) shoe (disguise or var. of) *zapato*

zarabanda spanking

zarape (orthog. var. of) *sarape* m.

zigzaquear or **zigzaquiar** (vars. of)

zigzaguear or *zigzaguiar*, resp.

zíper (Eng.) m. zipper (Std. *cremallera*)

zoncear or **zonciar** vn. to fool around; to joke

zoncera foolishness

zopilote (slang, pej.) m. policeman

zoquetal m. mudhole

zoquete m. mud; (fig.) good-for-nothing, worthless person

zoquetera mud-guard (aut.); mudhole

zoquetoso -sa muddy

zuca f. (rus.) (var. of) *azúcar* (m. or f. in Std.)

zucadero -ra (vars. of) *azucarero -ra*

zumbar va. to win; to conquer; (slang) to eat up; **zumbarle a alguien el aparato/el mango** to excel in something (esp. in sports); **zumbarle a alguien el coco** to be daffy, screwy, slightly crazy

zumbido gossip, wagging of tongues; running around (usually in search of sexual adventures)

zurum(b)ado -da (vars. of) *zurum-(b)ato -ta*

zurumbático -ca daffy, screwy, slightly crazy; dumb, stupid

zurrar vr. to get angry, become infuriated

Appendix A: Proverbs and sayings
Apéndice A: Proverbios y refranes

A

¡A buena hora!   (iron.) High time!:
"¡A buena hora vas llegando!" 'A
fine time to be arriving!'

A buen entendedor, pocas palabras
A word to the wise is sufficient

A buen hambre no hay mal pan
Hunger is the best sauce

A buen santo te encomiendas   The
blind are leading the blind (A fine
choice of a guide you've made)

**A caballo dado no hay que mirarle
el colmillo/los dientes**   One should
never look a gift horse in the
mouth (also: **A caballo rega-
lado no hay que mirarle el diente**
id.)

A cada santo se le llega su día
Every dog has his day (Everyone
gets his reward sooner or later)

A gustos se rompen panzas   Every
man to his own taste (Arguments
on likes and dislikes often provoke
fights)

A huevo ni los zapatos entran
You can lead a horse to water but
you cannot make him drink

A lo dado no se le busca lado
Don't look a gift horse in the
mouth

A mal tiempo buena cara   Keep a
stiff upper lip

A otro perro con ese hueso   Go tell
it to the marines

**A quien le venga el guante, que se
lo plante**   If the shoe fits, wear it

A quien madruga, Dios le ayuda
The early bird gets the worm /
God helps him who helps himself

A todo le tira, y a nada le da   Jack
of all trades, master of none

A ver si como roncan duermen
Talk is cheap / Let's see if they can
deliver the goods

**Al flojo lo ayuda Dios/Al flojo Dios
lo ayuda/Al perezoso lo ayuda
Dios/Al perezoso Dios lo ayuda**
Some people have all the luck
(comment directed to a lazy person who has had a much easier
time with a chore than was expected)

Al ojo del amo engorda el macho
A watched pot *does* boil / If you
want it done right, do it yourself

Al que habla, Dios lo oye   (var. of)
Al que no habla, Dios no lo oye
Faint heart never won fair lady

**Al que le aprieta el zapato que se lo
afloje/Al que le apriete el zapato
que se lo afloje**   God helps those
who help themselves

Al que le dé comezón que se rasque
God helps those who help themselves

**Al que le duela la muela que se la
saque/Al que le duele la muela
que se la saque**   God helps those
who help themselves

**Al que le quede el saco, que se lo
ponga**   If the shoe fits, wear it

**Al que le quede el zapato, que se lo
ponga**   If the shoe fits, wear it

Al que madruga, Dios le ayuda
The early bird gets the worm /
God helps him who helps himself

Al que no habla, Dios no lo oye
Faint heart never won fair lady

abeja: s. **Estar como ...**

abrazan: s. **De favor te ...**

Abrir el corazón   To bare one's
heart

abuela: s. **Cuéntaselo a tu ...**

Acá la madre de los borregos   Far,
far away / Way down yonder / East
of the twelfth of never

acaba: s. **El que aprisa vive,
pronto ...**

acaba: s. **La muerte lo acaba todo**

acaba: s. **Quien mal anda, mal ...**

Acostarse con las gallinas (y levantarse con los gallos) Early to bed and early to rise / To go to bed with the chickens and wake up with the roosters

acuerdo: s. **No lloro, pero me ...**

agua: s. **No le muevas al ...**

Agua que no has de beber, déjala correr Don't meddle in matters that don't concern you, mind your own business

aguante: s. **El que no ...**

aguante: s. **No hay mal que dure cien años ...**

Ahora es cuando, yerbabuena, le has de dar sabor al caldo Strike while the iron is hot / Now is the time to make one's move

Ahora que entierran dioquis Get it while the getting's good

Ahora sí baila mi hija con el doctor/con el señor Now you're talking! (indicates complete accord between speaker and listener)

Ahora sí chispas, quémenme Strike while the iron is hot / Now is the time to make the move

Ahora va la mía/la tuya/la suya (etc.) Now it's my turn / your turn (etc.)

ajena: s. **Cuida tu vida y deja ...**

amigo: s. **El que presta a un amigo ...**

amistad: s. **La amistad vale más que el dinero**

amistad: s. **El negocio es una cosa y ...**

amolar: s. **Para acabarla de ...**

Amor con amor se paga by love is love repaid / As you sow, so shall you reap

Amor de lejos, amor de pendejos Out of sight, out of mind

Amor que no es atrevido nunca logra sino olvido Faint heart never won fair lady

amor: s. **En el ...**

amores: s. **Ni besos ni apachurrones ...**

amos: s. **El que sirve (a) dos ...**

amos: s. **Es por demás, nadie puede servir a dos ...**

anda: s. **Quien mal ...**

Andar vuelta y vuelta to pace the floor

andas: s. **Dime con quien ...**

Antes de hablar es bueno pensar Think before you act/Look before you leap

Antes que te cases, mira lo que haces Look twice before you leap

aparezca: s. **De lo perdido ...**

aprender: s. **Nunca es tarde para ...**

aprieta: s. **El que mucho ... / Quien mucho abarca poco ...**

aprisa: s. **El que ...**

apures: s. **No te ...**

árbol: s. **El árbol se conoce por su fruta**

arriba: s. **Buscar algo de ...**

Arrieros somos y en el camino andamos We are all the children of God (expression used to admonish someone who is criticizing deficiencies he himself will inevitably come to possess)

arriesga: s. **El que no se arriesga, no cruza ...**

arriesga: s. **El que no ...**

astilla: s. **De tal palo tal ...**

atienda/atiende: s. **Quien tiene tienda ...**

atole: s. **Correrle a alguien ...**

atrevido: s. **Amor que no es ...**

Aunque la mona se vista de seda, mona se queda You can't make a silk purse from a sow's ear /

Clothes do not make the man (see
also **El hábito (no) hace ...**)
aventar: s. **Hay hasta para ...**
ayuda: s. **Al flojo lo ayuda Dios**
Ayúdate, que Dios te ayudará
God helps those who help themselves
azul: s. **El que quiera ...**

B

baila: s. **Con (Por) la plata baila
el perro**
baila: s. **Por dinero baila el
perro ...**
**Bajársele a alguien la sangre a los
pies (talones)**   To be scared stiff
barrio ajeno: s. **Estar como perro
en ...**
beber: s. **Agua que no has ...**
beber: s. **Mamar y ...**
bien: s. **El que mal haga, ...**
bitoque: s. **La jeringa ...**
boca: s. **Del plato a ...**
boca: s. **El que tiene ...**
borregos: s. **Acá la madre de
los ...**
botica: s. **Hay de todo como en ...**
brazo: s. **Te dan la mano y quieres
todo el ...**
brincos: s. **¿Para que dar
tantos ...?**
broche: s. **Cerrar con ...**
bruto: s. **Tú te pareces a Canuto,
cuanto (mientras, entre) más
viejo, más ...**
buen: s. **A buen entendedor ...**
buena: s. **A mal tiempo buena
cara**
buenos: s. **Cumplir como los
meros ...**
burra: s. **Cuando digo que ...**
burrada: s. **Hacer una ...**

Buscar algo de arriba a abajo   To
look high and low for something
Buscarle tres patas al gato   To
complicate matters

C

cabeza: s. **Echar(le) a alguien
por ...**
**Cada chango a su mecate y a darse
vuelo**   Let each one mind his own
business and get on with it / Keep
your nose to yourself
Cada oveja con su pareja   Birds of
a feather flock together
Cada pobrete lo que tiene mete
(general meaning: The poor must
use all the resources at their
disposal)
Cada uno es como Dios lo hizo
We are all as God made us
**Cae más pronto un hablador que
un cojo**   A liar is more likely to
slip up than a lame person
caliente: s. **Manos frías, corazón ...**
calientes: s. **Manos ...**
calzón: s. **Pon, pon, pon un nicle
pa' jabón**
**Camarón que se duerme se lo lleva
la corriente**   Opportunity only
knocks once
camino: s. **Arrieros somos y en
el ...**
camposanto: s. **Vale más sucio en
casa ...**
canasta: s. **Quitarle a alguien
la ...**
**Candil de la calle, oscuridad de la
casa**   A saint abroad and a devil
at home
canta: s. **Quien canta, ...**
Canta y canta y nada de ópera

Much ado about nothing
cántaro: s. **Tanto va el ...**
Canuto: s. **Tú te pareces a ...**
capitán: s. **Donde manda ...**
cara: s. **A mal tiempo buena cara**
caro: s. **Lo barato es ...**
carretilla: s. **Te dan una hebrita y quieres toda la ...**
casa: s. **Vale más sucio en ...**
cascarón: s. **No salir del ...**
cases: s. **El martes ni te ...**
Cerrar con broche de oro To end a program or event with a bang / with a grand finale
ciego: s. **El amor es ...**
cien: s. **Más vale un toma ...**
ciencia: s. **La experiencia es la madre de ...**
cobija: s. **Taparse con la misma colcha (...)**
cocina: s. **Si no te quieres quemar, salte ...**
cochinos: s. **El que no quiera ruidos ...**
cola de rana: s. **Sana, sana, ...**
colcha: s. **Taparse con la misma ...**
Colmarle a alguien la paciencia To cause someone to run out of patience
colmillo: s. **A caballo dado no hay que mirarle ...**
Comer frijoles y repetir pollo Weak to perform though mighty to pretend (ref. to person who tries to give the impression that he is better off than he really is)
comer: s. **No hay que morder la mano ...**
comer: s. **No muerdas la mano ...**
comezón: s. **Al que le dé comezón ...**
como: s. **Cada uno es ...**
comprar: s. **Si no van a ...**
Con el tiempo y un ganchito hasta

las verdes se alcanzan All things come to him who waits
Con (por) la plata baila el perro (var. of) *Por dinero baila el perro / Por dinero baila el perro y por pan si se lo dan* Money talks, money is power
Con la vara que midas serás medido As you sow, so shall you reap
conoce: s. **El árbol se conoce por su fruta**
conocer: s. **Más vale lo malo conocido que lo bueno por ...**
consejo: s. **Dar el ...**
consuelo: s. **Mal de muchos, ...**
coraje: s. **No siendo verdad ni ...**
corazón: s. **Abrir el ...**
corazón: s. **Ojos que no ven, ...**
corazón: s. **Manos calientes, ...**
corazón: s. **Manos frías, ...**
corazón: s. **Panza llena, ...**
corazones: s. **Por las acciones se juzgan los ...**
correr: Agua que no has de beber, déjala ...
Correrle a alguien atole por las venas To be extremely patient / To be slow as molasses
corriente: s. **Camarón que se duerme ...**
cortita: s. **Traérsela a alguien muy ...**
Cosa mala nunca muere A bad penny always turns up
cosa: s. **Decir una ...**
cosa: s. **El negocio es una ...**
costa: s. **Hay moros en ...**
creer: s. **Ver es ...**
crie: s. **El que no quiera ruidos ...**
cruza: s. **El que no se arriesga, no ...**
Cual más cual menos Six of one, half dozen of the other
Cuando digo que la burra es parda,

es porque traigo los pelos en la mano When I say it's so, it's because I have the proof right here in my hand

Cuando más se tiene, más se quiere The more one has, the more one wants

Cuando una puerta se cierra, otra se abre There are other fish in the sea

Cuando uno anda de malas hasta los perros lo mean When it rains, it pours

Cuando yo tenía dinero me llamaban don Tomás, y ahora que no tengo me llaman Tomás nomás Wealth makes worship / A rich man has many friends

cuentas: s. En resumidas ...

Cuanto más (Mientras más, Entre más) viejo, más pendejo The older you get, the dumber you become

cuentes: s. No cuentes tus gallinas ...

Cuéntaselo a tu abuela Tell it to the marines

Cuento chino tall tale, fish story

Cuida tu vida y deja la ajena/la del prójimo/la del vecino Go mind your own business

cuidado: s. Si quieres vivir sin ...

culecas: s. Son más las ...

Cumplir como los meros buenos To live up to one's word / To fulfill one's commitments to the letter

cura: s. La cura es peor ...

CH

Chávez: s. Tú sabes quien trae las llaves, ...

chingues: s. No me chingues ...

chino: s. cuento ...

chispas: s. Ahora sí ...

D

da: s. No siendo verdad ni coraje ...

dan: s. Te dan la mano y quieres todo el brazo

dan: s. Te dan una ...

dan: s. Por dinero baila el perro...

daño: s. Hasta lo que no comes te hace ...

Dar el consejo y quedarse sin él Not to practice what one preaches

Dar gato por liebre to deceive someone, to give someone a song and a dance

daré: s. Más vale un toma ...

dé: s. Al que le dé comezón...

De favor te abrazan, y quieres que te aprieten They give you an inch and you want a mile

¡De la que me escapé! That was a close shave / close call!

De lo perdido a lo que aparezca Something is better than nothing (lit. 'From having lost it to whatever may appear')

De músico, poeta y loco, todos tenemos un poco Everyone is a little bit crazy

De noche todos los gatos son pardos All cats are gray in the dark, the darkness of night obscures all distinguishable features; the darkness conceals all flaws or defects

De tal palo tal astilla Like father like son, A chip of the old block

De una mentira nacen muchas One lie leads to a thousand

De un día para otro Any day now,

Any time soon

De un momento para otro any minute now, any time soon

debe: s. **El que nada …**

dejes: s. **No dejes para mañana …**

Del árbol caído todos hacen leña Everyone kicks a man when he's down

Del dicho al hecho hay mucho trecho Sooner said than done

Del plato a la boca a veces se cae la sopa There's many a slip between the cup and the lip

Decir por derecho To call a spade a spade / To tell it like it is

Decir una cosa y hacer otra To say one thing and do another / To not practice what one preaches

déjala: s. **Agua que no has de beber, …**

Dejarse tratar con la punta del pie to let someone walk all over you

derechito: s. **Sangre de perrito …**

derecho; s. **Decir por …**

desea: s. **La suerte de la fea …**

deshonra: s. **El ser pobre no es …**

día: s. **A cada santo se le llega …**

día: s. **De un …**

diente: s. **A caballo dado no hay que mirarle …**

diferente: s. **La jeringa …**

digo: s. **Haz lo que yo …**

Dime con quien andas y te diré quien eres A man is known by the company he keeps

dinero: s. **El que presta a un amigo …**

dinero: s. **La amistad vale más que el …**

dinero: s. **Por dinero baila el perro …**

Dinero llama dinero Money begets money / The rich get richer (and the poor get poorer)

Dinero trae dinero (id. to **Dinero llama dinero)**

Dios todo lo puede All things are possible with God, God is all powerful

Dios: s. **A quien madruga, …**

Dios: s. **Al flojo lo ayuda …**

Dios: s. **Al que habla …**

Dios: s. **Al que madruga, …**

Dios: s. **Al que no habla, …**

Dios: s. **Ayúdate, que …**

Dios: s. **Cada uno es como …**

Dios: s. **Donde …**

Dios: s. **El hombre propone y …**

Dios: s. **El que no habla …**

diré: s. **Dime con quien andas …**

dolor: s. **Donde hay (gran) amor, hay (gran) …**

Donde comen dos, comen tres There's always room for one more / Two can live as cheaply as one

Donde Dios es servido On the other side of nowhere / Beyond the twelfth of never

Donde hay (gran) amor, hay (gran) dolor Where there is (a great) love, there is (great) pain.

Donde manda capitán, no manda marinero Too many cooks spoil the broth (There can be only one boss)

dos s. **Más vale que haiga …**

duela/duele: s. **Al que le …**

dures: s. **No te apures pa(ra) que …**

E

Echar el gato a retozar to steal; **echar la casa por la ventana** to go for broke, to shoot the works

Echar(le) a alguien por la cabeza To let the cat out of the bag (give someone away, betray someone)

Echar mentiras para sacar verdades   To tell a lie and learn the truth

El amor es ciego   Love is blind

El árbol se conoce por su fruta   By their fruits ye shall know them

El burro por delante para que no se espante   "Me first" (said to a person who always mentions his/ her name before the names of others, e.g., "Yo y mis amigos lo hicimos")

El comal le dijo a la olla: qué cola tan prieta tienes   The pot is calling the kettle black

El hábito (no) hace al monje   Clothes (don't) make the man (see also **Aunque la mona ...**)

El hombre propone y Dios dispone   Man proposes, (but) God disposes

El lunes ni las las gallinas ponen   On Mondays not even the hens lay (eggs) (ref. to blue Monday)

El martes ni te cases ni te embarques   (folk wisdom): Don't marry or set sail on Tuesdays

El muerto al pozo y el vivo al negocio/El muerto al pozo y el vivo al retozo   Let the dead bury the dead / Life must go on

El negocio es una cosa y la amistad otra   Business is business

El ser pobre no es deshonra   Poverty is no sin

El tiempo es oro   Time is money

El que a hierro mata, a hierro muere   He who lives by the sword dies by the sword

El que aprisa vive, pronto acaba   He who lives fast, dies young

El que canta, sus males espanta   He who sings chases away his blues

El que la hace la paga   As you sow

so shall you reap

El que mal haga, bien no espere   As you sow so shall you reap

El que mucho aprieta, poco abarca/ El que mucho abarca, poco aprieta   Don't bite off more than you can chew

El que nada debe, nada teme   If your hands are clean you have nothing to fear

El que no aguante (que) no juegue   He who can't take it shouldn't dish it out

El que no arriesga, no gana/El que no arriesga no pasa la mar   Nothing ventured, nothing gained

El que no habla Dios no lo oye   God helps those who help themselves

El que no llora no mama   One must speak up to be heard/God helps those who help themselves

El que no quiera ruidos que no críe cochinos/El que no quiere ruidos que no críe cochinos   If you can't stand the heat, stay out of the kitchen (lit. 'He who wants no noise should not raise hogs')

El que no se arriesga, no cruza el río   Nothing ventured, nothing gained

El que nunca ha tenido y llega a tener loco se quiere volver   When a man who has never had anything of value finally acquires it, he is in danger of losing his mind

El que poco habla, poco yerra   Silence is golden/He who speaks less, errs less

El que presta a un amigo, pierde el dinero y pierde el amigo   Neither a borrower nor a lender be (lit. 'He who lends money to a friend loses both money and friend')

El que quiera azul celeste que le

cueste   One must pay for what one wants (='Take what you want and pay for it, says God'--Spanish proverb)

El que ríe último, ríe mejor   He who laughs last, laughs best

El que se halla (se encuentra) en el lodo quisiera meter a otro   Misery loves company

El que sirve (a) dos amos, con alguno queda mal   No one can serve two masters/One who tries to serve two masters will do a disservice to one (of them)

El que tiene boca a Roma va   Speak up loud and you'll draw a crowd (He who speaks up is heard / is listened to)

En boca cerrada no entran moscas   Silence is golden

En el amor todo se vale or todo se vale en el amor   All's fair in love and war

En la unión hay fuerza   In unity there is strength/United we stand, divided we fall

en resumidas cuentas   when all is said and done

En tierra de ciegos el tuerto es rey   In the land of the blind the one-eyed is king

encontrarse (hallarse) la horma con su zapato   for one to meet one's match

encuentra: s. **El que se halla (se ...) ...**

encueras: s. **¿Qué esperas que no ...**

enfermedad: s. **La cura es peor ...**

engañan: s. **Las apariencias ...**

Enseñar la oreja   To show one's ignorance

entendedor: s. **A buen ...**

entiendes: s. **¿Me ...**

entierran: s. **Ahora que ...**

entrarle parejo   To go for broke (to go all out for something)

eres: s. **Dime con quien andas ...**

Es mejor andar solo que mal acompañado   Better to travel alone than to keep bad company

Es mejor que haya un tonto y no dos   You've made enough of a fool of yourself already (and you'll make more of one of yourself if you keep doing what you are doing)

Es por demás, nadie puede servir a dos amos   No one can serve two masters

escapé: s. **¡De la que me ...!**

espanta: s. **Quien canta, sus males...**

espanta: s. **El que canta, sus males ...**

espante: s. **El burro por delante ...**

esperas: s. **¿Qué esperas que no ...**

Estar como la abeja, que volando pica   (ref. to the person who enjoys malicious insinuation)

Estar como perro en barrio ajeno   To be like a fish out of the water

estar tamañito   to have one's heart in one's mouth, to feel "just so big"

experiencia: s. **La experiencia es madre ...**

explico: s. **¿Me entiendes, Méndez o te ...**

F

falta: s. **Nunca falta ...**

Farol de la calle, oscuridad de la casa   A saint abroad and a sinner at home

fea: s. La suerte de la ...

Federico: s. ¿Me entiendes, Méndez o te explico ...

flojo: s. Al flojo lo ayuda Dios

fregaste: s. Te casaste, te ...

frías: s. Manos ...

frío: s. Manos calientes, corazón ...

fuerza: s. En la unión hay ...

fuerza: s. Más vale maña que ...

G

Galván: s. No lo entenderá ...

gallina: s. Más vale...

gallinas: s. No cuentes tus ...

gallinas: s. Acostarse con las ...

gallo: s. Más claro no canta ...

gallo: s. Más vale gallina viva que ...

ganchito: s. Con el tiempo y ...

ganso: s. Me canso dijo un ...

garrote: s. Limosnero ...

gato: s. Buscarle tres patas ...

gato: s. Hay ...

gatos: s. De noche todos ...

guante: s. A quien le venga ...

Guatemala: Ir de Guatemala a guatepeor/Salir de Guatemala para ir a guatepeor to go from bad to worse

gustos: s. A gustos se rompen panzas

H

ha tenido: s. El que nunca ...

habla: s. Al que habla ...

habla: s. El que no habla ...

habla: s. El que poco ...

hablador: s. Cae más pronto un ...

hablar: s. Antes de ...

hace: s. La práctica ...

Hacer algo a como dé lugar To do something by hook or crook

Hacer de las suyas To be up to one's tricks

Hacer una burrada To pull a real boner

hacer: s. No es lo mismo decir que ...

hago: s. Haz lo que yo digo ...

haiga: s. Más vale que ...

halla: s. El que se ...

Hallarse (encontrarse) la horma con su zapato For one to meet one's match

hambre: s. A buen hambre ...

has: s. Agua que no ...

¡Hasta lo que no comes te hace daño! Busybodies never lack a bad day/If you look for trouble you will find it

hasta: s. Nadie sabe lo que tiene ...

Hay de todo como en botica (Here) there's a little bit of everything

Hay gato encerrado There's something rotten in Denmark / There's something fishy going on

Hay hasta para aventar pa' arriba There is enough (here) to take care of an army

Hay moros en la costa The walls have ears

Hay muertos que no hacen ruido y son mayores sus penas Silent rivers run deep

hay: s. Donde hay (gran) amor ...

hay: s. No hay mal que ...

Haz bien y no mires a quien Charity is its own reward

Haz lo que yo digo, y no lo que yo hago Do as I say, not as I do

hebrita: s. Te dan una ...
hermosa: s. La suerte de la fea ...
hermoso: s. Quien a feo ama ...
hierro: s. El que a ...
hija: s. Ahora sí baila mi ...
hincan: s. Ven la tempestad y no se ...
hizo: s. Cada uno es como Dios lo ...
hocico: s. Perro huevero aunque le quemen...
hombre: s. No sólo de pan vive ...
hora: s. A buena ...
horma: Encontrarse (Hallarse) ...
Hoy por ti, mañana por mí One good turn deserves another
hoy: s. No dejes para mañana lo que puedes hacer ...
hueso: s. A otro perro con ese ...

I

importa: s. No importa que nazcan chatos ...
incomoda: s. La verdad no mata, pero...
inundado: s. No le muevas al agua que el río está ...
Ir por lana y salir trasquilado (lit. 'To go to buy wool and to come back sheared'; the sense is that one has gone with the intent of winning but returns a complete loser)

J

jicotera: s. Mover la ...
Juan Domingues: s. no me chingues...

juegue: s. El que no aguante que no...
Justos pagan por pecadores The just pay for the sins of the guilty

L

La amistad vale más que el dinero Friendship is worth more than money/Change not a friend for money
La cura es peor que la enfermedad The cure is worse than the disease
la enema: s. La jeringa ...
La experiencia es la madre de la ciencia Experience is the mother of wisdom
La gracia es andar entre las llamas y no quemarse The real trick is to emerge unscathed from flame and fire
La jeringa/La lavativa/La enema es la misma, sólo el bitoque es diferente (mildly vulg.) The more things change, the more they stay the same
La mala yerba nunca muere The bad penny keeps coming back
La mentira dura hasta que la verdad llega The truth will always come out in the end
La muerte a nadie perdona Death pardons no man
La muerte lo acaba todo Death puts an end to everything
La práctica hace al maestro Practice makes perfect
La suerte de la fea la hermosa la desea The grass is always greener on the other side (lit. 'The beautiful woman envies the good fortune of the ugly one')

La verdad no mata, pero incomoda
The truth sometimes hurts
Las apariencias engañan You
can't judge a book by its cover
lado: s. **A lo dado no se le
busca ...**
lado: s. **Sangre de venado ...**
ladre: s. **No tener ni padre...**
ladrón: s. **Más peca la víctima ...**
lana: s. **Ir por ...**
lavativa: s. **La jeringa ...**
leche: s. **Mamar y beber ...**
lejos: s. **Poco a poco se va ...**
leña: s. **Del árbol caído todos
hacen ...**
liebre: s. **Dar gato por ...**
Limosnero y con garrote Beggars
can't be choosers
limpio: s. **Vale más sucio en
casa ...**
**Lo barato cuesta caro/Lo barato es
caro** Cheap goods cost dear in
the long run
Lo cortés no quita lo valiente
Civility never detracted from valor
Lo que pasó voló Let bygones be
bygones/No use crying over
spilled milk
Lo que siembras recoges (var. of)
Quien bien siembra, bien recoge As
you sow, so shall you reap
loco: s. **El que nunca ha tenido y
llega a tener ...**
loco: s. **De músico, poeta y ...**
locos: s. **Los niños y los ...**
lodo: s. **El que se halla (se
encuentra) ...**
logra: s. **Amor que no es atrevido
nunca ...**
**Los niños y los locos dicen la
verdad** Children and crazy
people always tell the truth /
Words form the mouth of babes
lugar: s. **Hacer (algo) a como
dé ...**

luna: s. **Ser más viejo que la ...**
lunes: s. **El lunes ni las gallinas
ponen**

LL

llamas: s. **La gracia es andar
entre ...**
llega: s. **El que nunca ha tenido
y ...**
llora: s. **El que no ...**

M

macho: s. **Al ojo del amo
engorda ...**
macho: s. **Taparle el ojo al ...**
madre: s. **La experiencia es ...**
madre: s. **No tener ni padre ...**
maestro: s. **La práctica hace ...**
mal: s. **A mal tiempo buena cara**
mal: s. **No hay mal que ...**
mal: s. **El que sirve a dos amos,
con alguno queda ...**
mal: s. **Quien mal anda ...**
mal acompañado: s. **Es mejor
andar solo que.../Más vale andar
solo que ...**
Mal de muchos, consuelo de tontos
Misery loves company / Fools are
comforted by the misfortunes of
others
mal: s. **Un mal nunca viene solo**
males: s. **Para alivio de mis ...**
males: s. **Quien canta, sus ...**
malluguen: s. **Si no van a comprar
no ...**
mama: s. **El que no llora ...**
Mamar y beber leche to have
one's cake and eat it too (coll.),
have it both ways (ref. to the

desire to receive the maximum benefit(s) possible)

mandados: s. **Unos nacieron para mandar …**

mano: s. **Te dan la mano …**

mano: s. **Te dan una …**

mano: s. **No hay que morder la …**

mano: s. **No muerdas la …**

Manos calientes, corazón frío Warm hands, cold heart

Manos frías, corazón caliente Cold hands, warm heart

mañana: s. **Hoy por ti, …**

mañana: s. **No dejes para …**

Más claro no canta un gallo As clear as the nose on your face

Más peca la víctima que el ladrón (roughly equivalent to 'The coward dies a thousand deaths, the valiant only one', though the literal meaning shows a variation on that theme: 'The victim sins more than the thief' [because the victim suspects and blames everyone whereas the thief only sinned during the single act of thievery])

Más vale algo que nada Every little bit helps

Más vale andar solo que mal acompañado It is better to be alone than in bad company

Más vale gallina viva que gallo muerto It's better to be a live coward than a dead hero

Más vale (lo) malo por conocido que (lo) bueno por conocer Better safe than sorry / Better the devil you know than the devil you don't know / Better a lean agreement than a fat sentence

Más vale maña que fuerza The pen is mightier than the sword

Más vale pájaro en mano que cien volando A bird in the hand is worth two in the bush

Más vale que haiga un tonto y no dos (roughly equivalent to): Two wrongs do not make a right (lit. 'Better for there to be just one fool than two')

Más vale tarde que nunca Better late than never

Más vale un toma que cien te daré A bird in hand is worth two in the bush

mata: s. **El que a hierro …**

matanceros: s. **Nadie quiere ser chivo, todos quieren ser …**

Me canso/Me canso, dijo un ganso/ Me canso dijo un ganso cuando volar no pudo (ritualistic response given--usually by a child--to someone ordering him/her to cease any particularly taxing form of behavior; the sense of the refrain is 'I'll do what I'm doing as long as I feel like doing it')

¿Me entiendes, Méndez, o te explico, Federico? (expression used to emphasize the speaker's desire to be understood; rough Eng. equivalent would be 'Ya see what I mean, Gene, or must I tell it all, Paul?')

mecate: s. **Cada chango a su …**

Méndez: s. **¿Me entiendes, …**

menos: s. **Cual más cual …**

mentira: s. **De una …**

mete: s. **Cada pobrete lo que tiene …**

meter: s. **El que se halla (se encuentra) en el lodo quisiera …**

mira: s. **Antes que te cases, …**

mires: s. **Haz bien y no …**

misma: s. **La jeringa …**

misma: s. **Ser pájaros de la misma pluma**

misma: s. **Taparse con la …**

momento: s. **De un …**

mona: s. **Aunque la …**

monje: s. **El hábito (no) hace …**

moscas: s. **En boca cerrada no entran …**

mosco: s. **Ya te conozco …**

mover la jicotera to stir things up/ to start a commotion

muela: s. **Al que le duela la muela…**

muerde: s. **Perro que ladra no …**

muere: s. **Cosa mala nunca …**

muere: s. **El que a hierro mata, a hierro …**

muere: s. **Yerba mala nunca …**

muerto: s. **Más vale gallina viva que gallo …**

muevas: s. **No le …**

N

nacieron: s. **Unos nacieron para mandar …**

nada: **Más vale algo que …**

Nadie quiere ser chivo; todos quieren ser matanceros Everyone wants to be a chief and no one an Indian

Nadie sabe lo que tiene hasta que lo pierde No one appreciates what he has until he loses it

Nadie sabe por quien trabaja One never knows who will reap the rewards of one's labor.

nazcan: s. **No importa que …**

negocio: s. **El negocio …**

Ni besos ni apachurrones son amores Actions speak louder than words

No cuentes tus gallinas antes de tenerlas Don't coun't your chickens before they're hatched

No dejes para mañana lo que puedes hacer hoy Don't leave for tomorrow what you can do today

No es el león como lo pintan/No es la leona coma la pintan Things are seldom what they seem

No es lo mismo decir que hacer Actions speak louder than words

No es oro todo lo que reluce All that glitters is not gold

No hay cosa/no hay persona tan mala que para algo no sirva There's a little bit of gold in every mine / There's some good in everyone

No hay mal que dure cien años ni enfermo que los aguante Nothing can last forever / Everything must have an end

No hay mal que por bien no venga Every cloud has a silver lining/It's a blessing in disguise

No hay que morder la mano que nos da de comer Don't bite the hand that feeds you

No importa que nazcan chatos con tal que tengan resuello Handsome is as handsome does/You can't judge a book by its cover (lit. It doesn't matter if they're born flat-nosed just as long as they can breathe through it)

No le muevas al agua que el río está inundado Leave well enough alone

No lo entenderá Galván If he doesn't know, nobody will

No lloro, pero me acuerdo I may not be crying, but I can remember the pain

No me chingues, Juan Domínguez (rough Eng. equivalent): Don't try to cheat, Pete (Don't try to get the better of me)

No muerdas la mano que te da de comer Don't bite the hand that feeds you

No salir del cascarón (todavía) To be (still) wet behind the ears

No siendo verdad ni coraje da Since what they say about me isn't true, I'm not angry in the least/ Sticks and stones may break my bones, but words will never hurt me

No sólo de pan vive el hombre Man does not live by bread alone

No te apures pa(ra) que dures Take it easy, and you'll live longer

No tener uno ni padre ni madre ni perrito que le ladre to be all alone in this world

No vengo a ver si puedo sino porque puedo vengo (lit. 'I haven't come to see if I am able but because I know I'm able, I'm here')

noche: s. **De ...**

nunca: s. **Amor que no es atrevido ...**

nunca: s. **El que ...**

nunca: s. **Un mal nunca viene solo**

nunca: **Nunca falta un yoloví** There's always going to be someone watching/There will always be a witness

Nunca es tarde para aprender It's never too late to learn

nunca: s. **Más vale tarde que ...**

O

Ojos que no ven, corazón que no siente Out of sight, out of mind

ojos: s. **Pelar tamaños ...**

olvido: s. **Amor que no es atrevido nunca logra ...**

olla: s. **El comal le dijo a ...**

ópera: s. **Canta y canta y nada**

de ...

oreja: s. **Enseñar ...**

oro: s. **El tiempo es ...**

oscuridad: s. **Candil de la calle.../ Farol de la calle ...**

otros: s. **Unos nacieron para mandar...**

oye: s. **Al que habla Dios no lo ...**

oye: s. **El que no habla Dios no lo ...**

P

paciencia: s. **Colmarle a alguien...**

paga: s. **Amor con amor se ...**

paga: s. **El que la hace ...**

pájaros: s. **Ser pájaros de la misma pluma**

palabras: s. **A buen entendedor ...**

pan: s. **Por dinero baila el perro ...**

Panza llena, corazón contento A full stomach makes a happy heart

panzas: s. **A gustos se rompen ...**

Para acabarla de amolar On top of everything else / To top it all off

Para alivio de mis males To make matters worse / On top of everything else

¡¿Para qué dar tantos brincos estando el suelo tan parejo?! (ref. to the folly of excessive pride, egotism, etc.)

pareces: s. **Tú te ...**

pardos: s. **De noche todos los gatos son ...**

pareja: s. **Cada oveja con su ...**

parejo: s. **Entrarle ...**

parejo: s. **¡¿Para qué dar tantos brincos ...?!**

pasó: s. **Lo que pasó voló**

peca: s. **Más peca la víctima ...**

pecadores: s. **Justos pagan por ...**

pedito: s. **Sana, sana, cola de rana ...**

Pelar tamaños ojos   to open one's eyes very wide (as in astonishment)

penas: s. **Hay muertos que no hacen ruido ...**

pendejo: s. **Cuanto más (Mientras más/Entre más) viejo, ...**

pendejos: s **Amor de lejos ...**

peor: s. **La cura es ...**

perdido: s. **De lo ...**

perdona: s. **La muerte a nadie ...**

perro: s. **Con (Por) la plata baila ...**

perro: s. **Por dinero baila ...**

Perro huevero aunque le quemen el hocico   Once a ____ always a ____

perrito: s. **No tener ni padre ...**

perrito: s. **Sangre de perrito ...**

perro: s. **Por dinero baila el ...**

perro: **Perro que ladra no muerde**   A barking dog never bites

perros: s. **Cuando uno anda de malas...**

pie: s. **Dejarse tratar con la punta ...**

pie: s. **Te dan la mano y quieres ...**

pierde: s. **El que presta a un amigo ...**

pierde: s. **Nadie sabe lo que tiene hasta que lo ...**

pintan: s. **No es el león ...**

plata: s. **Con (Por) ...**

plato: s. **Del ...**

pluma: s. **Ser pájaros de la misma ...**

pobrete: s. **Cada pobrete lo que tiene mete**

pocas: s. **A buen entendedor ...**

poco: **El que ...**

Poco a poco se va lejos   Rome wasn't built in a day / Little by little one goes a long way

poder: s. **Querer es ...**

pollo: s. **Comer frijoles y repetir ...**

Pon, pon, pon un nicle pa' jabón, pa' lavar tu calzón   Every little bit helps (expression hopefully encouraging contributions into a general fund, as at a church bazaar, etc.)

ponen: s. **El lunes ni las gallinas ...**

ponga: s. **Al que le quede el saco que ...**/s. **Al que le quede el zapato que ...**

Por dinero baila el perro/Por dinero baila el perro y por pan si se lo dan   Money talks

Por las acciones se juzgan los corazones   Actions speak louder than words

Por un oído le entra y por el otro le sale   In one ear, out the other

pozo: s. **El muerto al ...**

práctica: s. **La práctica ...**

presta: s. **El que presta a un amigo ...**

prestado: s. **Si quieres vivir sin cuidado, no pidas nunca ...**

pronto: s. **El que aprisa vive ...**

puede: s. **Dios todo ...**

puerta: s. **Cuando una ...**

Q

¿Qué esperas que no te encueras?   (vulg.) What are you waiting for, doomsday?

queda: s. **El que sirve (a) dos amos, con alguno ...**

quede: s. **Al que le ...**

quemar: s. **Si no te quieres ...**

Querer es poder Where there's a will there's a way

quiebra: s. **Tanto va el cántaro al agua hasta ...**

quien: s. **Dime con ...**

quien: s. **Nadie sabe por ...**

Quien a feo ama, hermoso le parece Love makes even the ugly look beautiful

Quien bien siembra, bien recoge As you sow, so shall you reap

Quien canta, sus males espanta (var. of) *El que canta, sus males espanta* He who sings chases away his blues

Quien mal anda, mal acaba He who lives by the sword shall die by the sword/As you sow so shall you reap

Quien más tiene, más quiere The more you have, the more you want

Quien mucho abarca, poco aprieta Your eyes are bigger than your stomach

Quien no oye consejos no llega a viejo Heed my advice or pay the price

Quien tiene tienda y no la atienda, que la venda/Quien tiene tienda y no la atiende, que la venda (lit. 'He who has a store and doesn't attend to business should sell the store')

quien: s. **Quien más tiene, ...**

quieres: s. **Si no te ...**

quieres: s. **Te dan la mano y ...**

quieres: s. **Te dan una ...**

quisiera: s. **El que se halla (se encuentra) en el lodo ...**

Quitarle a alguien la canasta To cut the umbilical cord (= to withdraw financial or other type of support)

Quitarse alguien la venda de los ojos To see things the way they really are

R

rasque: s. **Al que le dé comezón ...**

recoge: s. **Quien bien siembra ...**

recoges: s. **Lo que siembras ...**

reluce: s. **No es oro todo lo que ...**

resuello: s. **No importa que nazcan chatos ...**

retozar: s. **Echar el gato ...**

ríe: s. **El que ...**

río: s. **El que no se arriesga, no cruza ...**

río: s. **No le muevas al ...**

rompen: s. **A gustos se rompen panzas**

roncan: s. **A ver si como ...**

ruido: s. **Hay muertos que no hacen ...**

ruidos: s. **El que no quiera ...**

S

sabe: **Nadie sabe lo que ...**

sabe: s. **Nadie sabe por ...**

saco: s. **Al que le quede ...**

sale: s. **Por un oído le entra y por el otro le ...**

salir: s. **Ir por lana y salir trasquilado**

Salir de Guatemala para ir a guatepeor To go from bad to worse

salte: s. **Si no te quieres quemar ...**

Sana, sana, cola de rana, tira un pedito para ahora y mañana (expression said to children when one applies medicine to their cuts and bruises or when one simply kisses the wound to "make it better")

sangre: s. **Bajársele a alguien ...**

Sangre de perrito que se vaya derechito (said to or by a person trying to hit the target he is shooting at)

Sangre de venado que se vaya por un lado (said to someone to cause him to miss a target he is shooting at)

santo: s. **A buen santo ...**

saque: s. **Al que le duela la muela ...**

Ser más viejo que la luna to be older than Mathuselah

Ser pájaros de la misma pluma To be birds of a feather

¡Si fuera víbora te mordiera! It's staring at you right in the face! (said of a sought object)

Si no te quieres quemar, salte de la cocina (Ang.?) If you can't stand the heat, get (stay) out of the kitchen

Si no van a comprar, no malluguen If you're not going to buy, don't handle the merchandise

Si quieres vivir sin cuidado, no pidas nunca prestado Neither a borrower nor a lender be

siembra: s. **Lo que siembras recoges**

sirva: s. **No hay cosa tan mala que para algo no ...**

sirve: s. **El que ...**

sólo: s. **La jeringa ...**

solo: s. **Un mal nunca viene solo**

Sólo el tiempo dirá Only time will tell

Son más las culecas que las que están poniendo There are more birds in the barn than eggs in the nest (expression used to crtiticize

pretense, exaggerated claims, etc.)

sopa: s. **Del plato a la boca a veces se cae ...**

sucio: s. **Vale más sucio en casa ...**

T

Tanto va el cántaro al agua hasta que se quiebra The pitcher went to the well once too often/You'll get yours (= your just desserts) sooner or later

Taparle el ojo al macho to keep up appearances

Taparse con la misma colcha (cobija) to be birds of a feather (coll.), practice the same brand of politics, shady deals, etc.

tarde: s. **Más vale tarde que nunca**

tarde: s. **Nunca es ...**

Te casaste, te fregaste (jodiste, chingaste) (vulg.) A man's troubles begin when he gets married/Wedlock is padlock

Te dan la mano y quieres el pie They give you an inch and you want a mile

Te dan la mano y quieres todo el brazo They give you an inch and you want a mile

Te dan una hebrita y quieres toda la carretilla They give you an inch and you take a mile

tempestad: s. **Ven la tempestad ...**

tener: s. **El que nunca ha tenido y llega ...**

tener: s. **No tener ni padre ...**

tenerlas: **No cuentes tus gallinas antes ...**

tiempo: s. **A mal tiempo buena cara**

tiempo: s. **Sólo el ...**

tienda: s. Quien tiene …

tiene: s. Cuando más se …

tiene: s. Nadie sabe lo que …

tira: s. A todo le …

toda: s. Te dan una hebrita y quieres…

todo: s. Dios …

todo: s. En el amor …

todo: s. Te dan la mano y quieres …

todo   s. La muerte lo acaba todo

toma: s. Más vale un toma …

Tomás: s. Cuando yo tenía dinero me llamaban …

tonto: s. Es mejor que haya …

tonto: s. Más vale que haiga …

trabaja: s. Nadie sabe por quien …

trabaja: s. Uno nunca sabe por quien …

Traérsela a alguien muy cortita   to keep a tight rein on someone/ to keep someone on a short leash

trasquilado: s. Ir por lana y salir …

trecho: s. Del dicho al hecho …

tres: s. Donde comen dos …

Tú sabes quien trae las llaves, Chávez   You know who runs the show around here / You know who's boss, Hoss

Tú te pareces a Canuto, cuanto (mientras, entre) más viejo más bruto   You are like Canuto, the older you get, the dumber you become

tuerto: s. En tierra de ciegos, …

U

Un mal nunca viene solo   When it rains it pours

unión: s. En la unión hay fuerza

Uno nunca sabe por quien trabaja   One never knows who will reap the rewards of one's labor

Unos nacieron para mandar y otros para ser mandados   Some were born to command, others to be commanded/Some were born to be chiefs and others Indians

V

vale: s. Más vale gallina viva …

vale: s. Más vale que haiga …

vale: s. Más vale tarde que nunca

vale: s. Más vale un toma …

vale: s. En el amor todos …

vale: s. La amistad …

Vale más sucio en casa y no limpio en el camposanto (approx. equivalent to): Better a messy house than an early death (lit. 'It's better to be dirty at home than clean in the cemetery')

valiente: s. Lo cortés no quita lo …

van: s. Si no …

vara: s. Con la …

vaya: s. Sangre de perrito …

vaya: s. Sangre de venado …

Ven la tempestad y no se hincan   They don't know enough to come in out of the rain

venado: s. Sangre de venado …

venda: s. Quien tiene tienda …

venda: Quitarse uno la …

venga: s. No hay mal que por bien …

ventana: s. Echar la casa por …

Ver es creer   Seeing is believing

verdad: s. La mentira dura hasta que…

verdad: s. No siendo …

verdades: s. Echar mentiras para ...

víbora: s. ¡Si fuera ...!

víctima: s. Más peca la víctima ...

viejo: s. Cuanto (Mientras, Entre) más ...

viejo: s. Ser más ...

viejo: s. Quien no oye consejos ...

viene: s. Un mal nunca viene solo

viva: s. Más vale gallina ...

vive: s. El que aprisa ...

volando: s. Más vale pájaro en mano...

voló: s. Lo que pasó voló

vuelta: s. Andar ...

Yerba mala nunca muere A bad penny always shows up

yerba: s. La mala ...

yerbabuena: s. Ahora es cuando, ...

yerra: s. El que poco habla, poco ...

yoloví: s. Nunca falta ...

Z

zapato: s. Encontrarse (Hallarse) la horma ...

zapato: s. Al que le quede ...

zapato: s. A huevo ni ...

Y

Ya te conozco mosco I've seen through you

Appendix B: Verbs in -ear/-iar
Apéndice B: Verbos en -ear/-iar

Verbs in -ear/-iar

One of the most widespread phonetic variations observable in Texas Spanish (and one which affects the speech of all social levels) concerns verbs whose infinitives end in -ear in "standard" Spanish. The two "strong" (low) vowels are diphthongized and thereby simplified in a process which converts *e* into *i*. This trajectory is observed in the infinitive and in the past and present participles as well as in most forms of the simple tenses. There follows the partial conjugation of the verb *desear* as an example:

Verbos en -ear/-iar

Uno de los cambios fonéticos de mayor difusión social que se halla en el español de Tejas se relaciona con la terminación verbal *-ear*. Las dos vocales "fuertes" (bajas) se diptongan por un proceso de simplificación que convierte la *e* en *i*. Dicha transformación se realiza en el infinitivo y en los participios pasivos y presentes, así como en muchas formas de los tiempos sencillos. Conjugamos a continuación el verbo *desear* como ejemplo:

INFINITIVE/INFINITIVO: desiar
PAST PARTICIPLE/PARTICIPIO PASIVO: desiado
PRESENT PARTICIPLE/GERUNDIO (PARTICIPIO PRESENTE):
desiando
PRESENT INDICATIVE/PRESENTE DE INDICATIVO:
deseo
deseas
desea
desiamos
desean
PRESENT SUBJUNCTIVE/PRESENTE DE SUBJUNTIVO:
desee
desees
desee
desiemos the second form is used more, even though it is morphologically unmarked as a subjunctive / desiamos la segunda forma se usa más, a pesar de no marcarse como subjuntivo
deseen
FUTURE INDICATIVE/FUTURO DE INDICATIVO:
desiaré, desiarás, etc.
CONDITIONAL/POTENCIAL:
desiaría, desiarías, etc.

PRETERITE/PRETÉRITO:
desié, desiaste, desió, desiamos, desiaron
PAST SUBJUNCTIVE/IMPERFECTO DE SUBJUNTIVO:
desiara, desiaras, etc.
IMPERFECT/IMPERFECTO:
desiaba, desiabas, etc.

On the other hand we observe the "decomposition" of diphthongs occuring in verbs whose infinitives end in -iar in "standard" Spanish, for example, *copiar*. Overcorrection variously converts *i* to *e* in simple tenses:

En el polo opuesto encontramos la "descomposición" del diptongo de *i* más *a, e* u *o* que se halla en los verbos que terminan en -iar en el español "estándar," por ejemplo, *copiar*. La ultracorrección convierte la *i* en *e* en los tiempos sencillos:

PRESENT INDICATIVE/PRESENTE DE INDICATIVO:
copeo, copeas, copea, copiamos, copean
PRESENT SUBJUNCTIVE/PRESENTE DE SUBJUNTIVO:
copee, copees, copee, copiemos/copiamos, copeen

In effect, both variant conjugations appear to reflect a resistance in the slot immediately to the left of the designation of number and person towards all but high vowel *i*, unless the stress falls on the slot on the left, in which case a non-high vowel must occur. The distinction, then, between -*ear* and -*iar* verbs appears to have been eliminated.

Parece, por lo tanto, reflejarse en la casilla a la izquierda de la designación de número y persona, una resistencia de parte de ambas conjugaciones variantes hacia toda vocal que no sea la alta *i*, a menos que se coloque el énfasis en la casilla a la izquierda; en este caso tiene que aparecer la vocal no alta. Así que la distinción entre los verbos -*ear* e -*iar* parece haberse eliminado.

Appendix C: Bibliography
Apéndice C: Bibliografía

Bibliography

Each of the following secondary sources is annotated (for the most part critically) in: Richard V. Teschner, Garland D. Bills and Jerry R. Craddock, *Spanish and English of United States Hispanos: A Critical, Annotated, Linguistic Bibliography*, Arlington, Va.: Center for Applied Linguistics, 1975, xxii, 352 pp. The user is urged to consult that source for information on these and more than 600 other books, articles, monographs, dissertations, theses, etc., pertinent to the Spanish of Texas, the Southwest and other regions of the United States as well.

Bibliografía

Cada una de las siguientes obras de consulta se encuentra anotada (la mayor parte, de manera crítica) en: Richard V. Teschner, Garland D. Bills and Jerry R. Craddock, *Spanish and English of United States Hispanos: A Critical, Annotated, Linguistic Bibliography*, Arlington, Va.: Center for Applied Linguistics, 1975, xxii, 352 pp. Al lector se le recomienda encarecidamente la consulta de esa fuente bibliográfica para más informes relacionados con las obras aquí citadas y las más de 600 libros, artículos, monografías, tesinas, etc. adicionales que versan sobre el español de Tejas, el Sudoeste estadounidense y demás regiones de los Estados Unidos.

Atwood, E. Bagby. *The Regional Vocabulary of Texas.* Austin: Univ. of Texas Press, 1962. 273 pp.

Bough, Lila. "A Study of Pre-School Vocabulary of Spanish-Speaking Children." MA Thesis, Univ. of Texas, Austin, 1933. 129 pp.

Braddy, Haldeen. "Narcotic Argot Along the Mexican Border." *American Speech* 30.84–90 (1955).

_____. "Smugglers' Argot in the Southwest." *American Speech* 31.96–101 (1956).

_____. "The Pachucos and Their Argot." *Southern Folklore Quarterly* 24.255–271 (1960).

Carrow(-Woolfolk), Elizabeth (Sister Mary Arthur). "Comprehension of English and Spanish by Preschool Mexican-American Children." *Modern Language Journal* 55.299–306 (1971).

_____. "Auditory Comprehension of English by Monolingual and Bilingual Preschool Children." *Journal of Speech and Hearing Research* 15.407–412 (1972).

Castillo Nájera, Francisco. "Breves consideraciones sobre el español que se hable en Méjico." *Revista Hispánica Moderna* 2.157–169 (1936).

Cerda, Gilberto, Berta Cabaza and Julia Farias. *Vocabulario español de Texas.* Univ. of Texas Hispanic Studies, Vol. 5 (Austin: Univ. of Texas Press, 1953). 347 pp. (Reprinted unrevised, Austin: Univ. of Texas Press, 1970.)

Cervantes, Alfonso. "A Selected Vocabulary of Anglicisms Used by First Grade Students of Elementary Schools of Del Rio, Texas." M.A. Thesis, Southwest Texas State Univ., San Marcos, 1973. vi, 68 pp.

Coltharp, Lurline. "The Influence of English on the 'Language' of the Tirilones.": Ph.D. Diss., Univ. of Texas, Austin, 1964. (Subsequently published with occasional revisions as: *The Tongue of the Tirilones.* Alabama: Univ. of Alabama Press, 1965. 186 pp.)

_____. "Some Additions: Lexicon of 'Tongue of the Tirilones.'" In Ralph W. Ewton, Jr. and Jacob Ornstein, eds., *Studies in Language and Linguistics 1969–70*, El Paso: Texas Western Press, 1970, pp. 69–78.

_____. "'Invitation to the Dance': Spanish in the El Paso Underworld." In Glenn G. Gilbert, ed., *Texas Studies in Bilingualism*, Berlin: Walter e Gruyter Co., 1969, pp. 18–41.

Cornejo, Ricardo Jesús. "Bilingualism: Study of the Lexicon of the Five-Year-Old Spanish-Speaking Children of Texas." Ph.D. Diss., Univ. of Texas, Austin, 1969. 228 pp.

Elías Olivares, Lucía E. "Study of the Oral Vocabulary of Ten High-School Mexican-American Students in Austin, Texas." M.A. Thesis, Univ. of Texas, Austin, 1970. 100 pp.

Fody, Michael III. "A Glossary of Non-Standard Spanish Words and Idioms Found in Selected Newspapers of South Texas During 1968." M.A. Thesis, Southern Illinois Univ., Carbondale, 1969. 154 pp.

Frausto, Manuel. "Vocabulario español de San Marcos, Texas." M.A. Thesis, Southwest Texas State Univ., San Marcos, 1969. 55 pp.

Galván, Roberto A. "Un estudio geográfico de algunos vacablos usados por los habitantes de habla española de San Antonio, Texas." M.A. Thesis, Univ. Of Texas, Austin, 1949. 142 pp.

_____. "El dialecto español de San Antonio, Texas." Ph.D. Diss., Tulane Univ., New Orleans, 1955. 315 pp.

_____. "Más observaciones sobre el argot de Baranquilla." *Hispania* 49.483–485 (1966).

_____. "'Chichecano', neologismo jergal." *Hispania* 53.86–88 (1970).

_____. "More on 'Frito' as an English Loan-Word in Mexican Spanish." *Hispania* 54.511–514 (1971).

García, Anita H. "Identification and Classification of Types of Common Deviations from Standard Spanish Made by Representative Native Speakers in South Texas." M.A. Thesis, Texas A & I Univ., Kingsville, 1969. 110 pp.

García, Lucy. "Vocabulario selecto del español de Brownsville, Texas." M.A. Thesis, Southwest Texas State Univ., San Marcos, 1972. 64 pp.

Gonzáles, Gustavo. "A Linguistic Profile of the Spanish-Speaking First-Grader in Corpus Christi, Texas." M.A. Thesis, Univ. of Texas, Austin, 1968. 83 pp.

_____. "The Acquisition of Spanish Grammar by Native Spanish Speakers." Ph.D. Diss., Univ. of Texas, Austin, 1970. 178 pp.

Harrison, Helene. "A Methodological Study in Eliciting Linguistic Data from Mexican-American Bilinguals." Ph.D. Diss., Univ. of Texas, Austin, 1967. 119 pp.

Ivey, Alfred Joe. "A Study of the Vocabulary of Newspapers Printed in the Spanish Language in Texas." M.A. Thesis, Univ. of Texas, Austin, 1927. iii, 137 pp.

January, William Spence, Jr. "The Chicano Dialect of the Mexican-American Communities of Dallas and Fort Worth." M.A. Thesis, Texas Christian Univ., 1971. 242 pp.

Keever, Mary, Alfredo Vásquez and Anna Padilla. *Glossary of Words and Expressions, Irregular in Form or Meaning, Encountered in the Examination of Spanish Mail on the Mexican Border.* El Paso, Texas: El Paso Office of the United States Office of Censorship, 1945. vii, 46 pp. mimeographed. (Location: Library of Congress, PC 4832.U5.)

Kelly, Rex Robert. "Vocabulary as Used on the Mexican Border." M.A. Thesis, Baylor Univ., Waco, Texas, 1938. 39 pp.

_____ and George W. Kelly. *Farm and Ranch Spanish.* N. place: Authors, 1961. xv, 241 pp.

Kercheville, Francis M. "A Preliminary Glossary of Southwestern and Rio Grande Spanish Including Semantic and Philological Peculiarities." Unpublished Ms., Kingsville: Texas A & I Univ., 1967. 71 pp.

Lance, Donald M., ed. and chief contributor. *A Brief Study of Spanish-English Bilingualism.* Bethesda, Maryland: U.S. Dept. of Health, Education and Welfare, 1969. 104 pp. (ERIC System No. Ed 032 529.)

León, Aurelio de. *Barbarismos comunes en México*. 2 vols. México D.F.: Imprenta Mundial, (1: 1936, 2: 1937). 80 +/92 pp.

Luna, Juanita J. "A Selected Vocabulary of the Spanish Spoken in Sabinal, Texas." M.A. Thesis, Southwest Texas State Univ., San Marcos, 1970. 101 pp.

Marambio, Juan. "Vocabulario español de Temple, Texas." M.A. Thesis, Southwest Texas State Univ., San Marcos, 1970. 110 pp.

Marrocco, Mary Anne W. "The Spanish of Corpus Christi, Texas." Ph.D. Diss., Univ. of Illinois, Champaign-Urbana, 1972. 502 pp.

McKee, Okla Markham. "Five-Hundred Non-Dictionary Words found in the El Paso-Juárez Press." M.A. Thesis, Univ. of Texas-El Paso, 1955. 75 pp.

Montemayor, Elsa Diana. "A Study of the Spanish Spoken By Certain Bilingual Students of Laredo, Texas." M.A. Thesis, Texas Women's Univ., Denton, 1966. 106 pp.

Ornstein, Jacob S. "Sociolinguistics and New Perspectives in the Study of Southwest Spanish." In Ralph W. Ewton, Jr. and Jacob Ornstein, eds., *Studies in Language and Linguistics 1969–70*, El Paso: Texas Western Press, 1970, pp. 127–184.

_____. "Language Varieties Along the U.S.-Mexican Border." In *Applications of Linguistics: Selected Papers of the Second International Congress of Applied Linguistics*, edited by G.E. Perren and J.L.M. Trim, New York et alibi: Cambridge Univ. Press, 1971, pp. 349–362.

Patterson, Maurine. "Some Dialectal Tendencies in Popular Spanish in San Antonio." M.A. Thesis, Texas Women's Univ., Denton, 1946. 120 pp.

Ramírez, Carina (Karen). "Lexical Usage of and Attitude Toward Southwest Spanish in the Ysleta, Texas, Area." Graduate Paper, Univ. of Texas-El Paso, 1971. 84 pp. (Circulates through Library, Univ. of Texas-El Paso.)

_____. "Lexical Usage of and Attitude Toward Southwest Spanish in the Ysleta, Texas Area." *Hispania* 56.308–315 (1973).

Ramón, René Simón. "Vocabulario selecto del español regional de Del Río, Texas." M.A. Thesis, Southwest Texas State Univ., San Marcos, 1974 vii, 70 pp.

Reséndez, Víctor. "Vocabulario español de Seguín, Texas." M.A. Thesis, Southwest Texas State Univ., San Marcos, 1970. 81 pp.

Reynolds, Selma Fay. "Some Aspects of Spanish as Spoken and Written by Spanish-Speaking Students of a Junior High School in (Corpus Christi), Texas." M.A. Thesis, Texas Women's Univ., Denton, 1945. 105 pp.

Romano-V., Octavio I. "Donship in a Mexican-American Community in Texas.: *American Anthropologist* 62.966–976 (1960).

Rubel, Arthur J. *Across the Tracks: Mexican-Americans in a Texas City.* Austin: Univ. of Texas Press, 1966. xxvii, 266 pp.

Said, Sally Eugenia Sneed. "A Descriptive Model of Austin Spanish Syntax." M.A. Thesis, Univ. of Texas, Austin, 1970. 62 pp.

Sawyer, Janet Beck. "A Dialect Study of San Antonio, Texas: A Bilingual Community." Ph.D. Diss., Univ. of Texas, Austin, 1957. 325 pp.

Sharp, John M. "Some El Paso Spanish Etymologies." In Ralph W. Euton, Jr. and Jacob Ornstein, eds. *Studies in Language and Linguistics 1969–70*, El Paso: Texas Western Press, 1970, pp. 207–232.

Simón, Alphonse, O.M.I. *Pastoral Spanish.* San Antonio: Standard Printing Co., 1945. xxii, 511 pp.

Vásquez, Librado Keno and María Enriqueta Vásquez. *Regional Dictionary of Chicano Slang.* Austin, Texas: Jenkins Publishing Co./The Pemberton Press, 1975. 111 pp.

Wagner, Max Leopold. "Ein Mexikanisch-amerikanischer Argot: Das Puchuco." *Romanistiches Jahrbuch* 6.237–266 (1953–54).

Ward, Hortense Warner. "Ear Marks." *Texas Folklore Society. Publications* 19.106–116 (1944).

Wesley, Howard D. "Ranchero Sayings of the Border." *Texas Folklore Society. Publications* 12.211–220 (1935).

Other useful sources/Otras fuentes útiles

Aranda, Charles, comp. *Dichos: Proverbs and Sayings from the Spanish.* Santa Fe, NM: Sunstone Press, 1975.

Beltramo, Anthony Fred. "Lexical and Morphological Aspects of Linguistic Acculturation by Mexican Americans in San José, California." Ph.D. Diss., Stanford University, 1972.

Blanco, S., Antonio. *La lengua española en la historia de California.* Madrid: Ediciones Cultura Hispánica, 1971.

Corominas, J. *Diccionario etimológico del español*, 4 vols., Madrid: Gredos, 1954.

Domínguez, Domingo. "A Theoretical Model for Classifying Dialectal Variations of Oral New Mexican Spanish." Ph.D. Diss., University of New Mexico, 1975.

Fuentes, Dagoberto, and José A. López. *Barrio Language Dictionary: First Dictionary of Caló.* Los Angeles/La Puente, CA: Southland Press/El Barrio Publications; Lubbock, TX: Trucha Publications, 1974.

Gross, Stuart Murray. "A Vocabulary of New Mexican Spanish." M.A. Thesis, Stanford University, 1935.

Kay, Margarita Artschwager; John D. Meridith; Wendy Redlinger: and Alicia Quiroz Raymond. *Southwestern Medical Dictionary: Spanish-English/English-Spanish.* Tucson, AZ: University of Arizona Press, 1977.

Riegelhaupt-Barkin, Florence. "The Influence of English on the Spanish of Bilingual Mexican American Migrants in Florida." Ph.D. Diss., SUNY-Buffalo, 1976.

Ross, Lyle Ronald. "La lengua castellana en San Luis, Colorado." Ph.D. Diss., University of Colorado, 1975.

Santamaría, Francisco J., *Diccionario de mejicanismos*, 1959.

Serrano, Rodolfo G. *Dictionary of Pachuco Terms.* Bakersfield, CA: Sierra Printers, 1976.

Teschner, Richard V.; Garland D. Bills; and Jerry R. Craddock, eds. *Spanish and English of United States Hispanos: A Critical, Annotated, Linguistic Bibliography.* Arlington, VA: Center for Applied Linguistics, 1975.

_____. "Current Research on the Language(s) of U.S. Hispanos." *Hispania*, 60 (1977): 347–58.

Webb, John Terrance. "A Lexical Study of Caló and Non-Standard Spanish in the Southwest." Ph.D. Diss., University of California, Berkeley, (Dec.) 1975.